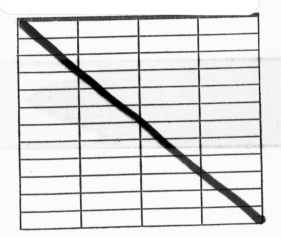

CONSCIENCE AND THE CONSTITUTION

CONSCIENCE AND THE CONSTITUTION

HISTORY, THEORY, AND LAW OF THE RECONSTRUCTION AMENDMENTS

David A. J. Richards

PRINCETON UNIVERSITY PRESS

PRINCETON, NEW JERSEY

LIBRARY OF CONGRESS CATALOGING-IN-PUBLICATION DATA
RICHARDS, DAVID A. J.
CONSCIENCE AND THE CONSTITUTION : HISTORY, THEORY, AND LAW OF THE
RECONSTRUCTION AMENDMENTS / BY DAVID A. J. RICHARDS.
P. CM.
INCLUDES BIBLIOGRAPHICAL REFERENCES AND INDEX.
ISBN 0-691-03231-9
1. UNITED STATES—CONSTITUTIONAL LAW—AMENDMENTS—13TH—
HISTORY. 2. UNITED STATES—CONSTITUTIONAL LAW—AMENDMENTS—14TH—
HISTORY. 3. UNITED STATES—CONSTITUTIONAL LAW—AMENDMENTS—15TH—
HISTORY. 4. CIVIL RIGHTS—UNITED STATES—HISTORY. 5. ABOLITIONISTS—
UNITED STATES. 6. RECONSTRUCTION. I. TITLE.
KF4757.R5 1993 342.73'03—DC20 [347.3023] 92-42895 CIP

THIS BOOK HAS BEEN COMPOSED IN LINOTRON CALEDONIA

PRINCETON UNIVERSITY PRESS BOOKS ARE PRINTED
ON ACID-FREE PAPER AND MEET THE GUIDELINES FOR
PERMANENCE AND DURABILITY OF THE COMMITTEE ON
PRODUCTION GUIDELINES FOR BOOK LONGEVITY
OF THE COUNCIL ON LIBRARY RESOURCES

PRINTED IN THE UNITED STATES OF AMERICA
1 3 5 7 9 10 8 6 4 2

IN LOVING MEMORY OF MY MOTHER

Josephine Cona Richards,
1904–1991

I am myne owene womman.
—Geoffrey Chaucer, *Troilus and Criseyde*

Let every American, every lover of liberty, every well wisher to his posterity, swear by the blood of the Revolution, never to violate in the least particular, the laws of the country; and never to tolerate their violation by others. As the patriots of seventy-six did to the support of the Declaration of Independence, so to the support of the Constitution and Laws, let every American pledge his life, his property, and his sacred honor; . . . in short, let it become the *political religion* of the nation; and let the old and the young, the rich and the poor, the grave and the gay, of all sexes and tongues, and colors and conditions, sacrifice unceasingly upon its altars.

—Abraham Lincoln, Address to Young Men's Lyceum,
January 27, 1838

CONTENTS

ACKNOWLEDGMENTS

THIS BOOK was largely researched and written during a full sabbatical year taken from the New York University School of Law during the academic year of 1990–91. That full sabbatical leave and associated summer researches were made possible by generous research grants from the New York University School of Law Filomen D'Agostino and Max E. Greenberg Faculty Research Fund. A book of this sort could not have been written without the support that the New York University School of Law gives to interdisciplinary scholarly work and research as a central mission of the school of law in a university; and I am grateful to my colleagues and our former dean, Norman Redlich, and current dean, John Sexton, for forging a culture hospitable to such work.

My thinking about the issues of this book profited from a seminar on equal protection given at the New York University School of Law in the spring term of 1990. I am grateful to all the students in the seminar, among whom Taina Bien-Aime, Seth Harris, Annette Hurst, and Derek Q. Reeves deserve special mention; Derek Reeves also rendered valuable research assistance. My colleague Paulette Caldwell graciously attended the seminar, and I am most grateful to her for her many probing and challenging comments. The manuscript also profited from critical discussion at two distinguished interdisciplinary colloquia sponsored by the School of Law. I must thank my superb colleagues Ronald Dworkin, Thomas Nagel, Lawrence Sager, Lewis Kornhauser, Christopher Eisgruber, and Lawrence Crocker for their helpful comments at the Colloquium in Law, Philosophy, and Political Theory; I am very much in the debt of my generous colleague William E. Nelson for his challenging criticisms at the Colloquium in Legal History and his continuing support and help over the years, and among the distinguished non-NYU historians participating in the colloquium, Paul Finkelman and Robert J. Kaczorowski for their especially helpful criticisms and comments. My colleague Sylvia Law also read and wisely criticized this work. Over the period I have been at the NYU School of Law, I have also learned much about relevant historical matters from my colleague John Reid and from such distinguished antebellum and Reconstruction period historians visiting at the School of Law for long periods as Harold Hyman and Michael Les Benedict.

Michael Dowdle was an excellent research assistant during the research stage of my work on this book, and also helped me at a later stage prepare the bibliography. My former secretary, Patricia Rinaldi-Johnson, also assisted me in gathering research materials used in writing this book; and my current secretary, Lynn Gilbert, has ably continued her good work.

The readers of this manuscript for Princeton University Press, Harold Hyman and Mark Tushnet, very greatly assisted me in working on the manuscript through their probing criticisms and comments; the book is a better work because of them. Thanks also are due to my supportive editor at Princeton, Ann Wald, and to my able copy editor, Lois Krieger. Parts of Chapter 4 of this book appeared as an article, "Revolution and Constitutionalism in America," published in *Cardozo Law Review* 14, pp. 577–634 (1993); permission to publish the material here is gratefully acknowledged.

Conversations with Donald Levy, professor of philosophy at Brooklyn College, nurtured and sustained all my work on this book. I am grateful as well for the support and encouragement of my sister and friend, Diane Rita Richards.

The dedication of a book about conscience and law to my recently deceased mother, Josephine Cona Richards, fitly memorializes many of her remarkable qualities as a person—ethical rigor and demanding standards, independence and spirit, and a great and loving heart.

New York, N.Y.
July 1992

CONSCIENCE AND THE CONSTITUTION

ONE

AIMS AND METHODOLOGIES

THE INTERPRETATION of the Reconstruction Amendments (the thirteenth, fourteenth, and fifteenth amendments to the Constitution of the United States) is at stage center of the American drama, our agon of public discourse about the basic terms of American identity, the values of equality and human rights. In this book, I argue that the interpretation of these amendments is too important to be left to either the historians or the lawyers or the political theorists and philosophers. Rather, we need a new interdisciplinary approach to the understanding of these amendments and their interpretation, one that brings arguments of history, law, and political theory into a fruitful working relationship that defines forms of public argument reasonably accessible and available to all as free and equal persons. If successful, my argument will give critical normative content to the idea of the people's Constitution as supremely authoritative law in the United States.

To do justice to these amendments, we must take seriously their continuity with the revolutionary constitutionalism of the founding and with the antebellum debates about American political and constitutional theory. At the heart of it all lies the ethical, political, and constitutional controversy over slavery and the remarkable ethical impartiality of the abolitionist challenge to it. Abolitionists forged the critical ethical arguments through which the revolutionary constitutionalism of the Reconstruction Amendments conceived and framed the mission of constitutional reconstruction. The constitutional power of abolitionist dissent was grounded in the way such dissent made arguments based on the right to conscience, a central value of American constitutionalism, and brought those arguments to bear on the interpretation and criticism of antebellum constitutionalism.

The Founders of 1787 had analyzed the inadequate constitutionalism of the British Constitution and the Articles of Confederation in the light of political experience and revolutionary political theory; in the same spirit, the founders of 1865 drew upon abolitionist argument to reflect on the sources of antebellum constitutional decadence and civil war. Their work, the Reconstruction Amendments, memorialized a struggle for moral growth and constitutional rebirth; American political community was reconstituted on ethical terms of respect for universal human rights. The interpretation of these amendments today imposes correlative responsibilities on our generation to make the best sense in our circumstances of this ethical vision of dissenting conscience and moral growth. This book tries to show how and why this is so by advancing a study of constitutional law as an interdisciplinary humane discipline of the American political philosophy of democratic constitutionalism, interpretive history, and law.

The approach taken in this work is a further testing and elaboration of the perspective on constitutional interpretation of my two previous books, *Toleration and the Constitution* (hereafter referred to as *Toleration*)[1] and *Foundations of American Constitutionalism* (referred to as *Foundations*).[2] Epistemically powerful theories, in law as elsewhere, must not only explain the domain of facts central to their immediate subject matter (for example, free speech), but should also lead, in comparison to competitive approaches, to more fruitful research programs in the whole domain of inquiry (constitutional law as such). This work offers an argument of this sort for the fertility of the approach taken in these earlier works. What is that approach, and what kind of testing of it do I offer here?

Toleration offered a political theory of toleration (based on the inalienable right to conscience) as a central value of American constitutionalism. The theory interpretively clarified the nature, weight, and interconnected structure of central historical and contemporary principles of religious liberty, free speech, and privacy under American public law.

Foundations proposed a more general formulation of that political theory, historically rooted in Lockean political theory. Here the theory explained the interpretive weight for American constitutionalists today of the Founders of 1787—how the great work of the Founders, the Constitution of 1787, had been understood and interpretively elaborated over time (including the place of amendments in that interpretive process). The ambition of *Foundations* was to offer a general account of the complex empirical and normative assessments central to the genre of American republican constitutionalism.

The American revolutionary and constitutional project was fundamentally conceived as a common enterprise.[3] Leading advocates of the American Revolution (John Adams and Thomas Jefferson) saw constitutionalism at both the state and national levels as the test of the very legitimacy of the revolution. Accordingly, Jefferson wrote no less than three constitutions for Virginia, and Adams was the main author of the Massachusetts constitution of 1780, which was centrally used by the Founders in 1787.[4] The success

[1] New York: Oxford University Press, 1986.

[2] New York: Oxford University Press, 1989.

[3] The following discussion of American revolutionary and constitutional thought is an abbreviated summary of the lengthy treatment of these matters in Richards, *Foundations*. For pertinent supporting arguments and citations, I refer the reader, in the text that follows, to the discussions in *Foundations*.

[4] See Richards, *Foundations*, pp. 19–20, 95, 106, 123, 124, 141.

of American constitutionalism was, for Adams and Jefferson, literally the test of the legitimacy of the revolution.

The six critical normative and empirical ingredients of American revolutionary constitutionalism were: (1) The ultimate tests for the political legitimacy of a constitutional order were specified by the Lockean political principles of the revolution, namely, respect for inalienable human rights and pursuit of the public good. (2) These objective principles of political right were also interpreted to be implicit in historically evolving legal common law and constitutional principles. Under this view, the British Parliament not only had violated principles of political right, but had pathologically misinterpreted the British Constitution itself. (3) The analysis of the sources of the interpretive decadence of British constitutionalism led to the prominence in American constitutional analysis of human nature in politics (for example, the theories of faction and fame), inferred not only from the history of British constitutionalism, but from the larger practice of republican and federal experiments over time. (4) Americans also prominently used comparative political science in the construction of new structures of government free of the mistakes both of the British Constitution and republican and federal experiments in the past. (5) Constitutional reflection also put weight on the experiments in the American states and in the nation between 1776 and 1787 in thinking about institutional alternatives. (6) Finally, Americans self-consciously recognized and seized their historically unique opportunity in 1787 to develop a novel republican experiment that established a new kind of argument (constitutional argument) more politically legitimate than the arguments of ordinary politics.

My task here is to bring the interpretive approach of these works fruitfully to bear on the Reconstruction Amendments.[5] This ambition defines the two critical tests that the argument of this book must meet. First, do the substantive arguments of political theory (in particular, the argument for toleration) central to my approach fundamentally clarify the constitutional aims of the Reconstruction Amendments? Second, do the critical interpretive methodologies of my account advance public understanding of the interpretive debates over the meaning of these amendments, which have preoccupied the nation since their ratification? In both cases, the benchmark of comparison must be the alternative approaches to these matters currently available today. Two approaches are prominent—one emphasizing history, the other political theory. The inspiration for my own interpretive approach to the Reconstruction Amendments is a constructive

---

[5] A brief chapter of *Foundations* made some schematic interpretive suggestions about how the general approach might, in comparison with other approaches, offer a more fruitful understanding of the Reconstruction Amendments in general and the fourteenth amendment guarantee of equal protection in particular. See chap. 7, pp. 248–86.

response to certain critical defects in the attempts of others to bring history or political theory to bear on the interpretation of these amendments. What are these attempts, and what are the defects in them?

The Reconstruction Amendments as History

The Reconstruction Amendments are the most important amendments to the U.S. Constitution since the Bill of Rights of 1791. They include the thirteenth amendment (ratified in 1865), abolishing slavery; the fourteenth amendment (ratified in 1868), extending citizenship to all persons born in the United States, and forbidding the states to violate the privileges and immunities of citizens, due process, and equal protection; and the fifteenth amendment (ratified in 1870), forbidding deprivation of the right to vote on the basis of race. The Reconstruction Amendments constitute, as a unit, the ultimate constitutional resolution of the long constitutional crisis that culminated in secession and the American Civil War of 1861–65. The amendments set out the new terms of principle on the basis of which the Union, in the wake of the Civil War, was to be reconstructed.[6]

The Reconstruction Amendments have been well studied by historians both in the context of the immediate events of the Civil War and its aftermath and in the larger context of the controversies of the antebellum period.[7] Some of that history has been taken to bear directly on interpretive questions about how the meaning of the amendments should be understood today. But there is no reasonable consensus among advocates of such views as to how history properly bears on such interpretive issues.

One such school of thought, which calls itself originalist, takes history to be relevant in terms of the particular concrete things (including practices) in the world to which the language of an amendment would or would not have been applied at the time the language was drafted, discussed, and ratified; the things included define the meaning of the constitutional terms, the things excluded are not within the meaning.[8] There are difficulties in-

---

[6] See Eric Foner, *Reconstruction: America's Unfinished Revolution, 1863–1877* (New York: Harper & Row, 1988).

[7] See, e.g., Harold M. Hyman, *A More Perfect Union: The Impact of the Civil War and Reconstruction on the Constitution* (New York: Knopf, 1973); Harold M. Hyman and William M. Wiecek, *Equal Justice under Law: Constitutional Development, 1835–1875* (New York: Harper & Row, 1982); Eric L. McKitrick, *Andrew Johnson and Reconstruction* (New York: Oxford University Press, 1960); Michael Les Benedict, *A Compromise of Principle: Congressional Republicans and Reconstruction 1793–1869* (New York: W. W. Norton, 1974); Foner, *Reconstruction*.

[8] See, e.g., Raoul Berger, *Government by Judiciary: The Transformation of the Fourteenth Amendment* (Cambridge: Harvard University Press, 1977); Robert Bork, *The Tempting of America: The Political Seduction of the Law* (New York: Free Press, 1990); Earl M. Maltz, *Civil Rights, The Constitution, and Congress, 1863–1869* (Lawrence: University Press of Kansas, 1990).

ternal to this approach, not well appreciated by its practitioners, about how we are to determine what the approach requires us to ascertain, namely, controlling intentions of a group of Founders—for example, whose intentions? Expressed when and how? At what level of generality? With what authority?

Aside from such difficulties, some of the originalist school's more notable advocates, such as Robert Bork, flatly refuse to follow this approach when it leads to results inconsistent with settled contemporary interpretive views (for example, that state-sponsored racial segregation is unconstitutional).[9] Indeed, they not only fail to offer good arguments of political or constitutional legitimacy that lend reasonable force to its way of interpreting the Constitution over competing views,[10] but they regard the question as unanswerable: "I do not know of any ultimate philosophic reason why it [the Constitution] should [be regarded as law]."[11] American constitutionalism, one of the greatest works of democratic public reason, is thus denatured to arbitrary, positivistic fiat. This makes no sense of the Constitution as supreme law and even less sense of the claims of authority that it has made on generations of Americans, including our own.

Another increasingly important school of historically based interpretive thought makes history interpretively relevant in a very different and more interesting way. Building on the pathbreaking work of Jacobus tenBroek[12] and Howard Graham,[13] interpretive attention has been drawn not to a contingent historical consensus on the scope of particular applications, but to the larger patterns of moral, political, and constitutional argument of the abolitionist movement and the role such arguments played in the drafting, ratification, and early interpretation of the Reconstruction Amendments.[14]

---

[9] On Robert Bork's specious attempt to offer an originalist argument for the unconstitutionality of state-sponsored racial segregation, see David A. J. Richards, "Originalism without Foundations," *New York University Law Review* 65, no. 5 (November 1990): 1379–82.

[10] I develop this criticism at greater length in Richards, *Toleration*, pp. 34–45; *Foundations*, pp. 5–11.

[11] See Bork, *The Tempting of America*, p. 174.

[12] See Jacobus tenBroek, *Equal under Law* (New York: Collier, 1969) (originally published as *The Antislavery Origins of the Fourteenth Amendment* in 1951 by University of California Press).

[13] See Howard Jay Graham, *Everyman's Constitution* (Madison: State Historical Society of Wisconsin, 1968).

[14] See Hyman, *A More Perfect Union*, Hyman and Wiecek, *Equal Justice under Law*, Robert J. Kaczorowski, *The Nationalization of Civil Rights: Constitutional Theory and Practice in a Racist Society, 1866–1883* (New York: Garland, 1987); Robert J. Kaczorowski, *The Politics of Judicial Interpretation: The Federal Courts, Department of Justice and Civil Rights, 1866–1876* (New York: Oceana, 1985); Robert J. Kaczorowski, "Searching for the Intent of the Framers of Fourteenth Amendment," *University of Connecticut Law Review* 5, no. 5 (Winter 1972–73): 368; Robert J. Kaczorowski, "Revolutionary Constitutionalism in the Era of the Civil War and Reconstruction," *New York University Law Review* 61, no. 5

There is, however, no reasonable consensus among these scholars about how abolitionist arguments interpretively clarify central terms of the Reconstruction Amendments (for example, the privileges and immunities clause of the fourteenth amendment).[15]

These disagreements are symptomatic of a more fundamental defect. Historians pay relatively little attention to the deeper questions of moral, political, and constitutional theory critically pressed by leading abolitionists both against one another and the larger political community. It simply fails to do justice, even historical justice, to the integrity of normative argument in politics, especially abolitionist rights-based moral and political argument, to dismiss it as "political rhetoric rather than legal analysis."[16] In fact, such argument articulated some of the most reasonable and critically rigorous moral argument of the age (or, for that matter, of any age) and must be understood in such terms. We need, at this point, the serious use of political theory to make sense of these arguments, something historians have not given us. This book will explore the dimensions of what we require.

This lapse in historical argument is, I believe, understandable in light of the interest of historians in contingent contextual explanation (with its tendency to relativism as a method of inquiry). The historical study of the Reconstruction Amendments has led some of the best historians of our generation quite properly to find a crucial part of the causal explanation in the power of ideas, in particular, the power of American abolitionist criticism as part of the larger Western movement of thought and action culminating in the abolition of slavery and the slave trade in Europe, the British West Indies, the United States, Latin America, and Russia.[17] The historian's interest in causation extends as well to the role such ideas play, however am-

---

(November 1986): 863; Paul Finkelman, "Prelude to the Fourteenth Amendment: Black Legal Rights in the Antebellum North," *Rutgers Law Journal* 17 (1986): 415; Paul Finkelman, "The Constitution and the Intentions of the Framers: The Limits of Historical Analysis," *University of Pittsburgh Law Review* 50, no. 2 (Winter 1989): 349; Michael Kent Curtis, *No State Shall Abridge: The Fourteenth Amendment and the Bill of Rights* (Durham, N.C.: Duke University Press, 1986); William E. Nelson, *The Fourteenth Amendment: From Political Principle to Judicial Doctrine* (Cambridge: Harvard University Press, 1988).

[15] Cf., e.g., Curtis, *No State Shall Abridge* (clause incorporates Bill of Rights and unenumerated rights against the states); and Nelson, *The Fourteenth Amendment* (clause arguably requires only equality among rights that states guarantee).

[16] See Nelson, *The Fourteenth Amendment*, p. 26.

[17] See David Brion Davis, *The Problem of Slavery in Western Culture* (Ithaca: Cornell University Press, 1967); David Brion Davis, *The Problem of Slavery in the Age of Revolution 1770–1823* (Ithaca: Cornell University Press, 1975); David Brion Davis, *Slavery and Human Progress* (New York: Oxford University Press, 1984); C. Duncan Rice, *The Rise and Fall of Black Slavery* (New York: Harper & Row, 1975).

bivalently, in actual interpretive practice.[18] But it is not a historical question to ask what sense should properly be made of history from the perspective of American constitutional interpretation as a distinctive genre of interpretation.[19] American constitutional interpretation centrally deploys arguments of political theory about the nature and scope of legitimate political power;[20] and the aims of this interpretation motivate the kind of interest we take in historical argument. We need, therefore, to ask what contribution political theory may and should make to the use of history in constitutional argument.

The Reconstruction Amendments as Political Theory

Contemporary political theory cannot advance interpretive understanding of the meaning of history if it is fundamentally antagonistic to the central normative arguments implicit in history or if it ascribes to history itself a kind of interpretive significance that it cannot reasonably bear. John Hart Ely and Bruce Ackerman develop procedural accounts of the Reconstruction Amendments that illustrate one or the other of these defects.

Ely stands out among contemporary constitutional theorists by virtue of his serious attention to both good arguments of critical historiography and his honesty in acknowledging the normative arguments central to that history, in particular, arguments protective of both enumerated and unenumerated basic human rights.[21] An interpretivist theory of the Constitution would, Ely argues, fully protect rights, including an unenumerated right such as the constitutional right to privacy extended to a woman's right to an abortion in *Roe v. Wade*.[22] Ely argues, however, that the historically based interpretivist theory of the Constitution must be critically assessed in light of the best political theory of democratic constitutionalism, a theory Ely associates with the Reconstruction Amendments in general and the equal protection clause of the fourteenth amendment in particular. If the interpretivist theory yields a result inconsistent with the political theory, that result is wrong; *Roe v. Wade*, though having a sound interpretivist basis in American constitutional history, is wrong because the judicial decision cannot be supported by what Ely takes to be the best democratic political theory.

[18] See, e.g., Nelson, *The Fourteenth Amendment*, pp. 148–200; Kaczorowski, *The Politics of Judicial Interpretation*.

[19] See Ronald Dworkin, *Law's Empire* (Cambridge: Harvard University Press, 1986). See also Richards, *Toleration*, pp. 20–45; and *Foundations*, pp. 131–71.

[20] See ibid.

[21] See John Hart Ely, *Democracy and Distrust: A Theory of Judicial Review* (Cambridge: Harvard University Press, 1980).

[22] 410 U.S. 113 (1973).

The two parts of Ely's theory work at critical cross purposes in this way because of the nature of the political theory that he takes to be the best democratic political theory of equal protection. That theory is skeptical about arguments of human rights because Ely finds contemporary theories of rights to be so controversial.[23] In the past, such forms of rights skepticism have been advocated by constitutional theorists such as Learned Hand as a consequence of Bentham's utilitarian skepticism about rights ("nonsense on stilts").[24] The utilitarian requirement of maximizing the net balance of pleasure over pain of all sentient beings may often, according to this view, require that some minority's interests be sacrificed to the extent required to secure a greater aggregate overall. Arguments of human rights, which often protect certain interests from such sacrifice, are invalid because they frustrate the utilitarian imperative; they are nonsense on stilts because they have no foundation in the only solid basis ethics can have, namely, utilitarianism. Ely does not expressly avow utilitarianism as the basis for his skepticism about rights, including it (with rights-based ethical theories) as one among the unacceptably controversial political theories now in the field.[25] Ely's version of the best democratic political theory is presented as an appropriately noncontroversial, because nonsubstantive, political theory, namely, fair representation.

Fair representation interprets the values of political democracy in terms of whether the persons in the relevant political community affected by the state's actions have been fairly represented in the political process leading to these actions. The theory is strongly supportive of political democracy because it clearly calls for equal political rights as one way of ensuring the required fair representation; it supports the institutions of constitutional democracy because it requires judicial intervention in a democratic political process when that process expresses prejudices that fail fairly to give fair representation to the interests of a minority victimized by such prejudices. Ely identifies two relevant kinds of such prejudice: first-order prejudice, such as blind racial hatred, which is aggressively hostile to the interests of a racial minority; and second-order prejudice, which expresses itself in the use of stereotypes—"those involving a generalization whose incidence of counterexample is significantly higher than the legislative authority appears to have thought it was."[26] *Roe v. Wade*, however well rooted in interpretivist constitutional history, is illegitimate because it does not, in the required way, rectify unfair representation; indeed, according to

[23] See Ely, *Democracy and Distrust*, pp. 56–60.
[24] See Learned Hand, *The Bill of Rights* (New York: Atheneum, 1968). For Bentham's classic criticism of rights, see Jeremy Bentham, "Anarchical Fallacies," *The Works of Jeremy Bentham*, ed. John Bowring, book 2 (Edinburgh: W. Tait 1843), pp. 491–529.
[25] See Ely, *Democracy and Distrust*, p. 58.
[26] Ibid., p. 157.

some views, the decision unfairly fails to give weight to relevant interests (those of fetuses).[27]

The appeal of Ely's version of democratic political theory is its putatively nonsubstantive, procedural character. Legitimate judicial intervention rests on the alleged procedural unfairness of two kinds of prejudice and the institutional competence of the judiciary (versus the legislature) to identify and rectify the unfair presence of such prejudice in politics. But the theory's proceduralism is suspect, resting on some substantive normative metric that delegitimates the frustration of certain human interests (those of victimized minority groups) by certain kinds of motivated political action by dominant majorities.

Why these interests and those motivations? One natural explanation would be that some appropriately defined utilitarian principle forbids such actions by the state in order to realize the higher net aggregate of pleasure over pain produced by limiting the severe frustration of human interests for no correspondingly weighty gain by others in the pursuit of their welfare. If so, Ely's rights skepticism rests on an unexamined commitment to utilitarianism at one remove. Or it rests on some other form of evaluation (weighing certain interests more heavily than others) that is clearly substantive in nature.

Ely's proceduralism, allegedly attractive because of its nonsubstantive character, assumes a policy-based substantive political theory; and the judiciary, *pace* Ely, enjoys no greater institutional competence at making such policy judgments than the legislature. Ely's repudiation of substantive moral theory rests on a substantive theory, one that apparently substitutes labels (procedure versus substance) for the kind of careful weighing of substantive moral arguments that the issue surely deserves if it is to be the Archimedean point from which interpretive history is to be criticized and sometimes rejected.

The theoretical incoherence of Ely's argument undermines the interpretive cogency of his affirmative case for when judicial intervention is justified. The first kind of prejudice, overt racial hostility, captures only the most blatantly obvious evils of racial discrimination; it fails clearly to articulate the nature of the political evil even in so clearly unconstitutional a practice as state-sponsored racial segregation,[28] which has been justified (the doctrine of separate but equal) as the best way of assuring the interests of all alike.[29] The second kind of prejudice, resting on factually inaccurate stereotypes, fails to take seriously the powerful constitutional objections to

[27] See John Hart Ely, "The Wages of Crying Wolf: A Comment on *Roe v. Wade*," *Yale Law Journal* 82, no. 5 (April 1974): 920.

[28] See *Brown v. Board of Education*, 347 U.S. 483 (1954).

[29] For a good recent history of the doctrine, see Charles A. Lofgren, *The Plessy Case: A Legal-Historical Interpretation* (New York: Oxford University Press, 1987).

factually accurate stereotypes that rest on and therefore legitimate a prior history of unjust subjugation.[30] Ely's quasi-utilitarian account of prejudice is aspect blind to the nature of the political evil (the insult to human rights) central to much equal protection jurisprudence, and to the institutional competence of the judiciary (versus the legislature) in affording a forum of principle for the protection of basic rights.

It was surely Ely's central purpose to defend equal protection jurisprudence in contrast to the substantive due process jurisprudence that he meant to condemn. He has neither well defended the one nor fairly attacked the other. Certainly, Ely's attempt to edit and revise an interpretivist reading of American constitutional history (that takes seriously its commitment to the protection of human rights both enumerated and unenumerated) fails. He has offered a freestanding political theory, against which interpretivist history is found wanting, but he has not given us a well-argued political theory and thus a good reason for subverting interpretivism. The challenge must be, in the wake of these defects, to investigate whether we may construct both a better political theory and, at the same time, a better interpretation of our rights-based constitutional tradition.

If Ely argues for the priority of political theory over history in constitutional interpretation, Bruce Ackerman exactly reverses that priority. Ackerman has independently offered what he takes to be the best substantive political theory;[31] the measure of correct constitutional interpretation is not, he argues, such a freestanding substantive political theory but historical events that satisfy certain procedural tests required by constitutional theory. Ackerman identifies these historical events as Publian moments of constitutional politics, that is, not only the Constitution of 1787 and subsequent amendments, but periods of widespread public argument over higher-order constitutional issues that culminate in a new consensus on these issues reflected in the concurrence among relevant authorities (for example, the president, Congress, and the Supreme Court of the United States);[32] he calls these latter changes in constitutional views structural amendments. Publian moments, including structural amendments, are the higher lawmaking procedure of the supreme law of American constitutionalism, against which ordinary politics is to be tested for its validity as law.

Ackerman has made an important contribution to constitutional theory

[30] See *Craig v. Boren*, 429 U.S. 190 (1976).

[31] See Bruce A. Ackerman, *Social Justice in the Liberal State* (New Haven: Yale University Press, 1980).

[32] See Bruce Ackerman, "The Storrs Lectures: Discovering the Constitution," *Yale Law Journal* 93, no. 6 (May 1984): 1013; "Constitutional Politics/Constitutional Law," *Yale Law Journal* 99, no. 3 (December 1989): 453; *We the People* (Cambridge: Harvard University Press, 1991).

by urging attention to nonjudicial forms of public argument in the development of American constitutionalism; he has, however, not given this phenomenon the interpretive characterization it requires. If Ely's proceduralism rests on an inadequately defended political theory, Ackerman's rests on defective interpretive history. His theory of structural amendments claims that certain important American constitutional developments cannot be understood as properly interpretive; he fails, however, adequately to defend this claim.[33]

For example, Ackerman revives interpretive doubts about the constitutional validity of the ratification of the fourteenth amendment and then justifies it as a structural amendment. The interpretive claim is that the required ratification of the amendment by three-fourths of the states was inadequate because, in contrast to the thirteenth amendment, the unreconstructed southern states rejected it; these states ratified it only after having been both reconstructed by Congress and denied admission to Congress until they ratified the amendment.[34] How, Ackerman asks, if the ratifications of southern state governments were valid for purposes of ratification of the thirteenth amendment, can they be held invalid for purposes of ratification of the fourteenth?

But Ackerman fails to engage serious investigation of the complexities both of interpretation and legitimacy surrounding the drafting, congressional approval, and state ratification of the fourteenth amendment. Such an investigation requires taking seriously what Ackerman denies, the role of substantive political theory in the interpretation of constitutionally legitimate government.

Secession and civil war—the most tragic failure of American constitutional institutions to resolve constitutional controversy deliberatively as a free and democratic people—required Americans to reflect on the form of constitutional government, both its interpretation and legitimacy, in a way they had not done since the Constitution of 1787. By comparison, the previous amendments basically clarified the 1787 consensus (the Bill of Rights)[35] or corrected judicial mistake in light of that consensus[36] or at-

---

[33] There may be amendment procedures to the U.S. Constitution beyond those textually specified, but Ackerman's structural amendments are not among them. For a recent argument that there are such amendments, see Akhil Reed Amar, "Philadelphia Revisited: Amending the Constitution Outside Article V," *University of Chicago Law Review* 55, no. 4 (Fall 1988): 1043; see also Akhil Reed Amar, "Of Sovereignty and Federalism," *Yale Law Journal* 96, no. 7 (June 1987): 1425.

[34] See Ackerman, "Constitutional Politics/Constitutional Law," pp. 500–507.

[35] See U.S. Constitution, Amendments I–X (ratified 1791); for commentary, see Bernard Schwartz, *The Great Rights of Mankind* (New York: Oxford University Press, 1977). For fuller discussion of the integral relationship between the Bill of Rights and the Constitution of 1787, see Richards, *Foundations*, pp. 220–22.

[36] See U.S. Constitution, Amendment XI (ratified 1798), depriving federal judiciary of

tended to electoral details.[37] In the wake of the Civil War, however, Americans fundamentally questioned the ways in which the Constitution had been interpreted in the antebellum period. Indeed, they revived the kinds of questions central to the deliberations of the Founders of 1787—the legitimacy of political power and the role of constitutional institutions in securing such legitimacy (including doubts about the Constitution itself).[38] Two interpretive issues regarding the validity of the fourteenth amendment's ratification turn on arguments of political theory.

First, the dominant theory of congressional reconstruction was the clause of the Constitution making the United States a guarantor of the republican form of government in all the states.[39] The interpretation of that theory by the Reconstruction Congress must be seen in the light of abolitionist constitutional theories, some of which had prominently developed an interpretation of the clause empowering Congress to attack slavery in the states.[40] Under this view, slavery in the southern states, depriving persons of their inalienable human rights, made those states nonrepublican; and Congress had an enforcement power to end slavery there and take whatever further steps were required to guarantee to all persons in those states protection of their equal rights (including ratification of the fourteenth amendment). In effect, only republican states have the constitutional power of ratification in such a union, and Congress has the power to ensure that states are republican in the required way (including readmission to Congress only after ratification of the fourteenth amendment). Such a congressional judgment regarding ratification of the fourteenth amendment was not inconsistent with its judgment about ratification of the thirteenth in view of the constitutionally relevant difference—in the one case resistance

---

power over certain suits against states; for commentary, see John V. Orth, *The Judicial Power of the United States: The Eleventh Amendment in American History* (New York: Oxford University Press, 1987).

[37] See U.S. Constitution, Amendment XII (ratified 1804), specifying procedures for elections of president.

[38] See, e.g., Sidney George Fisher, *The Trial of the Constitution* (Philadelphia: J. B. Lippincott, 1862).

[39] See U.S. Constitution, Art. IV, sec. 4: "The United States shall guarantee to every state in this union a republican form of government." For authoritative discussion of the background and interpretation of the clause, including its uses in the constitutional debates over reconstruction, see William M. Wiecek, *The Guarantee Clause of the U.S. Constitution* (Ithaca: Cornell University Press, 1972). For a good discussion of the range of alternative constitutional theories of reconstruction, see McKitrick, *Andrew Johnson and Reconstruction*, pp. 93–119.

[40] For a good general discussion, see Wiecek, *The Guarantee Clause*, pp. 155–65. One such theory had been powerfully stated by Theodore Parker, a major influence on the thought of Senator Charles Sumner of Massachusetts, shortly before the Civil War. See Theodore Parker, *The Relation of Slavery to a Republican Form of Government* (Boston: William L. Kent, 1858). For the influence of this argument on Sumner, see Hans L. Trefousse, *The Radical Republicans: Lincoln's Vanguard for Racial Justice* (New York: Knopf, 1969), p. 267.

and in the other acceptance of reasonable congressional guarantees of the republican character of the states in question.

Second, Ackerman's theory of structural amendments displaces attention from the real issues of constitutional and political legitimacy that were at stake in the Reconstruction Amendments. Comparable issues had arisen over the validity of the ratification of the Constitution of 1787 by three-fourths of the states in light of the requirement of the Articles of Confederation that any constitutional change should be unanimous by state governments (not, as the Constitution of 1787 required, by constitutional conventions separately elected for the purpose by the people of the state). In response to arguments of this sort, Madison in *The Federalist* had impatiently described the thinking of the Founders as resting on "the transcendent and precious right to the people to 'abolish or alter their governments as to them shall seem most likely to effect their safety and happiness'" (citing Declaration of Independence).[41] Madison also went on to offer a "perhaps"[42] valid argument that the Articles may, by its own terms as a treaty among states, be no longer valid, and therefore not legally bar the new procedures of ratification of the Constitution. The degree to which various states have defaulted in their obligations under the Articles dissolved, under the law of treaties, the obligation of other parties to regard them as any longer bound. Madison thus combined both an argument of revolutionary political theory and an interpretive argument about the meaning of the Articles.

The American Civil War is now conventionally termed by American historians "the second American Revolution."[43] If the circumstances of the nation were revolutionary, we need to ask, as did Madison, how that fact should affect both the legitimacy and the interpretation of the Constitution to which, as we shall see, all sides appealed in defense of their revolutionary activity. Both the fourteenth amendment and its procedures of ratification may reasonably be regarded not only as a sound interpretation of the Constitution (as we earlier saw), but a politically legitimate and appropriate expression of American revolutionary constitutionalism. If Americans had the revolutionary right to disown the Articles of Confederation (including its ratification procedures) and establish a more legitimate Union, Ameri-

[41] See Jacob E. Cooke, ed., *The Federalist Papers No. 40* (Middletown, Conn.: Wesleyan University Press, 1961), p. 265. Madison later repeats his citation to the arguments of the revolutionary legitimacy of the Declaration of Independence in explicit response to the argument of the alleged invalidity of any ratification of the Constitution in light of the Articles. See *The Federalist No. 43*, p. 297.

[42] See *The Federalist No. 43*, p. 297.

[43] See, e.g., James M. McPherson, *Abraham Lincoln and the Second American Revolution* (New York: Oxford University Press, 1990). For an early statement of the view, see Charles A. Beard and Mary R. Beard, *The Rise of American Civilization* (New York: Macmillan, 1930), 2:53ff.

cans in 1865 had at least the same revolutionary right to disown the Constitution (and its ratification procedures)—which had so egregiously violated basic human rights—in order to establish a Union that respected rights.

Ackerman's misguided concern, following Ely, to develop procedural models for constitutional doctrine explains as well the inadequacy of his attempt to analyze equal protection as a corrective for political powerlessness alone—roughly, according a politically disfavored group the political weight it would be accorded were it a group of that size not disfavored in political bargaining.[44] The account regards the gains in political solidarity of groups subjected to deep racial or religious prejudice as a reason for not regarding them as objects of special equal protection concern at least when political action by them has reached a certain level of power and achievement; and conversely, the view warrants equal protection concern for political groups that are less effective than their numbers would warrant (women, the poor, and homosexuals). The view proves too little and too much; it fails to protect the groups most deserving of protection from irrational prejudice *for that reason alone* (including, as we shall see, women, homosexuals, and the poor); and it extends protection to any political group (though subject to no such prejudice) solely because it has not been as politically successful as it might have been (say, dentists). Again, a model of fair democratic procedure suppresses the underlying substantive moral judgments central to how equal protection has been and should be interpreted.

Procedural models of American constitutionalism, such as Ely's and Ackerman's, have significantly advanced our understanding of democracy and constitutionalism. The common defect of their theories, however, is their suppression of the essential issues of the protection of human rights, in terms of which the American theory of democracy, as Lincoln correctly understood it,[45] should be construed. A theory of our democratic constitutionalism will surely do a better job if it can fruitfully engage the issue, integrating interpretive history, law, and rights-based political theory.

An Alternative Approach

The study of constitutional interpretation in the United States must bring history, law, and political theory into a fruitful working relationship. In

[44] See Bruce Ackerman, "Beyond *Carolene Products*," *Harvard Law Review* 98, no. 4 (February 1985): 713.

[45] "As I would not be a *slave*, so I would not be a *master*. This expresses my idea of democracy. Whatever differs from this, to the extent of the difference, is no democracy." Don Fehrenbacher, ed., *Abraham Lincoln: Speeches and Writings, 1832–1858* (New York: Library of America, 1989), p. 484.

Toleration and *Foundations*, I argued that American constitutionalism, consistent with Dworkin's interpretive methodology of fit and background rights,[46] should be interpreted as a complex genre (defined by the six ingredients of American revolutionary constitutionalism) that both best fits its traditions and, in periods of fundamental interpretive controversy, offers the best normative articulation of the abstract background rights in terms of which such controversies should be understood and resolved.

Consistent with this perspective, American constitutionalism should be understood in terms of historically evolving interpretive practices that aspire to narrative integrity in telling the constitutional story of a people's self-consciously historical struggle to achieve a politically legitimate government that would guarantee persons their equal human rights. Constitutional interpretation must make use of historical argument constructively to articulate the thread of legal texts, principles, and institutions that constitute over time the struggle for a political community in the genre of American revolutionary constitutionalism. Such interpretation must use the best available political theory of human rights to make contextual sense of the ultimate rights-based normative ends of the constitutional project.

The Reconstruction Amendments were the expression of the greatest struggle of the American people since the founding to remember and recover the narrative thread of their story of themselves as a people constituted by their revolutionary constitutionalism. Antebellum American political history set the stage for the amendments; but the dramatic focus for our purposes was the interpretive agon over the meaning of the U.S. Constitution as a central feature of that political history.

Constitutional democracy is an essentially contestable normative concept,[47] and its interpretation is correspondingly contestable. The Reconstruction Amendments reflected a complex interpretive contest over both the normative justification of constitutional democracy and the proper interpretation of the U.S. Constitution as a putatively legitimate institutional expression of constitutional democracy. This contest was expressed in terms of competing constitutional theories, namely, proslavery constitutionalism, the theory of Union, radical disunionism, and moderate and radical antislavery (see Chapters 2–3). If the legitimacy of the American Revolution required a form of constitutionalism (in contrast to the corrupt British Constitution) adequate to its normative demands, the legitimacy of the Civil War required a comparably probing reflection on constitutional decadence (the Constitution of 1787) adequate to its demands for a rebirth of rights-based constitutional government. Antebellum antislavery constitutional

---

[46] See Dworkin, *Law's Empire*.

[47] See W. B. Gallie, "Essentially Contested Concepts," in his *Philosophy and the Historical Understanding*, 2d ed. (New York: Schocken Books, 1968), chap. 8.

theories offered, consistent with the genre of American revolutionary constitutionalism, remedies that were regarded as the most justifiable way to correct central defects in the Constitution of 1787. The Reconstruction Amendments self-consciously embodied these remedies as constitutional law and are best understood and interpreted against this background (see Chapter 4).

Constitutional interpretation today may reasonably take an interest in the political and constitutional theories of the antebellum period because they are central to the continuing narrative of the genre of American revolutionary constitutionalism carried forward by the Reconstruction Amendments. Otherwise, we forget and therefore obliviously betray, as Americans did in the antebellum period, our role in the continuing American story of constitutional liberties and responsibilities under American public law. The special contribution of antebellum political and constitutional theory to this unfolding narrative is its focus on constitutional interpretation itself in light of the history and text of the Constitution of 1787 and its background political theory (see Chapters 3–4). The Reconstruction Amendments continue the story of American revolutionary constitutionalism against that background. The argument of this book is that our generation must cultivate the interdisciplinary competence to tell this story of American political and constitutional theory truly in all its range and depth, learn from it, and understand our conservative interpretive responsibilities accordingly.

Constitutional interpretation today of the Reconstruction Amendments may productively take an interest in the arguments of political and constitutional theory in the antebellum period for the same reason that political and moral philosophers take an interest in the pivotal developmental periods of modern normative ideals and arguments (for example, of toleration); in both domains, such study clarifies the distinctive force and originality of the foundational normative arguments central to our moral and political culture. That kind of interpretive enterprise should not, in turn, be sharply separated from the state of contemporary rights-based political theory because its contemporary meaning (including its relevance to constitutional theory) often clarifies, and is clarified by, its historical tradition. Indeed, to the extent that the best contemporary political theory yields a better understanding of what the enduring values of the tradition are, it enables us to read the moral meaning of great normative struggles such as that over slavery and racism in historically truer and more illuminating ways. We may understand them not as shallow polemics (as historians sometimes suppose), but as the great morally transformative developments in humane political conscience that they were. We may thus better understand and meet our responsibilities today to interpret this great legacy of humane moral intelligence on comparably transformative terms in our circumstances (for example, in the areas of gender or homosexuality or poverty; see Chapters 5–7). Contemporary political theory and interpretive history must work together in service of the integrity of constitutional argument.

The Reconstruction Amendments must be understood not only as an expression of the moral, political, and constitutional arguments of the abolitionists (as many historians also argue), but as an expression of a general political theory of human rights (centering on the argument for toleration based on the right to conscience) that leading abolitionist and related thinkers powerfully developed in both the moral criticism of slavery and racism and the political and constitutional criticism of the direction American institutions took in the antebellum period. Contemporary rights-based contractualist political theory illuminates these developments; it affords the kind of political theory that clarifies[48] and, unlike Ely's, does not distort the interpretive history of our constitutionalism and our interpretive responsibilities today to make the best sense we can of the principles of the Reconstruction Amendments in our circumstances. Suitably understood, this political theory fits our traditions and, in times of conflict over the meaning of our traditions, has given and gives the best interpretation of the values of human rights in terms of which such disputes are and should be resolved.

The interpretive fertility of my account will be played out in several domains. One of the principles of the Reconstruction Amendments, that of the equal protection clause of the fourteenth amendment, has been interpreted to attack the expression of forms of prejudice through law. A political theory of the Reconstruction Amendments that can clarify the sources and nature of the judgment of the evil of racism (clarifying, for example, common elements in the abolitionist criticism of racism and anti-Semitism) will advance interpretive understanding of the many issues of constitutional law that turn upon the expression of prejudice through public law (see Chapter 5). The theory also illuminates the principle, stated either in the privileges and immunities or due process clause of the fourteenth amendment, that has been interpreted to nationalize the protection of human rights (see Chapter 6); and it informatively advances discussion of the recurrent constitutional controversies that have arisen over the degree to which, if at all, the principles of the fourteenth amendment do or do not protect economic rights and interests (see Chapter 7). Finally, an account of these amend-

---

[48] For theories along similar lines, see, e.g., Judith A. Baer, *Equality under the Constitution: Reclaiming the Fourteenth Amendment* (Ithaca: Cornell University Press, 1983); Kenneth L. Karst, *Belonging to America: Equal Citizenship and the Constitution* (New Haven: Yale University Press, 1989).

ments that does justice to their roots in radical moral and political rights-based criticism of conscience in light of public reason enables us better to grasp our interpretive responsibilities today in preserving and elaborating the constitutional tradition of morally independent criticism and dissent that these amendments make centrally American (see Chapter 8).

TWO

PROSLAVERY CONSTITUTIONALISM VERSUS
THE THEORY OF UNION

THE AMERICAN CIVIL WAR, the second American Revolution, was understood by both parties to it as a controversy over the political theory of the first revolution and the constitutionalism in terms of which the revolution justified its claims. The Reconstruction Amendments were the culminating constitutionalism of this controversy, and we need to explore the competing constitutional theories central to this controversy.

I begin with the roots of the antebellum constitutional crisis in the founding itself and then turn to examine two important early competing constitutional theories—proslavery constitutionalism and the theory of Union. The next chapter will examine abolitionism and the range of constitutional theories to which it gave rise—radical disunionism and moderate and radical antislavery. Each form of antebellum constitutional theory will be examined in light of the variant interpretation it gives of the six ingredients of American revolutionary constitutionalism—its political theory of inalienable human rights, the interpretation of constitutional principles as embodying that theory, the analysis of political psychology, use of comparative political science, appeal to American political experience, and the treatment of constitutional argument as supreme over ordinary democratic politics.

Antebellum Constitutional Crisis: Slavery and the Founding

Leading Founders such as Madison presciently anticipated the weight they would have as Founders in later American constitutional controversy. In *The Federalist No. 49*, Madison (disagreeing with Jefferson) argued against a more easily amendable constitution of the sort Jefferson had proposed for Virginia on the ground that appeals to a written constitution rather than easy appeals to the people were more likely to ensure "[a] reverence for the laws" congruent with "the voice of an enlightened reason."[1]

The issue at stake in *No. 49* was not the reasonableness of the Consti-

[1] See *The Federalist No. 49*, p. 340.

tution, but what amendment procedure was more likely, after ratification, to sustain a public opinion supportive of such constitutional reasonableness over time.[2] In view of the power of faction in ordinary politics, Madison knew that appeals to reason would not be enough later on to preserve allegiance to constitutional reason: "a nation of philosophers is as little to be expected as the philosophical race of kings wished for by Plato."[3] The historical weight of a moment such as the American founding, understood not to be easily subject to change, could usefully forge a consensus of tradition that, if not itself based on reason, would be consistent with reason against distortions of constitutionalism motivated by political factions. If constitutional controversies should be resolved by such factions, "the *passions* . . . not *the reason*, of the public, would sit in judgment," but it was "the reason of the public alone that ought to controul and regulate the government."[4]

The U.S. Constitution, last amended in 1804, became during the antebellum period exactly the kind of venerated interpretive object that Madison anticipated. But there was a dark side to Madison's success, one anticipated by his very real private doubts about the compromises that led to the Constitution of 1787. Understanding these doubts yields a clarifying Founder's perspective not only on the internal tensions and even contradictions in the Constitution, but on the difficulties its interpretation would raise for Americans who came to venerate it.

Madison expressed these doubts at length in an important letter to Jefferson of October 24, 1787;[5] his primary doubt was the Constitution's failure to deal adequately with the degree to which state laws under the Articles of Confederation had violated rights. Madison characterized this concern as the central motivation leading to the Convention: "A reform therefore which does not make provision for private rights, must be materially defective."[6] What was needed was an instrumentality of federal control over state laws, which Madison identified with a congressional negative over such laws. The Convention's failure to adopt such a negative was the reason for Madison's blunt negative judgment on the work of the Convention expressed in an earlier letter to Jefferson: "I hazard an opinion nevertheless that the *plan should* it *be adopted* will neither effectually *answer*

[2] Madison had also explored this theme with Jefferson in their correspondence over Jefferson's principle "'that the earth belongs in usufruct to the living': that the dead have neither powers nor rights over it." For citation and discussion, see Richards, *Foundations*, pp. 134ff.

[3] *The Federalist No. 49*, p. 340.

[4] Ibid., p. 343.

[5] See James Madison, *The Papers of James Madison, 1787–1788*, ed. Robert A. Rutland et al. (Chicago: University of Chicago Press, 1977), 10:206–19.

[6] Ibid., 10:212.

its *national object* nor prevent the local *mischiefs* which every where *excite disgusts* agst the *state governments."*[7]

Madison's theory of faction identified a political psychology of group in-sularity and oppression that could be rendered consistent with the ends of republican government (the protection of rights and securing the public good) by the self-conscious constitutional design of political institutions that allowed expression to tendencies to faction only on terms likely to secure republican ends.[8] Madison's argument to Jefferson, later classically stated publicly in *The Federalist No. 10,* was that democratic representation in a large territory had the required constitutional properties; one such prop-erty was that diverse factions in various states and regions could only achieve their political ends democratically through nationwide coalitions based on respect for common rights and interests. The whole thrust of Mad-ison's argument was that only national institutions could be trusted to de-toxify the republican poison of faction. Local state politics, unmediated by any national representative principle, would be motored by faction run riot. The failure of the Constitution to afford any national institution to address this problem was, for Madison, a fundamental defect in constitutional design.

From this perspective, Madison's initial disinterest in a federal bill of rights makes sense.[9] Federal institutions, regulated by a principle of rep-resentation of national scope, were not the institutions most to be feared for potential abuse of human rights; their representative structure was likely to ensure an impartiality on issues of rights and the public interest. A federal bill of rights might thus be unnecessary. Much more to the point would be a nationally enforceable bill of rights applicable to the states along the lines of one of Madison's original proposals for a bill of rights, an amend-ment limiting state power over the rights to conscience, speech, and trial by jury in criminal cases.[10] Madison's proposal was, however, rejected in favor of language of the first amendment applicable only at the federal level: "Congress shall make no law."[11] For the Madison of the 1787 letters to Jef-ferson, the Bill of Rights of 1791 no more met the needs of the nation for an enlightened constitutionalism than the Constitution of 1787. Both were fundamentally flawed.

---

[7] Ibid., 10:163–64 (letter of Madison to Jefferson of 6 September 1787).

[8] For fuller analysis, see Richards, *Foundations,* pp. 32–49.

[9] For pertinent discussion and citations, see ibid., 220, 222, 227–28.

[10] Madison had recommended such an amendment in the following terms: "No State shall violate the equal rights of conscience, or the freedom of the press, or the trial by jury in criminal cases." See Leonard Levy, "No Establishment of Religion: The Original Understand-ing," in Leonard Levy, *Judgments: Essays on American Constitutional History* (Chicago: Quadrangle Books, 1972), p. 179.

[11] See U.S. Constitution, Amendment I.

The dark message of the Jefferson letter forebode an even darker un-spoken and perhaps unspeakable worry about the constitutionalism we now call Madisonian, namely, that it might be interpreted to give expression to the worst evils of state political faction. Madison's worries about consti-tutionally untrammeled state faction applied, a fortiori, to the form of property-based faction supporting slavery that he had described at the Constitutional Convention as "the mere distinction of colour made . . . a ground of the most oppressive dominion ever exercised by man over man."[12]

The Constitution did not merely fail to supply any national power (either a congressional negative or bill of rights) that might constrain this "most oppressive" of state factions. It extended to the property interest in slavery *constitutional* protections:[13] three-fifths additional representation for each slave,[14] a requirement that fugitive slaves be returned,[15] and a twenty-year moratorium on federal prohibition of the international slave trade.[16] Mad-ison successfully insisted that the language of such clauses not contain the word *slave*, objecting that "he thought it wrong to admit in the Constitution the idea that there could be property in men."[17] Madison's surgery was purely cosmetic; while he objected to the twenty-year moratorium clause,[18]

[12] See Max Farrand, ed., *The Records of the Federal Convention of 1787* (New Haven: Yale University Press, 1966), 1:135 (speech of 6 June 1787).

[13] See Paul Finkelman, "Slavery and the Constitutional Convention: Making a Covenant with Death," in Richard Beeman, Stephen Botein, and Edward Carlos Carter, eds., *Beyond Confederation: Origins of the Constitution and American National Identity* (Chapel Hill: University of North Carolina Press, 1987), pp. 188–225; Herbert J. Storing, "Slavery and the Moral Foundations of the American Republic," in Robert H. Horwitz, *The Moral Foundations of the American Republic*, 3d ed. (Charlottesville: University Press of Virginia, 1986), pp. 313–32.

[14] U.S. Constitution, Art. I, sec. 2: "Representatives and direct taxes shall be apportioned among the several states which may be included within this union, according to their re-spective numbers, which shall be determined by adding to the whole number of free persons, including those bound to service for a term of years, and excluding Indians not taxed, three-fifths of all other persons."

[15] U.S. Constitution, Art. IV, sec. 2: "No person held to service or labor in one state, under the laws thereof, escaping into another, shall, in consequence of any law or regulation therein, be discharged from such service or labor, but shall be delivered up on claim of the party to whom such service or labor may be due."

[16] U.S. Constitution, Art. I, sec. 9: "The migration or importation of such persons as any of the states now existing shall think proper to admit, shall not be prohibited by the Congress prior to the year 1808, but a tax or duty may be imposed on such importations, not exceeding ten dollars for each person."

[17] Farrand, *Records of the Federal Convention*, 2:417 (25 August 1787).

[18] "Twenty years will produce all the mischief that can be apprehended from the liberty to import slaves. So long a term will be more dishonorable to the National character than to say nothing about it in the Constitution." See ibid., 2:415.

he supported the general idea of some special constitutional protection for current property interests in slaves.[19] Indeed, no one at the Convention spoke more presciently than Madison of the real differences in interests among the states in future American politics (namely, slaveholding); and no one more realistically urged the need constitutionally to accommodate such differences in light of the principle: "Wherever there is danger of attack there ought be given a constitutional power of defence."[20]

Madison clearly included "the case of Black slaves in Modern times" as a paradigm example of "the danger of oppression to the minority from unjust combinations of the majority"[21]—indeed, in his already cited words at the Convention, "the most oppressive dominion ever exercised by man over man." Madison's constitutional thought, however, especially in 1787–88, gave independent normative weight to the rights of property; the unjust violations of such rights (for example, by state laws relieving debtors of obligations) were central political evils against which his constitutionalism was directed,[22] a fact Madison emphasized in *The Federalist No. 10*: "The most common and durable source of factions, has been the various and unequal distribution of property."[23] Indeed, property rights were, for Madison, so often unjustly abridged by popular factions that their protection required, so he argued at the Convention, that voters satisfying property qualifications were "the safest depositories of Republican liberty."[24]

Madison's concern for the injustices to property owners of popular factions must have carried over to slave owners; and we need, in light of his views about the injustice of property in slaves, to ask why.[25] Perhaps there is no really satisfying answer to this question of the sort that could relieve Madison and others of the charge of a morally defective understanding of

[19] In the Virginia Convention, Madison defended the fugitive slave clause as "expressly inserted, to enable owners of slaves to reclaim them. This is a better security than any that now exists." See Jonathan Elliot, *The Debates in the Several State Conventions on the Adoption of the Federal Constitution* (Philadelphia: J.B. Lippincott, 1836), 3:453.

[20] Farrand, *Records of the Federal Convention*, 1:486 (speech of 30 June 1787).

[21] James Madison, "Notes for the National Gazette Essays," in *The Papers of James Madison*, ed. Rutland et al., 14:160.

[22] For good general discussion of Madison's views on rights during this period, see Jack N. Rakove, "The Madisonian Theory of Rights," *William & Mary Law Review* 31, no. 2 (Winter 1990):245. See also Jack N. Rakove, "The Madisonian Moment," *University of Chicago Law Review* 55, no. 2 (Winter 1988):473.

[23] See *The Federalist No. 10*, p. 59.

[24] See Farrand, *Records of the Federal Convention*, 2:203.

[25] For a probing recent argument that the main flaw in Madisonian constitutionalism is the central place he accords property (Madison's treatment of slavery being an example of this more general problem), see Jennifer Nedelsky, *Private Property and the Limits of American Constitutionalism: The Madisonian Framework and Its Legacy* (Chicago: University of Chicago Press, 1990).

basic human rights.[26] We can at least understand, though not endorse, Madison's position along the following interpretive lines.

Madison would have thought of slave ownership on the model of himself and Jefferson in the circumstances of 1787 (the year that Jefferson's *Notes on the State of Virginia* was published). From this perspective, Madison might not unreasonably believe that some constitutional protection for this form of property would enable leaders like themselves, consistent with the argument in Jefferson's book,[27] better to abolish slavery on terms fair to all.

Under the influence of the revolutionary ideology of universal human rights, movements of abolition, some already successful, were well advanced in northern states.[28] Jefferson had now hopefully initiated such a movement in the South; and Congress had in 1787 finally agreed to prohibit slavery in the Northwest Territory (Jefferson's Ordinance of 1784 would have prohibited slavery in all territories).[29] Jefferson, both in an early draft of the Declaration of Independence[30] and now in *Notes*,[31] conspicuously blamed the British for foisting slavery on allegedly resisting Americans; and he was at great pains to advocate long-term gradual abolition in preference to immediate abolition; in the circumstances of Virginia, the latter would be culpably wrong (the political community could not reasonably accommodate freed slaves, and thus more harm would be done from immediate emancipation than from slavery itself).[32]

Not every act that is unjust is blameworthy, a proposition that Lincoln, not only Jefferson or Madison, believed to be true of southern slavery.[33] From this perspective, morally independent southern leadership—associated by Madison with the political independence of their property own-

[26] See, in general, Finkelman, "Slavery and the Constitutional Convention." See also Finkelman, "The Constitution and the Intentions of the Framers," pp. 392–93.

[27] See Thomas Jefferson, *Notes on the State of Virginia*, ed. William Peden (New York: W. W. Norton, 1982), pp. 87, 137–43, 162–63.

[28] See Arthur Zilversmit, *The First Emancipation: The Abolition of Slavery in the North* (Chicago: University of Chicago Press, 1967).

[29] See John Chester Miller, *The Wolf by the Ears: Thomas Jefferson and Slavery* (New York: Free Press, 1977), pp. 23–30. On Congress's treatment of the territories, see Donald L. Robinson, *Slavery in the Structure of American Politics, 1765–1820* (New York: Harcourt Brace Jovanovich, 1971), pp. 378–423.

[30] See Miller, *The Wolf by the Ears*, pp. 7–8.

[31] See Jefferson, *Notes on the State of Virginia*, p. 87.

[32] See ibid., pp. 137–43.

[33] "I have no prejudice against the Southern people. They are just what we would be in their situation. If slavery did not now exist amongst them, they would not introduce it. If it did now exist amongst us, we should not instantly give it up. . . . I surely will not blame them for not doing [abolishing slavery] what I should not know how to do myself." Abraham Lincoln, "Speech on Kansas-Nebraska Act," 16 October 1854, in Fehrenbacher, *Abraham Lincoln: Speeches and Writings, 1832–1858*, pp. 315–16.

ership—should be accorded constitutional protections for slavery that would enable them to resist the evil of immediate emancipation (advocated by certain factions) in order to end the injustice of slavery (on the model of Jefferson's recommendations of gradual emancipation) without culpably doing more injustice on balance than the institution itself.

This way of looking at the Constitution and slavery is, of course, an interpretive claim, a way of trying to make the best sense of the Constitution in light of the six ingredients of American revolutionary constitutionalism. The interpretation thus assumes that the Constitution should not be read as in flat contradiction to the revolutionary principles of natural rights[34] or the common-law principles of British constitutional liberty;[35] it reads the Constitution in light of a concern for the political psychology of faction and the use of comparative political science and American political experience to clarify the need for deliberative structures to limit the force of popular faction. The argument is put in terms that could be justifiable to all (that is, as better securing justice over all, including justice in the abolition of slavery).

But these six elements can be brought into some sensible working relationship in an overall interpretation of the Constitution only as long as slavery can reasonably be understood by all as a political evil on its way to abolition. Such views were not unanimously held even at the time of the American Revolution and the Constitution of 1787;[36] but in view of the long history of slavery and the brutality of the eighteenth century, that is not surprising. As Bernard Bailyn has recently insisted: "What is significant in the historical context of the time is not that the liberty-loving Revolutionaries allowed slavery to survive, but that they—even those who profited directly from the institution—went so far in condemning it, confining it, and setting in motion the forces that would ultimately destroy it."[37]

But the momentum for the abolition of slavery in the South had clearly

---

[34] James Otis in 1764 argued that "the colonists are by the law of nature freeborn, as indeed all men are, white or black." James Otis, "The Rights of the British Colonies Asserted and Proved" (Boston 1764), reprinted in Bernard Bailyn, ed., *Pamphlets of the American Revolution, 1750–1776* (Cambridge: Belknap Press, Harvard University Press, 1965), 1:439.

[35] Lord Mansfield's 1772 decision in *Sommersett v. Stuart*, King's Bench: 12 George III A.D. (1771–72) Lofft, 20 Howell's State Trials 1, had ruled that holding slaves in England, in the absence of sustaining parliamentary positive law, violated the common law. For further discussion of the case, see A. Leon Higginbotham, Jr., *In the Matter of Color: Race and the American Legal Process, The Colonial Period* (New York: Oxford University Press, 1978), pp. 313–68; Davis, *The Problem of Slavery in the Age of Revolution*, pp. 469–522.

[36] See, for good general studies, Duncan J. MacLeod, *Slavery, Race and the American Revolution* (Cambridge: Cambridge University Press, 1974); Robinson, *Slavery in the Structure of American Politics*.

[37] See Bernard Bailyn, *Faces of Revolution* (New York: Knopf, 1990), p. 222.

slowed in the first decades of the nineteenth century.[38] It decisively stopped in the South with the publication in 1832 of Thomas Dew's "Abolition of Negro Slavery,"[39] marking the 1831–32 heated and abortive debate in the Virginia legislature over emancipation. Dew rehearsed an argument very like that earlier ascribed to Madison searching for a mode of abolition that did not inflict greater injustice than slavery itself, but concluded, especially in light of the expense and cruelties of the colonization schemes for emancipated blacks, that retaining slavery was less unjust. Once slavery in the South was seen both in the South and North as not on its way to abolition, the six elements of American revolutionary constitutionalism fell into jangling disarray. The consequence was profound interpretive controversy over the Constitution, the venerated symbol of American national identity.

Proslavery Constitutionalism

When the two leaders of the Confederacy—its president, Jefferson Davis, and vice-president, Alexander Stephens—wrote their respective apologetics for their leadership in the wake of the Civil War, each justified his actions on the basis of an appeal to the Constitution of 1787.[40] Each emphatically denied that secession was motivated by the result-oriented preservation of slavery;[41] the point, rather, was a matter of interpretive principle about ultimate issues of constitutional power and authority.

Stephens had spoken in a different vein in 1861. Rejecting Jefferson's theories of equal human rights, he argued:

> Our new government is founded upon exactly the opposite idea; its foundations are laid, its corner-stone rests upon the great truth, that the negro is not equal to the white man; that slavery—subordination to the superior race—is his natural and normal condition. [Applause.]
>
> This, our new government, is the first, in the history of the world, based upon this great physical, philosophical, and moral truth.[42]

[38] On the responsibility of southern leaders such as Jefferson for the problem, see Miller, *The Wolf by the Ears*, see also Drew R. McCoy, *The Last of the Fathers: James Madison and the Republican Legacy* (Cambridge: Cambridge University Press, 1989).

[39] See Thomas Roderick Dew, "Abolition of Negro Slavery" (1832), reprinted in Drew Gilpin Faust, ed., *The Ideology of Slavery: Proslavery Thought in the Antebellum South, 1830–1860* (Baton Rouge: Louisiana State University Press, 1981), pp. 21–77.

[40] See Jefferson Davis, *The Rise and Fall of the Confederate Government* (Richmond, Va.: Garret & Massie, 1938), 2 vols., esp. 1:75–168; Alexander Stephens, *A Constitutional View of the Late War Between the States*, 2 vols. (Philadelphia: National Publishing Co., 1868–70).

[41] See Davis, *The Rise and Fall*, 1:65–72; Stephens, *A Constitutional View*, 1:9–12.

[42] See Alexander H. Stephens, "Sketch of the Corner-stone Speech" (21 March 1861 speech delivered in Savannah, Georgia), reprinted in Henry Cleveland, *Alexander H. Stephens, in Public and Private* (Philadelphia: National Publishing Co., 1866), p. 721.

Both Davis and Stephens acknowledged Calhoun to be the master of southern proslavery constitutional thought.[43] Such thought was essentially proslavery because the motivation of its interpretive attitude was to put the defense of the southern institution of slavery in the best possible constitutional light, indeed to make of southern secession and civil war legitimate expressions of American revolutionary constitutionalism.

At its origins, southern constitutionalism had not been ideologically proslavery or even distinctively southern; the original theory thus had appeal beyond the south, for example, to a New Yorker and Jacksonian Democrat such as Martin Van Buren.[44] The aim of this constitutionalism was to oppose the constitutional claims made on behalf of Federalists for national powers—for example, Hamilton's national bank, Adams's Alien and Sedition Act, and Marshall's Supreme Court.[45]

Jefferson and Madison, leading advocates of inalienable human rights and moral opponents to slavery, laid the foundations for the theory in their drafting of the 1798–99 Kentucky and Virginia Resolutions, resolutions by state legislatures challenging the constitutionality of the Alien and Sedition Act in part on grounds of its violation of the inalienable right of free speech.[46] Jefferson seminally framed the argument of the Kentucky Resolutions on the basis of state power under a compact theory of constitutionalism. Against unconstitutional actions by the national government, Jefferson asserted, "as in all other cases of compact among parties having no common judge, *each party has an equal right to judge for himself, as well of infractions as of the mode and measure of redress.*"[47] Madison, in contrast, phrased his claim as a political appeal "to the temperate consideration and candid judgment of the American public."[48]

Similarly, in his important 1803 edition of Blackstone's *Commentaries,* St. George Tucker, a law professor at William and Mary, argued that slavery violated American revolutionary principles in general and the Virginia bill of rights in particular, and proposed an emancipation scheme to abolish

[43] See Davis, *The Rise and Fall,* 1:13, 161; Stephens, *A Constitutional View,* 1:299–300, 340–44.

[44] See Martin Van Buren, *Inquiry into the Origin and Course of Political Parties in the United States* (New York: Hurd & Houghton, 1867). Van Buren's theory is self-consciously Jeffersonian, rights based, and court skeptical. He accordingly defends American Jacksonian political democracy as having led to a nation more rights respecting than any other. See ibid., pp. 88–89. See also Andrew E. Norman, ed., *The Autobiography of Martin Van Buren* (New York: Confucian Press, 1981).

[45] See, in general, John C. Miller, *The Federalist Era, 1789–1801* (New York: Harper & Row, 1960); Marshall Smelser, *The Democratic Republic, 1801–1815* (New York: Harper & Row, 1968).

[46] See Miller, *The Federalist Era,* pp. 228–42.

[47] See "Kentucky Revolutions of 1798 and 1799," reprinted in Elliot, *Debates,* 4:540.

[48] See "Madison's Report on the Virginia Resolutions," in Elliot, *Debates,* 4:548.

slavery in Virginia.[49] But on the basis of an appeal to the Lockean contractualist principles of the American Revolution, Tucker then argued that
the Constitution was a compact among states with each state, on the basis
of its role in ratification, having a right to secede when the government
violated constitutional principles. Consistent with the Constitution's status
as a treaty among states, the powers granted to the national government
should be narrowly construed.[50]

The most elaborate development of such a rights-based Jeffersonian constitutional theory was offered by John Taylor of Caroline. Taylor propounded a general political theory of inalienable human rights against the
allegedly aristocratic theories of John Adams;[51] the Virginia and Kentucky
Resolutions—directed against the Adams administration—exemplified
"the best restraint"[52] on aristocratically motivated unconstitutional usur-
pations. In his later, fuller developments of a distinctively constitutional
theory,[53] Taylor used an expressly Lockean contractualist theory of equal
inalienable natural rights and the right to revolution.[54] A Lockean theory
of the inalienable right to conscience was the model for the understanding
of other rights (for example, the right to property).[55]

Taylor spun an intricate web of argument that interpreted the U.S. Constitution in light of Lockean political theory and the other five ingredients
of American revolutionary constitutionalism. The distinctive virtues of the
American constitutional project were thus counterpointed to the class
balances of the British Constitution.[56] The pathologies of religious and

[49] See St. George Tucker, *Blackstone's Commentaries with Notes of Reference to the Constitution and Laws of the Federal Government of the United States and of the Commonwealth of Virginia* (Philadelphia: Birch & Small, 1803), Appendix Note H, "On the State of
Slavery in Virginia," 2:31–85.

[50] See ibid., Appendix Note B, "Of the Several Forms of Government," 1:7–78; on Locke,
see 1:7; on the inalienable right to reform government, see 1:20–21; on the right of secession,
see 1:73–75; on the Constitution as a compact among states, see 1:140–41, 150–55; on its
narrow construction as a treaty, see 1:143.

[51] See, in general, John Taylor, *An Inquiry into the Principles and Policy of the Government of the United States* (1814; reprint, New Haven: Yale University Press, 1950). Adams's
theory of constitutionalism, much misunderstood by Taylor, had been stated in his monumental *Defence of the Constitutions of Government of the United States of America*, reprinted in Charles Francis Adams, ed., *Works of John Adams* (Boston: Little, Brown, 1851),
4:278–588, 5:3–496, 6:3–220. For Adams's bemused responses to Taylor's misunderstandings,
see John Adams, "Letters to John Taylor," in 6:447–521. For commentary on Adams, see
Richards, *Foundations*, pp. 22, 93, 124.

[52] See Taylor, *An Inquiry*, p. 556.

[53] See John Taylor, *Construction Construed and Constitutions Vindicated* (1820; reprint,
New York: Da Capo Press, 1970), *New Views of the Constitution of the United States* (1820;
reprint, New York: Da Capo Press, 1971).

[54] See Taylor, *Construction Construed*, pp. 52, 53–58.

[55] See ibid., pp. 9–10, 19, 203–5, 230–31.

[56] See Taylor, *New Views*, pp. 46–48, 57, 208, 213–14; *Construction Construed*, pp. 59–
63.

economic faction were central concerns of constitutional argument.[57] Comparative political science and recent American political experience (particularly, the national bank) were consulted to draw lessons on how to understand constitutional principles.[58] And the force of the general interpretive argument was a higher-order reasonable justification of the Constitution to all persons in light of its contractualist principles of respect for human rights.[59] Taylor's interpretive argument was originalist: recapturing the meaning of America's revolutionary constitutionalism from what he took to be Hamilton's and Madison's distortions in *The Federalist*[60] and from the misinterpretations of John Marshall's Supreme Court.[61]

Taylor's treatment of Madison shows that his argument was not, like Abel Upshur's later originalist appeal,[62] essentially a strained reading of history; Taylor offered what he took to be the best interpretation of constitutional institutions in light of their background contractualist political theory, which he assumed to be interpretively prior to originalist history. His model of legitimate constitutional action was the kind of state resistance on grounds of constitutional principle exemplified by the Virginia and Kentucky Resolutions,[63] a use of state political power deliberatively to mobilize public opinion to bring federal institutions (including the Supreme Court) into line with respect for constitutional principles of inalienable rights such as free speech. Taylor accordingly argued for a compact theory of American constitutionalism.[64] Under this theory, each state had the right to interpose its deliberative judgment on constitutional issues between its own citizens and the federal government;[65] an ultimate right of appeal lay to the constitutional judgment of three-fourths of the states (exercising the amendment power)[66] or, if necessary, to revolt and secession.[67]

Taylor had stated the essential elements of Calhoun's later articulated doctrine of nullification, but he did not rest his argument on Calhoun's

[57] See, e.g., Taylor, *Constitutions Construed*, pp. 9–10.

[58] For discussion of the bank question, see Taylor, *Construction Construed*, pp. 79–202; on the Missouri Compromise, see ibid., pp. 291–314; on American political science and the history of republican governments, see Taylor, *New Views*, pp. 238–42, 284–85; and *An Inquiry*, pp. 158–61.

[59] See Taylor, *Construction Construed*.

[60] See Taylor, *New Views*, pp. 63–169.

[61] See Taylor, *Construction Construed*, pp. 79–201.

[62] See Abel P. Upshur, *A Brief Enquiry into the Nature and Character of Our Federal Government Being a Review of Judge Story's Commentaries* (1840; reprint, Philadelphia: John Campbell, 1863).

[63] See Taylor, *Construction Construed*, pp. 133–34.

[64] See Taylor, *New Views*, pp. 136–37.

[65] See ibid., pp. 70–71.

[66] See ibid., at pp. 254–47.

[67] See Taylor, *Construction Construed*, p. 243 (unimportant whether right to resist is natural only or natural and constitutional).

rights skepticism and theory of sovereignty. Rather, he made a functional inquiry into states as the best available deliberative institutions to protect inalienable rights, asking: "Which will act with most knowledge, discretion, legality, and effect, in maintaining the rights of the people, mobs or state governments?"[68] Since the Constitution was best interpreted as a compact among states, its grant of power to the national government should, consistent with principles governing the interpretation of treaties, be interpreted narrowly.[69] No federal power over slavery could, for example, be inferred.[70] Only the states with slavery could, Taylor argued, reasonably understand whether and how to abolish or otherwise how to ameliorate the institution.[71]

John C. Calhoun had, of course, read and learned much from Taylor,[72] but Calhoun's interpretive version of American revolutionary constitutionalism preserved mainly the high style of the tradition he claimed to be interpreting. In fact, Calhoun's argument denigrated or inverted each of the six substantive ingredients of American revolutionary constitutionalism.

First, Calhoun was aggressively skeptical about the existence of equal inalienable human rights in general and thus of the ethical appeal of the Declaration of Independence in particular—"the most dangerous of all political errors," Jefferson's "utterly false view."[73]

Second, American constitutionalism was interpreted not in light of the vices but of the virtues of Britain's class-balanced constitution.[74]

Third, Calhoun made no use of the theory of faction of *The Federalist No. 10*, that is, the tendency of the political psychology of groups to denigrate the rights and interests of individuals as outsiders. His constitutional thought conceptualized politics as "an aggregate, in fact, of communities, not of individuals,"[75] and took the protection of communities as

---

[68] See ibid., at p. 188.

[69] See ibid., pp. 49, 144, 150–51, 243.

[70] See ibid., pp. 126, 142, 167, 284; Taylor, *New Views*, pp. 276–77.

[71] See Taylor, *Construction Construed*, pp. 293–94, 300–301. For Taylor's ambivalent views on slavery as a basic evil but with many more ancillary goods than Jefferson acknowledged (including heightening the love and competence for freedom of nonslaves), see John Taylor, *Arator*, ed. M. E. Bradford (1818; reprint, Indianapolis: Liberty Classics, 1977), pp. 115–25.

[72] See August O. Spain, *The Political Theory of John C. Calhoun* (New York: Bookman Associates, 1951), pp. 35–36, 50–55; Charles M. Wiltse, *John C. Calhoun: Sectionalist, 1840–1850* (Indianapolis: Bobbs-Merrill, 1951), p. 420.

[73] John Calhoun, "Speech on the Oregon Bill," delivered in the Senate, 27 June 1848, reprinted in *The Works of John C. Calhoun*, ed. Richard K. Cralle, 4 vols. (New York: D. Appleton, 1861–64), 4:511–12.

[74] See John C. Calhoun, *A Disquisition on Government*, ed. Richard K. Cralle (1853; reprint, New York: Peter Smith, 1943), pp. 63, 98–103, 105–6.

[75] John C. Calhoun, "Remarks on the State Rights' Resolutions in regard to Abolition," speech delivered in the Senate, 27 December 1837, in *Works*, 3:180.

normatively central. Indeed, Calhoun stated the *moral* end of politics to be "the preservation and perpetuation of the race";[76] the prejudice Madison had termed the most oppressive of factions defined the *end* of Calhoun's constitutionalism.

Fourth, in contrast to a Madisonian constitutionalism based on learning from the pathologies of political psychology under classical republicanism, Calhoun's distinctive contribution, the theory of concurrent majorities, was based on ancient institutions of the Roman republic;[77] and his concepts of ethics and politics notably drew inspiration from the Greeks (Aristotle in particular).[78]

Fifth, Calhoun's argument drew none of its force from the cumulative democratic political experience at the state and national levels from which American revolutionary constitutionalism had learned so much. Indeed, the not entirely unfriendly critic Frederick Grimke pointed out that Calhoun's main substantive claim, the veto power of states over national legislation applicable to them, called for a constitutional principle at the national level that experience at the state level had not suggested or supported.[79]

Sixth, Calhoun's argument was profoundly sectional: it could not and did not reasonably appeal to the nation at large as an argument stating a constitutionally legitimate constraint on ordinary factionalized politics; indeed, its very popularity in the South marked the decisive emergence of what Carpenter has called "the south as a conscious minority."[80] Leading politicians outside the South, such as Senator Stephen Douglas, certainly took political positions on some issues in support of the South, but not on all issues in the terms required by Calhoun's rigorously sectional logic.[81]

In the genre of constitutional argument, Calhoun's theory has enjoyed respect because of the brilliance and clarity of its statement of the problem

[76] See Calhoun, *A Disquisition on Government*, p. 58.

[77] See John C. Calhoun, "Speech on the Force Bill," delivered in the Senate, 15–16 February 1833, in *Works*, 257–57, where the inference is quite clearly made.

[78] See Spain, *The Political Theory of John C. Calhoun*, pp. 94–95, 105, 227–29, 263–64.

[79] See Frederick Grimke, *The Nature and Tendency of Free Institutions* (1848; reprint, Cambridge: Belknap Press, Harvard University Press, 1968), p. 493. While Grimke criticizes the theory of nullification cogently, (pp. 477–502), he offers a race-based justification for southern slavery (pp. 417–37) and defends the constitutional right of secession (pp. 503–17).

[80] See Jesse T. Carpenter, *The South as a Conscious Minority, 1789–1861* (New York: New York University Press, 1930).

[81] For Douglas's strained attempt to defend popular sovereignty against both southern and northern critics as the best reading of American constitutional traditions, see Stephen A. Douglas, "The Dividing Line between Federal and Local Authority: Popular Sovereignty in the Territories," *Harper's New Monthly Magazine* (September 1859): 519. For background, see Robert W. Johannsen, *Stephen A. Douglas* (New York: Oxford University Press, 1973).

of constitutional government and the ingenuity with which he solved it.[82] The problem was that the normative goal of politics ("one that would embrace the consent of every citizen or member of the community") was not achieved by simple majority rule, "government of a part,—the major over the minor portion."[83] The constitutional scheme of concurrent majorities assumed that the consent of all relevant persons (the normative goal of politics) could be identified with homogeneous interest groups (in which, by definition, all persons have the same interests). The ingenuity of the scheme was constitutionally to require all such interest groups to consent as a way of better approximating the underlying normative goal. Calhoun defended nullification as an interpretation of the U.S. Constitution because it allowed each state (a homogeneous interest group) to have the power it should have under this constitutional theory (namely, to veto national political action applicable to it).

Calhoun stated the normative end of constitutional argument in terms of contractualist equality, but he repudiated, as we have seen, any rights-based interpretation of such equality. His interpretation was, rather, utilitarian: "To enlist the individual on the side of the social feelings to promote the good of the whole, is the greatest possible achievement of the science of government."[84] The utilitarian interpretation of equality gives equal weight to all pleasures and pains irrespective of their sources or objects, and then requires those actions that lead to the greatest aggregate of pleasure over pain of all sentient beings. Calhoun was evidently exploiting the natural tendency of utilitarian thought to allow the pains of a few (for example, slaves) to be subordinated to the greater aggregate satisfaction of all.[85] Many utilitarians (notably, Bentham), as hostile to the language and thought of rights as Calhoun, did not draw the conclusions he did about slavery.[86] But Calhoun, like others in the South who invoked rights-skeptical utilitarianism to similar effect,[87] did draw these conclusions, find-

---

[82] For a respectful treatment, see Spain, *The Political Theory of John C. Calhoun*; cf. Louis Hartz, *The Liberal Tradition in America* (New York: Harcourt, Brace & World, 1955), pp. 145–200. For a recent philosophical treatment of secession that pays tribute to at least some ingredients of the southern position (its claims of redistributive justice against national tariffs, not, of course, its ultimate defense of slavery), see Allen Buchanan, *Secession: The Morality of Political Divorce from Fort Sumter to Lithuania and Quebec* (Boulder: Westview Press, 1991), pp. 69, 157–58.

[83] See Calhoun, *A Disquisition of Government*, p. 29–30.

[84] Ibid., p. 70.

[85] Cf. Spain, *The Political Theory of John C. Calhoun*, pp. 108, 263.

[86] See Ross Harrison, *Bentham* (London: Routledge & Kegan Paul, 1983), pp. 152–53.

[87] For standard rights-skeptical utilitarian justifications of southern slavery, see Albert Taylor Bledsoe, *Liberty and Slavery: Or, Slavery in the Light of Moral and Political Philosophy*, in E. N. Elliott, ed. *Cotton Is King, and Pro-Slavery Arguments* (Augusta, Ga.: Pritchard, Abbott & Loomis, 1860), pp. 271–458, esp. pp. 286–87; William Harper, "Memoir on Slavery," in Faust, *Ideology of Slavery*, pp. 78–135, esp. pp. 88–90.

ing utilitarian equality to be a natural interpretation of the normative ends of constitutional government consistent with the legitimation of slavery.

Calhoun's argument, an interpretive appeal to a venerated tradition of Founder's intent, is a straightforward example of Madison's worry that an interpretation of the Constitution, in fact motivated by factionalized ordinary politics, would become the measure of constitutional legitimacy. Calhoun's argument makes a great deal of interpretive sense if one, as a leading senator from the South, took the view that Calhoun defiantly did take in 1837 in the U.S. Senate in response to abolitionist petitions, namely, that slavery "is, instead of an evil, a good—a positive good."[88] Slavery, a positive good for southern society, must not be a constitutional evil in any sense; in particular, Congress must lack the power to forbid slavery in the territories.[89]

Taking these views to be fixed interpretive points, a theorist must wholly remove from the landscape of constitutional morality the normative concepts (equal human rights) that would critically challenge slavery; and then decisive constitutional weight must be accorded southern interests in fostering this positive good against hostile national action. The answer, a veto power, was the point of Calhoun's theory of concurring majorities: National action would require majorities in both the North and South to concur. Since the South would not concur on actions hostile to its positive good (including prohibition of slavery in the territories), such actions would be ruled out. In effect, Calhoun's constitutional theory was ruthlessly motivated by a factionalized judgment of ordinary politics (here, southern self-consciously sectional politics).

Calhoun's rights skepticism motivated, finally, the unusual emphasis that his constitutional theory, in contrast to Taylor's rights-based theory,[90] gave the idea of sovereignty. Rights-based political and constitutional theories regard the protection of rights as a fundamental normative end of a legitimate polity, and thus are hostile to theories of sovereignty whose legitimacy is not assessed in the required rights-based way. Calhoun, precisely because of his hostility to natural rights, adopted a Hobbesian theory of undivided and indivisible ultimate sovereignty.[91] Sovereignty under Amer-

[88] John C. Calhoun, "Speech on the Reception of Abolition Petitions," delivered in the Senate, 6 February 1837, in *Works*, 2:631.

[89] For Calhoun's constitutional argument to this effect, see John C. Calhoun, "Speech on the Oregon Bill," in *Works*, pp. 4:479–512.

[90] "If the people are sovereign, their governments cannot also be sovereign." Taylor, *Construction Construed*, p. 143.

[91] Calhoun was studying Hobbes's *Leviathan* prior to giving his views their first important statement. See John Niven, *John C. Calhoun and the Price of Union* (Baton Rouge: Louisiana State University Press, 1988), p. 136. For these statements, see John C. Calhoun, "The South Carolina Exposition," adopted with alteration by South Carolina legislature, December 1828, in *Works*, 6:1–59; "Address on the Relation which the States and General Government Bear to Each Other," dated 1831, in ibid., 6:59–94.

ican constitutionalism could not, under this view, be divided; "to divide, is,—to destroy it."[92] States alone were, for Calhoun, sovereign in the United States; states accordingly have the right of nullification[93] and, if necessary, secession.[94] Calhoun defended the nullification procedure as, in contrast to judicial review,[95] the most adequate ultimate expression of the idea of a reasonable and deliberative constitutionalism.[96]

Calhoun's theory of sovereignty was positivistic: Law and authority were to be understood as the posited will of the sovereign. But positivism was not, for Calhoun, an axiomatic legal or political theory; it arose, in the structure of his views, fairly late in the argument as a kind of theorem that his interpretive argument had proven. American constitutionalism was interpreted in light of what Calhoun took to be the best account of its governing political theory of equality (namely, utilitarian equality). The constitutional theory of concurrent majorities (serving functionally the same role as Ely's theory of fair representation) offered the best account of American history and institutions understood in that light. Finally, states were accorded the status of sovereign because the ascription of that status gives them the power that the theory of concurrent majorities required them to have.[97]

Calhoun's theory of sovereignty was based on a highly contestable interpretation of American constitutionalism, in which his political theory of utilitarian rights skepticism is pivotal. His uncomprehending rejection of any theory of sovereignty less absolute than his included the theory of divided constitutional powers that James Madison, now an elder statesman, proposed in 1830 in response to South Carolina's doctrine of nullification.

Madison defended divided powers as a sounder interpretation both of the U.S. Constitution and the Virginia and Kentucky Resolutions (in both of which events Madison had been a central participant).[98] While Madison

[92] John C. Calhoun, A Discourse on the Constitution and Government of the United States, in Works, 1:146.

[93] The power of nullification allowed a state constitutionally to invalidate a federal law applicable to them by state constitutional convention subject to three-fourths of the states amending the Constitution to apply it to the resisting state. For a good statement of the view, see Calhoun, "The South Carolina Exposition," in Works, 6:1–59.

[94] See Calhoun, A Discourse on the Constitution, in Works, 1:300–301.

[95] See Calhoun, "The South Carolina Exposition," in Works, 6:45–46.

[96] See, e.g., ibid., 6:49; "Address on the Relation which the States and General Government Bear to Each Other," in ibid., 6:74–75.

[97] For a clear statement of this argument, see John C. Calhoun, "Speech on the Revenue Collection (Force) Bill," delivered in the Senate on 15–16 February 1833, in Works, 2:254–55.

[98] See James Madison, letter to Edward Everett, August 1830, in Letters and Other Writings of James Madison (New York: R. Worthington, 1884), 4:95–106. Madison's letter was printed in Everett's North American Review in 1830; see Madison's letter to Edward Everett, 7 October 1830, in ibid., pp. 115–16. For the historical background of the nullification debates during the period, see William W. Freehling, Prelude to Civil War: The Nullification Con-

accepted the view of the Constitution as a compact among states, he argued that it must be fairly interpreted according to its terms; it was not, in his view, a fair interpretation to put "it in the power of the smallest fraction over one-fourth of the United States—that is, of seven States out of twenty-four—to give the law and even the Constitution to seventeen States, each of the seventeen having, as parties to the Constitution, an equal right with each of the seven to expound it and to insist on the exposition."[99]

From a Madisonian perspective, the Constitution must be interpreted from the rights-based perspective so crucial to its proper understanding. State-centered factions—a central concern motivating the authors of the Constitution of 1787—could hardly afford the kind of impartial interpretation of the Constitution that was required. Madison accepted the right to revolution (when properly claimed) as a matter of abstract right; but he regarded this "as an extra and ultra constitutional right."[100] The difference between Calhoun and Madison on the constitutionality of nullification and presumably secession was not an abstract disagreement about legal theory, but an interpretive disagreement about the best account of American constitutionalism. The pivotal issue at every stage was one of background political theory: Madison's revolutionary political morality of inalienable human rights, Calhoun's rights skepticism.

The crisis of American constitutionalism, signaled by the Madison-Calhoun controversy, was a crisis over the ethical foundations of American constitutionalism. To defend southern proslavery constitutionalism, the ethical impulses central to the Declaration of Independence and the American Revolution had to be displaced from stage center in the discussion of politics and society in the South. Calhoun himself struck this note when he formulated his rights skepticism in terms of an attack on the demands of contractualist ethical impartiality, that is, testing political legitimacy by whether free and equal persons could reasonably agree to certain principles or institutions. Calhoun interpreted the test as making a claim that man once existed outside society; but "such a state is purely hypothetical,"[101] that is, false; and therefore the ethical criterion was false.

Of course, contractualist ethics makes no such historical claim,[102] and therefore Calhoun's argument is fallacious. The social nature of humankind is presumably a fact of human circumstances that any plausible ethical cri-

---

troversy in South Carolina, 1816–1836 (New York: Harper & Row, 1968); Richard E. Ellis, *The Union at Risk: Jacksonian Democracy, States' Rights, and the Nullification Crisis* (New York: Oxford University Press, 1987).

[99] See James Madison, August 1830 letter to Edward Everett, in *Letters,*, p. 102.

[100] *Letters,* at p. 101.

[101] See Calhoun, *A Disquisition on Government,* p. 58.

[102] See David A. J. Richards, *A Theory of Reasons for Action* (Oxford: Clarendon Press, 1971).

terion, including contractualism, must take seriously. Calhoun's strategy was to displace attention from ethical argument to ethically neutral social facts, "that men . . . are born in the social and political state; and of course, instead of being born free and equal, are born subject, not only to parental authority, but to the laws and institutions of the country where born." Social facts of this sort were "the natural state of man,"[103] and the task of politics and of constitutionalism was to accommodate natural facts of subjection and hierarchy. Ethical argument was, in short, being turned into a kind of social science of natural hierarchy.

This displacement of ethical argument—so fundamental to the integrity of southern proslavery constitutionalism—pervaded characteristically southern thought after Calhoun. Henry Hughes[104] and George Fitzhugh[105] analyzed the institution of southern slavery as an enlightened form of economic and social science (preferable, for example, to northern capitalism); Josiah Nott,[106] Samuel Cartwright,[107] and others, enthusiastically supported by Calhoun,[108] developed American ethnology, a putatively "hard" physical science supporting the racial inferiority of blacks. The circle of Simms, Ruffin, Tucker, Holmes, and Hammond studied and improved slavery as a matter of Baconian science and technology.[109] And Thornton Stringfellow argued that the legitimacy of slavery turned on a literal reading of the

[103] See Calhoun, A Disquisition on Government, p. 58.

[104] See Henry Hughes, "Treatise on Sociology," first published 1854, in Faust, Ideology of Slavery, pp. 239–71.

[105] See George Fitzhugh, Cannibals All! or, Slaves without Masters, (1857), ed. C. Vann Woodward (Cambridge: Belknap Press, Harvard University Press, 1960); Sociology for the South (1854), in Harvey Wish, ed., Antebellum: Writings of George Fitzhugh and Hinton Rowan Helper on Slavery (New York: Capricorn Books, 1960), pp. 43–95; "Southern Thought" (1857), in Faust, Ideology of Slavery, pp. 272–99.

[106] See Josiah C. Nott, "Two Lectures on the Natural History of the Caucasian and Negro Races" (1844), in Faust, Ideology of Slavery, pp. 206–38; "Types of Mankind" (1854), in Eric L. McKitrick, ed., Slavery Defended: The Views of the Old South (Englewood Cliffs, N.J.: Prentice-Hall, 1963), pp. 126–38.

[107] Samuel A. Cartwright, "Slavery in the Light of Ethnology," in Elliott, Cotton Is King, pp. 691–728.

[108] See William Stanton, The Leopard's Spots: Scientific Attitudes toward Race in America, 1815–59 (Chicago: University of Chicago Press, 1960), pp. 52–53, 61–62.

[109] See Drew Gilpin Faust, A Sacred Circle: The Dilemma of the Intellectual in the Old South, 1840–1860 (Philadelphia: University of Pennsylvania Press, 1977); James Henry Hammond and the Old South: A Design for Mastery (Baton Rouge: Louisiana State University Press, 1982). For writings, see James Henry Hammond, "Letter to an English Abolitionist" (1845), in Faust, Ideology of Slavery, pp. 168–205; "'Mud-Sill' Speech," speech delivered in Senate, 4 March 1858, in McKitrick, Slavery Defended, pp. 121–25; Edmund Ruffin, "The Political Economy of Slavery" (1853), in McKitrick, Slavery Defended, pp. 69–85; George Frederick Holmes, "Review of Uncle Tom's Cabin" (1852), reprinted in McKitrick, Slavery Defended, pp. 99–110.

Bible.[110] Ethical argument, to the extent it existed at all as an independent mode of argument, was reduced to some hard fact (for example, a vague general good to which all rights give way, or race differences, or a literalist interpretation of the Bible).[111] Historical argument appealed not to American revolutionary freedom as its model, but to the ancient Greek and Roman examples of slavery and freedom[112] or to a romantic, paternalistic medievalism of knights and serfs.[113] The southern mind, once capable of the critical impartiality of a Jefferson and Madison, was increasingly polemical and insular, centering on whatever kind of argument could sustain slavery as a fixed point in the southern landscape.[114]

But southern proslavery constitutional thought could not remorselessly follow Calhoun's rights-skeptical logic. When the South neared the moment of truth over secession and civil war, it was not always Calhoun's logical rigor that moved them, but more often a right to revolution rooted in the Declaration of Independence that Calhoun had mocked.[115] Southern slave owners increasingly articulated their sense of indignation, as had the revolutionaries of 1776, in terms of unjust political enslavement by the North.[116.] Burke had observed in 1775 how slavery had paradoxically heightened southern slave owners' valuation of their own freedom: "In such a people, the haughtiness of domination combines with the spirit of freedom, fortifies it, and renders it invincible."[117] The language and thought of rights were too fundamental to what most deeply moved Americans in their constitutionalism to be struck from the hearts and minds of such liberty-

[110] See Thornton Stringfellow, "A Brief Examination of Scripture Testimony on the Institution of Slavery" (1850), in Faust, Ideology of Slavery, pp. 136–67; Stringfellow, "The Bible Argument: Or, Slavery in the Light of Divine Revelation," in Elliott, Cotton Is King, pp. 461–546.

[111] See, e.g., Bledsoe, "Liberty and Slavery," in Elliott, Cotton Is King, pp. 286–88, 295–96, 299, 315, 378–79.

[112] See William Sumner Jenkins, Pro-slavery Thought in the Old South (Chapel Hill: University of North Carolina Press, 1935), pp. 53, 86, 178, 190–95, 290–91; Larry E. Tise, Proslavery: A History of the Defense of Slavery in America, 1701–1840 (Athens, Ga.: University of Georgia Press, 1987), pp. 49, 191, 246, 283, 340, 354.

[113] See, e.g., John Hope Franklin, The Militant South, 1800–1861 (Cambridge: Belknap Press, Harvard University Press, 1956). Southern thinkers particularly admired, in this respect, Carlyle's criticisms of the capitalist excesses of the British Industrial Revolution. See Thomas Carlyle, Latter-day Pamphlets (London: Chapman & Hall, 1850), and citation to Fitzhugh, Cannibals All!, p. 10.

[114] See Jenkins, Pro-slavery Thought in the Old South; Tise, Proslavery; Franklin, The Militant South; William R. Taylor, Cavalier and Yankee: The Old South and American National Character (New York: George Braziller, 1961); for later developments as well, see W. J. Cash, The Mind of the South (New York: Vintage Books, 1969).

[115] See Carpenter, The South as a Conscious Minority, pp. 194–200.

[116] For a general treatment, see Greenberg, Masters and Statesmen.

[117] Edmund Burke, "Speech on Moving His Resolutions for Conciliation with the Colonies," 22 March 1775, in The Works of Edmund Burke, 6th ed. (Boston: Little, Brown, 1880), 2:124.

loving southerners by the mere logic of their most articulate constitutional theorist.

Jefferson Davis thus justified secession and civil war on the basis of "the eternal principles of the *Declaration of Independence* . . . and the unalienable rights of man,"[118] and Alexander Stephens located the justification of the Confederacy in the "immutable principles" of the Declaration of Independence, invoking the same right to revolution against the Constitution that had been claimed by the Founders of that Constitution against the Articles of Confederation.[119] Indeed, when pressed for the justification of the southern view of absolute state sovereignty, Stephens did not follow Calhoun's aridly abstract conceptualism of sovereignty[120] but appealed to a rights-based argument, such as Taylor's, that allegiance fundamentally bound Americans to their states as the best institutional protection of one's rights.[121]

From this perspective, secession and civil war were justified by the South not exclusively on the basis of a rights-skeptical interpretation of the Constitution, but also on a rights-based interpretation—a view of what rights people had and of threats to those rights. Alexander Stephens's 1861 speech, earlier quoted, clearly stated that blacks, as a class, were racially inferior and thus were not bearers of rights within the contemplation of Jefferson's principle of equal inalienable human rights in the Declaration of Independence. But the excision of one class of beings from the scope of the principle left the principle intact within its proper scope, that is, non-blacks. Southern whites had inalienable rights, and one of these rights was, in appropriate circumstances, property rights in blacks under the terms of American slavery.

Southern proslavery apologists defended such claims as moral and legal rights, indeed as a kind of intimate domestic relationship: "nothing but the mere relations of husband and wife, parent and child, brother and sister, . . . produce a closer tie, than the relation of master and servant,"[122] "one of the most intimate relations of society."[123] A political threat to such re-

---

[118] See Davis, *The Rise and Fall*, 2:644.

[119] See Stephens, *A Constitutional View*, 1:205, 427–29.

[120] Calhoun's view rested, as we have seen, on a rights-skeptical utilitarianism, which Stephens, in fact, rejected. Stephens thus wrote in a letter in 1864: "No doctrine or principle is more unjust or pernicious than that 'of the greatest good to the greatest number.' The true rule is the greatest good to all, to each and every one, without injury to any. No one hundred men on earth have the moral right to govern any other ninety-nine men or, less number, and to make the interests of the ninety-nine, or less number, subservient to the interests of the hundred, because thereby the greatest good to the greatest number will be promoted." Quoted in Carpenter, *The South as a Conscious Minority*, p. 82.

[121] See Stephens, *A Constitutional View*, 1:492–94.

[122] See Dew, "Abolition of Negro Slavery," in Faust, *Ideology of Slavery*, p. 65.

[123] See William Harper, citing Dew in his "Memoir on Slavery" (1852), in Faust, *Ideology of Slavery*, p. 100.

lations was, according to this view, a threat to inalienable rights centering on intimate domestic life and would justify the right to revolution, other things being equal, to protect such rights.

Not all southerners took this interpretation of abstract natural rights; and many undoubtedly thought that slavery should, over the long term, be abolished.[124] Jefferson Davis, for example, believed that southern slaveowners had a constitutional right to take slaves into the territories,[125] but he also believed, as Jefferson and Madison had come to believe in the 1820s,[126] that such expansion would lead to the quicker end of slavery over time.[127] Such southerners may have favored abolition over time on reasonable terms formulated by the southern states, but resisted the imposition of ill-considered abolition schemes by the national government that would, in their view, have led to more injustice than the injustice of slavery itself.

By the time of secession, the U.S. Supreme Court, in *Dred Scott v. Sanford*,[128] had significantly supported central claims of southern proslavery constitutionalism (for example, the right of southern slave owners to introduce slavery into the territories); and northern criticism of that decision (by Lincoln among others)[129] led some such southerners to regard both their moral and constitutional rights as being placed significantly at threat. The right to revolution of the Declaration of Independence was thus invoked, as it was by Davis, to defend moral and constitutional rights now allegedly at risk.

Of course, it does not follow from the fact that one's rights are threatened that revolution is always justified if nonrevolutionary means might equally well secure one's rights or if revolution will clearly fail or inflict a balance of injustice (for example, loss of innocent life) greater than the injustice under attack.[130] Alexander Stephens, who defended the abstract constitu-

[124] For the complexities in southern views on these matters, see David M. Potter, *The Impending Crisis, 1848–1861*, ed. Don E. Fehrenbacher (New York: Harper & Row, 1976); William W. Freehling, *The Road to Disunion: Secessionists at Bay, 1776–1854* (New York: Oxford University Press, 1990).

[125] See Davis, *The Rise and Fall*, 1:70.

[126] See Miller, *The Wolf by the Ears*, pp. 234–42. For Madison's view, see James Madison, "Slavery in the West: The Missouri Crisis," in Marvin Meyers, *The Mind of the Founder: Sources of the Political Thought of James Madison*, rev. ed. (Hanover, N.H.: University Press of New England, 1981), pp. 319–27; see McCoy, *The Last of the Fathers*.

[127] See Davis, *The Rise and Fall*, 1:4–6.

[128] 19 Howard 393 (1857).

[129] See, e.g., Abraham Lincoln, "Speech at Columbus, Ohio," delivered 16 September 1858, in Fehrenbacher, *Abraham Lincoln: Speeches and Writings, 1858–1865*, pp. 31–58.

[130] See John Locke, *The Second Treatise of Government*, in John Locke, *Two Treatises of Government*, ed. Peter Laslett (Cambridge: Cambridge University Press, 1960), pp. 424–46 (sec. 211–43); for commentary, see Ruth W. Grant, *John Locke's Liberalism* (Chicago: University of Chicago Press, 1987), pp. 136–78; Richard Ashcraft, *Locke's Two Treatises of Government* (London: Allen & Unwin, 1987), pp. 196–230.

tional right of southern secession, had argued before the Georgia legislature in 1860 that secession was in fact not needed to achieve redress of southern grievances.[131] But Stephens, who felt bound by the decision of his state to secede, defended at length the moral and constitutional right of the South to revolt from the Union as, in principle, a constitutionally and morally justified revolution. Southern secession and civil war was, for leaders of the South and many others, an expression of American revolutionary constitutionalism.

Stephens wrote of Lincoln's opposing constitutionalism: "The Union with him in sentiment, rose to the sublimity of a religious mysticism," and he wrote to Lincoln in December 1860 that the abolitionist attempt to forbid slavery in the territories was functionally the same as trying to forbid a certain religion in the territories.[132] Stephens did not understand the constitutional theory of Union to which Lincoln and others appealed against the doctrines of nullification and secession, and he certainly did not take seriously abolitionist moral and constitutional theory. We need to understand and investigate both as interpretations of American revolutionary constitutionalism that fundamentally contested southern proslavery constitutionalism.

The Constitutionalism of Union

The constitutional theory of Union crystallized, as a distinctive interpretation of American revolutionary constitutionalism, in response to the primacy accorded the states by southern constitutionalism. At the bottom of the interpretive crisis lay slavery. The nullification controversy in South Carolina was ostensibly about unjust tariff burdens, but the underlying worry was that national principles and institutions, uncabined by Calhoun's constitutional principle of concurrent majorities, would undertake policies that eroded slavery as an institution.[133] Northern states were also concerned about national power, but about power used to advance not erode slavery. In particular, northern states were increasingly hostile to such national legislation (the Fugitive Slave Act of 1793, later superseded by the Fugitive Slave Act of 1850) and had tried to hobble national policy by passing personal liberty laws that insisted on observance of state procedures protective of rights of their citizens (for example, the right to jury trial).[134]

[131] See Stephens, *A Constitutional View*, 1:495–522, 532–39, 2:279–300.
[132] Ibid., 2:448, 2:268–69.
[133] See Freehling, *The Prelude to Civil War*; Ellis, *The Union at Risk*.
[134] See, e.g., Potter, *The Impending Crisis*, pp. 138–39; see Robert Cover, *Justice Accused: Antislavery and the Judicial Process* (New Haven: Yale University Press, 1975), pp. 159–91.

The constitutional theory of Union sought to forge a sense of American national identity, rooted in the Founding, that would be strong enough to enforce the Constitution's long-term values both of substance and procedure against short-term state factions (both pro- and antislavery) that distorted constitutional interpretation to their own immediate political ends. The proponents of this view appealed to the Founders very much in the way Madison had anticipated in *The Federalist No. 49*. The theory asserted the ultimate interpretive role of national institutions in general and the judiciary in particular as a way of best securing over time the enduring values of American revolutionary constitutionalism, the protection of rights, and advancing the public good. In this connection, the theory's leading proponents—John Quincy Adams, Daniel Webster, Joseph Story, Francis Lieber, and Abraham Lincoln—were all morally opposed to slavery and favored abolition as the morally required long-term goal.

Adams, Webster, and Story: Foundations of Theory of Union

The constitutional theory of Union took as its starting point Madisonian constitutionalism in the terms we have already discussed: The Constitution was interpreted in light of the six ingredients of revolutionary constitutionalism with particular emphasis placed on Madison's theory of faction and the special threat of state faction to the interpretive integrity of American constitutionalism. The immediate stimulus to its development was Calhoun's theory of state sovereignty and defense of constitutional rights of nullification and secession. Prior to Calhoun, constitutional thinkers, such as Tucker[135] and Rawle,[136] had construed the compact theory and right of secession loosely as roughly equivalent to the reserved right to revolution required by the Lockean political theory of American constitutionalism. Madison himself assumed the compact theory in his earlier mentioned 1830 refutation of Calhoun's interpretation of the view. But in response to Calhoun's radical defense of ultimate state sovereignty, both John Quincy Adams and Daniel Webster, leading political figures of the North, argued that the best interpretation of American revolutionary constitutionalism required rejection of the compact theory altogether.

In his July 4 oration in Quincy in 1831, John Quincy Adams, echoing the views once articulated by his revolutionary father, John Adams, reminded his audience that the American Revolution had been fought on the ground of an interpretation of the British Constitution that repudiated the role parliamentary supremacy had been accorded by the British government.

[135] See Tucker, *Blackstone's Commentaries*, Appendix Note A, 1:20–21, 73–75, 78, 140–41.

[136] See William Rawle, *A View of the Constitution of the United States of America* (Philadelphia: H. C. Carey & I. Lea, 1825), pp. 85–88, 288–90, 295–301.

American revolutionary constitutionalism, consistent with its foundations in the Declaration of Independence (America's "primitive social compact"), repudiated any theory of absolute sovereignty (such as Calhoun's), because it was inconsistent with the Constitution's ultimate commitment to "the first principle of natural right."[137]

For John Quincy Adams, the foundation of American constitutionalism was not state sovereignty, but a union, forged on the basis of experience of factions in the states and elsewhere,[138] and based on a moral covenant committing a people to principles and institutions that protect human rights. The demands of union rested on its institutional articulation and enforcement of the abstract ethical demands of the American Revolution: "Without them, our revolution would have been but successful rebellion. Right, truth, justice, are all abstractions. The Divinity that stirs within the soul of man is abstraction. The Creation of the universe is a spirit, and all spiritual nature is abstraction."[139] The doctrine of nullification was inconsistent with the deliberative impartiality that constitutional argument—in light of our history, experience, and values—required.[140]

Daniel Webster, in his great Senate speeches against the doctrine of nullification,[141] rejected Calhoun's absolutism of state sovereignty on the same basis: "The government owes high and solemn duties to every citizen of the country. It is bound to protect him in his most important rights and interests."[142] The basis of the American "social compact" was the rights of the people, and the Constitution's permanence rested on the enduring principles of human rights that it guaranteed to the American people over generations. South Carolina's claim to constitutional protection as a state minority against a national majority was unprincipled because its doctrine of state absolutism extended no protection for the rights of minorities abridged by the state. The Constitution—based on the protection of rights of the person and the fair distribution of the benefits and burdens of na-

[137] See John Quincy Adams, *An Oration Addressed to the Citizens of the Town of Quincy* (Boston: Richardson, Lord, & Holbrook, 1831), pp. 11–12, 7, 13.

[138] See ibid., pp. 26–28, 33–36.

[139] See ibid., p. 18.

[140] See ibid., pp. 36–39. For a good general treatment of Adams's views and role in American politics, see Samuel Flagg Bemis, *John Quincy Adams and the Union* (New York: Knopf, 1956).

[141] See Daniel Webster, "The Reply to Hayne," delivered in the Senate on 26–27 January 1830, in Edwin P. Whipple, *The Great Speeches and Orations of Daniel Webster* (Boston: Little, Brown, 1899), pp. 227–72; "The Constitutional Not a Compact between Sovereign States," delivered in the Senate on 16 February 1833, reprinted in Whipple, *The Great Speeches*, pp. 273–306. For Henry Clay's related support of the idea of union, see George Rawlings Poage, *Henry Clay and the Whig Party* (Chapel Hill: University of North Carolina Press, 1936).

[142] See Webster, "The Constitution Not a Compact," in Whipple, *The Great Speeches*, p. 286.

tional citizenship—could not reasonably be interpreted to allow one state to be the ultimate judge of such responsibilities.[143]

Joseph Story, a justice of the U.S. Supreme Court and Harvard law professor, wove these arguments into an interpretive history of American constitutionalism supportive of a broad construction of national powers in his important *Commentaries on the Constitution of the United States*.[144] Story offered an alternative interpretation to that of St. George Tucker of the historical background of the Constitution: in particular, its roots in the inadequacies of the Articles of Confederation, its ratification by specially called state conventions, the arguments of *The Federalist*, and its text.[145] Story's history did not persuade southern apologists, who gave strained responses that essentially repeated Tucker.[146] But his interpretive history plausibly supported a constitutional theory of Union that saw national representative institutions as the best Madisonian solution to the republican dilemma of faction, in particular, state factions. The ultimate authority of the Constitution was not the sovereignty of the states, but the supremacy of law rooted directly in the people and their rights, "resting on . . . a solemn recognition and admission of those rights, arising from the law of nature and the gift of Providence, and incapable of being transferred or surrendered."[147]

The great importance of Story's argument was its integration of a plausibly Madisonian interpretation of American constitutional history with a general theory of constitutional interpretation that defended the approach to constitutional interpretation taken by Story's acknowledged judicial master, John Marshall. Story reasonably made a case for the proposition that the Constitution was not a compact among nations and thus not subject to the principle of strict construction of treaties.[148] On that basis, he could argue plausibly that the Constitution should be interpreted broadly in order to make the best sense to the American people, the source of its authority, as a security for protection of their rights and advancing their common interests. In particular, the Constitution must be interpreted with contextual sensitivity to changing circumstances so that it imposes reasonable requirements in such circumstances.[149] For Story, the work of Chief Justice

---

[143] See ibid., pp. 290–91, 296–97, 297–98.

[144] See Joseph Story, *Commentaries on the Constitution of the United States*, ed. Melville M. Bigelow, 2 vols., 5th ed. (1833; reprint, Boston: Little, Brown, 1891). See also James Kent, *Commentaries on American Law*, ed. Oliver W. Holmes, Jr., vol. 1 (1826; reprint, Boston: Little, Brown, 1873).

[145] See Story, *Commentaries*, 1:144–387.

[146] See Upshur, *A Brief Enquiry*.

[147] See Story, *Commentaries*, 1:245.

[148] See ibid., 1:313–17.

[149] See ibid., 1:321–26.

John Marshall on the U.S. Supreme Court illustrated how such interpretive responsibilities should be understood by the judiciary.[150]

Such a broad interpretation of national power extended as well, for Story, to the fugitive slave clause and the Fugitive Slave Act of 1793. Justice Story's 1842 opinion for the Supreme Court in *Prigg v. Pennsylvania*[151] interpreted broadly the constitutional power exercised by Congress under the Fugitive Slave Act of 1793 to invalidate a Pennsylvania kidnapping statute that forbade the forcible removal of a Negro or mulatto; the Court held that the state law unconstitutionally conflicted with the scope of federal power.[152] Story had written of the fugitive slave clause in the *Commentaries* as a sectional compromise.[153] While his own views on political morality were clearly antislavery,[154] Story's opinion in *Prigg* illustrates the price he thought must be demanded of the northern states if the southern states were fairly to be expected to comply with a broad construction of national powers in other areas (including, for example, the power of congressional abolition of slavery in the territories, which might eventually lead to the long-term demise of slavery).[155] In both cases—whether southern nullification of antislavery laws or northern nullification of proslavery laws—the constitutional theory of Union must impartially maintain the higher-order reasonableness of the Constitution over such factionalized interpretive distortions.

Francis Lieber

The question of the terms of national unity was one of the great questions of both American and European politics in the nineteenth century.[156]

---

[150] See, for commentary, R. Kent Newmyer, *Supreme Court Justice Joseph Story: Statesman of the Old Republic* (Chapel Hill: University of North Carolina Press, 1985); James McClellan, *Joseph Story and the American Constitution* (Norman: University of Oklahoma Press, 1971); Gerald T. Dunne, *Justice Joseph Story and the Rise of the Supreme Court* (New York: Simon & Schuster, 1970). For a good general treatment of constitutional theory in the antebellum period, see Elizabeth Kelley Bauer, *Commentaries on the Constitution, 1790–1860* (New York: Columbia University Press, 1952).

[151] 41 U.S. (16 Pet.) 539 (1842).

[152] For commentary on *Prigg*, including the other judicial opinions, see Cover, *Justice Accused*, pp. 166–68.

[153] See, e.g., Story, *Commentaries*, 2:589.

[154] See Cover, *Justice Accused*, p. 239.

[155] For criticism of Story's formalism, see ibid., 234–35, 240–41.

[156] See Yehoshua Arieli, *Individualism and Nationalism in American Ideology* (Cambridge: Harvard University Press, 1964); E. J. Hobsbawm, *Nations and Nationalism since 1780* (Cambridge: Cambridge University Press, 1990). For important recent developments, see Benedict Anderson, *Imagined Communities: Reflections on the Origin and Spread of Nationalism* (London: Verso, 1983); Ernest Gellner, *Nations and Nationalism* (Ithaca: Cornell University Press, 1983).

Americans were well aware of European aspirations to national unity and self-determination (in, for example, Germany, Italy, and Hungary), and indeed found in the work of Francis Lieber (a neo-Kantian German liberal nationalist who fled to the United States from persecution in his native country) the most probing philosophical student of America's evolving constitutional theory of Union.[157]

Like Adams, Webster, and Story, Lieber identified the moral ideal of Union with the aspiration to national institutions protective of basic human rights. Teaching as a professor in South Carolina for much of the antebellum period,[158] however, Lieber did not publicly state his own abolitionist views[159] or their implications for American constitutionalism[160] until he moved to the North before the Civil War (to teach at Columbia). At that time, he became a prominent figure among the Radical Republicans, worked for the Lincoln administration, and argued for constitutional amendments along the lines of the Reconstruction Amendments.[161]

Lieber interpreted the constitutional theory of the American Union in terms of an interpretation of the six ingredients of American revolutionary constitutionalism that gave the most powerful answer to Calhoun's theory of the Constitution in the antebellum period.

First, Lieber offered a Kantian theory of inalienable human rights that he argued gave a sounder foundation for such rights than Locke had offered.[162] Human rights were not inferred empirically (as Locke supposed); rather, they were expressions of our internal moral powers of reasonable conscience exercised in terms of the Kantian conception of ethical impartiality.[163] The state was as necessary for human life as language and must

---

[157] See Francis Lieber, *Manual of Political Ethics*, 2 vols. (Boston: Little and Brown, 1838–39); *On Civil Liberty and Self-government* (Philadelphia: J. B. Lippincott, 1859). For commentary, see Frank Freidel, *Francis Lieber: Nineteenth-Century Liberal* (Baton Rouge: Louisiana State University Press, 1947); Bernard Edward Brown, *American Conservatives: The Political Thought of Francis Lieber and John W. Burgess* (New York: Columbia University Press, 1951), pp. 13–100.

[158] See Freidel, *Francis Lieber*.

[159] On Lieber's unpublished draft letters to Calhoun on this matter, see Freidel, *Francis Lieber*, pp. 238–41.

[160] See Francis Lieber, "What Is Our Constitution—League, Pact, or Government?" (two lectures originally delivered 1860–61), in Francis Lieber, *The Miscellaneous Writings of Francis Lieber* (Philadelphia: J. B. Lippincott, 1880), 2:87–123. Lieber did publish an antisecession address in South Carolina in 1851; see Lieber, "An Address on Secession," in ibid., pp. 125–36.

[161] See Freidel, *Francis Lieber*; for Lieber on constitutional reform, see Francis Lieber, "Amendments of the Constitution" (1865), in Lieber, *Miscellaneous Writings*, 2:139–79.

[162] See Lieber, *Manual of Political Ethics*, 1:26–29

[163] See ibid., 1:24–26, 38–40, 51–52. For Lieber, human rights are "the rights which man has according to his inherent, inalienable ethical nature." Lieber, ibid., 1:58. Rights are determined "scientifically" by Kant's test: "Act always in such a manner that the immediate

be tested for its legitimacy in terms of whether it guaranteed equal protection for basic rights. Such rights included the rights to conscience and speech, to life and health, locomotion, reputation, intimate family life, and to property.[164]

Second, these principles of human rights were fundamental not only to the legitimacy, but to the proper interpretation of the genre of American and British constitutionalism—"Anglican liberty."[165] Lieber regarded such constitutionalism as the best available institutions protective of human rights that history had yet produced, and thus as properly to be interpreted in terms of rights-based political theory.

Third, Lieber powerfully developed Madison's rights-sensitive theory of faction into a theory of the pathology he called "democratic absolutism." On this theory, majorities tended to regard their actions as self-validated by their majoritarian character alone; this tendency corrupted conscience itself not even to "feel so distinctly their responsibility" for egregious oppressions of the rights or interests of minorities. Such democratic absolutism, which Lieber associated with Jacksonian democracy, was politically illegitimate by the test of equal protection of human rights. The task of constitutional government was to limit and frame such absolutist democratic power to serve legitimate ends.[166]

Fourth, Lieber extensively employed comparative political science to clarify forms of republican political power inconsistent with human rights (in particular, ancient Greece and Rome and "Gallican liberty").[167]

Fifth, American political experience—in particular, the excesses of democratic absolutism—was consulted as a test for more legitimate constitutional forms.[168]

And sixth, while Lieber rejected the idea of a historical contract, contractualism would be acceptable if understood as a test for institutions that could be justified to all on terms of respect for their equal rights.[169] The constitutional practices that could be justified in this way were nationally representative institutions, bicameralism, and an independent judiciary resting on common-law reasoning about the meaning of civil liberties.[170]

---

motive or maxim of thy will may become a universal rule in an obligatory legislation for all intelligent beings." See Lieber, ibid., 1:45.

[164] See ibid., 1:185–86, 60, 153, 167–68, 191–214.

[165] See Lieber, *On Civil Liberty and Self-government*, pp. 54–55, 295–300.

[166] See Lieber, *Manual of Political Ethics*, 2:368, 2:3, 1:377–93.

[167] See ibid., 1:73–74, 401–6; Lieber, *On Civil Liberty and Self-government*, pp. 45–52, 283–300.

[168] See Lieber, *Manual of Political Ethics*, 1:368–72, 407.

[169] See ibid., 1:320–21, 324.

[170] See ibid., 2:488–97, Lieber, *On Civil Liberty and Self-government*, pp. 197–203, 206–17.

Sovereignty should have political force only as a term for the rights of the people in society; and national representative institutions, not the states, would be regarded as the more reasonable way to secure more abstract impartial reflection about the meaning and protection of such human rights.[171] From this perspective, the moral deformity of the constitutional theory of secession was its inversion of the language and thought of rights; the appeal to state's rights rested on the egregious violation of human rights (for example, slavery). In effect, the "centralization and consolidation of power within their respective states"[172] promoted "local absolutism and local oppression."[173]

Lieber deepened the constitutional theory of Union by bringing to bear on its interpretation a general political theory of human rights and an institutional theory that accorded national institutions the central role in the more impartial articulation and enforcement of those rights on terms of principle. In his *Legal and Political Hermeneutics* Lieber argued, consistent with Story's interpretive theory, that a constitution like that of the United States must be interpreted broadly. It was in the nature of interpretation, Lieber argued, to apply general language to different things in light of changing circumstances; and the value he placed on common law reasoning led him to disfavor interpretation on the model of a closed code in favor of one sensitive to evolving principles.[174]

For Lieber, interpretation by the judiciary was central to the protection of civil liberties, and the interpretation of a Constitution whose terms were general and intended to endure must be construed reasonably to apply in circumstances unforeseen by its founders.[175] Such reasonable interpretation must be guided by the weight and nature of the underlying normative values at stake. Human rights were so central to the legitimacy of government and so often subjected to political abuse that their judicial interpretation should be expansive: "In short, with a manly nation, let every thing that is in favor of power be closely construed; every thing in favor of the security of the citizen and the protection of the individual, comprehensively, for the simple reason, that power is power, which is able to take care of itself, and tends, by its nature, to increase, while the citizen wants protection."[176]

[171] See Lieber, *Manual of Political Ethics*, 1:233–42, 423–24, 2:566–69.

[172] See Lieber, "What Is Our Constitution—League, Pact, or Government?" in *Miscellaneous Writings*, p. 119.

[173] Lieber, "Amendments of the Constitution," in *Miscellaneous Writings*, p. 164.

[174] Francis Lieber, *Legal and Political Hermeneutics*, ed. William G. Hammond (1837–38; reprint, St. Louis: F. H. Thomas, 1880), pp. 23–26, 37–38, 44–45, 130–34, 32, 35–36, 155–58.

[175] See ibid., pp. 36–42, 76–77, 155–56, 192–93, 44, 110–11, 125–30, 194–95.

[176] See ibid., pp. 178–79.

Abraham Lincoln

At an early stage of his political career in his justly famed 1838 address to the Young Men's Lyceum, Lincoln struck the theme of constitutional memory to which he was to return throughout his political life.[177] We are told immediately: "We find ourselves under the government of a system of political institutions, conducing more essentially to the ends of civil and religious liberty, than any of which the history of former times tells us."[178] And we are warned of our unworthiness of our institutions in view of "the increasing disregard for law which pervades the country"—"the mobocratic spirit." A generation of Americans—that of the Founders—immortalized themselves by bequeathing us a successful experiment in "*the capability of a people to govern themselves*," but our generation, lacking memory, may devote itself to a "towering genius [that] disdains a beaten path . . . emancipating slaves, or enslaving freemen." Such romantically inspiring leadership is not our need: "Reason, cold, calculating, unimpassioned reason, must furnish all the materials for our future support and defence."[179]

Lincoln's prophetic worries make sense against the background of the constitutional theory of Union he assumed and the political threats to that theory he saw about him. As we have seen, the appeal of Union for its proponents was based on the moral ideals of the protection of human rights to which it aspired and the role national institutions, properly understood, played in the long-term service of that goal. Some of these rights had been guaranteed by the Constitution itself (for example, by the Bill of Rights applicable against the federal government); others had been recognized later under the influence of the ideals of the Constitution (for example, state acceptance of the antiestablishment principles of the first amendment,[180] and abolition of slavery in the northern states).[181]

Under this view, both the substantive principles of the Constitution and the democratic procedures of debate and deliberation in light of those principles would, if properly understood and interpreted, lead to the fuller rec-

[177] See Abraham Lincoln, "Address to the Young Men's Lyceum of Springfield, Illinois," delivered 27 January 1838, in Fehrenbacher, *Abraham Lincoln: Speeches and Writings, 1832–1858,*, pp. 28–36. The best general study of Lincoln's moral and constitutional thought, from which I have much profited, is Harry V. Jaffa, *Crisis of the House Divided: An Interpretation of the Issues in the Lincoln-Douglas Debates* (Chicago: University of Chicago Press, 1982).

[178] See Lincoln, "Address to the Young Men's Lyceum," in Fehrenbacher, *Abraham Lincoln: Speeches and Writings, 1832–58*, p. 28.

[179] See ibid., pp. 29, 31, 34, 36.

[180] For example, Connecticut accepted the antiestablishment principle in 1818 and Massachusetts accepted the principle in 1833. See Leonard W. Levy, *Establishment Clause: Religion and the First Amendment* (New York: Macmillan, 1986), pp. 44, 37–38.

[181] See Zilversmit, *The First Emancipation*.

ognition and protection of human rights over time. Proponents of the theory of Union often believed, as Lincoln certainly did, that slavery morally violated human rights, and thought the Constitution, here as elsewhere, could be invoked in ways leading to the long-term abolition of slavery (for example, by congressional abolition of slavery in the territories). But Lincoln, as early as 1838, had come to fear that American public opinion had lost faith in what he pointedly called "the *political religion* of the nation."[182]

The age of Jackson and Calhoun had been shrewdly observed and described by two European visitors, Harriet Martineau of Britain[183] and Alexis de Tocqueville of France,[184] in terms that clarify Lincoln's growing constitutional anxieties in 1838. Martineau painfully recorded the degree to which democratic Americans were oppressed by a "servitude to opinion," reinforced in the South by an absence of free speech and reasonable public debate about slavery. The consequence was a nation, ostensibly committed to human rights, in which people displayed "an inability even to comprehend them"; indeed, the mere exercise of rights of free speech was met by "terrorism."[185] And de Tocqueville wrote of the "tyranny of the majority" in America, with the consequence that "I know of no country in which there is so little independence of mind and real freedom of discussion as in America."[186]

Lincoln's condemnation of mob rule certainly embraced the kinds of Jacksonian mobs (often antiabolitionist and led by "gentlemen of property and standing")[187] that Martineau observed and condemned, but he strikingly made his point in a more general way in terms of an anticonstitutional political leader "emancipating slaves, or enslaving freemen."[188] Lincoln despised slavery and believed that the Constitution, properly interpreted, should place it "in the course of ultimate extinction."[189] But his first allegiance was to the theory of Union, and he resisted mob rule as anticonstitutional in its principle, whatever the ultimate merits of its substantive ends.

For Lincoln, everything turned on whether the Constitution was indeed

[182] See Lincoln, "Address to Young Men's Lyceum," in Fehrenbacher, *Abraham Lincoln: Speeches and Writings, 1832–1858*, p. 32.

[183] See Harriet Martineau, *Society in America*, 3 vols. (London: Saunders & Otley, 1837).

[184] See Alexis de Tocqueville, *Democracy in America*, ed. Phillips Bradley (New York: Vintage Press, 1945; originally published in 2 vols. in 1835 and 1840).

[185] See Martineau, *Society in America*, 3:18, 2:344–45, 343, 349.

[186] See de Tocqueville, *Democracy in America*, 1:269, 273.

[187] See Leonard L. Richards, *"Gentlemen of Property and Standing": Anti-Abolition Mobs in Jacksonian America* (New York: Oxford University Press, 1970).

[188] See Lincoln, "Address to Young Men's Lyceum," in Fehrenbacher, *Abraham Lincoln: Speeches and Writings, 1832–1858*, p. 34.

[189] See Abraham Lincoln, in Robert W. Johannsen, *The Lincoln-Douglas Debates of 1858* (New York: Oxford University Press, 1965), p. 55 (first joint debate, Ottawa, 21 August 1858).

properly interpreted in terms of both national powers and the guarantee of such basic human rights as free speech so that a reasonable public debate could be conducted. As Martineau and de Tocqueville document, however, Jacksonian America had increasingly given play to an anticonstitutional majoritarianism that had, both at the national and state levels (with the complicity of Jackson himself), abridged rights of free speech on slavery (its evils and abolition).[190] In effect, the Constitution's most essential and clearly articulated principles—guarantees of freedom of conscience, speech, and reasonable public inquiry and debate—had been subverted in the name of a constitutionally decadent public opinion that would not tolerate public debate on the nation's great evil. Lincoln's concluding appeal to "reason, cold, calculating, unimpassioned reason"[191] was motivated by one of the deepest anxieties a constitutionalist may have, namely, that the interpretation of the Constitution—one of the greatest expressions of public reason in human history—might be mangled by populist political faction and fad into an instrument of majoritarian irrationalism: polemical, insular, prejudiced.

Proponents of the theory of Union had already grappled with one expression of such a distortion of the Constitution in Calhoun, whose defense of minorities was, as Lieber clearly saw, merely cosmetic (in effect, entrenching oppressive majorities at the state level with no remedy for minorities whatsoever). Lincoln's monumental importance to American constitutionalism was the way in which he arrested the public mind of the nation by his powerfully reasoned criticisms of two later proponents of such constitutional irrationalism: Senator Stephen Douglas and Chief Justice Roger Taney.

Lincoln's dramatic reentry into national politics was triggered by the Kansas-Nebraska Act of 1854 (repealing the prohibition of slavery in the territories), which had been engineered by Senator Stephen Douglas of Illinois.[192] Douglas justified the repeal on the basis of the principle of popular sovereignty, the right of people in the territories democratically to decide the issue of slavery. For Lincoln, as for the many Americans he and others mobilized in forming the Republican Party,[193] it was one thing to admit that the Constitution protected slavery in the states and even that

---

[190] For a superb general study, see Russel B. Nye, *Fettered Freedom: Civil Liberties and the Slavery Controversy, 1830–1860*, rev. ed. (East Lansing: Michigan State College Press, 1949); see also Clement Eaton, *The Freedom-of-Thought Struggle in the Old South* (New York: Harper & Row, 1940).

[191] See Lincoln, "Address to Young Men's Lyceum," in Fehrenbacher, *Abraham Lincoln: Speeches and Writings, 1832–1858*, p. 36.

[192] See Potter, *The Impending Crisis*, pp. 145–76.

[193] See William E. Gienapp, *The Origins of the Republican Party, 1852–1856* (New York: Oxford University Press, 1987).

it empowered Congress to pass the Fugitive Slave Act of 1850.[194] But it violated both a fair interpretive reading of the scope of national powers and the background constitutional morality of respect for human rights for the Congress of the United States to repeal a prohibition on slavery in the territories.

For constitutionalists such as Lincoln, the comparison to Great Britain was particularly galling. Britain, unencumbered by the U.S. Constitution's powerful guarantees of representation of slave owners in the federal government, abolished the institution of West Indian slavery in 1833.[195] The British Constitution, once condemned as illegitimate by American revolutionaries on grounds of its betrayal of human rights, now appeared to abolitionist Americans to be a shining example of constitutional decency, which shamed America. Thus, radical abolitionists such as Garrison and Phillips could now plausibly condemn the U.S. Constitution as "a covenant with death and an agreement with hell" and urge disunion.[196]

Lincoln rejected the disunionism of the radical abolitionist view of the Constitution. His explosion of rage at the Kansas-Nebraska Act, however, reflected a similar sense that American political indifference to slavery expressed a loss of faith in the promise of American constitutionalism that humiliated America before the world, especially the European world:

> This *declared* indifference, but as I must think, covert *real* zeal for the spread of slavery, I can not but hate. I hate it because of the monstrous injustice of slavery itself. I hate it because it deprives our republican example of its just influence in the world—enables the enemies of free institutions, with plausibility, to taunt us as hypocrites—causes the real friends of freedom to doubt our sincerity, and especially because it forces so many really good men amongst ourselves into an open war with the very fundamental principles of civil liberty—criticising the Declaration of Independence, and insisting that there is no right principle of action but *self-interest*.[197]

For Lincoln, growing public acceptance of the rights skepticism of Calhoun (who had criticized the Declaration of Independence), now supported by northern politicians such as Douglas in the name of a majoritarian interpretation of democracy (popular sovereignty), reflected a further deepen-

[194] Many political abolitionists, however, balked at this later claim. See e.g., Richard H. Sewell, *Ballots for Freedom: Antislavery Politics in the United States, 1837–1860* (New York: Oxford University Press, 1976), pp. 236–39.

[195] See Davis, *Slavery and Human Progress*, pp. 108, 116, 204–5.

[196] Wendell Phillips Garrison and Francis Jackson Garrison, *William Lloyd Garrison, 1805–1879*, 4 vols. (New York: Century Co., 1889), 3:88.

[197] Abraham Lincoln, "Speech on Kansas-Nebraska Act," delivered at Peoria, Illinois, on 16 October 1854, in Fehrenbacher, *Abraham Lincoln: Speeches and Writings, 1832–1858*, p. 315.

ing of the crisis of constitutional morality that he had predicted in 1838. Douglas was precisely the kind of talented anticonstitutional Jacksonian politician Lincoln had so prophetically described.

Douglas had based the Kansas-Nebraska Act on the political principle of popular sovereignty,[198,] reserving to the U.S. Supreme Court the ultimate interpretive issue of the scope of congressional constitutional powers over the territories. In *Dred Scott v. Sanford,* the Supreme Court adopted Calhoun's view that Congress could not constitutionally forbid slavery in the territories,[199] and also held that blacks "had no rights which the white man was bound to respect."[200]

Chief Justice Taney's opinion for the Court was self-consciously originalist: "It [the Constitution] must be construed now as it was understood at the time of its adoption."[201] But Taney's appeal—in a style of originalism above factionalized politics that imitated *The Federalist No. 49*—was itself the ultimate triumph of the factionalized reading of the Founders that Lincoln so feared. Calhoun's rights skepticism triumphed in *Dred Scott* with a vengeance, giving a reading both of the powers of Congress and of the rights of black Americans that Justice Curtis showed in his dissent to be without solid basis in history, precedent, or text.[202] Lincoln's anxieties now extended not only to ambitious politicians without constitutional scruples, but to the institution that proponents of the theory of Union had historically supposed to be the most pivotally important of national deliberative institutions, the Supreme Court of the United States itself. If the Supreme Court could so willfully distort the memory of the Founders, the time had come to challenge American institutions—on the ground of America's revolutionary constitutionalism—for failure to protect the basic rights of the person.

Lincoln rose to make this challenge in the Lincoln-Douglas debates,[203,] "one of the most important intellectual discussions of the slavery question that occurred during three decades of almost uninterrupted contro-

---

[198] For Douglas's later strained attempt to justify popular sovereignty as a sound interpretation of the American constitutional tradition, see Douglas, "The Dividing Line," p. 519. In fact, the principle was for Douglas "essentially pragmatic and expedient." Johannsen, *Stephen A. Douglas,* p. 240.

[199] For Calhoun's views, see, e.g., "Speech on the Oregon Bill," delivered in the Senate, 27 June 1848, in *Works,* 4:479–512.

[200] *Dred Scott v. Sanford,* 19 Howard 393, 407 (1857).

[201] Ibid., p. 426.

[202] See ibid., p. 564 (Curtis, J., dissenting); for the authoritative contemporary discussion of the background and fallacies of the opinion, see Don E. Fehrenbacher, *The Dred Scott Case: Its Significance in American Law and Politics* (New York: Oxford University Press, 1978).

[203] See Johannsen, *The Lincoln-Douglas Debates.*

versy."[204] Lincoln believed and argued cogently that *Dred Scott* was wrongly decided,[205] but the burning issue of public reason that he placed unforgettably before the conscience of the nation was the enormity of the abandonment of the rights-based morality of American revolutionary constitutionalism implicit in the majoritarianism of Douglas and the originalism of Taney: "When he [Douglas] invites any people, willing to have slavery, to establish it, he is blowing out the moral lights around us. When he says he 'cares not whether slavery is voted down or voted up'—that it is a sacred right of self-government—he is, in my judgment, penetrating the human soul and eradicating the light of reason and the love of liberty in this American people."[206]

The consequence of such a view was grotesque distortion not only of the history of American revolutionary constitutionalism (for example, Douglas's[207] and Taney's[208] claim that Jefferson could not have meant the Declaration of Independence to apply to black Americans), but of the essential moral meaning of the Declaration, namely, that "there is no just rule other than that of moral and abstract right!"[209] The interpretive consequence of such crippling rights skepticism would be preparation of the public mind of the nation for a "new Dred Scott decision, deciding against the right of the people of the States to exclude slavery"; for "to prepare the public mind for this movement, operating in the free States, where, there is now an abhorrence of the institution of slavery, could you find an instrument so capable of doing it as Judge Douglas? or one employed in so apt a way to do it?"[210]

Lincoln's point was cogent. Such a decision would be as interpretively wrong as *Dred Scott*, but its acceptability would be prepared, just as *Dred Scott* was prepared, by the further elaboration of the rights-skeptical subversion of American constitutional morality by such politicians as Douglas

[204] See Potter, *The Impending Crisis*, p. 331. For excellent commentary and analysis, see ibid., pp. 328–55; Jaffa, *Crisis of the House Divided*; David Zarefsky, *Lincoln, Douglas and Slavery in the Crucible of Public Debate* (Chicago: University of Chicago Press, 1990).

[205] For Lincoln's most expansive historical defense of this view, see Abraham Lincoln, "Address at Cooper Institute, New York City," delivered 27 February 1860, reprinted in Fehrenbacher, *Abraham Lincoln: Speeches and Writings, 1858–1865*, pp. 111–30. For the Lincoln-Douglas debates, see Johannsen, *Lincoln-Douglas Debates*, pp. 54–67, 145–59, 197–200, 255, 279–81, 301–2, 320–22.

[206] See Abraham Lincoln, in Johannsen, *Lincoln-Douglas Debates*, p. 67 (first debate, Ottawa, 21 August 1858).

[207] See Stephen Douglas, in ibid., pp. 215–16 (delivered at Galesburg debate, 7 October 1858). For Douglas's attempt to argue that popular sovereignty was implicit in American revolutionary constitutionalism, see Douglas, "The Dividing Line," pp. 521, 522, 527, 529.

[208] See *Dred Scott*, pp. 409–10.

[209] See Abraham Lincoln, in Johannsen, *Lincoln-Douglas Debates*, pp. 219–20, 221 (delivered at Galesburg, 7 October 1858).

[210] See Abraham Lincoln, in ibid., pp. 231, 233.

and such judges as Taney, both products and instruments of Jacksonian democracy.[211] Lincoln concluded the debates starkly:

> That is the issue that will continue in this country when these poor tongues of Judge Douglas and myself shall be silent. It is the eternal struggle between these two principles—right and wrong—throughout the world. . . . The one is the common right of humanity and the other the divine right of kings. . . . It is the same spirit that says, "You work and toil and earn bread, and I'll eat it." No matter in what shape it comes, whether from the mouth of a king who seeks to bestride the people of his own nation and live by the fruit of their labor, or from one race of men as an apology for enslaving another race, it is the same tyrannical principle.[212]

Lincoln made his appeal to the revolutionary foundations of American constitutionalism within the framework of the constitutional institutions of deliberative public argument that he cherished. Though he lost the election for the Senate in 1858,[213] he became a national figure and won the presidency in 1860 in part on the basis of such arguments (including publication in book form of the Lincoln-Douglas debates).[214] He made clear in his first inaugural address—consistent with the constitutional theory of union—that he believed secession to be unconstitutional and the claim to a moral right to revolution, on the part of the South, to be frivolous.[215] The election of 1860 had been conducted as a form of majority rule embedded in constitutional institutions according full protection for "all the vital rights of minorities, and of individuals."[216] A democratic election, conducted within such a framework, was politically and constitutionally legitimate, and must be respected.[217] The South must now abide by the fair rules of the game and could not justly or constitutionally withdraw because it had fairly lost one play.

Lincoln had argued to the American people that their politicians and judges had so betrayed their constitutionalism that their rights were not adequately protected. That was a revolutionary claim made in the context of democratic elections, and his success indicated that other forms of rev-

---

[211] For a view of some of the egalitarian merits of Jacksonian democracy, see Arthur M. Schlesinger, Jr., *The Age of Jackson* (Boston: Little, Brown, 1945).

[212] See Abraham Lincoln, in Johannsen, *Lincoln–Douglas Debates*, p. 319 (delivered at Alton on 15 October 1858).

[213] See Don E. Fehrenbacher, *Prelude to Greatness: Lincoln in the 1850's* (Stanford: Stanford University Press, 1962).

[214] See Johannsen, *Lincoln-Douglas Debates*, pp. v–vi.

[215] See Abraham Lincoln, "First Inaugural Address," delivered 4 March 1861, in Fehrenbacher, *Abraham Lincoln: Speeches and Writings, 1858–1865*, pp. 219–10.

[216] See ibid., p. 219.

[217] For Lincoln's views and actions during this period, see David M. Potter, *Lincoln and His Party in the Secession Crisis* (New Haven: Yale University Press, 1942).

olutionary action were not yet necessary. In fact, as we shall see, some of the more pessimistic abolitionists were right. America, in the face of a southern sectional intransigence that now sought to entrench its violations of human and constitutional rights behind the wall of the Confederacy,[218] was ripe for revolutionary action in the name of the rights-based Constitution. We need, now, to understand the abolitionists' prophetic moral, political, and constitutional wisdom.

[218] On Confederate constitutionalism, see Emory M. Thomas, *The Confederate Nation, 1861–1865* (New York: Harper & Row, 1979); Don E. Fehrenbacher, *Constitutions and Constitutionalism in the Slaveholding South* (Athens, Ga.: University of Georgia Press, 1989).

THREE

THE ARGUMENT FOR TOLERATION IN ABOLITIONIST

MORAL, POLITICAL, AND CONSTITUTIONAL THOUGHT

T HE ABOLITIONISTS were a small but internally highly contentious, fissaparous group of probing social critics, often most energetic in criticism of one another.[1] They disagreed on matters of substance and strategy, not least, as we shall see, on the interpretive attitude to be taken to the U.S. Constitution and on what political strategy, if any, they should adopt.[2]

[1] For a fascinating and strikingly objective account by a leading abolitionist of their internal disagreements, see William Goodell, *Slavery and Anti-Slavery: A History of the Great Struggle in Both Hemispheres* (New York: William Goodell, 1855). For early, important studies of abolitionists and their background, see Mary Stoughton Locke, *Anti-Slavery in America from the Introduction of African Slaves to the Prohibition of the Slave Trade (1619–1808)* (Boston: Ginn & Co., 1901); Alice Dana Adams, *The Neglected Period of Anti-Slavery in America, 1808–1831* (Boston: Ginn & Co., 1908); Gilbert Hobbs Barnes, *The Antislavery Impulse, 1830–1844* (New York: D. Appleton-Century Co., 1933); Dwight Lowell Dumond, *Antislavery: The Crusade for Freedom in America* (Ann Arbor: University of Michigan Press, 1961); Dwight Lowell Dumond, *Antislavery Origins of the Civil War in the United States* (Ann Arbor: University of Michigan Press, 1939). Both Barnes and Dumond are critical of Garrison in contrast to Theodore Weld; for later, more sympathetic accounts of Garrison, see Aileen S. Kraditor, *Means and Ends in American Abolitionism: Garrison and His Critics on Strategy and Tactics, 1834–1850* (1967; reprint, Chicago: Elephant Paperbacks, 1989); Lewis Perry, *Radical Abolitionism: Anarchy and the Government of God in Antislavery Thought* (Ithaca: Cornell University Press, 1973). Important recent studies of the movement include Louis Filler, *The Crusade against Slavery, 1830–1860* (New York: Harper & Row, 1960); Martin Duberman, ed., *The Antislavery Vanguard: New Essays on the Abolitionists* (Princeton: Princeton University Press, 1965); James Brewer Stewart, *Holy Warriors: The Abolitionists and American Slavery* (New York: Hill & Wang, 1976); Ronald G. Walters, *The Antislavery Appeal: American Abolitionism after 1830* (New York: W. W. Norton, 1978); Merton L. Dillon, *The Abolitionists: The Growth of a Dissenting Minority* (New York: W. W. Norton, 1974); Louis S. Gerteis, *Morality and Utility in American Antislavery Reform* (Chapel Hill: University of North Carolina Press, 1987); Robert William Fogel, *Without Consent or Contract: The Rise and Fall of American Slavery* (New York: W. W. Norton, 1989). For an excellent collection of articles, see Paul Finkelman, ed., *Antislavery* (New York: Garland, 1989). For good collections of abolitionist thought, see William H. Pease and Jane H. Pease, *The Antislavery Argument* (Indianapolis: Bobbs-Merrill, 1965); Louis Ruchames, *The Abolitionists: A Collection of Their Writings* (New York: Capricorn Books, 1964); John L. Thomas, *Slavery Attacked: The Abolitionist Crusade* (Englewood Cliffs, N.J.: Prentice-Hall, 1965); Louis Filler, ed., *Abolition and Social Justice in the Era of Reform* (New York: Harper & Row, 1972).

[2] On the political abolitionists, see Sewell, *Ballots for Freedom*.

Their great importance in American moral, political, and constitutional thought was not only the substantive moral issue on which they aimed to fasten the public attention of the nation, but a mode of argument basic to the integrity of American revolutionary constitutionalism: namely, argument based on the demands of the right of free conscience. The abolitionists not only opposed the tyranny of unreflective majoritarian opinion of the age of Jackson, but their voice was its proclaimed public enemy, the object of the antiabolitionist mobs. These mobs, often led by Jacksonian community leaders, subjected courageous early abolitionist leaders such as Weld and Garrison—who asked only to be heard—to unremitting violence, threats of death, insult, ridicule, and in the case of Elijah Lovejoy, murder.[3] It was their appeal to conscience that was met by the age of Jackson's repression of free speech both at the state and national levels; such repression deprived the South and, for a long period, the nation of reasonable public discussion of the moral evils of slavery and of the merits and strategies of abolition.[4] It was the abolitionist attack on the political and constitutional pathology behind the deprivation of these constitutional liberties that eventually was to awaken the public mind of the nation to the underlying constitutional principles of human rights that condemned equally the repression of conscience and the institution of slavery.[5]

To understand the importance of abolitionist thought to American political and constitutional development, we must interpret their thought in light of the political theory of toleration central to their intellectual, moral, and political project; that theory gives pivotal weight to the inalienable right to conscience and to the primacy of ethical reflection. The theory of toleration enables us to understand the power of their ethical criticism of both slavery and racism, and how they connected that criticism to a larger conception of political and constitutional legitimacy rooted in American revolutionary constitutionalism.

Abolitionist Ethical Criticism of Slavery: The Analogy of Anti-Semitism

Theodore Weld, one of the most important and influential of the early abolitionists, presented in his widely circulated *American Slavery as It Is*[6] not only a factual picture (gathered largely from southern newspapers) of

---

[3] For an excellent study, see Richards, *"Gentlemen of Property and Standing."*

[4] See Nye, *Fettered Freedom*; Eaton, *The Freedom-of-Thought Struggle.*

[5] See Nye, *Fettered Freedom*; Sewell, *Ballots for Freedom.*

[6] *"American Slavery as It Is* sold more copies than any other antislavery pamphlet ever written: more than 100,000 copies within a year." Dumond, *Antislavery,* p. 256. Cf. Barnes, *The Antislavery Impulse,* pp. 139, 163.

life in the South under slavery, but a normative argument in light of which those facts should be interpreted.[7]

The normative argument took it to be fundamental that persons have

> inalienable rights, of the ownership of their own bodies, of the use of their own limbs and muscles, of all their time, liberty, and earnings, of the free exercise of choice, of the rights of marriage and parental authority, of legal protection, of the right to be, to do, to go, to stay, to think, to feel, to work, to rest, to eat, to sleep, to learn, to teach, to earn money, and to expend it, to visit, and to be visited, to speak, to be silent, to worship according to conscience, in fine, their rights to be protected by just and equal laws, and to be *amenable to such only.*[8]

The abridgment of such inalienable rights (including "free speech and rights of conscience, their right to acquire knowledge")[9] required a heavy burden of justification.

Weld identified an important analogy between the inadequacies of the justifications in fact offered by southerners and the comparably inadequate arguments offered in support of religious persecution, whether Puritan persecutions of the Quakers or Roman persecution of Christians or Christian persecutions of pagans and heretics. Weld was struck by the fact that persons, just and generous "with those of their own grade, or language, or nation, or hue," practiced "towards others, for whom they have contempt and aversion, the most revolting meanness, perpetrate robbery unceasingly, and inflict the severest privations, and the most barbarous cruelties." In language and thought very similar to Madison's theory of faction and its application by Madison (as we have seen in Chapter 2) to race prejudice, Weld observed: "Arbitrary power is to the mind what alcohol is to the body; it intoxicates. Man loves power. It is perhaps the strongest human passion; and the more absolute the power, the stronger the desire for it; the more it is desired, the more its exercise is enjoyed: this enjoyment is to human nature a fearful temptation,—generally an overmatch for it." The key to understanding the political evil of both religious persecution and slavery was the intrinsic corruptibility of human nature by political power over certain kinds of questions. The worst corruption was of conscience itself—

[7] On Weld and his importance in the early abolitionist movement, see Barnes, *The Antislavery Impulse*; for other important works by Weld, see Theodore Weld, *The Bible against Slavery* (1838; reprint, Pittsburgh: United Presbyterian Board of Publication, 1864); "The Power of Congress over Slavery in the District of Columbia" (1838), in tenBroek, *Equal under Law* Appendix A, pp. 243–80; "Persons Held to Service, Fugitive Slave, &c." (originally in published, 1843?), in *The Influence of the Slave Power with other Anti-Slavery Pamphlets* (Westport, Conn.: Negro Universities Press, 1970), no. 12, pp. 1–8.

[8] See Theodore Dwight Weld, *American Slavery as It Is* (1839; reprint, New York: Arno Press and the New York Times, 1968), p. 123; see also pp. 7–8, 143–44, 151.

[9] Ibid., pp. 7–8.

a fact, he argued, well reflected in the cumulative blinding of southern public morality to the evils of slavery.[10]

In the most important studies of the morality of slavery by an American philosopher in the antebellum period, William Ellery Channing had temperately stated the ethical dimensions of the abolitionist case for both the evil of slavery and the need for abolition in a similar way.[11] Like Weld, Channing based his argument on the fact that "all men have the same rational nature and the same power of conscience," a capacity for the powers of moral personality that he characterized, following Kant, as man's nature as "an end in himself," moral capacities of responsible moral freedom that reflect that we are "created in God's image . . . ; because created to unfold godlike faculties and to govern himself by a divine law written on his heart." Our equal moral capacity to know and effectuate that moral law was "the foundation of human rights in human nature,"[12] from which

> particular rights may easily be deduced. Every man has a right to exercise and invigorate his intellect or the power of knowledge, for knowledge is the essential condition of successful effort for every good; and whoever obstructs or quenches the intellectual life in another inflicts a grievous and irreparable wrong. Every man has a right to inquire into his duty, and to conform himself to what he learns of it. Every man has a right to use the means given by God and sanctioned by virtue for bettering his condition. He has a right to be respected according to his moral worth; a right to be regarded as a member of the community to which he belongs, and to be protected by impartial laws; and a right to be exempted from coercion, stripes, and punishment, as long as he respects the rights of others. He has a right to an equivalent for his labor. He has a right to sustain domestic relations, to discharge their duties, and to enjoy the happiness which flows from fidelity to these and other domestic relations.[13]

The fundamental wrong of slavery was that it deprived persons of the very foundation of human rights, freedom of conscience in knowing and acting on one's moral rights and duties. The test of political legitimacy was

[10] See ibid., pp. 112–13, 118–20, 115, 113–17, 120–21, 123–25, 146, 184–86.

[11] See *Slavery* (1836), pp. 688–743, *Remarks on the Slavery Question* (1839), pp. 782–820, and *Emancipation* (1842), pp. 820–53, in William E. Channing, *The Works of William E. Channing* (1882; reprint, New York: Burt Franklin, 1970). For commentary on Channing and his background, see Andrew Delbanco, *William Ellery Channing: An Essay on the Liberal Spirit in America* (Cambridge: Harvard University Press, 1981); Daniel Walker Howe, *The Unitarian Conscience: Harvard Moral Philosophy, 1805–1861* (Middletown, Conn.: Wesleyan University Press, 1988). See also D. H. Meyer, *The Instructed Conscience: The Shaping of the American National Ethic* (Philadelphia: University of Pennsylvania Press, 1972).

[12] See *Slavery*, in Channing, *Works*, pp. 693, 696, 695, 698.

[13] See ibid., pp. 698–99.

the Lockean test of whether a state respected the inalienable rights that must, in principle, be reserved from political power. The idea that such rights were not reserved from political power was "the logic of despotism." The American constitutional republic, in contrast to the Athenian democracy and Roman republic, rested on the distinctive mission of securing respect for the principles of Lockean political legitimacy. While "the oppressions of ages have nowhere wholly stifled" the idea of human rights, the existence of slavery today rested on the subversion of the idea of republican human rights,[14] whose force "is darkened, weakened among us, so as to be to many little more than a sound."[15] The ultimate degradation was that slaves were so deprived of the "consciousness of rights" that their docility was taken to show they have no rights. In fact, "the quiet of slavery is . . . the stillness of death."[16]

Such subversion required people to ignore the "self-evident truth"[17] that man cannot be owned, a truth that Channing characterized in a way Lincoln was later to echo:

LINCOLN: If slavery is not wrong, nothing can be wrong.[18]

CHANNING: And if this impression [that slavery is wrong] is a delusion, on what single moral conviction can we rely?[19]

In order to understand such subversion, Channing, like Weld, drew an analogy to the history of religious persecution, whose injustice often rested on the corruption of conscience.[20] In the same way Lincoln would later distinguish the wrongness of slavery from the blameworthiness of slaveowners,[21] Channing, making pointed reference to anti-Semitism, argued:

I maintain that we can never argue safely from the character of a man to the system he upholds. It is a solemn truth, yet not understood as it should be, that the worst institutions may be sustained, the worst deeds performed, the

---

[14] See ibid., pp. 699, 700, 740, 702, 716–18, 698.

[15] See *Emancipation*, in Channing, *Works*, p. 843.

[16] See *Slavery*, in Channing, *Works*, p. 714.

[17] See ibid., p. 692.

[18] See letter to Albert G. Hodges, 4 April 1864, in Fehrenbacher, *Abraham Lincoln: Speeches and Writings, 1858–1865*, p. 585.

[19] See *Slavery*, in Channing, *Works*, pp. 692–93.

[20] See ibid., pp. 704–5, 714, 715, 722; see also *Emancipation*, in Channing, *Works*, pp. 839–43, 840, 843.

[21] "I have no prejudice against the Southern people. They are just what we would be in their situation. If slavery did not now exist amongst them, they would not introduce it. If it did now exist amongst us, we should not instantly give it up. . . . I surely will not blame them for not doing what I should not know how to do myself." Lincoln, "Speech on Kansas-Nebraska Act," 16 October 1854, in Fehrenbacher, *Abraham Lincoln: Speeches and Writings, 1832–58*, pp. 315–16.

most merciless cruelties inflicted, by the conscientious and the good. . . . For ages the Jews were thought to have forfeited the rights of men, as much as the African race at the South, and were insulted, spoiled, and slain, not by mobs, but by sovereigns and prelates, who really supposed themselves avengers of the crucified Saviour."[22]

Channing drew instruction from the history of religious persecution because it exemplified both an abridgment of inalienable human rights and a familiarly inadequate way in which such abridgments have been justified. Proslavery views exemplified the same structure of argument and should be condemned for the same reason.

Other abolitionists, such as Frederick Douglass,[23] Charles Sumner,[24] and James Russell Lowell,[25] also drew pointed analogies between the evil of slavery and the evil of intolerance exemplified by anti-Semitism. And George William Curtis, addressing the abolitionist moral challenge before the nation at the end of the American Civil War, spoke of "the bitter prejudice against the colored race, which is as inhuman and unmanly as the old hatred and contempt of Christendom for the Jews."[26]

We need now to explore this abolitionist argument and the role the example of the wrongness of anti-Semitism played in it.

The Argument for Toleration

The argument for toleration assumed by both Weld and Channing was an American elaboration of the argument for universal toleration that had been stated, in variant forms, by Pierre Bayle and John Locke.[27] The context and motivations of the argument were those of radical Protestant intellectual and moral conscience reflecting on the political principles requisite to protect its enterprise against the oppressions of established churches, both Catholic and Protestant.

That enterprise arose both from a moral ideal of the person and the need to protect that ideal from a political threat that had historically crushed it. The ideal was of respect for persons by virtue of their personal moral powers both rationally to assess and pursue ends and reasonably to adjust and

<hr/>

[22] See *Emancipation*, in Channing, *Works*, p. 840.

[23] See "Colored Men of America Demand Equal Rights as Americans," in Pease and Pease, *The Antislavery Argument*, p. 278.

[24] See "Charles Sumner Argues for School Desegregation," in ibid., p. 293.

[25] See "James Russell Lowell Condemns the Prejudice of Color," in ibid., p. 313.

[26] See "The Good Fight," in Charles Eliot Norton, ed., *Orations and Addresses of George William Curtis* (New York: Harper & Bros., 1894), p. 168.

[27] For fuller examination of the argument in Locke and Bayle and its American elaboration, notably by Jefferson and Madison, see Richards, *Toleration*, pp. 89–128.

constrain pursuit of ends in light of the equal moral status of persons as bearers of equal rights. The political threat to this ideal of the person was the political idea and practice that the moral status of persons was not determined by the responsible expression of their own moral powers, but specified in advance of such reflection or the possibility of such reflection by a hierarchical structure of society and nature in which they were embedded. That structure, classically associated with orders of being,[28] defined roles and statuses in which people were born, lived, and died, and exhaustively specified the responsibilities of living in light of those roles.

The political power of the hierarchical conception was shown not only in the ways in which people behaved, but in the ways in which it penetrated into the human heart and mind, framing a personal, moral, and social identity founded on roles specified by the hierarchical structure. The structure—religious, economic, political—did not need to achieve its ends by massive coercion precisely because its crushing force on human personality had been rendered personally and socially invisible by a heart that felt and mind that imaginatively entertained nothing that could render the structure an object of critical reflection. There could be nothing that might motivate such reflection (life being perceived, felt, and lived as richly natural).

Of course, such a political order, being human, would make use of our rational powers when contexts and roles might call for the exercise of practical rationality (for example, in the organization of farming or in war). A few persons might even achieve a remarkably high level of competence in the exercise of critical moral powers (as in the literate elites of ancient hierarchical societies such as those of Babylonia, Egypt, and the Maya). But the general life of society placed no value or weight on a more extended exercise of such powers.

In light of the moral pluralism made possible by the Reformation, liberal Protestant thinkers such as Bayle and Locke subjected the political power of the hierarchical conception to radical ethical criticism in terms of a moral ideal of the person having moral powers of rationality and reasonableness; the hierarchical conception had subverted the ideal and, for this reason, distorted the standards of rationality and reasonableness to which the ideal appealed.

Both Bayle and Locke argued as religious Christians. Their argument naturally arose as an intramural debate among interpreters of the Christian tradition about freedom and ethics. An authoritative Pauline strand of that tradition had given central weight to the value of Christian freedom. That tradition, like the Jewish tradition from which it developed, had a powerful ethical core of concern for the development of moral personality; Augustine

---

[28] See Arthur O. Lovejoy, *The Great Chain of Being* (Cambridge: Harvard University Press, 1964).

of Hippo thus had interpreted the trinitarian nature of God, in whose image we are made, on the model of moral personality, that is, the three parts of the soul—will, memory, and intelligence. Indeed, the argument for toleration arose from an internal criticism by Bayle of Augustine's argument for the persecution of the heretical Donatists; to wit, Augustine had misinterpreted central Christian values of freedom and ethics.[29] The concern was that religious persecution had corrupted ethics and, for this reason, the essence of Christianity's elevated and simple ethical core of a universal brotherhood of free people.

The argument for toleration was a judgment of and response to perceived abuses of political epistemology. The legitimation of religious persecution by both Catholics and Protestants (drawing authority from Augustine, among others) had rendered a politically entrenched view of religious and moral truth the measure of permissible ethics and religion, including the epistemic standards of inquiry and debate about religious and moral truth. By the late seventeenth century (when Locke and Bayle wrote), there was good reason to believe that politically entrenched views of religious and moral truth (resting on the authority of the Bible and associated interpretive practices) assumed essentially contestable interpretations of a complex historical interaction between pagan, Jewish, and Christian cultures in the early Christian era.[30]

The Renaissance rediscovery of pagan culture and learning reopened the question of how the Christian synthesis of pagan philosophical and Jewish ethical and religious culture was to be understood. Among other things, the development of critical historiography and techniques of textual interpretation had undeniable implications for reasonable Bible interpretation.[31] The Protestant Reformation both assumed and further encouraged these new modes of inquiry, and encouraged as well the appeal to experiment and experience, which were a matrix for the methodologies associated with the rise of modern science.[32] These new approaches to thought and inquiry had made possible the recognition that there was a gap between the politically entrenched conceptions of religious and moral truth and inquiry and the kinds of reasonable inquiries that the new approaches made available. The argument for toleration arose from the recognition of this disjunction between the reigning political epistemology and the new epistemic methodologies.

The crux of the problem was that politically entrenched conceptions of

---

[29] See Richards, *Toleration*, pp. 86–95.

[30] See ibid., pp. 25–27, 84–98, 105, 125.

[31] See ibid., pp. 125–26.

[32] For a recent review of the question, see I. Bernard Cohen, ed., *Puritanism and the Rise of Modern Science: The Merton Thesis* (New Brunswick, N.J.: Rutgers University Press, 1990).

truth had, on the basis of the Augustinian legitimation of religious persecution, made themselves the measure both of the standards of reasonable
inquiry and of who could count as a reasonable inquirer after truth. But in
light of the new modes of inquiry now available, such political entrenchment of religious truth was often seen to rest not only on the degradation
of reasonable standards of inquiry, but on the self-fulfilling degradation of
the capacity of persons to conduct such inquiries. In order to rectify these
evils, the argument for toleration forbade, as a matter of principle, the enforcement by the state of any such conception of religious truth. The scope
of legitimate political concern must, rather, rest on the pursuit of general
ends such as life and basic rights and liberties (for example, the right to
conscience). The pursuit of such goods was consistent with the full range
of ends free people might rationally and reasonably pursue.[33]

A prominent feature of the argument for toleration was its claim that
religious persecution corrupted conscience itself, a critique we have already noted in the American abolitionist thinkers who assume the argument. Such corruption, a kind of self-induced blindness to the evils one
inflicts, is a consequence of the political enforcement at large of a conception of religious truth that immunizes itself from independent criticism in
terms of reasonable standards of thought and deliberation. In effect, the
conception of religious truth, though perhaps having once been importantly shaped by more ultimate considerations of reason, ceases to be held
or to be understood and elaborated *on the basis of reason.*

A tradition, which thus loses a sense of its reasonable foundations, stag-
nates and depends increasingly for allegiance on question-begging appeals
to orthodox conceptions of truth and the violent repression of any dissent
from such conceptions as a kind of disloyal moral treason. The politics of
loyalty rapidly degenerates, as it did in the antebellum South's repression
of any criticism of slavery, into a politics that takes pride in widely held
community values solely because they are community values. Standards of
discussion and inquiry become increasingly parochial and insular; they
serve only a polemical role in the defense of the existing community values
and are indeed increasingly hostile to any more impartial reasonable assessment in light of independent standards.[34]

Such politics tends to forms of irrationalism in order to protect its now
essentially polemical project. Opposing views relevant to reasonable public
argument are suppressed, facts distorted or misstated, values disconnected
from ethical reasoning, indeed deliberation in politics denigrated in favor
of violence against dissent and the aesthetic glorification of violence. Paradoxically, the more the tradition becomes seriously vulnerable to inde-

[33] See Richards, *Toleration*, pp. 119–20.
[34] See Franklin, *The Militant South*; cf. Cash, *The Mind of the South.*

pendent reasonable criticism (indeed, increasingly in rational need of such criticism), the more it is likely to generate forms of political irrationalism (including scapegoating of outcast dissenters) in order to secure allegiance.

This paradox of intolerance can be understood by reference to the epistemic motivations of Augustinian intolerance. A certain conception of religious truth was originally affirmed as true and politically enforced on society at large because it was supposed to be the epistemic measure of reasonable inquiry (that is, more likely to lead to epistemically reliable beliefs). But the consequence of the legitimation of such intolerance over time was that standards of reasonable inquiry, outside the orthodox measure of such inquiry, were repressed. In effect, the orthodox conception of truth was no longer defended on the basis of reason, but was increasingly hostile to reasonable assessment in terms of impartial standards not hostage to the orthodox conception. Indeed, orthodoxy was defended as an end in itself, increasingly by nonrational and even irrational means of appeal to community identity and the like. The paradox appears in the subversion of the original epistemic motivations of the Augustinian argument. Rather than securing reasonable inquiry, the argument now has cut off the tradition from such inquiry. Indeed, the legitimacy of the tradition feeds on irrationalism precisely when it is most vulnerable to reasonable criticism, contradicting and frustrating its original epistemic ambitions.

The history of religious persecution amply illustrates these truths; and as the abolitionists clearly saw, no aspect of that history more clearly so than Christian anti-Semitism. The relationship of Christianity to its Jewish origins has always been a tense and ambivalent one.[35] The fact that many Jews did not accept Christianity was a kind of standing challenge to the reasonableness of Christianity, especially in its early period (prior to its establishment as the church of the late Roman Empire), when Christianity was a proselytizing religion that competed for believers with the wide range of religious and philosophical alternative belief systems available in the late pagan world.

In his recent important studies of anti-Semitism[36] the medievalist Gavin Langmuir characterizes as anti-Judaism Christianity's longstanding worries about the Jews because of the way the Jewish rejection of Christianity discredited the reasonableness of the Christian belief system in the pagan

---

[35] For a useful study of the early Christian period, see John A. Gager, *The Origins of Anti-Semitism: Attitudes toward Judaism in Pagan and Christian Antiquity* (New York: Oxford University Press, 1983). The classic general study is Leon Poliakov, *The History of Anti-Semitism*, trans. Richard Howard, Natalie Gerardi, Miriam Kochan, and George Klin, 4 vols. (Oxford: Oxford University Press, 1965–85).

[36] See Gavin I. Langmuir, *Toward a Definition of Antisemitism* (Berkeley: University of California Press, 1990); and *History, Religion, and Antisemitism* (Berkeley: University of California Press, 1990).

world. Langmuir argues that the Christian conception of the obduracy of the Jews and the divine punishment of them for such obduracy were natural forms of anti-Judaic self-defense, resulting in the forms of expulsion and segregation from Christian society that naturally expressed and legitimated such judgments on the Jews. In contrast, Langmuir calls anti-Semitism proper the totally baseless and irrational beliefs about ritual crucifixions and cannibalism of Christians by Jews that were "widespread in northern Europe by 1350";[37]; such beliefs led to populist murders of Jews usually (though not always) condemned by both church and secular authorities.

Langmuir suggests, as does R. I. Moore,[38] that the development of anti-Semitism proper was associated with growing internal doubts posed by dissenters in the period 950–1250 about the reasonableness of certain Catholic religious beliefs and practices (for example, transubstantiation) and the resolution of such doubts by the forms of irrationalist politics associated with anti-Semitism proper (often centering on fantasies of ritual eating of human flesh that expressed the underlying worries about transubstantiation). The worst ravages of anti-Semitism illustrate the paradox of intolerance, which explains the force of the example for abolitionists. Precisely when the dominant religious tradition gave rise to the most reasonable internal doubts, these doubts were displaced from reasonable discussion and debate into blatant political irrationalism against one of the more conspicuous, vulnerable, and innocent groups of dissenters.

Langmuir's distinction between anti-Judaism and anti-Semitism proper is an unstable one. Both attitudes rest on conceptions of religious truth that are unreasonably enforced on the community at large. Certainly, both the alleged obduracy of the Jews and their just punishment for such obduracy were sectarian interpretations of the facts and not reasonably enforced at large. Beliefs in obduracy are not as unreasonable as beliefs in cannibalism; and segregation is not as evil as populist murder or genocide. But both forms of politics are, on grounds of the argument for toleration, unreasonable in principle. More fundamentally, anti-Judaism laid the corrupt political foundation for anti-Semitism. Once it became politically legitimate to enforce at large a sectarian conception of religious truth, reasonable doubts about such truth were displaced from the reasonable discussion and debate they deserved to the irrationalist politics of religious persecution. The Jews have been in the Christian West the most continuously blatant victims of that politics, making anti-Semitism "the oldest prejudice in Western civilization."[39]

The radical criticism of political irrationalism implicit in the argument

---

[37] See Langmuir, *Toward a Definition of Antisemitism*, pp. 57–62, 302.

[38] See R. I. Moore, *The Formation of a Persecuting Society: Power and Deviance in Western Europe, 950–1250* (Oxford: Basil Blackwell, 1987).

[39] Langmuir, *Toward a Definition of Antisemitism*, p. 45.

for toleration, once unleashed, could not be limited to religion proper, but was naturally extended by John Locke to embrace politics as such.[40] Reflection on the injustice of religious persecution by established churches was generalized into a larger reflection on how political orthodoxies of hierarchical orders of authority and submission (for example, patriarchal political theories of absolute monarchy such as Filmer's)[41] had been unreasonably enforced at large. In both religion and political theory, political enforcement at large of one view not only degraded standards of argument to the exclusive measure of the orthodox one; it also retained a hold on political power by stunting people's capacity to know, understand, and give effect to their inalienable human rights of reasonable self-government. The generalization of the argument for toleration naturally suggested the political legitimacy of some form of constitutional democracy (in which the principle of toleration would play a foundational central role) as a political decision procedure more likely to secure a reasonable politics that respected human rights and pursued the common interests of all persons alike.[42]

The argument for toleration was motivated by a general political skepticism about enforceable political epistemologies. Such politics enforced at large sectarian conceptions of religious, moral, and political truth at the expense of denying the moral powers of persons to assess these matters in light of reasonable standards and as reasonable persons.

The leading philosophers of toleration thus tried to articulate some criteria or thought experiment in terms of which such sectarian views might be assessed and debunked from a more impartial perspective. Bayle thus argued:

> Since passions and prejudices only too often obscure the ideas of natural equity, I would advise a person who intends to know them well to consider these ideas in general and as abstracted from all private interest and from the customs of his country. It can happen that a fond and deeply rooted passion will persuade a man that an action he envisages as profitable and pleasant for him is consonant with the dictates of right reason. It can happen that the force of custom and the turn given to the soul while instructing it in earliest infancy, may cause honesty to be found where there is not any. To surmount both these obstacles, therefore, I would like whoever aims at knowing distinctly this natural light with respect to morality to raise himself above his own private interest or the custom of the country, and to ask himself in general: "*Is such a practice just in itself? If it were a question of introducing it in a country*

---

[40] See Richards, *Toleration*, pp. 98–102; and *Foundations*, pp. 82–90.

[41] See Robert Filmer, *Patriarcha* (1680), in Filmer, *Patriarcha and Other Writings*, ed. Johann P. Sommerville (Cambridge: Cambridge University Press, 1991), pp. 1–68.

[42] See Richards, *Foundations*, pp. 78–97.

*where it would not be in use and where he would be free to take it up or
not, would one see, upon examining it impartially that it is reasonable
enough to merit being adopted?"*[43]

Bayle's use of a contractualist test was generalized by Locke into a comprehensive contractualist political theory.[44] Though Locke is not clear on
the point, contractualism has nothing to do with history; nothing in the
argument turns on the actual existence of a state of nature. Rather, as Jeffrey Reiman has strikingly put it, in contractualism "the state of nature is
the moral equivalent of the Cartesian doubt."[45] Descartes was not, of
course, an ultimate epistemological skeptic, but rather a philosopher of
knowledge worried by the unreliable ways in which beliefs were conventionally formed. He was, for this reason, concerned heuristically to discover
what could count as a reasonable basis on which reliable beliefs may be
formed, and the Cartesian doubt was a way of articulating what he took
that basis to be.

In the same way, neither Bayle nor Locke were moral, political, or religious skeptics; they were concerned, rather, by the unreliable appeals to
politically enforceable conceptions of sectarian truths (that is, politically
enforceable epistemologies) and articulated a thought experiment of abstract contractualist reasonableness to assess what might legitimately be
enforced through law. Bayle's use of a contractualist test made this point
exactly: Abstracting from your own aims and the particular customs of your
society, what principles of legitimate politics would all persons reasonably
accept? The test is, of course, very like Rawls's abstract contractualist test
in the absence of knowledge of specific identity and serves exactly the same
political function.[46]

Such a contractualist test assumes that persons have the twin moral powers of rationality and reasonableness in light of which they may assess human ends, their own and others.[47] The principles of prudence enable us to
reflect on the coherence and complementarity among our ends and the
more effective ways to pursue them subject to principles of epistemic rationality. The principles of moral reasonableness enable us to regulate the
pursuit of our ends in light of the common claims of all persons to the forms
of action and forbearance consistent with equal respect for our status in
the moral community. These self-originating powers of reason enable us
not only to think for ourselves from our own viewpoint, but also from the

[43] Pierre Bayle, *Philosophical Commentary*, trans. Amie Godman Tannenbaum (New York:
Peter Lang, 1987), p. 30.

[44] See Richards, *Foundations*, pp. 82–90; and *Toleration*, pp. 98–102.

[45] Jeffrey Reiman, *Justice and Modern Moral Philosophy* (New Haven: Yale University
Press, 1990), p. 69.

[46] See John Rawls, *A Theory of Justice* (Cambridge: Harvard University Press, 1971).

[47] For a fuller account of these powers, see Richards, *A Theory of Reasons for Action*.

moral point of view that gives weight or should give weight to the view-points of everyone else.

Reason—epistemic and practical—can have the power that it does in our lives because it enables us to stand back from our ends, to assess crit-ically how they cohere with one another and with the ends of others, and to reexamine and sometimes revise such judgments in light of new insights and experience and to act accordingly. Reason can only reliably perform this role when it is itself subject to revision and correction in light of public standards open, accessible, and available to all. Public reason—a resource that better enables all persons to cultivate their moral powers—requires a public culture that sustains high standards of independent, critically tested and testable, revisable argument accessible to all. In order to perform the role that it should play in the exercise of our internal moral powers, public reason cannot be merely or even mainly polemical. It must afford sufficient public space within which we may comfortably express what doubts we may have or should have about our ends, lives, and communities, and delib-eratively discuss and resolve such doubts.[48]

The claim that this conception rests on a false and superficial meta-physical picture of an agent with no deep ends fails to take seriously the account of our moral freedom that it offers.[49] Nothing in the account denies the obvious social facts of our upbringing, our socialization, or the com-munities with whom we profoundly identify. Indeed, implicit in this view is an illuminating understanding of human personality and our ends and the ways in which our moral powers flourish only through the language and public culture that give expression to the life of reason. Our moral freedom, to the extent we cultivate it, is not an anomic freedom to eschew and adopt ends arbitrarily, but the freedom of exercising our moral powers by appeal to reason with all that implies about perspective on and impartiality about our ends.[50]

Respect for our capacity for reason, thus understood, requires a politics that respects the principle of toleration. Forms of traditional wisdom—which have a basis in public reason—will not be subject to the principle. But the principle does deny that convictions of sectarian truth *can be en-forced through law solely on that basis* (the role of such convictions in private life is, of course, another matter). The principle thus limits the force

[48] For a useful discussion of all these points, see Onora O'Neill, *Constructions of Reason* (Cambridge: Cambridge University Press, 1989). For Kant on public reason, see "An Answer to the Question: 'What Is Enlightenment?'" in Hans Reiss, ed., *Kant's Political Writings* (Cambridge: Cambridge University Press, 1970), p. 55: "The *public* use of man's reason must always be free."

[49] See Michael J. Sandel, *Liberalism and the Limits of Justice* (Cambridge: Cambridge University Press, 1982).

[50] See Susan Wolf, *Freedom within Reason* (New York: Oxford University Press, 1990).

in *political* life of convictions that draw their strength solely from the certainties of group loyalty and identification that tend, consistent with the paradox of intolerance, most to self-insulate themselves from reason when they are most reasonably subject to internal doubts.

Nothing in the account suggests that religious views or even convictions about truth of dominant religions are unreasonable, but only that certain facts of political psychology about human nature in politics lead to a kind of political corruption of the religious enterprise as an inquiry into ultimate truth. Exercises of political power enforcing views of religious truth tend not to do so on the basis of reason. Indeed, consistent with the paradox of intolerance, precisely when the tradition may need most to entertain, discuss, and resolve reasonable doubts about its truth, it tends to make war on its reasonable doubts by the despicable forms of political irrationalism exemplified by the history of religious persecution.

Contractualism, thus understood as a hypothetical test for public reason in politics, must tend in the nature of its enterprise to identify the more abstract features that characterize our moral powers as reasoning agents. Since the motivation of the entire enterprise is the degree to which the idea and practice of hierarchical orders of authority has been permitted to subvert our moral powers of rationality and reasonableness, the reclamation of such powers requires a demanding test of political legitimacy that constrains and limits political power in the ways that we have good reason, in light of our historical experience, to believe require limitation in order to do justice to the reasonable demands of our moral natures.

Contractualism offers us such a test, asking us to think hypothetically in abstraction from our current particular ends and situations about the more general features of living a rational and reasonable life and what constraints on politics are required in order for all persons to be secure in living such a life. The idea of general goods or resources or capacities—all familiar in the contractualist literature—are corollaries of such a test;[51] they identify the kind of abstract features of living a life that reasonable persons, in the contractualist choice situation, would regard as properly subject to a distributive principle of a just politics. The principle of toleration is one such principle, concerned with the foundational principles that make possible

---

[51] See, e.g., Rawls, *A Theory of Justice*; Richards, *A Theory of Reasons for Action*; T. M. Scanlon, "Preference and Urgency," *Journal of Philosophy* 72, no. 19 (November 6, 1975) 655; Amartya Sen, *The Standard of Living* (Cambridge: Cambridge University Press, 1987); Ronald Dworkin, "What Is Equality? Part I: Equality of Welfare," *Journal of Philosophy and Public Affairs* 10, no. 3 (Summer 1981) 185; "What Is Equality? Part II: Equality of Resources," *Journal of Philosophy and Public Affairs* 10, no. 4 (Fall 1981): 283; "What Is Equality? Part III: The Place of Liberty," *Iowa Law Review* 73, no. 1 (Fall 1987): 1; "What Is Equality? Part IV: Political Equality," *University of San Francisco Law Review* 22, no. 1 (Fall 1987): 1.

both a politics of reason and a conception of political community that dignifies the capacity for reasonableness of all persons to be self-governing moral agents.

Slavery as a Political Evil

John Locke began his great refutation of Filmer's patriarchalism with a broad condemnation of the advocacy of natural slavery Filmer espoused as "so vile and miserable an Estate of Man . . . that 'tis hardly to be conceived, that an *Englishman*, much less a *Gentleman*, should plead for't."[52] Locke's constructive development of a general contractualist political theory based on the protection of inalienable human rights prominently drew the consequence:

> The *Natural Liberty* of Man is to be free from any Superior Power on Earth, and not to be under the Will or Legislative Authority of Man, but to have only the Law of Nature for his Rule. . . . This *Freedom* from Absolute, Arbitrary Power, is so necessary to, and closely joyned with a Man's Preservation, that he cannot part with it, but by what forfeits his Preservation and Life together. For a Man, not having the Power of his own Life, *cannot*, by Compact, or his own Consent, *enslave himself* to any one, nor put himself under the Absolute, Arbitrary Power of another, to take away his Life, when he pleases.[53]

Locke's exception to his general rights-based condemnation of slavery was for cases of forfeiture of rights. Certain kinds of culpable wrongdoing led to forfeiture of rights as just punishment; and if death may be just punishment (for example, for culpably fighting an unjust war), slavery—a less severe punishment—may be just as well.[54] Locke had drafted the Fundamental Constitutions of Carolina, which provided: "Every freeman of Carolina shall have absolute power and authority over his negro slaves, of what opinion or religion soever."[55] He apparently believed that the African slave trade rested on captives taken in a just war, who had forfeited their lives "by some act that deserves Death."[56]

Locke's judgment about the legitimacy of American black slavery was not supported by the facts even when he wrote. The slave trade was not

[52] See Locke, *The First Treatise of Government*, in Locke, *Two Treatises*, p. 159 (sec. 1).

[53] See Locke, *Second Treatise of Government*, in Locke, *Two Treatises*, pp. 301–2 (secs. 22–23).

[54] See ibid., pp. 302–3 (secs. 23–24), 340–41 (sec. 85).

[55] See John Locke, The Fundamental Constitutions of Carolina," in *The Works of John Locke*, 10 vols. (London: Tomas Tegg, 1823), 10:196.

[56] See Locke, *Second Treatise of Government*, in Locke, *Two Treatises*, p. 302 (sec. 23). For commentary, see ibid., pp. 302–3, note; Davis, *The Problem of Slavery*, pp. 118–21.

the product of just wars.[57] Even if it were, the theory could not justify the American practice of continuing the enslavement of offspring; the children of slaves were born as free as any other person by any reading of Locke.[58] Both points were clearly made by later highly influential proponents of Lockean political contractualism such as Francis Hutcheson. Hutcheson forcefully demolished the idea that enslavement could justifiably be regarded as a just punishment even in a just war,[59] and underscored the clear wrongness of enslaving the children of slaves: "Grant that the parents might have been put to death justly, yet their children come into life innocent, they are rational beings of our species, the workmanship of the same God in their bodies and souls, of the same materials with ourselves and our children, and endued with like faculties."[60]

American contractualist political thought was also much moved by Montesquieu's ethically skeptical way of trying to even state the case for American slavery: "It is impossible for us to suppose these creatures to be men, because, allowing them to be men, a suspicion would follow that we ourselves are not Christians." Consistent with his general interest in climactic determinants of political culture, Montesquieu rejected Aristotle's theory of natural slaves as unsupported; he suggested, however, that environmental factors such as climate might justify its existence in very warm locales. But again, he urged skepticism in view of the very ease with which the argument came to him: "I know not whether this article be dictated by my understanding or by my heart."[61]

Such skepticism appealed to American contractualist thought because it naturally raised the same kinds of questions about the sectarian rationalization of entrenched power and hierarchy so central to their own revolutionary claims. James Otis could not have been clearer on this point:

> The colonists are by the law of nature freeborn, as indeed all men are, white or black. No better reasons can be given for enslaving those of any color than such as Baron Montesquieu has humorously given as the foundation of that cruel slavery exercised over the poor Ethiopians, which threatens one day to

---

[57] On the motives and effects of the Atlantic slave trade, see Barbara L. Solow, ed., *Slavery and the Rise of the Atlantic System* (Cambridge: Cambridge University Press, 1991); Joseph E. Inikori and Stanley L. Engerman, eds., *The Atlantic Slave Trade: Effects on Economies, Societies, and Peoples in Africa, the Americas, and Europe* (Durham: Duke University Press, 1992).

[58] See Grant, *John Locke's Liberalism*, p. 68, n. 68.

[59] See Francis Hutcheson, *A System of Moral Philosophy* (1755; reprint, Hildesheim: Georg Olms Verlagsbuchhandlung, 1969), pp. 204–5; *A Short Introduction to Moral Philosophy* (1747; reprint, Hildesheim: Georg Olms Verlagsbuchhandlung, 1969), pp. 273–74.

[60] See Hutcheson, *A System of Moral Philosophy*, p. 210; cf. *A Short Introduction to Moral Philosophy*, p. 226.

[61] See Baron de Montesquiueu, *The Spirit of the Laws*, trans. Thomas Nugent (New York: Hafner, 1949), p. 239, 240, 241.

reduce both Europe and America to the ignorance and barbarity of the darkest ages. Does it follow that 'tis right to enslave a man because he is black? Will short curled hair like wool instead of Christian hair, as 'tis called by those whose hearts are as hard as the nether millstone, help the argument? Can any logical inference in favor of slavery be drawn from a flat nose, a long or a short face? Nothing better can be said in favor of a trade that is the most shocking violation of the law of nature, has a direct tendency to diminish the idea of the inestimable value of liberty, and makes every dealer in it a tyrant. . . . It is a clear truth that those who every day barter away other men's liberty will soon care little for their own.[62]

It was no accident but fundamental to their vindication of the right to conscience against majoritarian American complacency that the abolitionists—the most principled nineteenth-century advocates of the argument for toleration in the United States—should, following Otis, have come to see the abolition of slavery as the central critical test for American contractualism. The existence of slavery—resting on the denial of the human rights of some—undermined the kind of value appropriate to respect for any human rights at all.[63] Having the political conviction appropriate to the wrongness of slavery was, for the abolitionists, the test for having any political convictions of moral wrongness at all.

Slavery was a moral wrong of a qualitatively distinctive kind; it deprived persons of their inalienable human rights—rights to freedom of conscience and speech, to intimate family life, to free labor, to security of life and property, and the like. Such a wrong, if it was to be justified at all, was to be justified on the basis of public reasons not themselves hostage to the institution under critical assessment. In fact, the failure of American politics to meet this latter requirement or even to take it seriously led abolitionists critically to challenge American identity as a nation that ostensibly took rights seriously. Theodore Parker, abolitionist and transcendentalist, was an exemplary and often profound critic along these lines.

Parker saw the evil of slavery as the test for America's commitment to the principles of the Protestant Reformation. He could see how the Catholic Church could tolerate slavery, but "it seems amazing that American Christians of the puritanic stock, with a philosophy that transcends sensationalism, should prove false to the only principle which at once justifies the

[62] See Otis, *The Rights of the British Colonies* (1764), in Bailyn, *Pamphlets*, at p. 439.

[63] For another attack on slavery in light of revolutionary political morality, see Samuel Hopkins, *Timely Articles on Slavery* (1776; reprint, Miami: Mnemosyne, 1969). For a comparable southern view, see St. George Tucker, *A Dissertation on Slavery with a Proposal for the Gradual Abolition of It, in the State of Virginia* (1796; reprint, Westport, Conn.: Negro Universities Press, 1970), reprinted in Tucker's *Blackstone's Commentaries* (1803), 2:31–89, Note H; see also Jefferson, *Notes on the State of Virginia*, pp. 137–43, 162–63.

conduct of Jesus, of Luther, and the Puritans themselves."[64] Consistent
with the arguments of Weld and Channing on the evil of slavery as a kind
of religious persecution, Parker's appeal to Protestant principle was to the
argument for toleration central to the enterprise of Bayle and Locke, a tradition Parker and the abolitionists took to be ethically fundamental. The
task of a life of conscience was to question politically entrenched epistemologies to assess whether they illegitimately degraded both standards of
argument and persons in order to maintain their power. The demands of
ethical impartiality accordingly required more abstract questions of justification to be raised in light of independent standards of public reason,
standards not hostage to the political epistemology under examination.

The Bible was, of course, no exception. Parker was thus a leading American Protestant advocate of making available to religious inquiry the broadest range of reasonable methodologies, including the most advanced
German techniques of Bible interpretation and historiography. He brought
to the interpretation of the Bible, consistent with Bayle and Locke, an interest primarily in what he took to be its simple and elevated ethical truths
of a reasonable respect for the moral powers of all persons as equal bearers
of inalienable human rights.[65]

Parker's quest for an ethical impartiality on human rights motivated his
neo-Kantian transcendentalism: Our capacity for ethics was rooted in the
abstract deliberations of our internal moral powers, "a living principle
which of itself originates ideas."[66] Ethics demanded abstract respect for
these moral powers, however stunted and starved by the unjust coercions
of politically entrenched epistemologies. Parker's transcendentalism was
thus an appeal for an abstract respect for free moral personality. Such ethical deliberation could not be reduced, in the style of proslavery thought,
to impersonal facts such as sociology, or biblical literalism, or ancient or
medieval history, or to utilitarian aggregation. Utilitarian aggregation was,

[64] Theodore Parker, "The Rights of Man in America," delivered in 1854, in Theodore Parker, *The Rights of Man in America*, ed. F. B. Sanborn (Boston: American Unitarian Association, 1911), pp. 369–61.

[65] See Theodore Parker, "The Transient and Permanent in Christianity," in Theodore Parker, *The Transient and Permanent in Christianity*, ed. George Willis Cooke (Boston: Amer-
ican Unitarian Association, 1908). For commentary on Parker's life and thought, see Henry
Steele Commager, *Theodore Parker* (Boston: Little, Brown, 1936); John Edward Dirks, *The
Critical Theology of Theodore Parker* (New York: Columbia University Press, 1948). For
other examples of abolitionist Bible interpretation, see Weld, *The Bible against Slavery*;
Moses Stuart, *Conscience and the Constitution* (1850; reprint, New York: Negro Universities
Press, 1969); Francis Wayland, *The Elements of Moral Science*, ed. Joseph L. Blau (Cam-
bridge: Belknap Press, Harvard University Press, 1963), esp. pp. 192–96, 386–90.

[66] Theodore Parker, "Transcendentalism," in Theodore Parker, *The World of Matter and
the Spirit of Man*, ed. George Willis Cooke (Boston: American Unitarian Association, 1907),
p. 23.

for Parker, yet another kind of objectifying tendency; in this case, a sensationalist ethics of aggregate pleasures over pains justified slavery, as Calhoun believed, by supposing that, whatever its pains, it caused a greatest net aggregate of utility over all. Thus understood, utilitarianism was an ideology that rendered invisible to criticism the incommensurable moral evil that slavery was.[67] In effect, all the available justifications for slavery were themselves hostage to the politically enforced epistemology of proslavery, distorting or degrading impartial ethical assessment of the institution.

Parker clearly followed his teacher Channing's argument that the ethical consideration of slavery should not focus on external facts such as race but on the internal moral powers of all persons,[68] powers that gave rise to "the great political idea of America, the idea of the Declaration of Independence,"[69] the idea of universal human rights. Ethics, under this view, turned on the moral capacities people have, however degraded by tyranny and oppression. Accordingly, both Parker and Channing found no reason whatsoever in the actual situation of blacks under American slavery to justify the institution from the required contractualist point of view of ethical impartiality. The familiar proslavery arguments usually pointed out the actual situation of American slaves (their apparent happiness and docility, the satisfaction of their material and welfare interests by adequate food, housing, and care, and the like).[70] But these facts could have no more weight, from a contractualist perspective, than the comparable arguments should have in the case of populations historically subjugated by religious or political tyrannies based on a hierarchical order of natural authority. In all these cases, a politically entrenched conception of truth had been permitted unreasonably to subjugate persons to the terms of the conception and then justified its demands in terms of consequences of the subjugation.

The principle of toleration was central to the abolitionist criticism of slavery at several levels. As we saw earlier, abolitionists such as Weld and Channing took objection to the way in which American slavery had deprived slaves of the most elementary requirements of equal respect for their moral powers, including abridgment of the inalienable right to conscience—the formation of their own religious groups and the opportunities to learn to read and write in the exercise of their own moral powers. But the abolitionist political criticism cut deeper; the very structure of authority in southern life had come to depend on precisely what the argument for toleration forbade, namely, the political enforcement on society at large of a

[67] See ibid., p. 12.
[68] See *Slavery,* in Channing, *Works,* p. 691.
[69] See Parker, "Transcendentalism," in Parker, *World of Matter,* p. 26.
[70] See Faust, *Ideology of Slavery*; McKitrick, *Slavery Defended.*

self-consciously sectarian proslavery conception of religious and political truth.

As we have seen, in the attempt to defend slavery against abolitionist criticism, the South had undertaken a successful policy of forbidding any form of abolitionist advocacy in the South, put pressure on the North to discourage any such advocacy there, and in the 1840s undertook to limit public discussion in the Congress of the flood of abolitionist petitions sent there.[71] The consequence was not only the unpopularity of abolitionism both in the South and North but the removal of the serious discussion of slavery from public discussion by either of the great political parties (Democratic and Whig), each of which depended on retaining support in both the South and North. This silencing of reasonable public discussion and debate on the greatest issue of moral conscience of the age led to the debasement of public morality, which the argument for toleration had long identified as one of the greatest evils of the enforcement of sectarian views of normative truth.

That debasement of public morality affected not only political morality but, as we saw in Chapter 2, constitutional interpretation. In the South, increasingly insular proslavery thought defended slavery not only as a necessary evil, but as a positive good worthy of adoption anywhere in preference to the labor-capital relations of the North;[72] and Calhoun offered a rights-skeptical constitutional theory that would have constitutionally entrenched slavery indefinitely. In the North, where slavery had been abolished, the rights of free blacks were often egregiously abridged, and racism ran rampant,[73] albeit with some notable advances in protection of free blacks' rights.[74] Widespread public indifference to the evil of slavery made possible the successful advocacy by a northern politician, Stephen Douglas, of the congressional repeal of the prohibition of slavery in the territories. Such debasement of American public morality culminated in the wrong-headed and disastrous decision of the Supreme Court, *Dred Scott v. Sanford*. The Court both reflected and further promoted the debasement of both political and constitutional morality.[75] Lincoln, who much admired

---

[71] For an excellent general treatment of this period, see Nye, *Fettered Freedom*; see also Eaton, *The Freedom-of-Thought Struggle*.

[72] See, e.g., Fitzhugh, *Cannibals All!*; and *Sociology for the South*, in Wish, *Antebellum*.

[73] See Leon F. Litwack, *North of Slavery: The Negro in the Free States, 1790–1860* (Chicago: University of Chicago Press, 1961); V. Jacque Voegeli, *Free but Not Equal: The Midwest and the Negro during the Civil War* (Chicago: University of Chicago Press, 1967). For free blacks in the South, see Ira Berlin, *Slaves without Masters: The Free Negro in the Antebellum South* (New York: Pantheon Books, 1974).

[74] See Finkelman, "Prelude to the Fourteenth Amendment."

[75] For a superb treatment of this case, see Fehrenbacher, *The Dred Scott Case*.

Parker's political, religious, and ethical views,[76] was a leading political analyst and critic of this pathology.

The theory of toleration not only supplied the internal ideals of the supremacy of critical conscience that motored the abolitionist project, but supplied a diagnosis of the underlying political and constitutional problem. American constitutionalism, ostensibly based on the argument for toleration, had betrayed its own central ideals by allowing a politically entrenched sectarian conception of the religious and political legitimacy of slavery to be the measure of legitimate political debate on this issue. The consequence was what the argument for toleration would lead one to expect, the debasement of public reason about the political morality of slavery and about issues of constitutional interpretation relating to slavery. In the South, the paradox of intolerance ran amok—reasonable doubts about slavery were brutally suppressed, and the politics of group loyalty displaced these doubts into increasingly irrationalist pride and violence, which culminated in an unjust and illegitimate civil war.

Political abolitionists, such as Theodore Parker and the founders of the Republican party, developed a unified theory to explain the force of this debasement, namely, a slave power conspiracy that permeated the fabric of American political life.[77] Abolitionists brilliantly analyzed the political pathology of southern pride and violence and northern indifference and cowardice because they saw so clearly their common roots in an irrationalist intolerance that American constitutional institutions and traditions had proven unable to contain. In so doing, they articulated an argument of principle that rendered their defense of human rights not hostage to the abolition issue alone.

According to the abolitionist view, slavery was an intrinsic moral evil in itself because it unjustly deprived the slaves of their inalienable human rights; the deprivation of such rights required a heavy burden of justification in light of public reasons not themselves hostage to the institution under examination. Such reasons not only were not and could not be given, but the rights of conscience and free speech of all were abridged in order to stop serious and morally independent public discussion of the evils of slavery and the merits of abolition in terms not hostage to the dominant slave oligarchy of the South and its commercial allies in the North. The evil of slavery and the evil of repression of conscience and speech were not

[76] See William H. Herndon and Jesse W. Weik, *Herndon's Life of Lincoln* (1889) (New York: De Capo Press, 1983); pp. 292–94, 323, 359; see also pp. 102, 354–60, 432–33, 479.

[77] See Theodore Parker, *The Slave Power*, ed. James K. Hosmer (Boston: American Unitarian Association, 1916); David Brion Davis, *The Slave Power Conspiracy and the Paranoid Style* (Baton Rouge: Louisiana State University Press, 1969); Gienapp, *The Origins of the Republican Party*, pp. 353–65.

morally or politically independent. From the perspective of the argument
for toleration, they were integrally linked by virtue of the argument's identification of how the deprivation of basic rights was illegitimately justified
by sectarian arguments hostage to the politically entrenched epistemology
under examination. In similar fashion, the rights of northern free labor in
the territories were abridged on the ground of similarly factionalized political and constitutional arguments.

In effect, no rights were safe once some rights were unsafe. Abolitionists
crucially helped forge public argument, grounded in the argument for toleration, that explained how and why the defense of slavery had required
the deprivation of the human rights of nonslaves—not only free blacks but
the rights of whites to conscience and free speech and their right morally
to limit the spread of slavery to the extent permitted by constitutional guarantees. In the light of the radical turn of proslavery thought against the
very principles of human rights,[78] political abolitionists could cogently rest
their case on the broad foundation of the defense of the principle of human
rights of conscience and free labor of both whites and blacks.[79] Under the
impact of abolitionist moral and political criticism, the issue of slavery had
become the issue of the principle of human rights for all persons.

The Political Evil of Racism

American abolition of slavery was historically remarkable in that it was
shortly followed by immediate guarantees both of protection of basic rights
of the person and protection of rights to political participation.[80] The
breathtaking idealism of this accomplishment was followed, however, by
the brilliant but brief empowerment of the freedmen and the subsequent
betrayals of blacks' rights by both North and South. These facts of history
remind us of the depth of the bitter antebellum legacy that rendered America's commitments to the freedmen under the Reconstruction Amendments
hollow for a long period.

The question posed by the end of the Civil War was, in light of abolition,
what was the relationship of black Americans to be to the American political

---

[78] See, e.g., Fitzhugh, *Cannibals All!* Fitzhugh's views evidently shocked Lincoln into the
realization that the South was now undertaking an attack on the very idea of human rights,
an attack that required a forceful response. See Herndon and Weik, *Herndon's Life of
Lincoln*, pp. 297–98.

[79] See Eric Foner, *Free Soil, Free Labor, Free Men: The Ideology of the Republican Party
before the Civil War* (New York: Oxford University Press, 1970).

[80] See Eric Foner, *Nothing but Freedom: Emancipation and Its Legacy* (Baton Rouge:
Louisiana State University Press, 1983); cf. C. Vann Woodward, "Emancipations and Recon-
structions: A Comparative Study," in C. Vann Woodward, *The Future of the Past* (New York:
Oxford University Press, 1989), pp. 145–66.

community? Chief Justice Taney, writing for the Supreme Court in *Dred Scott v. Sanford*, had offered an originalist historical argument that no blacks were citizens at the time of ratification of the Constitution of 1787 and therefore all blacks were excluded from membership in the American political community. Justice Curtis, in dissent, decisively exploded the historical foundations of Taney's argument (blacks had clearly been citizens in a number of states in 1787, participating in ratification of the Constitution); under Curtis's view, states had the power to make blacks citizens.[81] Notably, a leading Republican critic of *Dred Scott* such as Lincoln merely noted quickly and in passing in his Charleston debate with Douglas that he, like Curtis, dissented to Taney's view that states lacked constitutional power to make blacks citizens, and then affirmed his own opposition to a state making blacks citizens. Later at Alton he denied "making any complaint of it [Taney's opinion on citizenship issue] at all."[82]

In fact, Lincoln long had hoped to solve the problem of abolition by colonizing blacks abroad, a point he made in an appalling 1862 address to blacks calling for their agreement to leave the country.[83] Lincoln only moved toward advocacy of black citizenship when black participation on the battlefields of the Civil War had rendered the elevation of the freedmen's status a moral and political imperative. These events prompted him near the end of his life publicly to urge his preference for a Reconstruction policy in the South that conferred the franchise on some blacks, namely, "on the very intelligent, and on those who serve our cause as soldiers"[84] (earlier he had urged this privately).[85]

One group of abolitionist Americans had long urged the full inclusion of

[81] Only Justice McLean, the second dissenter, made citizenship a matter of federal constitutional right. McLean took the simple view that all native-born persons in the United States are citizens of the United States and, for purposes of diversity jurisdiction, of the state wherein they reside. "The most general and appropriate definition of the term citizen is 'a freeman.' Being a freeman, and having his domicil in a State different from that of the defendant, he is a citizen within the act of Congress, and the courts of the Union are open to him." See *Dred Scott*, p. 531 (McLean, J., dissenting). McLean's views on this question were like those of radical antislavery constitutional theory, discussed later in this chapter. I am grateful to my colleague Christopher Eisgruber for bringing McLean's distinctive views to my attention.

[82] See Johannsen, *The Lincoln-Douglas Debates*, pp. 198, 302. Of the two dissenting justices in *Dred Scott*, Justice Curtis squarely affirmed that the states had authority to regulate the citizenship of native-born persons, leaving, as Lincoln did, the question of black citizenship to the discretion of the states. Only Justice McLean, the second dissenter, made citizenship a matter of federal constitutional right. See previous note.

[83] Lincoln said: "But for your race among us there could not be war, although many men engaged on either side do not care for you one way or the other." See Abraham Lincoln, "Address on Colonization," 14 August 1862, in Fehrenbacher, *Abraham Lincoln: Speeches and Writings, 1858–1865*, p. 354.

[84] Abraham Lincoln, "Speech on Reconstruction," 11 April 1865, in ibid., p. 699.

[85] See "Letter of Michael Hahn," 13 March 1864, in ibid., p. 579.

black Americans into the political community on terms of equal citizenship with white Americans. Their thought was understandably to be pivotally important once the nation embraced such inclusion. The argument for toleration was central to this claim and to its underlying political analysis of the evil of racism.

The key to the abolitionist position was their very unpopular attack on the colonization movement, the idea, advocated by Jefferson among others,[86] that abolition of slavery would be followed by colonization of freedmen abroad. Garrison prominently attacked colonization because it expressed and reinforced "those unchristian prejudices which have so long been cherished against a sable complexion" taking blacks to be "a distinct and inferior caste"[87]—what Lowell called "a depraved and unchristian public opinion."[88] The abolitionist accusation was that American conscience had assuaged its guilt about the evil of slavery by advocating a policy, abolition and colonization, that rested on the more fundamental evil of racism, the evil on which both the injustice of slavery and of discrimination against free blacks rested.

The most perceptive and probing abolitionist analysis of the moral evil of racial prejudice and its role in American politics was L. Maria Child's *An Appeal in Favor of Americans Called Africans.* Child offered the most elaborate abolitionist criticism of the common American racist assumption of the inferiority of blacks, urging, following Montesquieu, "that the present degraded condition of that unfortunate race is produced by artificial causes, not by the laws of nature." The evil of racial prejudice was to make of the product of unjust institutions, subject to criticism and reform, "a fixed and unalterable law of our nature, which cannot possibly be changed." In truth, "we made slavery, and slavery makes the prejudice." Correspondingly, the alleged inferior capacities of blacks were themselves the product of unjust cultural patterns and could not, without vicious circularity, justify unequal treatment: "The wrongs of the oppressed have been converted into an argument against them. We first debase the nature of man by making him a slave, and then very coolly tell him that he must always remain a slave because he does not know how to use freedom. We first crush people

---

[86] See Jefferson, *Notes on the State of Virginia*, pp. 135–36.

[87] William Lloyd Garrison, *Thoughts on African Colonization* (1832; reprint, New York: Arno Press and the New York Times, 1968). See also William Jay, *Inquiry into the Character and Tendency of the American Colonization, and American Anti-Slavery Societies* (1835), reprinted in William Jay, *Miscellaneous Writings on Slavery* (1853; reprint, New York: Negro Universities Press, 1968), pp. 7–206; James G. Birney, *Letter on Colonization Addressed to the Rev. Thornton J. Mills, Corresponding Secretary of the Kentucky Colonization Society* (New York, 1834).

[88] James Russell Lowell, "The Prejudice of Color," in *The Anti-Slavery Papers of James Russell Lowell*, 2 vols. (Boston: Houghton Mifflin, 1902), 1:19.

to the earth, and then claim the right of trampling on them for ever, because they are prostrate."[89]

The abolition of slavery in the North did not, Child argued, exempt the North from her criticism. The North practiced various discriminations against blacks (including laws requiring segregation and forbidding inter-marriage, schooling, voting, travel, and the like) resting on unjust racial prejudice. Her cogent criticism of antimiscegenation laws was, in her his-torical context, remarkable ("the government ought not to be invested with power to control the affections, any more than the consciences of citi-zens").[90] Anticipating de Tocqueville,[91] Child argued: "Our prejudice against colored people is even more inveterate than it is at the South. The planter is often attached to his negroes, and lavishes caresses and kind words upon them, as he would on a favorite hound: but our cold-hearted, ignoble prejudice admits of no exception—no intermission." Comparing the strength of racial prejudice in America with that in other countries (including countries that retained slavery), Child concluded: "No other people on earth indulge so strong a prejudice with regard to color, as we do."[92]

Such modern abolitionist critical insight into the cultural roots of racism (its essential confusion of culture with nature)[93] was integral to their crit-icism of slavery on the basis of the argument of toleration. The abolitionists were committed to the right of radical Protestant moral conscience, and they criticized slavery's dependence on the abridgment of the right to con-science, both of slaves and of anyone who would criticize the institution. They understood, in a way in which no other Americans of their generation did, the extent to which the political legitimation of slavery in Protestant America depended on, *indeed compelled* racist assumptions: Blacks were, in their nature, what Augustinian intolerance supposed could be only the product of a culpable defect in will, namely, blind heretics; the 1834 Synod of South Carolina described blacks in exactly such terms: "that heathen of this country, . . . [who] will bear comparison with the heathen of any part of the world."[94] Under the abolitionist view, racism was toleration's evil genius of unreason, arising and sometimes flourishing in reaction to what appear to be the greatest achievements of political reason (for example, a

[89] L. Maria Child, *An Appeal in Favor of Americans Called Africans* (1833; reprint, New York: Arno Press and The New York Times, 1968), pp. 148, 133, 134, 169; see also pp. 11, 66, 133–34.

[90] Ibid., p. 196.

[91] See de Tocqueville, *Democracy in America*, 1:373, 390–91.

[92] Child, *An Appeal*, pp. 195, 208.

[93] See, e.g., Pierre L. van den Berghe, *Race and Racism* (New York: John Wiley & Sons, 1967), p. 11.

[94] Cited in Theodore Parker, "A Letter on Slavery," in Parker, *The Slave Power*, p. 75.

constitution committed to universal toleration or, as we shall see in chapter 5, the abolition of American slavery or the emancipation of the European Jews).

The abolitionist insight captured an important truth about the origins of slavery in colonial America and perhaps a deeper truth about the enduring cultural roots of American racism and its modern European analogue, anti-Semitism. The point about origins was the early historical justification of slavery on the ground that blacks were heathen non-Christians,[95] perhaps an outgrowth of the Spanish and Portuguese association of blacks with the dangerous infidelity of the Moor and the putative legitimacy of enslavement of infidels.[96] Shakespeare's *Othello* certainly supports an English conflation of blacks and Moors, and suggests corresponding anxieties and fears centering on race and sex.[97] Desdemona's father, Brabantio, who had welcomed Othello into his house, is easily persuaded by Iago that the marriage was "against all rules of nature,"[98] which suggests prejudice easily rationalized as natural group boundaries not to be breached. Such a "folk bias"[99] against blacks thus probably antedated slavery in Britain's American colonies and hardened into racism under the impact of the special harshness, as we shall see, of American slavery. If Locke could so misinterpret his own views to justify black slavery in the Carolinas, less self-critical men could have found it all too natural to legitimate the permanent enslavement of blacks, even after their religious conversion, on racist assumptions. Blacks so lacked moral capacity that they were permanent heathens and thus permanently exiled from a political community whose condition of unity was the moral power fundamental to the principle of toleration.

The abolitionist theory of racism offers a cultural analysis of how this was done and how it was sustained. American racism arose reactively as a way of justifying cultural boundaries of moral and political community—ostensibly universalistic in their terms—that had already excluded a class of persons from the community. Slavery was such an excluding institution, and it was historically based on a folk bias against Africans that centered on their unfamiliar culture, for which color became a kind of proxy. A public culture based on the principle of toleration is and should be open to all persons on fair terms of freedom of conscience and moral and cultural plu-

[95] See Winthrop D. Jordan, *White over Black: American Attitudes toward the Negro, 1550–1812* (New York: W. W. Norton, 1977), pp. 56, 65, 91–98; Edmund S. Morgan, *American Slavery, American Freedom: The Ordeal of Colonial Virginia* (New York: W. W. Norton, 1975).

[96] See Davis, *The Problem of Slavery*, pp. 170, 195, 207–8, 214, 281, 246–47, 473.

[97] See Jordan, *White over Black*, pp. 37–38.

[98] See William Shakespeare, *Othello*, act 1, scene 3, line 101, in *Shakespeare: Complete Works*, ed. W. J. Craig (London: Oxford University Press, 1966), p. 947.

[99] See Carl N. Degler, *Out of Our Past: The Forces That Shaped Modern America*, 3d ed. (New York: Harper & Row, 1984), p. 30.

ralism. American slavery violently disrupted and intolerantly degraded the culture of African slaves. The peculiarly onerous conditions of American slavery (prohibitions on reading and writing, on religious self-organization, and on marriage, and limitations and eventual prohibitions on manumission)[100] deprived black slaves of any of the rights and opportunities that the public culture made available to others; in particular, black Americans were deprived of the respect for their creative moral powers of rational and reasonable freedom in public and private life. The nature of American slavery and the associated forms of racial discrimination against free blacks both in the South and North had socially produced an image of black incapacity that ostensibly justified their permanent heathen status (outside the community capable of Christian moral freedom).

For the abolitionists, consistent with the argument for toleration, slavery and discrimination were forms of religious, social, economic, and political persecution motivated by a politically entrenched conception of black incapacity. That conception enforced its own vision of truth against both the standards of reasonable inquiry and the reasonable capacities of both blacks and whites that might challenge the conception. A conception of political unity, subject to reasonable doubt as to its basis and merits, had unreasonably resolved its doubts, consistent with the paradox of intolerance, in the irrationalist racist certitudes of group solidarity on the basis of unjust group subjugation.

Black Americans were the scapegoats of southern self-doubt in the same way European Jews had been the victims of Christian doubt. Frederick Douglass, the leading black abolitionist, stated the abolitionist analysis with a classical clarity:

> Ignorance and depravity, and the inability to rise from degradation to civilization and respectability, are the most usual allegations against the oppressed. The evils most fostered by slavery and oppression are precisely those which slaveholders and oppressors would transfer from their system to the inherent character of their victims. Thus the very crimes of slavery become slavery's best defence. By making the enslaved a character fit only for slavery, they excuse themselves for refusing to make the slave a freeman. [101]

[100] On the special features of American slavery, in contrast to slavery elsewhere, see Stanley M. Elkins, *Slavery: A Problem in American Institutional and Intellectual Life*, 3d rev. ed. (Chicago: University of Chicago Press, 1976); Kenneth M. Stampp, *The Peculiar Institution* (New York: Vintage, 1956); Eugene D. Genovese, *The World the Slaveholders Made: Two Essays in Interpretation* (Middletown, Conn.: Wesleyan University Press, 1988); John W. Blassingame, *The Slave Community: Plantation Life in the Antebellum South*, rev. ed. (New York: Oxford University Press, 1979); Carl N. Degler, *Neither Black nor White: Slavery and Race Relations in Brazil and the United States* (Madison: University of Wisconsin Press, 1986); Peter Kolchin, *Unfree Labor: American Slavery and Russian Serfdom* (Cambridge: Harvard University Press, 1987).

[101] "The Claims of the Negro Ethnologically Considered," in Philip S. Foner, ed., *The Life*

The abolitionists thought of the political evil of racism in America as more fundamental an evil than slavery itself. It was the political evil in terms of which Americans justified slavery; and its evils, if unrecognized and un-remedied, would corrupt abolition by means of the illegitimate construc-tion of the boundaries of moral and political community on terms that excluded blacks (as colonization had).

Jefferson's treatment of the advocacy of slavery in *Notes on the State of Virginia* illustrates their point. Jefferson powerfully urged the depravity and injustice of slavery as an institution:

> The parent storms, the child looks on, catches the lineaments of wrath, puts on the same airs in the circle of smaller slaves, gives a loose to his worst of passions, and thus nursed, educated, and daily exercised in tyranny, cannot but be stamped by it with odious peculiarities. The man must be a prodigy who can retain his manners and morals undepraved by such circumstances. And with what execration should the statesman be loaded, who permitting one half the citizens thus to trample on the rights of the other, transforms those into despots, and these into enemies, destroys the morals of the one part, and the amor patriae of the other. [102]

But he advocated emancipation with colonization abroad.

Posing the query "Why not retain and incorporate the blacks into the state?" Jefferson first conceded the force of "deep rooted prejudices en-tertained by the whites"; then he superficially reviewed other features "physical and moral" [103] of blacks essentially observed by him under the conditions of slavery, hardly the appropriate standard of comparison for an impartial assessment. For all his tentativeness about his conclusions about race differences, [104] the force of the account, driven by a "geyser of libidinal energy" focusing on black sexuality, stood "until well into the nineteenth century . . . as the strongest suggestion of inferiority expressed by any na-tive American." [105] The argument is remarkable for its pseudoscientific, as-sured tone with little of the doubt that another Virginian, St. George Tucker, confessed to feeling about similar conclusions: "Early prejudices, had we more satisfactory information than we can possibly possess on the subject at present, would render an inhabitant of a country where negroe [sic] slavery prevails, an improper umpire between them [Hume versus Beattie on race differences]." [106]

---

and Writings of Frederick Douglass, 5 vols. (New York: International Publishers, 1975), 2:295.

[102] Jefferson, *Notes on the State of Virginia*, pp. 162–63.

[103] See ibid., p. 138.

[104] "I advance it therefore as a suspicion only." Ibid., p. 143.

[105] See Jordan, *White over Black*, pp. 458, 455.

[106] Tucker, *Blackstone's Commentaries*, Note H, "On the State of Slavery in Virginia,"

Both Jefferson and Tucker did argue for the abolition of slavery in Virginia, but the abolitionist point against them was that their failure to take racism seriously as a political evil subverted ostensibly abolitionist arguments into a kind of justification for the evil that in fact sustained the institution. Jefferson is thus not only a central figure in the history of scientific racism,[107] but his arguments about race were soon to be elaborated by southern proslavery apologists into a full-scale justification of black slavery itself.

The abolitionists were familiar with these antebellum arguments of the infant American "science" of ethnology, which pointed to alleged physical differences (for example, brain size) of blacks and whites to argue for differences in capacity. Ethnology appealed to the Protestant respect for experience and scientific method and was aggressively cultivated and used by southerners to suggest that racist assumptions were not unreasonable in the way that abolitionists had suggested.[108] But even in the relatively incoherent state of the human sciences in this period, abolitionists such as James Russell Lowell,[109] Frederick Douglass,[110] and Charles Sumner[111] questioned both the validity of the general approach, its interpretation of data and ignorance of other evidence, and its failure to take seriously moral ideas[112] and the importance of culture in the human sciences.[113]

The very ease and certitude with which proslavery apologists adopted this ostensibly scientific view suggest the increasingly polemical nature of southern thought, no longer able to sustain even a Jefferson's gesture of

---

p. 75, n. Tucker, however, agrees with Jefferson's conclusions about colonization, citing his discussion at some length (pp. 74–75, n.). For Hume's empirical argument for race differences, see David Hume, "Of National Character," in *Essays Moral Political and Literary,* ed. Eugene F. Miller (1777; reprint, Indianapolis: Liberty Classics, 1987), p. 208, n. 10; for James Beattie's attack on Hume's argument, see James Beattie, *An Essay on the Nature and Immutability of Truth,* ed. Lewis White Beck (1770; reprint, New York: Garland, 1983).

[107] For general treatments of the topic, see Jordan, *White over Black*; George M. Fredrickson, *The Black Image in the White Mind: The Debate on Afro-American Character and Destiny, 1817–1914* (Middletown, Conn.: Wesleyan University Press, 1971); Thomas F. Gossett, *Race: The History of an Idea in America* (New York: Schocken Books, 1965); Reginald Horsman, *Race and Manifest Destiny: The Origins of American Racial Anglo-Saxonism* (Cambridge: Harvard University Press, 1981).

[108] For a good general study, see Stanton, *The Leopard's Spots.*

[109] See "Ethnology," in *Anti-Slavery Papers of James Russell Lowell,* 2:26–32.

[110] See "The Claims of the Negro Ethnologically Considered," in Foner, *Life and Writings,* 2:289–309.

[111] See "The Question of Caste," in *Charles Sumner: His Complete Works,* 20 vols. (New York: Negro Universities Press, 1969), 17:131–83.

[112] See Douglass, "The Claims of the Negro Ethnologically Considered," in Foner, *Life and Writings,* 2:292, 307–8; Sumner, "The Question of Caste," in *Complete Works,* 17:138–39.

[113] See, esp., Douglass, "The Claims of the Negro Ethnologically Considered," in Foner, *Life and Writings,* 2:304–6.

tentativeness or a Tucker's doubts about impartiality. Some southerners notably could entertain such doubts, but they were often on the verge of moral revolt against and self-imposed exile from southern culture.

Moncure Conway, born into a Virginia slave-owning family, was a notable example. Conway had always believed blacks were inferior, but was searching for ways to justify his position. The new theory of Agassiz on race differences having appeared, Conway enthusiastically embraced it, giving a public lecture and writing an (unpublished) essay in support of it. Then, as Conway's biographer observes:

> Something, however, perhaps "the dumb answers of the coloured servants moving about the house, cheerfully yielding . . . unrequited services," soon brought about a reaction which proved to be "the moral crisis" of his life. Conway was shocked by "the ease with which I could consign a whole race to degradation." . . . The reaction constituted a religious conversion of the eighteenth-century variety, now extinct: "an overwhelming sense of my own inferiority came upon me" and "left me with a determination to devote my life to the elevation and welfare of my fellow-beings, white and black." Thus began Conway's long career in the antislavery movement."[114]

Conway had been reading Emerson and was much struck by his emphasis on transcendental moral conscience self-reliantly pursued in criticism of traditional culture and values.[115] His awakening interest in the primacy of ethical impartiality led Conway to experience a reasonable doubt and indeed a piercing sense of guilt that neither his polemical culture nor its hard science of ethnology could support or sustain.

Strikingly, Conway thought of women as having a superior moral sense,[116] an intuition about moral personality not corrupted by intellectual constructions such as ethnology and the like. Harriet Beecher Stowe had taken the same view in *Uncle Tom's Cabin*, appealing to heart over head[117] (the latter exemplified by proslavery interpretations of the Bible).[118] Both

---

[114] See Stanton, *The Leopard's Spots*, p. 111. See also Peter F. Walker, *Moral Choices: Memory, Desire, and Imagination in Nineteenth-Century American Abolition* (Baton Rouge: Louisiana State University Press, 1978), pp. 58–62.

[115] See John d'Entremont, *Southern Emancipator: Moncure Conway, the American Years, 1832–1865* (New York: Oxford University Press, 1987), pp. 43–56. On Emerson's abolitionism, see Len Gougeon, *Virtue's Hero: Emerson, Antislavery, and Reform* (Athens: University of Georgia Press, 1990).

[116] See d'Entremont, *Southern Emancipator*, pp. 18–19, 62–63.

[117] See Harriet Beecher Stowe, *Uncle Tom's Cabin or, Life among the Lowly*, ed. Ann Douglas (1852; reprint, New York: Penguin, 1981), pp. 153, 210, 437. See also Harriet Beecher Stowe, *The Key to Uncle Tom's Cabin* (1854; reprint, Salem, N.H.: Ayer Company, 1987).

[118] See Stowe, *Uncle Tom's Cabin*, pp. 183, 184, 200, 279, 508; and *The Key to Uncle Tom's Cabin*, pp. 460–73.

Conway and Stowe reflect the primacy of impartial ethical thought independent of the intellectual constructions that dominant political epistemologies tried to domesticate to the rationalizing ends of entrenched political power on the model of religious persecution.[119]

For the abolitionists, ethics was, as we have seen, an inward appeal to an abstract equal respect for the moral powers of all persons, and their interpretation of its moral ideal, in light of the argument for toleration, led them, uniquely among their generation, to suspect and question denials of moral capacity, such as those of the ethnologists, which so unreasonably confused the results of a corrupt culture with nature.[120] This insight led many abolitionists (some of them, such as the Grimke sisters, also early feminists)[121] to suppose as well that women, exercising free moral personality, could discover in their own subjugation a similar oppression to that of blacks and use that personal experience to achieve an ethical impartiality possessed of critical moral insights into the evils of slavery and racism.[122]

The abolitionists offered a theory of the evil of racism as part of their larger analysis of the responsibilities of ethical conscience in a community ostensibly committed to the argument for toleration. The moral point of their analysis was to articulate the extent of the ethical responsibility of such a community for the cultural construction over time of a form of intolerance violative of its own constitutive principles of national identity. Racism is not obviously religious persecution or even like it. It was the insight of the abolitionist analysis of racism to understand its cultural roots in longstanding patterns of intolerance that achieve pathological political force in a community whose intolerance has become subject to reasonable doubt. The transmogrification of a cultural into a racial intolerance was the key to the abolitionists' analysis.

Abolitionist Constitutional Theory

The abolitionist articulation of the evils of slavery and racism depended, as we have seen, on the argument for toleration: both slavery and racism

[119] See Stowe, *The Key to Uncle Tom's Cabin*, pp. 401–2, which identifies the analogy between proslavery thought and religious persecution.

[120] For later development of this insight in American social theory, see Carl N. Degler, *In Search of Human Nature: The Decline and Revival of Darwinism in American Social Thought* (New York: Oxford University Press, 1991).

[121] See Angelina Grimke, "Appeal to the Christian Women of the South" (1836), in Alice S. Rossi, ed., *The Feminist Papers: From Adams to de Beauvoir* (Boston: Northeastern University Press, 1988), pp. 296–304; Sarah Grimke, "Letters on the Equality of the Sexes and the Condition of Women" (1838), in Rossi, *Feminist Papers*, pp. 306–18; Angelina Grimke, "Letters to Catherine Beecher" (1836), in Rossi, *Feminist Papers*, pp. 319–22.

[122] See Stowe, *Uncle Tom's Cabin*, Introduction, pp. 19–20; Ellen Carol DuBois, *Feminism and Suffrage: The Emergence of an Independent Women's Movement in America, 1848–1869* (Ithaca: Cornell University Press, 1978).

were, at bottom, forms of unjust and unjustifiable intolerance that refused to accord their victims respect for the exercise of their moral powers on fair terms. Such criticism was in its nature an appeal to the Lockean political theory of American constitutionalism.

Theodore Weld put the point as clearly as anyone in his *American Slavery as It Is*:

> The *benefits* of law to the subject should overbalance its burdens—its protection more than compensate for its restraints and exactions—and its blessings altogether outweigh its inconveniences and evils—the former being numerous, positive, and permanent, the latter few, negative, and incidental. Totally the reverse of all this is true in the case of the slave. Law is to him all exaction and no protection: instead of lightening his *natural* burdens, it crushes him under a multitude of artificial ones. . . . The same law which makes him a *thing* incapable of obligation, loads him with obligations superhuman—while sinking him below the level of a brute in dispensing its *benefits,* he lays upon him burdens which would break down an angel.[123]

The central requirement of republican political theory was, Weld argued, equal protection of one's natural rights, and the wrongness of both slavery and racism were interpreted in light of their violation of this minimal requirement for the legitimacy of political power.[124]

Such criticism of slavery and racism in light of Lockean political theory necessarily raised questions about the meaning and limits of the U.S. Constitution as an expression of Lockean political theory. These questions were of two sorts. First, how, if at all, should Lockean political theory shape the proper interpretation of the Constitution's provisions bearing on slavery? Second, assuming the Constitution, properly interpreted, allowed or was consistent with slavery, how and in what ways should the Constitution be criticized in light of Lockean political theory? I shall hereinafter call the first question that of internal interpretive criticism (or internal criticism) and the second the question of external criticism of legitimacy (or external criticism).

Major proponents of abolitionist moral and political thought, such as Weld, Channing, and Parker, contributed to both forms of criticism. Weld's *American Slavery as It Is* was a highly influential appeal to the liberal conscience of America to take seriously both the facts of slavery and their own Lockean political morality; it was not, as such, a work of either internal or external constitutional criticism. But Weld elsewhere brilliantly har-

[123] See Weld, *American Slavery as It Is*, p. 150.
[124] See, e.g., ibid. pp. 150–51.

nessed his moral and political theory to related interpretive issues regarding both Bible interpretation[125] and constitutional interpretation.[126]

Channing's powerful moral analysis of the wrongness of slavery made an equally cogent case for how a rights-based Constitution such as that of the United States must be understood; the Constitution must recognize reserved rights not specifically enumerated, give rights a normative weight superior to the public good, and recognize its distinctive foundations, in contrast to the classical republics of Greece and Rome,[127] in respect for rights. Channing elsewhere cogently used his moral theory to make both internal and external constitutional criticisms of the annexation of Texas.[128]

Theodore Parker not only articulated highly influential abolitionist criticisms of both slavery and the slave power conspiracy,[129] but brought his transcendentalist ethical theory powerfully to bear on a general approach to the interpretation of the Bible[130] and the Constitution.[131] Lockean political theory and constitutional interpretation ran together for these abolitionists because they, like the proponents of the constitutional theory of Union, saw the Constitution as grounded in a political theory of respect for human rights that must be to some significant extent consulted in the interpretation of the Constitution's provisions.

In the harmonious and hopeful days of 1833, the Declaration of Sentiments of the American Anti-Slavery Convention, authored by Garrison, could articulate a common abolitionist view of the relationship between political theory and the Constitution. On grounds of Lockean political theory, slavery was morally wrong, and "all those laws which are now in force, admitting the right of slavery, are therefore, before God, utterly null and void." The Constitution was equally clear:

> Congress, under the present national compact, has no right to interfere with any of the slave States, in relation to this momentous subject:
> But we maintain that Congress has a right, and is solemnly bound, to suppress the domestic slave trade between the several States, and to abolish slavery in those portions of the territory which the Constitution has placed under its exclusive jurisdiction.

[125] See Weld, *The Bible against Slavery*.

[126] See Theodore Dwight Weld, "The Power of Congress over Slavery in the District of Columbia," and "Persons Held to Service, Fugitive Slaves, &c.," *The Bible against Slavery*.

[127] See Channing, *Slavery*, in Channing, *Works*, pp. 699, 700, 740, 700–702, 716–18.

[128] See William Ellery Channing, "A Letter to the Hon. Henry Clay on the Annexation of Texas" (1837), in Channing, *Works*, pp. 752–81; "The Duty of the Free States" (1842), in Channing, *Works*, pp. 853–907.

[129] See Parker, *The Slave Power*.

[130] See Theodore Parker, "The Transient and Permanent in Christianity," in *The Slave Power*; and *A Discourse of Matters Pertaining to Religion*, ed. Thomas Wentworth Higginson (Boston: American Unitarian Association, 1907).

[131] See Parker, *The Relation of Slavery*.

The various proslavery provisions of the Constitution (for example, the fugitive slave clause and the three-fifths clause) should be changed by "moral and political action."[132]

The Declaration of Sentiments appealed to the Declaration of Independence as authority for its principles, but it denied, in contrast to the earlier Declaration, the legitimacy of the use of revolutionary force or force of any kind. "Ours shall be . . . the opposition of moral purity to moral corruption . . . the abolition of slavery by the spirit of repentance." The abolitionist movement was only to make arguments appealing to the conscience of other Americans; all else were "carnal weapons" and therefore illegitimate.[133]

That claim may have made some larger political sense in 1833 when abolitionists might reasonably have believed that American constitutional principles of conscience and free speech would be extended on fair terms to them; and their message might persuasively lead to a change in dominant American public opinion that would put an end to slavery. But the age of Jackson (with its repression of abolitionist advocacy both by law and by mobs sponsored by civic leaders) led many Americans, consistent with Lincoln's speech to the Young Men's Lyceum, to question whether public opinion any longer adequately sustained constitutional principles and institutions. In light of these events, abolitionists also had to rethink the relationship of their political theory of conscience both to politics in general and to constitutional law in particular. Three important forms of constitutional theory arose within the abolitionist movement: radical disunionism, moderate constitutional antislavery, and radical constitutional antislavery.[134]

Finally, the growing despair over the direction of American constitutionalism, in light of the politics of Stephen Douglas and the judiciary of Roger Taney, moved some leading abolitionists, such as Theodore Parker, to believe and act on the belief that Lockean political theory now justified extraconstitutional revolutionary action against the South (notably, support for John Brown). By the time of secession and civil war, the South and the North confronted each other in terms of conflicting interpretations not only of their common constitution but of its underlying revolutionary principles.

Radical Disunionism

Radical disunionism, led by William Lloyd Garrison[135] and Wendell Phillips,[136] rested on both an internal and external criticism of the Constitution

---

[132] See William Lloyd Garrison, *Declaration of Sentiments of the American Anti-Slavery Convention*, reprinted in *Selections from the Writings and Speeches of William Lloyd Garrison* (Boston: R. F. Wallcut, 1852), pp. 68–69, 70.

[133] See ibid., p. 67.

[134] For an excellent general study, see William M. Wiecek, *The Sources of Antislavery Constitutionalism in America, 1760–1848* (Ithaca: Cornell University Press, 1977).

[135] See Garrison, *Selections*; Garrison and Garrison, *William Lloyd Garrison*.

[136] See Wendell Phillips, *Speeches, Lectures, and Letters* (Boston: Lothrop, Lee & She-

and a larger repudiation of the role of political action in securing abolitionist aims. For Garrison, disowning politics was increasingly rooted in a theory of moral anarchism, which repudiated the legitimacy of any kind of force (and thus the legitimacy of the state) in favor of appeals to free and informed conscience.[137] For Phillips, the repudiation of politics was altogether more strategic; he urged abolitionists not to vote or take office in current circumstances, conceding he would take a different view in other circumstances. The important point was political influence, and voting or not voting should be assessed in light of the optimal strategy to achieve that end.[138] Unlike Thoreau,[139] Phillips saw no good reason of principle why an abolitionist should not pay taxes.[140]

The objective of Garrison and Phillips was that "the public mind" be "thoroughly revolutionized,"[141] that is, that people's consciences be awakened to the enormity of the moral wrongs of slavery and racism and their personal culpability for complicity with these wrongs. Both their internal and external criticisms of the Constitution were strategies in service of this larger moral end.

Phillips, a lawyer, viewed the interpretation of the Constitution highly positivistically, claiming that "loose construction . . . leads . . . to absolute tyranny." The right to conscience, central to Phillips's moral aims, "exists in religion—but not in Government. Law is a rule *prescribed*."[142] It is no accident that Phillips (calling for disunion with the South) self-consciously echoed the arguments of proslavery constitutional theory in support of secession.[143] Both modes of argument took a rights-skeptical approach to the interpretation of the Constitution, leading to a positivistic focus on state

---

pard, 1863); *Speeches Lectures, and Letters*, 2d ser. (Boston: Lee & Shepard, 1905); *The Constitution a Pro-Slavery Compact* (1844; reprint, New York: Negro Universities Press, 1969); *Can Abolitionists Vote or Take Office under the United States Constitution?* (New York: American Anti-Slavery Society, 1845); Louis Filler, ed., *Wendell Phillips on Civil Rights and Freedom* (New York: Hill & Wang, 1965). Cf. William Bowditch, *The Constitutionality of Slavery* (Boston: Coolidge & Wiley, 1848).

[137] For a good general study, see Perry, *Radical Abolitionism*.

[138] See Phillips, *Can Abolitionists Vote*, pp. 6, 28.

[139] See Henry D. Thoreau, "Resistance to Civil Government," in Thoreau, *Henry D. Thoreau: Reform Papers*, ed. Wendell Glick (Princeton: Princeton University Press, 1973), pp. 63–90. For a good recent study of Thoreau's abolitionist thought that places him close to Theodore Parker (including support for the revolutionary activity of John Brown), see Daniel Walker Howe, "Henry David Thoreau on the Duty of Civil Disobedience," *An Inaugural Lecture Delivered before the University of Oxford on 21 May 1990* (Oxford: Clarendon Press, 1990).

[140] See Phillips, *Can Abolitionists Vote*, pp. 30–35.

[141] See ibid., p. 6.

[142] See ibid., pp. 15, 18.

[143] See Phillips, *The Constitution a Pro-Slavery Compact*, pp. 93–94, 108–11.

sovereignty and a narrow construction of national constitutional powers favorable to the reserved powers of the states (including a right to disunion). The difference was that Phillips was writing to enhance the powers of abolitionist Massachusetts, Calhoun to buttress proslavery South Carolina. The abolitionist strategy was polemically to rouse public conscience in the North by demonizing the Constitution ("a covenant with death and agreement with hell"). [144]

Phillips, unlike Calhoun, did not attack the political theory of human rights; indeed, his external criticism of the Constitution clearly depended on such a theory. But to achieve his polemical end, he had to adopt an internal interpretive attitude toward the Constitution that showed *it* (the Constitution) to be rights skeptical.

Phillips's argument to this effect was hardly an interpretive argument at all; it was, rather, a collation of all the passages from Madison's notes on the Constitutional Convention and from the state ratification debates that unambiguously confirmed the historical understanding of a sectional compromise over slavery. [145] But Phillips could only make a case for his internal interpretive analysis by completely ignoring the more general arguments of political theory, political science, and history central to the deliberations over and ratification of the Constitution and the many features of the Constitution that could only be plausibly understood in the light of Lockean political theory. [146] In effect, Phillips ignored much of the Constitution and then interpreted the rest in a positivistic style that only made ostensible sense—abstracted from the rest—as a positivistic expression of evil. Conscience, grounded in Lockean political theory, should revolt against such a Constitution founded on the deprivation of human rights; revolt against the Constitution was in order to recover our consciences.

Phillips's interest in the Constitution was not so much interpretive as strategic. His interpretive attitude, albeit in service of different ends, was as strategically motivated as Calhoun's. Phillips's internal and external stances on the Constitution were, however, divided, indeed incoherent, in a way Calhoun's were not. Calhoun's internal interpretive positivism was driven by an external rights-skeptical political theory that he clearly defended; Phillips's internal positivism rested on a rights skepticism he knew, as political theory, to be false.

It remains only to ask whether his strategy was a wise one in light of his ultimate abolitionist aims. Many abolitionists thought it was consummately bad strategy. [147] Disunion would leave the southern institution of slavery intact without any accountability whatsoever to the principles and insti-

---

[144] See Garrison and Garrison, *William Lloyd Garrison*, 3:88.
[145] See Phillips, *The Constitution a Pro-Slavery Compact*.
[146] See Richards, *Foundations*.
[147] See Goodell, *Slavery and Anti-Slavery*, p. 557.

tutions of the Union. That might enhance the northern sense of self-righteousness but would worsen the plight of southern black slaves, for whom all Americans bore an ethical, political, and constitutional responsibility. The abolitionist aim should not be disunion, but rather an interpretation of the terms of the Constitution that would allow abolitionists to achieve their aims politically under the Constitution. That ambition naturally gave rise to other kinds of abolitionist constitutional theory.

Moderate Constitutional Antislavery

As we have seen, the constitutional theory of Union emphasized the role of national constitutional principles and institutions in the overall protection of human rights. Its leading proponents, morally opposed to slavery, regarded the proper constitutional interpretation of the principles and powers of Union as instrumental to the long-term abolition of slavery in the United States. Accordingly, when leading abolitionists such as Theodore Weld turned to political action in addition to purely moral argument and advocacy, they naturally lent their considerable intellectual abilities for moral and political analysis to the development of interpretive argument that would assist the proponents of Union in advancing abolitionist aims at the national level.

Weld's *Power of Congress over Slavery in the District of Columbia* was a work of legal analysis of this sort.[148] The work powerfully constructed a cogently reasoned interpretive argument confirming in a particular area (namely, the power of Congress over the District of Columbia) what the constitutional theory of Union would lead one to believe in general, namely, that Congress had broad powers to abolish slavery and the slave trade in areas outside the relevant jurisdictional authority of slaveholding states. Weld, indeed, lent his research abilities and energies directly to the service of the abolitionist politics being forged in the House of Representatives by a leading proponent of the theory of Union, John Quincy Adams, and by Joshua R. Giddings.[149] In 1839, Adams proposed a constitutional amendment for the abolition of slavery everywhere in the Union, and he and Giddings led the long and politically important struggle against the gag rule on the discussion of abolitionist petitions in the U.S. Congress.[150]

[148] Reprinted in tenBroek, *Equal under Law*, pp. 243–80.

[149] On Weld's collaborative activities, see Barnes, *The Antislavery Impulse*, pp. 180–90. On Adams, see Bemis, *John Quincy Adams and the Union*; on Giddings, see James Brewer Stewart, *Joshua R. Giddings and the Tactics of Radical Politics* (Cleveland: Case Western Reserve University Press, 1970); George W. Julian, *The Life of Joshua R. Giddings* (Chicago: A. C. McClurg, 1892).

[150] See Barnes, *The Antislavery Impulse*, pp. 165–67; Filler, *The Crusade against Slavery*, pp. 96–107, 172–74.

The constitutional theory of moderate antislavery, developed by Joshua Giddings[151] and Salmon P. Chase,[152] sharply separated the interpretive questions of the constitutional powers of the national and state governments over the institution of slavery. The Constitution left in place "the slavery already existing in the states" subject to state power, but "all power to create or continue the system by national sanction" was "carefully withheld."[153] The Constitution was not, however, morally neutral on the long-term future of slavery in the United States.

Slavery was clearly violative of the political theory of the Constitution stated in "the Declaration of 1776"—"THE BASIS OF A NATIONAL POLITICAL FAITH," and therefore the understanding of the Founders was

> to keep the action of the national government free from all connection with the [slave] system; to discountenance and discourage it in the States; and to favour the abolition of it by State authority—a result, then, generally expected; and, finally, to provide against its further extension by confining the power to acquire new territory, and admit new States to the General Government, the line of whose policy was clearly marked out by the ordinance and preceding public acts.

Indeed, the constitutional limitation on national power was more direct; the Bill of Rights in general and the due process clause of the fifth amendment in particular forbade the federal government to "create or continue the relation of master and slave. Nor can that relation be created or continued in any place, district, or territory, over which the jurisdiction of the National Government is exclusive; for slavery cannot subsist a moment after the support of the public force has been withdrawn."[154]

Moderate antislavery constitutional theory was a natural abolitionist development of the theory of Union in light of the 1772 *Sommersett* decision in Great Britain.[155] If, consistent with *Sommersett*, slavery was contrary to the common law unless expressly authorized by positive law, then slavery could only legally exist in the United States to the extent mandated by positive law. Since the supreme law of the Constitution gave the national

[151] See, e.g., Joshua R. Giddings, *Pacificus: The Rights and Privileges of the Several States in Regard to Slavery* (1842), in Julian, *The Life of Joshua R. Giddings*, pp. 415–62.

[152] See, e.g., Salmon P. Chase, "The Address of the Southern and Western Liberty Convention" (1845), in Salmon Portland Chase and Charles Dexter Cleveland, *Anti-Slavery Addresses of 1844 and 1845* (1867; reprint, New York: Negro Universities Press, 1969). On Chase's importance in the formation of the Republican party, see Gienapp, *The Origins of the Republican Party*.

[153] See Chase, "The Address of the Southern and Western Liberty Convention," in Chase and Dexter, *Anti-Slavery Addresses*, p. 84.

[154] See ibid., pp. 79, 84–85, 87.

[155] See *Sommersett v. Stuart*, King's Bench: 12 George III A.D. (1771–1772) Lofft, 20 Howell's State Trials 1.

government no positive power to authorize slavery, slavery could legally exist, if at all, only under state law. Moderate antislavery theory, thus understood, was a reasonable interpretation both of *Sommersett* and the interpretation of American law in light of it. Many state judiciaries, including those in the South, had appealed to the authority of *Sommersett* in suits for the freedom of slaves taken to free states by their masters and then returned home. Such cases turned on common-law principles of the conflict of laws, and these principles were interpreted in light of *Sommersett* not to recognize slavery and thus to prefer freedom.[156]

The constitutional theory of Union, at least as developed and enforced by Justice Story in *Prigg*,[157] conferred an expansive federal power on Congress to enforce the fugitive slave clause over the objections of hostile states (including state-imposed requirements of a jury trial). Proponents of moderate antislavery such as Chase thought the fugitive slave clause should at least be interpreted to require a jury trial right[158]. But aside from this disagreement, the theories of moderate antislavery and of Union were generally convergent and complementary. It was no accident that a central exponent of the theory of Union, Abraham Lincoln, was the person who led to victory in 1860 the long struggle of political abolitionism to secure national recognition.[159]

Radical Constitutional Antislavery

We earlier noted that Theodore Weld, when analyzing the wrongness of slavery, invoked the Lockean political theory that legitimate government must protect equal rights. He made a similar appeal in explaining why Congress had power to abolish slavery in the District of Columbia, namely, "an axiom of the civilized world, and a maxim even with savages, that allegiance and protection are reciprocal and correlative."[160] The assumption of this view was that black Americans (slave or free) were working members of the American political community and, as such, subject to its governing Lockean principles of a fair balance of rights and obligations as a condition of allegiance.

But many Americans (Lincoln among them) wanted to distinguish the question of abolishing slavery in order to recognize the natural rights of

---

[156] For an able general discussion, see Paul Finkelman, *An Imperfect Union: Slavery, Federalism, and Comity* (Chapel Hill: University of North Carolina Press, 1981). See also Cover, *Justice Accused*.

[157] See *Prigg v. Pennsylvania*, 41 U.S. (16 Pet.) 539 (1842).

[158] See Cover, *Justice Accused*, pp. 164–65.

[159] For a good general study of this struggle, see Sewell, *Ballots for Freedom*.

[160] Theodore Weld, *The Power of Congress over Slavery in the District of Columbia*, in tenBroek, *Equal under Law*, p. 278.

slaves from the question of rights of membership in the American political community. This explains their view that the constitutional theory of Union, properly interpreted, would allow the national government to achieve its goals of respect for human rights by the long-term abolition of slavery and yet to combine abolition with colonization of the freedmen abroad (thus, not including them in the American political community). They were able to take this view by ascribing rights of American citizenship to the powers of the states alone; the national government might constitutionally achieve the long-term abolition of slavery and colonize the freedmen abroad without violating any constitutional rights.

But if one believed, like Weld and many abolitionists, that Lockean political theory guaranteed black Americans both their natural rights and their right to citizenship, the theories of Union and of moderate antislavery reconciled the Constitution and its background political theory in an unappealing way. The distinction between national and state power over slavery, fundamental to these views, could sensibly interpret the Constitution as in service of its political theory of respect for equal rights only if national power could be read as achieving such rights by abolition and colonization. But if Weld and the abolitionists were right, that interpretation of the Constitution would violate the rights of black Americans—earned by years of unremunerated labor in service of the national interest—to be free and to be citizens. Was there an interpretation of the Constitution that might better reconcile it with its background political theory?

Radical constitutional antislavery—the most important expression of uniquely abolitionist constitutional thought—responded to this question by interpreting the Constitution to forbid slavery both at the national and state levels. [161] Radical constitutional antislavery agreed with both the theories of Union and moderate antislavery that the proper interpretive attitude toward the U.S. Constitution must be Lockean political theory. It disagreed with them about the best account of such theory, in particular, about what rights black Americans in fact had in light of the wrongs inflicted on them by American slavery and racism. For radical antislavery, black Americans had both natural rights to liberty and a right to citizenship.

Taking the view of political theory that it did, radical antislavery rejected moderate antislavery's federal-state dichotomy on the slavery issue because it could not be reasonably justified in terms of protecting rights and ad-

<hr>

[161] See Alvan Stewart, *A Constitutional Argument on the Subject of Slavery* (1837), in tenBroek, *Equal under Law*, pp. 281–95; G.W.F. Mellen, *An Argument on the Unconstitutionality of Slavery* (Boston: Saxton & Peirce, 1841); Goodell, *Views*; Lysander Spooner, *The Unconstitutionality of Slavery* (New York: Burt Franklin, 1860); James G. Birney, *Can Congress, under the Constitution, Abolish Slavery in the States?* (1847), in tenBroek, *Equal under Law*, pp. 296–319; Joel Tiffany, *A Treatise on the Unconstitutionality of American Slavery* (1849; reprint, Miami: Mnemosyne, 1969).

vancing the common interest. Moderate antislavery's interpretation would allow abolition on terms that violated the rights of black Americans to be citizens (namely, colonization), and thus could not be reasonably justified.

The better interpretation—the one that overall enabled the Constitution to be read more coherently as in service of its political theory—was one that made all participants in the American political community national citizens and therefore bearers of the equal human rights of such citizenship. The national government—both the judiciary and Congress—thus had power, as the other theories contended, to achieve abolition of slavery, but in contrast to them, only on terms that recognized the rights of black Americans to be both free and citizens.

To make a plausible case for its thesis, radical theory had to make a negative case against two natural interpretive objections: first, the text of the Constitution that apparently protected southern slavery (for example, the fugitive slave clause, the three-fifths clause, and the slave trade clause); and second, the history of the founding (including the Constitutional Convention, *The Federalist*, state ratification debates) relevant to a compromise over slavery. The best radical theorists—William Goodell,[162,] Lysander Spooner,[163] and Joel Tiffany[164]—confronted these objections and argued that the answer to them required metainterpretive or philosophical reflection about the nature and distinctive purposes of constitutional interpretation in the United States. Constitutional text and history must, they argued, be appropriately weighted and understood in light of such reflection.

The constitutional text of a written constitution must, of course, be respected, but, they argued, respected as what it was, namely, textual constraints on ordinary political power to which all persons could appeal to ensure that such power conformed to the requirements of political legitimacy. If anything, the radicals gave the *text* of the Constitution a kind of authority it had not enjoyed under competing constitutional theories. The continuing contractualist authority of the Constitution required, Spooner thus argued, that "it must purport to authorize nothing inconsistent with natural justice, and men's natural rights. It cannot lawfully authorize government to destroy or take from men their natural rights: for natural rights are inalienable, and can no more be surrendered to government—which is but an association of individuals—than to a single individual."[165]

The authority of the Constitution as supreme law "was not, *in theory*, the exercise of a right granted to the people by the State legislatures, but of the *natural* original right of the people themselves, as individuals" to

[162] See Goodell, *Views*.
[163] Spooner, *Unconstitutionality*.
[164] Tiffany, *Treatise*.
[165] See Spooner, *Unconstitutionality*, p. 8.

protect their inalienable human rights. The contractualist foundations of constitutional legitimacy rested on the idea that "justice is evidently the only principle that *everybody* can be presumed to agree to, in the formation of government"; and accordingly the interpretation of the Constitution, to preserve its legitimacy as supreme law, "must not be construed, (unless such construction be unavoidable), so as to authorize anything whatever *to which every single individual of 'the people'* may not, as competent men, knowing their rights, reasonably be presumed to have freely and voluntarily assented." The supremacy of the text, thus interpreted, dictated that "*we certainly cannot go out of the constitution to find the parties to it,*" and therefore the actual nature of the consent to the Constitution ("a bare majority of the adult males, or about one tenth of the whole people") was interpretively irrelevant. The *text* of American constitutions "themselves assume, and virtually *assert,* that *all* 'the people' have agreed to them. They must, therefore, be construed on the theory that all have agreed to them."[166]

The authority of the Constitution, thus understood, was supreme law precisely because it assured guarantees of the rights and interests of all in a way in which majoritarianism did not. Spooner's penetrating anatomization of majoritarianism underscored how often it fraudulently gave effect to the interests of minorities alone.[167] He concluded that the appeal to majoritarian popular sovereignty, as the foundation of American constitutionalism (in the style of a Stephen Douglas), was "as disgusting as it is hypocritical."[168]

In light of this theory of constitutional legitimacy, the radicals argued that the constitutional text "must be construed '*strictly*' in favor of natural right."[169] This led them sharply to distinguish interpretation of constitutional text from interpretations of any persons who wrote or ratified the text. The reasonable interpretation of the text, in light of their interpretive

---

[166] See ibid., pp. 183, 143, 182–83, 184–85.

[167] Spooner observes: "Not more than one fifth of the people vote. A bare majority of that fifth (, being about one tenth of the whole,) choose the legislators. A bare majority of the legislators, (representing but about one twentieth of the people,) constitute a quorum. A bare majority of the quorum, (representing but about one fortieth of the people.) are sufficient to make the laws.

"Finally. Even the will of this *one fortieth* of the people cannot be said to be represented in the general legislation, because the representative is necessarily chosen for his opinions on one, or at most a few, important topics, when, in fact, he legislates on an hundred, or a thousand others, in regard to many, perhaps most, of which, he differs in opinion from those who actually voted for him. He can, therefore, with certainty, be said to represent nobody but himself." Spooner, *Unconstitutionality*, p. 154; cf. pp. 184–85.

[168] See ibid., p. 154.

[169] See ibid., pp. 18–19; for variant statements of the interpretive principle, see pp. 43–44, 58–59, 62.

principle, required asking not what some founder had concretely in mind, but what reading of the text (often in terms of a more abstract principle of human rights) enabled the interpreter in his or her circumstances to make the best sense of the Constitution as supreme law.[170]

Each of the clauses ostensibly about protecting southern slavery was construed, in light of this interpretive principle, strictly in favor of the protection of natural rights. Since the word *slave* was never expressly used but rather "three-fifths of all other persons"[171] or "migration or importation of such persons"[172] or "person held to service or labour,"[173] the radicals ascribed to these texts meanings that did not protect slavery. The fugitive slave clause, using the word *person,* could not apply to slavery, which rested on the denial of personality, but only to apprentices (Goodell);[174] the three-fifths clause applied not to southern slaves, but mainly to resident aliens (Spooner);[175] the slave trade clause was not really a limitation on congressional power to forbid the international slave trade for twenty years, but an acknowledgment of the power of Congress to forbid the interstate slave trade (Tiffany).[176]

In order to reach these interpretive results, the radicals had to come to terms with the history of both the Constitutional Convention and the ratification debates, which make clear, as Wendell Phillips had shown beyond any reasonable doubt,[177] that each of these provisions was historically very much about the protection of southern slavery as part of a sectional compromise. The response of the radicals, as one might expect, was to deny that the interpretation of the Constitution, in light of its background political theory, could be bound by such historical facts.

William Goodell, for example, questioned, on grounds of Lockean political legitimacy, how a later generation could authoritatively be bound by an earlier generation:

> My good father or grandfather, (peace to their ashes,) may have signed the compact, as they had a right to do, if they saw fit. But they stood in their own shoes, and I stand in mine—as truly a man as either of them, with the same unimpaired powers—with the same high responsibilities. . . . They had no

---

[170] See ibid., pp. 54–67, 222–26.

[171] See U.S. Constitution, Art. I, sec. 2, cl. 3.

[172] See U.S. Constitution, Art. I, sec. 9, cl. 1.

[173] See U.S. Constitution, Art. IV, sec. 2, cl. 3.

[174] See Goodell, *Views,* pp. 21–27.

[175] See Spooner, *Unconstitutionality,* pp. 73–81.

[176] See Tiffany, *Treatise,* pp. 64–7.

[177] See Phillips, *The Constitution a Pro-Slavery Compact;* and *Review of Lysander Spooner's Essay on the Unconstitutionality of Slavery* (1847; reprint, New York: Arno Press and the New York Times, 1969).

power to make me less of an independent man, and a voluntary free agent, than they were themselves. And they have not done it.[178]

The Constitution could not, consistent with its political theory, be interpreted positivistically in terms of what the Founders concretely meant in 1787, but like the common law,[179] in terms of the underlying human rights it protects. With respect to these rights, "When will men see that they can only *discover* and *obey*, not *construct*, the laws of the political world! That their paper constitutions can only *teach* and *declare*, not *originate*, the fundamental principles of a civil government!"[180]

A positivistic theory of law, Spooner argued,

had its origin in days of ignorance and despotism, when government was founded in force, without any acknowledgement of the natural rights of men. . . . What a shame and reproach, nay, what an unparalleled crime is it, that at this day, *and in this country*, . . . a definition of law should be adhered to, that denies all these self-evident and glorious truths, blots out all men's natural rights, founds government on force, buries all present knowledge under the ignorance and tyranny of the past, and commits the liberties of mankind to the custody of unrestrained power![181]

Spooner was responding to Wendell Phillips's criticism of his essay.[182] Phillips there repeated and further analyzed much of his earlier expressed collation of historical materials about the founding[183] and, in light of it, said of Spooner's interpretation of the proslavery clauses: "We hardly know of a more daring flight of genius in the whole range of modern fiction than this." Spooner was no doubt correct, in response, that much of Phillips's argument depended on an unreflective positivism. Phillips had thus urged, consistent with his positivism, that morality was only interpretively relevant when embedded in law; otherwise, positive law means "*arbitrary*, and is used as opposed to *moral*."[184] Spooner precisely denied, in the spirit of Dworkin's interpretive theory of law today, that his interpretive principles were external to American constitutionalism as a system of law,[185] a point Phillips did not engage.

One part of Phillips's criticism did not, however, turn on positivism, namely, the insistence of the radicals that interpretive weight may be de-

---

[178] See Goodell, *Views*, p. 146.

[179] See ibid., pp. 150–51.

[180] See ibid., p. 154.

[181] See Spooner, *Unconstitutionality*, p. 146.

[182] See Phillips, *Review*.

[183] See Phillips, *The Constitution a Pro-Slavery Compact* (1844); *Review* was originally published in 1847.

[184] See Phillips, *Review*, p. 32, 54–60, 64, 85.

[185] See Spooner, *Unconstitutionality*, pp. 155–56, n.

nied the public understanding of constitutional clauses both at the time of the founding and continuously later. If these materials are part of the canonical public understanding of American constitutionalism, as they appear to be, they must presumably be given at least some weight in the larger interpretive account (perhaps, as part of a theory of mistake or, as moderate antislavery proposed, a long-term ambition for the triumph of national principles at the state level). It seems interpretively question begging to dismiss them altogether as, in principle, irrelevant.

Having made their negative case against the proslavery reading of the Constitution, the radicals had then to make their case for the Constitution as antislavery at both the state and national levels. Goodell gave prominent weight to the due process clause of the fifth amendment (supposing it to be applicable to the states)[186] and to the guarantee clause[187] (slavery, an antirepublican institution, could be abolished by Congress).[188] Spooner inferred directly from the account he had given of constitutional legitimacy (based on the equal rights of all persons) that slaves were owed the natural rights of citizens, and that slavery was therefore unconstitutional; Congress, under the guarantee clause, also had the power to abolish slavery in the South as an antirepublican abridgment of rights.[189]

Joel Tiffany generalized arguments implicit in Goodell and Spooner into a general constitutional principle "for the equal protection of all, individually and collectively."[190] Consistent with the general methodology of the radicals, Tiffany interpreted the text of the Constitution in light of Lockean political theory understood, in Weld's terms, as a guarantee of equal protection of one's rights as the condition of allegiance.

Tiffany particularly emphasized the privileges and immunities clause of Article IV: "The citizens of each State shall be entitled to all privileges and immunities of citizens in the several States."[191] Consistent with Weld on equal protection, all persons born in the United States were equal citizens endowed with "the privileges and immunities which the American citizen has a right to demand of the Federal Government," namely, "those natural and inalienable rights which the Declaration of Independence asserted, the war of the Revolution maintained, and the adoption of the Federal Constitution secured." Accordingly, the federal government had the power to enforce such rights both under the privileges and immunities clause and the guarantee clause, that is, to abolish slavery in order to recognize the

---

[186] See Goodell, Views, pp. 57–63.

[187] "The United States shall guarantee to every State in this Union a Republican form of government." U.S. Constitution, Art. IV, sec. 4.

[188] See Goodell, Views, pp. 46–57.

[189] See Spooner, Unconstitutionality, pp. 90–95, 105–14.

[190] See Tiffany, Treatise, p. 87.

[191] See U.S. Constitution, Art. IV, sec. 2, cl. 1.

rights of blacks as American citizens. Consistent with the interpretive ingredients of American revolutionary constitutionalism, Tiffany's argument
gave weight to the important contrasts between rights-based American
constitutionalism and both British parliamentary supremacy and the ancient republics of Greece and Rome.[192]

Tiffany sharply posed the crisis of American constitutionalism in terms
of the despotic powers of states. It was not, *pace* Calhoun, the states that
required protection "but the *individual*, crushed, and overwhelmed by an
insolent, and tyranical [*sic*] majority, that needed such a guaranty [*sic*]; and
to him, as a citizen of the United States, whether in the majority, or minority, is that guaranty given, to secure him, not only from *individual*, but
also from *governmental oppression*." Indeed, "if its guarantys [*sic*] were
only intended to protect the citizen against its own [national] despotism, a
vast majority of the citizens would have been more secure without a union
government, than with it."[193] The language was pointedly revolutionary.

Legitimacy of Revolution

If slavery violated human rights, as many Americans had come to believe,
the natural question posed by American revolutionary constitutionalism
was whether such violations justified the abstract Lockean revolutionary
right to revolt.

The issue had long haunted abolitionist moral thought, which combined
argument both insisting that slavery violated human rights and denying
that it followed that revolution was legitimate. Channing thus began his
classic abolitionist moral analysis of the evil of slavery with unequivocal
moral condemnation of slave insurrection;[194] and Francis Wayland offered
an important moral condemnation of slavery as a violation of human rights,
but urged the religious duty of slaves to submit and good reasons for pre-
ferring suffering in a just cause to either forcible resistance or passive obe-
dience.[195] Elsewhere, Wayland considered the moral responsibilities of
third parties in such cases; he argued for the moral force of a legal rule
established by majority rule,[196] denied that the moral wrongness of slavery
in the South imposed a moral responsibility on others to end it, and even
suggested an affirmative moral obligation arising from the social contract

---

[192] See Tiffany, *Treatise*, pp. 87, 88, 107–14, 23–27, 35–37.

[193] See ibid., pp. 55–56, 110, 58.

[194] See Channing, *Slavery*, in Channing, *Works*, pp. 689–90; see also pp. 697, 730, 737.

[195] See Wayland, *The Elements of Moral Science*, pp. 182–96, 386–90, 197–98, 336–38.

[196] See Francis Wayland, *The Limitations of Human Responsibility* (New York: D. Appleton & Co., 1838), p. 124. For a good general discussion of the how the issue was conceived
during this period, see Edward H. Madden, *Civil Disobedience and Moral Law in Nineteenth-Century American Philosophy* (Seattle: University of Washington Press, 1968).

of the Union not morally to interfere with slavery or encourage slave resistance. Abolitionism, in particular, was counterproductive.[197]

The moral question of either the rights of slaves to revolt or of third parties to assist would not, however, go away. Theodore Parker put the haunting moral point clearly as a challenge to American revolutionary constitutionalism:

> In the last century your fathers cried out to God against the oppressions laid on them by England, justly cried out. Yet those oppressions were but little things—a tax on sugar, parchment, paper, tea; nothing but a tax, allowing no voice in the granting thereof or its spending. They went to war for an abstraction—the great doctrine of human rights. . . . What was the oppression the fathers suffered, to this their sons commit? . . . How then can you justify your oppression? How refuse to admit that the bondmen of the United States have the same right, and a far stronger inducement to draw the sword and smite at your very life? Surely you cannot do so, not in America; never till Lexington and Bunker Hill are wiped out of the earth; never till the history of your own Revolution is forgot; never till the names of the Adamses, of Jefferson, of Washington, are expunged from the memory of men.[198]

Against the background of successful slave revolts in Saint-Domingue and elsewhere in Latin America and the abortive slave revolts of Gabriel Prosser, Denmark Vesey, and Nat Turner in the United States,[199] black abolitionists had made the same point.[200] Walker's 1829 *Appeal* had asked unanswerably: "Now, Americans! I ask you candidly, was your sufferings under Great Britain, one hundredth part as cruel and tyrannical as you have rendered ours under you?"[201] And Frederick Douglass had bitterly celebrated July 4 in 1852: "You can bare your bosom to the storm of British artillery to throw off a three-penny tax on tea; and yet wring the last hard earned farthing from the grasp of the black laborers of your country."[202]

[197] See Wayland, *The Limitations of Human Responsibility*, pp. 167–68, 172–75, 191–92.

[198] See Theodore Parker, "A Letter on Slavery" (1848), in Parker, *The Slave Power*, pp. 108–10.

[199] For a good general study, see Eugene D. Genovese, *From Rebellion to Revolution: Afro-American Slave Revolts in the Making of the Modern World* (Baton Rouge: Louisiana State University Press, 1979). See also Herbert Aptheker, *American Negro Slave Revolts* (New York: International Publishers, 1952).

[200] For a good general study, see Benjamin Quarles, *Black Abolitionists* (London: Oxford University Press, 1969).

[201] See David Walker, *Walker's Appeal, in Four Articles: Together with a Preamble, to the Coloured Citizens of the World* (1829), reprinted in Herbert Aptheker, ed., *A Documentary History of the Negro People in the United States*, 4 vols. (New York: Citadel Press Books, 1990), 1:97.

[202] See Frederick Douglass, "The Meaning of July Fourth for the Negro," speech delivered 5 July 1852, reprinted in Foner, *Life and Writings*, 2:200.

The key to the early insistence of moral abolitionists such as Garrison that they eschewed "all carnal weapons"[203] was their clear-eyed public statement that, absent immediate abolition, slave owners *know* that oppression must cause rebellion."[204] A clear statement of the legitimacy of revolution was rendered at least palatable by Garrison's anarchist denial that coercion could ever be justified in principle for any cause or reason. Few abolitionists were, however, radical disunionists, and even fewer of them agreed with Garrison's principled moral anarchism (for Phillips, for example, political noninvolvement was basically strategic).

For most abolitionists, the question was not the abstract one of whether slaves had a moral right to revolt (they clearly had this right). The issue, rather, was whether, first, the right could be reasonably exercised without abridging other moral rights; and second, whether it was reasonably necessary to exercise the right and, if so, likely to succeed without unacceptable infliction of harms on innocent third parties. The second point was the fundamental one for American abolitionist constitutionalists, whether they were proponents of the theory of Union or of moderate or radical antislavery. Lincoln certainly believed, as we have seen, that the Constitution, properly interpreted in light of the theory of Union, would reasonably end slavery; and his own electoral success of 1860 might have led him to believe that constitutional institutions could be trusted to end slavery without appeal to the right to revolution.

But the developments in the nation that mobilized Lincoln into political action and leadership—namely, the Kansas-Nebraska Act, violence in Kansas, the brutal beating on the floor of the Senate of the great abolitionist senator Charles Sumner, and *Dred Scott*[205]—led other abolitionist Americans to think that constitutional institutions could no longer be trusted deliberatively to accord slaves their inalienable human rights. Proponents of radical antislavery thus argued that, if the Constitution was not properly interpreted in the way they argued it should be, "it would annul his [a slave's] allegiance . . . to a government that either will not, or cannot protect them."[206] Indeed, "if a state under this provision of the constitution is so entirely disrobed of authority as to be compelled to sit by and see these and the like enormities perpetrated upon its citizens, it is high time it was *known*—and *when known*, the time for a *second revolution* will have arrived, greater in cause and importance than the first."[207]

Theodore Parker had already notably argued for the moral right and duty

---

[203] See William Lloyd Garrison, "Declaration of Sentiments," in Garrison, *Selections*, p. 67.
[204] See Garrison, *Thoughts on African Colonization*, p. 94.
[205] See Potter, *The Impending Crisis*.
[206] See Spooner, *Unconstitutionality*, p. 271.
[207] See Tiffany, *Treatise*, p. 75.

of citizens to resist the requirements of the Fugitive Slave Act of 1850.[208] In view of his general views about the clear right of American slaves to revolt, Parker had gone so far as to ascribe to the backwardness of blacks (whether cultural or natural) failure to claim the right in the aggressive way white Americans, comparably situated, would have.[209] By the end of a decade of the politics of Douglas and the judiciary of Taney, Parker had come to believe that American constitutional institutions could no longer be depended on to vindicate the urgency of the underlying rights to liberty of American slaves: "I think now this terrible question must be settled, as all the preceding ones, by violence and the sword. I deplore it exceedingly. I hate war, but injustice worse than war."[210]

Parker argued in an 1859 letter written from Rome near the end of his life that the slave has "a natural right to kill every man who seeks to prevent his enjoyment of liberty" and "it may be a natural duty for the freeman to help the slaves to the enjoyment of their liberty, and as means to that end, to aid them in killing all such as oppose their natural freedom."[211] The U.S. Constitution, no longer properly interpreted consistent with its revolutionary political morality, was no longer legitimate. The time had come for Americans to appeal to the right to revolution to remedy the nation's greatest political evil. Parker had joined other abolitionists in support of the revolutionary activities of John Brown.[212]

[208] See Theodore Parker, "The Function of Conscience" (1850), in Parker, The Slave Power, pp. 287–315; Theodore Parker, "The Boston Kidnapping" (1852), reprinted in Parker, The Slave Power, pp. 316–85. See Theodore Parker, The Trial of Theodore Parker (1855; reprint, Freeport, N.Y.: Books for Libraries Press, 1971).

[209] For an implicit such comparison, see Theodore Parker, "A Letter on Slavery," in Parker, The Slave Power, pp. 108–11. For Parker's association of backwardness with successful enslavement, see, e.g., Theodore Parker, Social Classes in a Republic, ed. Samuel A. Eliot (Boston: American Unitarian Association, n.d.), pp. 142–43.

[210] Parker, The Relation of Slavery, p. 20.

[211] See Theodore Parker, letter to Francis Jackson of 24 November 1859, reprinted in F. B. Sanborn, "Parker in the John Brown Campaign," in Theodore Parker, Saint Bernard and Other Papers, ed. Charles W. Wendte (Boston: American Unitarian Association, 1911), pp. 422–23 (emphasis in original).

[212] See Sanborn, "Parker in the John Brown Campaign," in Parker, Saint Bernard, pp. 391–448. For Thoreau's speeches in praise of Brown, see "A Plea for Captain John Brown," in Thoreau, Reform Papers, pp. 111–38; "Martrydom of John Brown," in Thoreau, Reform Papers, pp. 139–43; "The Last Days of John Brown," in Thoreau, Reform Papers, pp. 145–53. For commentary on Thoreau's support of Brown and his abolitionist stance in general, see Daniel Walker Howe, "Henry David Thoreau on the Duty of Civil Disobedience."

FOUR

THE SECOND AMERICAN REVOLUTION AND THE

RECONSTRUCTION AMENDMENTS

T HE RECONSTRUCTION AMENDMENTS were the culminating expression of the moral, political, and constitutional crisis of the antebellum period discussed in the previous two chapters. That long national controversy may have been a necessary condition of the Reconstruction Amendments, but it was not sufficient. The moral and political world of 1864–70, which gave rise to these amendments, was not the nation of 1860–61. Two related facts in each period mark the moral chasm that separates these dates.

First, on March 2, 1861, the Congress of the United States, having given the required two-thirds approval in each house, transmitted to the states its proposed thirteenth amendment to the Constitution; the amendment, never ratified, would have constitutionally entrenched slavery in the states against federal interference.[1] Lincoln, in his first inaugural address, supported the amendment, observing: "Holding such a provision to now be implied constitutional law, I have no objection to its being made express, and irrevocable."[2] On June 15, 1865, the Congress, having approved it by the required two-thirds, sent the later ratified thirteenth amendment to the states; this amendment abolished slavery and involuntary servitude in the United States.[3] In his December 6, 1864, annual message to Congress, Lincoln had forcefully urged Congress to pass the then pending amendment.[4]

Second, in 1860, in light of the triumph of political abolitionism through constitutional processes, the leaders of the radical disunionist wing of the abolitionist movement (in particular, William Lloyd Garrison and Wendell Phillips) were a discredited and even despised minority within a minority (Phillips had even welcomed secession). But by 1864 they had become major leaders of a northern public opinion increasingly favorable to abolition

[1] See Potter, *Lincoln and His Party*, p. 301.

[2] Abraham Lincoln, First Inaugural Address, delivered 4 March, 1961, reprinted in Fehrenbacher, *Abraham Lincoln: Speeches and Writings, 1858–1865*, p. 222.

[3] See George H. Hoemann, *What God Hath Wrought: The Embodiment of Freedom in the Thirteenth Amendment* (New York: Garland, 1987), p. 130.

[4] See Abraham Lincoln, Annual Message to Congress, 6 December 1864, reprinted in Fehrenbacher, *Abraham Lincoln: Speeches and Writing, 1858–1865*, p. 658.

by constitutional amendment. Indeed, Phillips was an influential public advocate of related constitutional amendments guaranteeing equal rights, including voting rights. President Lincoln met with Garrison and Frederick Douglass and profited from their (though not Phillips's)[5] public political support in the election of 1864.

The chasm between these two periods was filled not only by public deliberative constitutional debate of the sort we have so far studied as the background of the Reconstruction Amendments,[6] but by the greatest and most tragic failure of constitutionalism in American history, namely, the Civil War.[7] To study the Reconstruction Amendments as if they were to be understood as simply continuous with the dominant constitutionalism and politics of the antebellum period is to study the Soviet state without reference to the Russian Revolution or the French republics without the French Revolution or, for that matter, the U.S. Constitution without the American Revolution.

The Reconstruction Amendments were not only made possible by the sectional conflict of arms between the North and South; they were the expression of essential public reflections on the moral and constitutional meaning of the Civil War in light of a constitutionalism that had tragically failed to bring public reason to bear on the underlying controversy. The most compelling interpretation of those events was that they fulfilled the abolitionist prophecy of "the time for a *second revolution.*"[8] Americans had appealed to the right of revolution against the decadent constitutionalism that had protected and expanded slavery and led to its entrenchment under the Confederacy. That interpretation required not only abolition of slavery, but a rethinking of our constitutionalism.

The Civil War had been fought originally by the North to defend the Union against the moral and constitutional illegitimacy of southern secession and not to secure the abolition of slavery;[9] Lincoln himself insisted on this very point in his 1862 letter to Greeley.[10] But as the Civil War wore

[5] See James M. McPherson, *The Struggle for Equality: Abolitionists and the Negro in the Civil War and Reconstruction* (Princeton: Princeton University Press, 1964), pp. 34–36, 271–72, 213, 260–2, 266, 268–70, 285.

[6] For a good collection of ongoing constitutional debates during the Civil War, including over the war itself, see Freidel, *Union Pamphlets.*

[7] See Phillip Shaw Paludan, *"A People's Contest": The Union and Civil War* (New York: Harper & Row, 1988); James M. McPherson, *Battle Cry of Freedom: The Civil War Era* (New York: Ballantine Books, 1988).

[8] Tiffany, *Treatise,* p. 75.

[9] See Lincoln, "First Inaugural Address," in Fehrenbacher, *Abraham Lincoln: Speeches and Writing, 1858–1865,* pp. 215–24.

[10] See Abraham Lincoln, letter to Horace Greeley, 22 August 1862, in ibid., pp. 357–58; for example, "I would save the Union. I would save it the shortest way under the Constitution. . . . If I could save the Union without freeing *any* slave I would do it, and if I could save it by freeing *all* the slaves I would do it; and if I could save it by freeing some and leaving others alone I would also do that" (p. 358).

on, the kinds of terrible human losses that the conflict required called for a moral justification more able and worthy to sustain the will and morale of the North.[11]

Lincoln, after various attempts to secure some form of voluntary compensated abolition with colonization of freedmen abroad, came to regard immediate uncompensated emancipation as necessary to win the war. He defended the Emancipation Proclamation in such terms; it had stimulated the presence of blacks (both free and slave) in the Union armies, and that presence was important to the increasingly successful war effort.[12] By the end of the war, most slaves had been effectively emancipated, and Lincoln recognized that only the constitutional abolition of slavery would and did give the war an enduring moral and constitutional meaning.[13] The Civil War was to be regarded as a revolutionary battle for human rights, and the constitutional abolition of slavery must be the symbol of that moral achievement.

The Civil War, the Second American Revolution, was, like the First American Revolution, a revolution over constitutional and moral ideals. It required, like its predecessor, a constitutional order that would conserve its astonishing accomplishments in a legacy of principle for posterity. Prior to the Civil War, there was a widely recognized sharp distinction between the question of the abstract requirements of justice (namely, that slavery was morally wrong and should not exist) and the question of the morally tolerable and reasonable burdens that could be imposed on the South to abolish slavery. Under this view, the institution of slavery had been foisted on the South by history; it had not been adopted by the present generation, many of whom would not have adopted it if adoption had been an open question.

Lincoln embraced the point in 1854: "When southern people tell us they are no more responsible for the origin of slavery, than we; I acknowledge the fact." Lincoln's initial suggestion was colonization. The other possibility, the immediate abolition of slavery, would impose severe economic and personal costs on slave owners, on society at large, and arguably even on the freedmen. Lincoln had problems with all the options:

> What then? Free them all, and keep them among us as underlings? Is it quite certain that this betters their condition? I think I would not hold one in slavery,

[11] See, e.g., Lewis Tappan, "The War, Its Cause and Remedy: Immediate Emancipation: The Only Wise and Safe Mode" (New York, 1861), in Freidel, *Union Pamphlets*, pp. 102–17; Orestes Augustus Brownson, "Brownson on the Rebellion" (St. Louis, 1861), in Freidel, *Union Pamphlets*, pp. 128–65.

[12] See Abraham Lincoln, letter to James C. Conkling, 26 August 1863, in Fehrenbacher, *Abraham Lincoln: Speeches and Writings, 1858–1865*, pp. 495–99.

[13] See Abraham Lincoln, "Annual Message to Congress," 6 December 1864, in ibid., pp. 657–58; "Second Inaugural Address," 4 May 1865, in ibid., pp. 686–87.

at any rate; yet the point is not clear enough for me to denounce people upon. What next? Free them, and make them political and socially, our equals? My own feelings will not admit of this; and if mine would, we well know that those of the great mass of white people will not. Whether this feeling accords with justice and sound judgment, is not the sole question, if indeed, it is any part of it. A universal feeling, whether well or ill-founded, can not be safely disregarded. We can not, then, make them equals."

Lincoln concluded: "It does seem to me that systems of gradual emancipation might be adopted; but for their tardiness in this, I will not undertake to judge our brethren of the south."[14]

In effect, such southern "brethren" might not unreasonably (or at least not blamably) conclude, as Thomas Dew had in 1832,[15] that all such schemes of abolition and colonization were unworkably unrealistic; the balance of reasons might favor continuing slavery subject to amelioration of its rigors. In the antebellum period, the judgment of the abstract injustice of slavery was thus consistent with a range of views about whether, when, or how slavery could or should be abolished in light of the balance of considerations of justice overall.

After the Civil War, the distinction between these questions had been subverted by new moral realities. Most slaves had been emancipated. More important from the vantage of the emerging conception of Union moral identity, many of them had fought well and nobly in a civil war to save the Union. In response to objections to his emancipation policy, Lincoln made clear the new moral weight black and white Americans now deserved in light of the great moral testing of this civil war over national identity:

The war has certainly progressed as favorably for us, since the issue of the proclamation as before. I know as fully as one can know the opinions of others, that some of the commanders of our armies in the field who have given us our most important successes, believe the emancipation policy, and the use of colored troops, constitute the heaviest blow yet dealt to the rebellion. . . . You say you will not fight to free negroes. Some of them seem willing to fight for you. . . . If they stake their lives for us, they must be prompted by the strongest motive—even the promise of freedom. And the promise being made, must be kept. . . . Peace does not appear so distant as it did. I hope it will come soon, and come to stay . . . then, there be some black men who can remember that, with silent tongue, and clenched teeth, and steady eye, and well-poised bayonet, they have helped mankind on to this great consum-

[14] Abraham Lincoln, "Speech on Kansas-Nebraska Act," delivered 16 October 1854, in ibid., p. 316.
[15] See Dew, "Abolition of Negro Slavery," Faust, *Ideology of Slavery*, pp. 21–77.

mation; while, I fear, there will be some white ones, unable to forget that, with malignant heart, and deceitful speech, they have strove to hinder it. [16]

If black Americans were now taken with a new moral seriousness by Lincoln and the public he led, the claims of southern defenders of slavery had, in contrast, negligible moral, political, and constitutional weight. Indeed, much could now be said and was said in favor of the constitutional disempowerment of the southern leadership that had precipitated and persevered in the conflict until its bitter end. [17] Their obduracy had led them unjustly and illegitimately to defend slavery as an institution by fighting a war essentially for its protection and expansion, a war whose successful prosecution had required the abolition of slavery. From the perspective of the now triumphant constitutional theory of Union, southern leaders had forfeited the protections they had long enjoyed under the Constitution of 1787; they had revolted against legitimate constitutional processes (namely, the result of the presidential election of 1860) in factionalized pursuit of short-term sectional advantage and pride.

In the antebellum period, the claim that the southern slave states were not republican in the way required by the guarantee clause was the view only of radical antislavery constitutional theorists or of increasingly radical political abolitionists such as Parker. Secession and civil war—the southern revolt against constitutional law and process—rendered the theory the dominant understanding of congressional power over reconstruction. [18] The very facts of secession and civil war were proof of the nonrepublican character of southern governments. Slavery—the institution, in the terms of Lincoln's second inaugural, "all knew . . . was, somehow, the cause of the war"[19]—was pivotal to the moral and constitutional understanding of the nonrepublican character of these states. The injustice of slavery was no longer an abstract question. Public reason—for the first time in our constitutional history alive to the claims of black Americans and no longer reasonably bound to the demands of the South—was now, in light of the de

---

[16] Abraham Lincoln, letter to James C. Conkling, 26 August 1863, in Fehrenbacher, *Abraham Lincoln: Speeches and Writings, 1858–1865*, pp. 497–99.

[17] Much of the congressional debate over the fourteenth amendment was not about the substantive terms of section 1, but the terms of political disempowerment of section 2; see Horace Edgar Flack, *The Adoption of the Fourteenth Amendment* (Baltimore: Johns Hopkins University Press, 1908); Joseph B. James, *The Framing of the Fourteenth Amendment* (Urbana: University of Illinois Press, 1956).

[18] See McKitrick, *Andrew Johnson and Reconstruction*, pp. 93–119; Benedict, *A Compromise of Principle* pp. 152, 169–70, 215; Foner, *Reconstruction*, pp. 232–33; Paludan, "A People's Contest," pp. 224–25, 252–53; J. G. Randall, *Constitutional Problems Under Lincoln*, rev. ed. (Gloucester, Mass.: Peter Smith, 1963), pp. 234–38.

[19] See Abraham Lincoln, "Second Inaugural Address," delivered 4 March 1865, in Fehrenbacher, *Abraham Lincoln: Speeches and Writings, 1858–1865*, p. 686.

facto wreckage of American slavery, required to act on the demands of justice.

America faced in 1865 the question of how the terms of political community and national unity and identity were to be understood in the light of the antebellum debates, the Civil War, and the emancipation of the millions of blacks that had been held in slavery in the South.

The antebellum mainstream understanding was reasonably clear and clearly racist. Chief Justice Roger Taney had given an authoritative interpretation of American national identity in *Dred Scott*. Blacks were "beings of an inferior order, and altogether unfit to associate with the white race, either in social or political relations; and so far inferior, that they had no rights which the white man was bound to respect." Blacks accordingly could not be citizens. Correspondingly, Taney argued that the words of the Declaration of Independence ("all men are created equal . . . [and] endowed with certain unalienable rights") "were not intended" to include "the enslaved African race."[20]

Both of Taney's originalist claims were historically doubtful: blacks had voted in states at the time of the 1787 Convention,[21] and the Declaration of Independence, understood as a statement of long-term ambition and aspiration, could reasonably be taken to mean what it said.[22] In his 1858 debates with Douglas, however, Lincoln thought it important to refute Taney's historical claims about the Declaration,[23] but stated Taney's views of black citizenship "without making any complaint of it at all."[24] Lincoln knew that Taney's history on this point was wrong as well, but made little of it because he agreed in substance with it. Though states had constitutional power to make blacks citizens of the state and of the nation, "I should be opposed to the exercise of it."[25] In effect, Taney offered a racial conception of American national identity as constitutionally compelled, Lincoln as permitted and desirable.

This antebellum world of racist complacency was shattered by the Civil War, which rendered imperative the reexamination of the terms of national unity in a new way. Americans were compelled critically to rethink both

[20] See *Dred Scott*, p. 407, 404–5, 410.

[21] See ibid., pp. 572–74, 576 (Curtis, J., dissenting).

[22] See id., at pp. 574–75 (Curtis, J., dissenting). For a discussion of the conflicting Founders' denotations in the North and South, see Finkelman, "The Constitution and the Intentions of the Framers," pp. 392–93 (1989); Finkelman questions whether such narrow originalism was in any case the appropriate interpretive attitude to be taken in *Dred Scott* (pp. 393–94).

[23] See Abraham Lincoln, Fifth Joint Debate, Galesburg, 7 October 1858, in Johannsen, *Lincoln-Douglas Debates*, pp. 219–20; Seventh Joint Debate, Alton, October 15, 1858, in ibid., p. 304.

[24] See Lincoln, Seventh Joint Debate, in ibid., p. 302.

[25] See Abraham Lincoln, Fourth Joint Debate, Charleston, 18 September 1858, in ibid., p. 198.

their revolutionary constitutionalism and the form it took in the Constitution of 1787. Drawing upon the antebellum moral, political, and constitutional controversies, Americans asked the kinds of fundamental questions about constitutionalism they had not discussed since 1787. The Reconstruction Amendments were the outcome of those deliberations.

Several important constitutional historians have persuasively argued that the Reconstruction Amendments are best understood both historically and constitutionally as a set of ramifying principles all interpretive of the central judgment of political morality at the heart of the abolitionist movement, namely, the fundamental moral wrongness of slavery on grounds of its abridgment of fundamental human rights.[26] According to this view, the thirteenth amendment's abolition of slavery and involuntary servitude were not merely negative prohibitions on certain institutions and practices. The amendment also affirmed the constitutionally enforceable judgment of political morality that made sense of these prohibitions, namely, a judgment about the substance, nature, and weight of the inalienable human rights of all persons subject to political power in the United States.[27]

Both the fourteenth and fifteenth amendments are to be understood as deliberative interpretations of this judgment of political morality along various normative dimensions. These include the guarantee of inalienable rights and liberties, the requirement that legitimate political power be justifiable to all persons as equals, the fair distribution of political power, and observance of the fair procedures of due process. The leaders of the Reconstruction Congress agreed about the desirability of constitutional protection for all these principles, disagreeing only on whether separate amendments (the fourteenth and fifteenth amendments, for example) were needed to secure them and on points of strategy about how to secure ratification of amendments guaranteeing such principles.[28] We need, then, to study the methodologies of analysis and justification used in the deliberations over these amendments as a unity, thus capturing the normative coherence that the amendments have and were understood to have.

Consistent with this historical understanding of the normative integrity of the Reconstruction Amendments, the six ingredients of American revolutionary constitutionalism, suitably interpreted in the context of 1865, were crucially brought to bear on deliberations about the amendments. To a remarkable extent, the Reconstruction Amendments were as much the

---

[26] See tenBroek, *Equal under Law*; Hyman, *A More Perfect Union*; Hyman and Wiecek, *Equal Justice under Law.*

[27] See Hoemann, *What Hath God Wrought.*

[28] See Benedict, *A Compromise of Principle.* For a useful anthology of relevant readings, see Harold M. Hyman, ed., *The Radical Republicans and Reconstruction, 1861–1870* (Indianapolis: Bobbs-Merrill, 1967).

result of internal reflections on the revolutionary constitutionalism of 1787–88 as they were external criticisms of that constitutionalism in light of the bitter experience of its antebellum decadence.

Revolutionary Principles

Lincoln's famous 1864 letter on the wrongness of slavery memorialized for the nation moral views central to the public mind deliberating on the constitutional abolition of slavery. One sentence in that letter, echoing a similar passage in Channing's great essay,[29] was conspicuously cited by proponents of the thirteenth amendment in the congressional debates: "If slavery is not wrong, nothing is wrong."[30] Lincoln referred to the antislavery views thus expressed as "my primary abstract judgment on the moral question of slavery";[31] and members of Congress thought of it similarly as expressing a "philosophical truth."[32]

That truth was a natural moral judgment about the origination of natural rights in moral personality, which no positive law of vested property rights could legitimately abridge: "What vested rights so high or so sacred as a man's right to himself, to his wife and children, to his liberty, and to the fruits of his own industry? Did not our fathers declare that those rights were inalienable? And if a man cannot himself alienate those rights, how can another man alienate them without being himself a robber of the vested rights of his brother-man?"[33] Democratically legitimate power cannot accept the claims of popular sovereignty of the

> right of one people to enslave another people to whom nature has given equal rights of freedom. Sir, civil liberty, in my judgment, has no such interpreta-

[29] "Is there any moral truth more deeply rooted in us, than that such a degradation [slavery] would be an infinite wrong? And, if this impression be a delusion, on what single moral conviction can we rely?" Channing, *Slavery,* in Channing, *Works,* pp. 692–93.

[30] Abraham Lincoln, letter to Albert G. Hodges, 4 April 1864, in Fehrenbacher, *Abraham Lincoln: Speeches and Writings, 1858–1865,* p. 585. For citations to this statement by Lincoln, see Representative Ashley, *Congressional Globe,* 38th Cong., 2d sess., 6 January 1865, p. 138: "My Speaker, '*If slavery is not wrong, nothing is wrong.*' Thus simply and truthfully has spoken our worthy Chief Magistrate." See also Representative Smith, *Congressional Globe,* 38th Cong., 2d sess., 12 January 1965, p. 237: "Mr. Speaker, in my judgment there never was a sounder or a more philosophical truth communicated by any man than that of the President of the United States, when he wrote to Colonel Hodges, of Frankfort, Kentucky, that 'if slavery is not wrong, nothing is wrong.'"

[31] See Lincoln, letter to Hodges, in Fehrenbacher, *Abraham Lincoln: Speeches and Writings, 1858–1865,* vol. 2, at p. 585.

[32] See Representative Smith, *Congressional Globe,* 38th Cong., 2d sess., 6 January 1985, p. 237.

[33] See Representative Farnsworth, *Congressional Globe,* 38th Cong., 2d sess., 10 January 1865, p. 200.

tion, no such meaning; and no man who regards himself as made in the image of his Maker, solely responsible to his Maker for his thoughts and actions, can recognize a sentiment which lowers him in his own estimation, in the estimation of Heaven, and before the face of the whole world.

Such distortions of legitimate democracy were "conceived more than thirty years ago, and John C. Calhoun was present at its conception." Its basis was "tyrannic and despotic power" of the sort "exercised abroad for the purpose of restricting liberty of opinion . . . where, . . . the despotism of Church and State attempted to control the minds of men."[34]

The abstract moral judgment, underlying the thirteenth amendment, expresses the truth, following Locke, that persons have inalienable human rights; the legitimacy of political power must be tested against respect for such rights, and revolution is justified against forms of political power that fail to respect such rights. Locke's argument for human rights and associated limits on political power must be construed within the structure of his seminal defense of an inalienable right to conscience (see Chapter 3); his argument for toleration called for skepticism about the uses of political power to entrench hierarchies of "natural" privilege that deprived persons of their reasonable moral freedom as democratic equals. All these elements of Lockean skepticism were crucially in play in the most philosophically elaborate defense of the thirteenth amendment, that made by Representative James Wilson introducing the amendment on the floor of the House of Representatives on March 19, 1864.[35]

Wilson began and ended his address by appealing to the great change in American public opinion stimulated by the Civil War: a "public opinion now existing in this country in opposition to this power [that] is the result of slavery overleaping itself, rather than of the determination of freemen to form it." The Civil War "awakened to its true and real life the moral sense of the nation," a sense that had lain dormant for "half a century . . . when slavery controlled the national mind." What we, in contrast to the Founders, have learned both from the antebellum controversies and from the Civil War is the imperative moral need for revolutionary political action against slavery: "We see that the death [of slavery] can only be accomplished by an executioner. Slavery will not kill itself."[36]

The nation, in fighting a just civil war now seen to be essentially against slavery, had recovered, as a people, the revolutionary political morality of

---

[34] See Representative Davis, *Congressional Globe*, 38th Cong., 2d sess., 7 January 1865, p. 154, 155 (citing examples of Holland, Spain, and Britain).

[35] See Representative James Wilson, *Congressional Globe*, 38th Cong., 1st sess., 19 March 1864, pp. 1199–1206.

[36] See ibid., pp. 1199, 1200, 1201, 1203.

the American Revolution that justified war on grounds of defending human rights:

> The spirit of patriotism has returned to us clothed with a resurrectional bright-ness like unto that which shall light the heirs of glory to the abode of the eternal Father. Manhood, as it stood proudly erect in the grand, colossal, sym-metrical proportions known to the early days of the Republic, again gives sub-limity to American character. . . . An awakened, invigorated concentrated national conscience revivifies our observance of justice. . . . Our Red Sea pas-sage promises to be as propitious as was that of God's chosen people when the waters parted and presented the sea-bed for their escape from the hosts upon whom these waters closed and effected the burial appointed by Him who had declared, "Let my people go."

The task now was to forge a constitutionalism that would memorialize and give adequate institutional expression to "the grand volcanic action that is upheaving the great moral ideas which underlie the Republic."[37]

Wilson's emphasis on a judgment of moral right forged by morally good action reflects the abolitionist distrust for the familiar proslavery uses of the intellect to distort or suppress the requirements of ethical impartiality: "We have tried to reason it [the wrongness of slavery] away, to practice arts which should carry us around it, or over it, or under it."[38] But he also offers an argument for why this judgment of political morality is sound, an argument, based on toleration, clearly derivative from the same argument made by the abolitionists (see Chapter 3).

The right to revolution was, in Lockean political theory, centrally linked to the right to conscience because only the required guarantees for the moral independence of critical conscience would enable it to make the kinds of judgments on the basis of which the right to revolution might legitimately be asserted; as Locke put the point, "I my self can only be Judge in my own Conscience."[39] The abridgment by the state of the rights to conscience and free speech would allow it illegitimately to determine what counted as valid or proper criticism of the state or, even worse, to set the critical in-tellectual and ethical standards of public reason. In effect, dominant polit-ical powers would entrench an epistemology that would immunize its powers from the kind of independent critical assessment central to the tests in terms of which the legitimacy of any political power should be assessed, namely, respect for rights and pursuit of the public interest. Abridgment of the right to conscience was, for this reason, one of the central grounds on the basis of which the right to revolution might be claimed.

[37] See ibid., p. 1203.
[38] See ibid., p. 1200.
[39] See Locke, *Second Treatise*, p. 300 (sec. 21); see also pp. 398 (sec. 168), 422–23 (sec. 209), 445 (sec. 242). For commentary, see Richards, *Foundations*, pp. 78–97.

The normative heart of Wilson's argument of revolutionary justification for the Civil War was thus put in terms of the illegitimate abridgment of the inalienable rights of conscience, free speech, and assembly. For example, with respect to freedom of conscience:

> The bitter, cruel, relentless persecutions of the Methodists in the South, almost as void of pity as those which were visited upon the Huguenots in France, tell how utterly slavery disregards the right to a free exercise of religion. No religion which recognizes God's eternal attribute of justice and breathes that spirit of love which applies to all men the sublime commandment, "Whatsoever ye would that men should do unto you, do ye even so to them," can ever be allowed free exercise where slavery curses men and defies God . . . where slavery dwarfs the consciences of men.[40]

And with respect to free speech:

> How much better has free discussion fared at the hands of the black censor who guards the interests of slavery against the expression of the thoughts of freemen? On what rood of this Republic cursed by slavery have men been free to declare their approval of the divine doctrines of the Declaration of Independence? Where, except in the free States of this Union, have the nation's toiling millions been permitted to assert their great protective doctrine, "The laborer is worthy of his hire?" What member of our great free labor force, North or South, could stand up in the presence of the despotism which owns men and combat the atrocious assertion that "Slavery is the natural and normal condition of the laboring man, whether white or black," . . . The press has been padlocked, and men's lips have been sealed. . . . [In the South] an organized element of death was surely sapping the foundations of our free institutions, reversing the theory of our Government, dwarfing our civilization, contracting the national conscience, compassing the destruction of everything calculated to preserve the republican character of our Constitution; and no man in the immediate presence of this rapidly accumulating ruin dared to raise a voice of warning. Submission and silence were inexorably exacted. Such, sir, is the free discussion which slavery tolerates.[41]

And the right of free assembly to protest grievances

> has been as completely disregarded as the other rights I have mentioned by the terrorism which guards the citadel of slavery. . . . Slavery could hold its assemblages, discuss, resolve, petition, threaten, disregard its constitutional obligations, trample upon the right of labor, do anything its despotic disposition might direct; but freedom and freemen must be deaf, dumb, and blind.

[40] See Wilson, *Congressional Globe*, 38th Cong., 1st sess., 19 March 1864, p. 1202.
[41] See ibid., p. 1202.

Throughout all the dominions of slavery republican government, constitutional liberty, the blessing of our free institutions were mere fables.[42]

From the contractualist perspective of Lockean political theory that Wilson assumes, the abridgment of such rights—at the very core of the inalienable human rights that government was instituted to secure—deprived political power of legitimacy and justified the right to revolution in order to secure those rights in a form of constitutionalism that would, at a minimum, better protect them. Americans in 1864–65 were thus, on grounds of abstract natural right, at least as well justified as the American revolutionaries of 1776 in rejecting the illegitimate political claims made on behalf of the southern slave power, revolting against such power, and forging new constitutional forms adequate to their just grievances.

Constitutional Principles of American Constitution

American constitutional revolutionaries such as Wilson in 1864 believed that their revolutionary principles were fundamental not only to the legitimacy but also to the proper interpretation of the U.S. Constitution. In the same way that the revolutionaries of 1776 justified themselves not only on the basis of natural rights but on the basis of a better interpretation of the principles of the constitution against which they were revolting (namely, the British Constitution), the revolutionaries of 1864 appealed interpretively to the American constitutionalism they still revered.

Their continuing reverence for the Constitution of 1787 underlies their failure to take seriously the more radical constitutional alternative of reconsidering the Founders' rejection of the model of British parliamentary supremacy, a proposal urged upon them by Sidney George Fisher in 1862.[43] Fisher's proposal was not frivolous.

The British Constitution had been rejected by Americans in 1776 on revolutionary grounds of violating natural rights. But this form of government had successfully and democratically abolished slavery in the West Indies in 1833–38. The institution of parliamentary supremacy, in which West Indian planters were not well represented, had sufficient power and incentive to act on humane moral principle when confronted by a well-organized and politically astute British abolitionist movement (a movement intimately connected to the American abolitionists).[44] In morally ironic con-

---

[42] See ibid., p. 1202.

[43] See Fisher, *The Trial of the Constitution*. For commentary on Fisher, see Phillip S. Paludan, *A Covenant with Death: The Constitution, Law, and Equality in the Civil War Era* (Urbana: University of Illinois Press, 1975), pp. 170–218.

[44] See Davis, *The Problem of Slavery*; and *Slavery and Human Progress*.

trast, the U.S. Constitution had been proposed and defended as a better constitutional process to protect inalienable human rights; but the Constitution had so entrenched southern slaveholding power (through the three-fifths clause)[45] that America was to abolish slavery after a deadly civil war comparatively late (only Brazil[46] and Cuba[47] were later), after even Imperial Russia.[48] The argument might certainly be reasonably made that, in light of the comparative experience of Britain and the United States on the greatest issue of human rights in the nineteenth century, British parliamentary democracy was, on grounds of Lockean political theory, the preferable constitutionalism. America, under this view, had taken a wrong turn in 1776 and 1787, and should now return to the parent constitutionalism it had unwisely rejected.

American revolutionary constitutionalists such as Wilson in 1864 knew that radical changes in American constitutionalism were needed. They framed their task, however, in terms of the various antebellum constitutional theories (see Chapter 3) that had criticized the interpretively mistaken direction in which American constitutionalism had been taken by the politics of Douglas and by the judiciary of Taney. To differing degrees and extents, the constitutional theories of Union, of radical disunion, and of moderate and radical antislavery criticized American constitutionalism both internally and externally. Internal criticism supplied a theory of interpretive mistake in light of which various influential and even authoritative interpretations of the Constitution could be reasonably regarded as wrong and mistaken. Such mistakes included Calhoun's theory of nullification and secession, Douglas's popular sovereignty, and Taney's views in *Dred Scott* of both citizenship and the national powers of Congress in the territories. Both radical disunionism and radical antislavery had questioned the Constitution of 1787 itself: disunionism by attacking it directly as proslavery and thus worthy of revolution, radical antislavery more circuitously by draining the proslavery clauses of their evident historical meaning. Otherwise (in the view of radical antislavery), revolutionary Americans of 1776 and 1787 "would sooner have had it [the Constitution] burned by the hands of the common hangman";[49] and it would have been incumbent on the present generation, when awake to our revolutionary rights of conscience, to demand, in Tiffany's words, *"change or revolution."*[50]

---

[45] On the political importance of the constitutionally enhanced representation of the South on crucial sectional issues, see Dumond, *Antislavery*, pp. 63–75, 106–7.

[46] Slaves in Brazil were emancipated in 1888. See Davis, *Slavery and Human Progress*, pp. 291–98.

[47] Slavery was abolished in Cuba in 1886. See ibid., pp. 285–91.

[48] Serfdom was abolished in Russia in 1861. See, Kolchin, *Unfree Labor.*

[49] See Spooner, *Unconstitutionality*, p. 119.

[50] See Tiffany, *Treatise*, p. 99.

Wilson in 1864, speaking to a nation now alive to its revolutionary rights and responsibilities, made his case for the thirteenth amendment not only on the abstract ground of natural rights, but on the interpretive grounds urged by radical antislavery, namely, the Constitution protected the inalienable rights of conscience, free speech, and assembly of persons against abridgment by the states. Borrowing an argument made by Goodell[51] and clearly stated by Tiffany,[52] Wilson suggested that the supremacy clause[53] and the privileges and immunities clause[54] extended the protections of the first amendment against the states; these protections had been egregiously abridged by the southern states because they were in political thrall to the slave power.

Wilson might have made this argument not as an interpretive one but as a claim of political theory; even if the Constitution did not extend the Bill of Rights to the states, the failure of the states to respect such rights deprived them of Lockean political legitimacy. From the revolutionary perspective of the nation in 1864, slavery should be abolished to remove the main temptation to such political illegitimacy. But Wilson's interpretive stance on the meaning of the Constitution was motivated by exactly what motivated radical antislavery (namely, an interpretation of the Constitution so that it would conform with Lockean political theory). The only difference was that he, unlike them, had behind him "the grand volcanic action"[55] of national revolutionary moral public opinion wrought by the Civil War. From the perspective of such revolutionary constitutionalism, the Constitution, to be worthy of allegiance, must be interpreted in this way, and slavery was to be abolished in order that such interpretive mistake might not recur.

Representative John A. Bingham, the architect of section 1 of the fourteenth amendment, had been a close friend of Joshua Giddings,[56] an important advocate of moderate not radical antislavery. Bingham correspondingly took the road not taken by Wilson, acknowledging more of a gap between political theory and the proper interpretation of the Constitution of 1787 than Wilson conceded. Bingham certainly believed and ar-

[51] See Goodell, *Views*, pp. 75–77.

[52] See Tiffany, *Treatise*, pp. 84–97.

[53] "This Constitution, and the laws of the United States which shall be made in pursuance thereof; and all treaties made, or which shall be made, under the authority of the United States, shall be the supreme law of the land; and the Judges in every State shall be bound thereby, anything in the Constitution or laws of any State to the contrary notwithstanding." U.S. Constitution, Art. VI, cl. 2, cited in Wilson, *Congressional Globe*, 38th Cong., 1st sess., 19 March 1864, p. 1202.

[54] "The citizens of each State shall be entitled to all privileges and immunities of citizens in the several States." U.S. Constitution, Art. IV, sec. 2, cl. 1, cited in ibid., p. 1202.

[55] See ibid., p. 1203.

[56] See Julian, *The Life of Joshua R. Giddings*, pp. 398–99.

gued that, as a matter of political theory, no state had the authority to violate inalienable human rights such as those guaranteed by the first amendment. But in contrast to Wilson, Bingham thought the Constitution, properly interpreted, had applied the standard to the states as a standard that they were to enforce and had not applied the principle against the states by adequate federally enforceable guarantees.

In the debate over the first version of section 1 introduced in the House of Representatives, Bingham pointed, like Wilson, to the supremacy clause and privileges and immunities clause (also the due process clause) as imposing obligations on the states to respect human rights. But "these great provisions of the Constitution, this immortal bill of rights embodied in the Constitution, rested for its execution and enforcement hitherto upon the fidelity of the States."[57] The point of section 1 was, Bingham argued, "to arm the Congress of the United States, by the consent of the people of the United States, with the power to enforce the bill of rights as it stands in the Constitution today,"[58]—that is, to give the federal government adequate power to guarantee respect for human rights by the states.

Bingham recognized as clearly as Wilson the revolutionary character of the constitutional moment. In response to the suggestion that the Congress could not constitutionally approve any amendment in the absence of the southern states from Congress, he noted an analogous argument had been made against the ratification of the Constitution of 1787 on terms forbidden by the Articles of Confederation; the same response applied here as there, namely, "that the right of the people to self-preservation justifies it; it rests upon the transcendent right of nature, and nature's God."[59] But the very legitimacy of the revolutionary moment required, for Bingham, clarity that section 1 of the fourteenth amendment worked revolutionary change, not merely a correction of interpretive mistake.

In the debate over the second version of section 1 introduced in the House,[60] Bingham made clear the gap between political legitimacy and constitutional guarantees that section 1 filled. With respect to political legitimacy: "No State ever had the right, under the forms or law or otherwise,

[57] The version read: "The Congress shall have power to make all laws which shall be necessary and proper to secure to the citizens of each State all privileges and immunities of citizens in the several States, and to all persons in the several States equal protection in the rights of life, liberty, and property." See *Congressional Globe*, 39th Cong., 1st sess., 26 February 1866, p. 1034.

[58] See ibid., 28 February 1866, p. 1088.

[59] See ibid., p. 1089.

[60] The second version read: "No state shall make or enforce any law which shall abridge the privileges or immunities of citizens of the United States; nor shall any State deprive any person of life, liberty, or property without due process of law, nor deny to any person within its jurisdiction the equal protection of the laws." See *Congressional Globe*, 39th Cong., 1st sess., p. 2461.

to deny to any freeman the equal protection of the laws or to abridge the privileges or immunities of any citizen of the Republic, although many of them have assumed and exercised the power, and that without remedy." Section 1 would fill this gap by enabling "the people . . . by express authority of the Constitution to do that by congressional enactment which hitherto they have not had the power to do; that is, to protect by national law the privileges and immunities of all the citizens of the Republic and the inborn rights of every person within its jurisdiction whenever the same shall be abridged or denied by the unconstitutional acts of any State."[61]

Bingham, like Wilson, nonetheless fitted his conception of the need for the Reconstruction Amendments very much within the framework of the principles of American constitutionalism (which section 1 extends in certain required ways). While they disagreed on points of internal criticism that largely reflect interpretive divergences in antebellum abolitionist constitutional theories, they agreed both in the ultimate revolutionary foundations of the amendments and the need—in light of the revolutionary moment—to see the amendments as bringing the Constitution of 1787 unambiguously in line with rights-based political theory.

Analysis of Political Psychology

For the revolutionary Americans of 1776, the betrayal by the British of their own constitutionalism required a complex historical analysis of political power and its corruptibilities. Such investigations led to the pivotal role in American constitutional thought of the theories of faction and of fame.[62] Neither theory rested on ultimate moral skepticism, but rather took seriously facts gathered from the study of comparative political science about political psychology, that is, man's nature in the group psychology characteristic of political life.

The great architects of American constitutionalism, James Madison and John Adams, did not believe, in contrast to Rousseau,[63] that man's political nature would be ethically transformed by the responsibilities of politics under a republican form of government; the political corruptibilities of group psychology in politics would persist, albeit in varying ways, under any form of politics, including republican politics. The task of an enlightened constitutionalism was to use these facts of political psychology in the design of constitutional institutions that, consistent with democratic rights

[61] See Representative Bingham, 39th Cong., 1st sess., 10 May 1966, p. 2542.

[62] For fuller discussion, see Richards, *Foundations*, pp. 32–39, 49–55.

[63] For an extended exploration of this comparison, see Richards, "Revolution and Constitutionalism in America and France," *University of Mississippi Law Journal* 60, no. 2 (Fall 1990): 311.

of voting and participation, would channel and structure republican political power in ways more likely to secure respect for inalienable human rights and the use of political power for the public good.

Madison in particular had anatomized the political psychology of faction acutely as a form of group identification and insularity that could corrupt conscience itself, respect for which was the foundation of inalienable human rights. Moreover, he had suggested two elaborations of the theory of faction that would be central to the thinking of the revolutionary constitutionalists of 1865 (see Chapter 2). First, Madison worried in his despairing October 24, 1787, letter to Jefferson that the Constitution of 1787 had not taken sufficient account of the need for national constitutional structures (such as a congressional veto over state laws) that might address what had proven under the Articles of Confederation to be the worst form of political pathology, namely, state factions. Second, Madison identified group political psychology based on race as one of the worst forms of faction—"the most oppressive dominion ever exercised by man over man."[64] To a remarkable degree, the thought on political psychology of the proponents of the Reconstruction Amendments worked within and analytically elaborated the framework of Madison's thought about these factions.

Proponents of the Reconstruction Amendments took different views of where the Constitution had gone wrong, some, such as Wilson, emphasizing interpretive mistakes, others, such as Bingham, focusing on foundational mistakes in institutional design. But they all shared the common interest, central to American revolutionary constitutionalism, of both understanding the nature of the political psychology that had led to the American revolutionary crisis of constitutional legitimacy and the framing of a constitutionalism adequate to this analysis.

Such an analysis had two components, one normative, the other empirical. The normative component rested on the central principles of political legitimacy—in particular, respect for inalienable human rights. The empirical component examined the main political threats to which various rights tended to be subject. In Lockean constitutional thought, religious persecution was a paradigm example of such a faction, and the argument for toleration correspondingly had both a normative and an empirical component to explain its nature and its appropriate constitutional remedy. The normative component was the inalienable right to conscience and the kind of justification for public power that it required; the empirical component was the political enforcement at large of sectarian views that both corrupted reasonable standards of critical inquiry and deprived persons of their moral powers to make such inquiries. Both components were crucial to the analysis of each of the factions central to the design of the Reconstruction

---

[64] Farrand, *The Records of the Federal Convention of 1787*, 1:134 (speech of 6 June 1787).

Amendments, namely, the slave power and irrational race prejudice (or racism).

The idea of a slave power was a central contribution of political abolitionism to antebellum moral and constitutional debate (see Chapter 3). Its normative component was defined by the unjustifiable abridgments of inalienable human rights required to maintain and expand the political power of the defenders of slavery; its empirical component was the political enforcement on society at large of sectarian moral and constitutional views that crippled reasonable standards of debate and deprived persons of their rights of personal and moral self-government. I have already cited at some length the most brilliant expression of this analysis in the congressional debates on the Reconstruction Amendments, James Wilson's speech proposing a thirteenth amendment to the House of Representatives.

Wilson's discussion of the unjustified abridgment by southern states of the inalienable rights of conscience, free speech, and assembly was offered by him as part of his larger analysis of the political faction that had grown up around the defense and expansion of slavery as an institution. The faction was identified as such both by its normative abridgment of the rights of all persons (slave and free) to conscience, free speech, and assembly and by its increasingly parochial and insular modes of essentially sectarian argument in terms of which such abridgments were thought to be justified. The distorted uses to which the Constitution of 1787 had been put in the antebellum period were then explained in terms of the political power that this faction had achieved under and in the name of the Constitution (for example, in *Dred Scott*).

Wilson argued that the Founders had also recognized the evil of slavery, but they mistakenly thought an institution "so directly opposed to justice, so distinctly arrayed against divine law, so utterly depraved and desperately wicked . . . would speedily accomplish its dissolution."[65] Experience had proven them tragically wrong; an institution such as slavery, itself based on the abridgment of human rights, had given rise to a political faction, precisely within the terms of Madison's theory, "a number of citizens . . . who are united and actuated by some common impulse of passion, or of interest, adverse to the rights of others citizens, or to the permanent and aggregate interests of the community."[66] This political faction, united by its economic interests in slavery as an institution, had abused the constitutional protections accorded slavery not to end it, but to entrench and extend it on terms that required further violations of inalienable human rights of conscience, free speech, and assembly. If Madison had thought that the representational political power accorded the South under the

---

[65] See Wilson, *Congressional Globe*, 38th Cong., 1st sess., 19 March 1864, p. 1203.
[66] See James Madison, *The Federalist No. 10*, p. 57.

Constitution would be used more reasonably to secure the abolition of slavery in the long term (see Chapter 2), he was tragically wrong.

The Constitution of 1787, designed to channel both faction and fame in service of a republican political theory of respecting rights and pursuit of the public good, was in this case itself responsible for the growth and effective political power of a pathological faction that had undermined its political legitimacy. The political science of the Founders, so wisely skeptical about the corruptibilities of political power, had recognized its corruption even of conscience itself; and thus the principle of toleration of the first amendment had removed from national power altogether the force of sectarian factions that threatened the very foundations of political legitimacy. But they had failed to act on the insight, so worrying to Madison, that the same argument applied at the state level.

As abolitionist criticism made clear, state-supported slavery, like religious persecution, had been in its nature corruptive even of conscience itself and thus could not be regarded as a normal form of political faction whose temptations to radical evil could be ameliorated and compromised by democratic politics. The theory of the slave power thus rested on the abolitionist argument about the radical and incommensurable republican evil of slavery. It drew from that normative argument an explanation of the nation's political and constitutional decadence, one that Lincoln brilliantly articulated for the American public mind in the Lincoln-Douglas debates. A constitution, structuring political power to respect rights and the public good, could not, Wilson argued in light of American experience, accord political power to the radical republican evil of slavery without undermining its own legitimacy. Indeed, as history had shown, the radical political evil of the institution, once accorded any constitutional protection at all, had gradually subverted constitutionalism itself. A legitimate constitutionalism and slavery could not coexist.

The abolition of slavery gave rise to a related elaboration of the theory of faction, namely, concern for the faction of irrational race prejudice. As we have seen, the Confederacy had been justified by its vice-president, Alexander Stephens, on the grounds of "the great truth, that the negro is not equal to the white man; that slavery—subordination to the superior race—is his natural and normal condition."[67] The force of this theory was so strong in the Confederacy that, in its dying days when leaders such as Jefferson Davis and General Lee urged the use of blacks in southern armies, its Congress refused. Davis acidly observed, "If the Confederacy falls, there should be written on its tombstone, 'Died of a theory.'"[68] The

[67] See Stephens, "Sketch of the Corner-Stone Speech," in Cleveland, *Alexander H. Stephens*, p. 721.

[68] Cited in Davis, *Rise and Fall*, 1: 443.

abolition of slavery did not morally transform the popularity in the South of the views defended by Stephens in 1861 and still powerful enough to die for near the end of the war; it gave new opportunities for their political perpetuation in the southern Black Codes designed, on racial grounds, to deprive the freedmen of rights.

Senator Trumbull, in proposing national legislation (eventually to be the Civil Rights Act of 1866) to strike down these laws, described the Black Codes:

> They provide that if any colored person, any free negro or mulatto, shall come into that State for the purpose of residing there, he shall be sold into slavery for life. If any person of African descent residing in the State travels from one county to another without having a pass or a certificate of his freedom, he is liable to be committed to jail and to be dealt with as a person who is in the State without authority . . . and one provision of the statute declares that for "exercising the functions of a minister of the Gospel free negroes and mulattoes, on conviction, may be punished by any number of lashes not exceeding thirty-nine on the bare back, and shall pay the costs." . . . The statutes of South Carolina make it a highly penal offense for any person, white or colored, to teach slaves.[69]

Trumbull argued that the enforcement clause of the thirteenth amendment conferred power on Congress to pass this legislation. But some Republicans, notably John A. Bingham[70] (opposed, strikingly, by James Wilson),[71] argued that the application of such legislation nationwide required a constitutional amendment. The fourteenth amendment was proposed and approved in part to quiet any constitutional doubts about national power to enforce such legislation.[72]

Section 1 of the fourteenth amendment reads:

> All persons born or naturalized in the United States, and subject to the jurisdiction thereof, are citizens of the United States and of the State wherein they reside. No State shall make or enforce any law which shall abridge the privileges or immunities of citizens of the United States; nor shall any State deprive any person of life, liberty, or property, with due process of law; nor deny to any person within its jurisdiction the equal protection of the laws.[73]

[69] See Senator Lyman Trumbull, *Congressional Globe*, 39th Cong., 1st sess., 29 January 1866, p. 474.

[70] See Representative Bingham, *Congressional Globe*, 39th Cong., 1st sess., 9 March 1866, pp. 1291–92.

[71] See Wilson, *Congressional Globe*, 38th Cong., 1st sess., 19 March 1864, pp. 1294–95.

[72] See Flack, *The Adoption of the Fourteenth Amendment*; James, *The Framing of the Fourteenth Amendment*.

[73] U.S. Constitution, Amendment XIV, sec. 1.

Its citizenship clause constitutionalized the once radical abolitionist argument that persons subject to political power should be citizens; and its remaining clauses constitutionalized the related radical abolitionist argument of Lockean political theory that all such persons should be guaranteed equal protection of their basic rights as the reasonable reciprocal condition of the duties of allegiance.

Its clear constitutional legitimation of the Civil Rights Act of 1866 was pointed to by Senator Howard, introducing the amendment in the Senate, in terms that reveal concern for the faction of race prejudice:

> This abolishes all class legislation in the States and does away with the injustice of subjecting one caste of persons to a code not applicable to another. It prohibits the hanging of a black man for a crime for which the white man is not to be hanged. It protects the black man in his fundamental rights as a citizen with the same shield which it throws over the white man. Is it not time, Mr. President, that we extend to the black man, I had almost call it the poor privilege of the equal protection of the law?[74]

In light of the experience of the Civil War, Republicans had come to regard "prejudice against race," of the sort clearly articulated in Stephens's defense, as irrational and unjust.[75] Its expression through laws such as the southern Black Codes was for this reason unconstitutional under section 1 of the fourteenth amendment and thus within the power of Congress to strike down under section 5, the enforcement clause of the amendment.

Of course, the Republicans, who agreed that racial prejudice was irrational, had a range of varying views about what counted as unreasonable race prejudice and thus how the concept should be interpreted and applied.[76] But in light of antebellum mainstream views on racial questions both in the North and the South, the identification of racial prejudice (or racism) as a faction at all confirms the remarkable impact on public constitutional thought of the Civil War. Prior to the war, only some of the abolitionists had generated any views critical of American racism as such (see Chapter 3). The same constitutional analysis of the antebellum period that had led to the theory of the slave power evolved—under the impact of the Civil War, abolition, and the southern reaction—into the theory of racism as a political faction; that analysis, of course, had direct antebellum antecedents in abolitionist moral and political thought.

The underlying analysis tracked rather exactly the comparable analysis

[74] See Senator Howard, *Congressional Globe*, 39th Cong., 1st sess. 23 May 1866, p. 2766.

[75] See Senator Henderson, *Congressional Globe*, 39th Cong., 1st sess., 8 June 1866, p. 2034 (citing and discussing Stephens). For the generality of the view, see Nelson, *The Fourteenth Amendment*, pp. 124–25.

[76] See, e.g., Nelson, *The Fourteenth Amendment*, pp. 133 (antimiscegenation laws), 133–36 (state-sponsored racial segregation).

of the slave power, from which it derived. The normative component of the analysis was the abridgment of rights of the person by institutions and practices such as slavery and racial discrimination. Such practices had not only been immunized from impartial criticism and assessment, but unjustly fostered the kinds of cultural differences (now interpreted as natural) on the basis of which subjugation and discrimination were ostensibly justified. The empirical component illustrated the paradox of intolerance so clearly displayed in American antebellum politics. An intolerant exclusion of a racial minority from the political community immunized itself from reasonable criticism by manufacturing a conception of national identity, as intrinsically racial, based on irrationalist distortion of fact and history (see *Dred Scott* and Stephens's defense of Confederate national identity). Racist degradation could, no more than slavery or religious intolerance, be permitted political expression if American revolutionary constitutionalism was, in light of experience, to forge a constitutionalism that was politically legitimate.

All these themes were forcefully analyzed in Senator Charles Sumner's long speech in the Senate of February 5–6, 1866, later published as *The Equal Rights of All*.[77] Sumner's aim was, even without constitutional amendments such as the fourteenth and fifteenth, constitutionally to defend the extension of the franchise to black Americans by national law on the ground of the guarantee clause and the enforcement clause of the thirteenth amendment. He put his argument in terms of an American revolutionary constitutionalism, derived from Locke, that self-consciously united the revolutionaries of 1776 and 1866. American revolutionaries such as Otis and constitutionalists such as Madison (citing Madison on racism as the worst faction) had recognized the claims of blacks to equal inalienable rights. The recent abolition of slavery had, however, unleashed on the freedmen the hatred of an embittered South.[78] It was now incumbent on American revolutionary constitutionalists to accord them adequate protections against this vicious form of faction.

Sumner directly analogized race hatred to a kind of religious persecution:

---

[77] See Charles Sumner, *The Equal Rights of All: The Great Guaranty and Present Necessity for the Sake of Security, and to Maintain a Republican Government*, reprinted in Sumner, *Complete Works*, 13:115–269. Sumner's speech was actually offered in opposition to what he took to be the inadequacies of the fourteenth amendment (in particular, its failure to extend the franchise to the freedmen), and was bitterly resented by other Republicans for failure to support the great practical advance that the fourteenth amendment represented: securing the freedmen's rights. The speech's general analysis of issues of principle was, nonetheless, admired even by those Republicans, such as Representative Dawes, who condemned Sumner's failure to apply the principles properly to the current situation. See David Donald, *Charles Sumner and the Rights of Man* (New York: Knopf, 1970), p. 246.

[78] See Sumner, *The Equal Rights of All*, in Sumner, *Complete Works*, 13:215–19, 155, 156, 158, 159, 164, 180, 131–32, 222–23.

It is nothing less than a caste, which is irreligious as well as unrepublican. A caste exists only in defiance of the first principles of Christianity and the first principles of a republic. It is heathenism in religion and tyranny in government. The Brahmins and the Sudras in India, from generation to generation, have been separated, as the two races are still separated in these States. If a Sudra presumed to sit on a Brahmin's carpet, he was punished with banishment. But our recent Rebels undertake to play the part of Brahmins, and exclude citizens, with better title than themselves, from essential rights, simply on the ground of caste, which, according to its Portuguese origin (*casta*), is only another term for race.[79]

The constitutional task before us, Sumner concluded, was to ensure that the Constitution would never again be distorted by "the Gospel according to Calhoun," namely, "that this august Republic, founded to sustain the rights of Human Nature, is nothing but 'a white man's government.'" Constitutional interpretation must recover its roots in ethical impartiality: "The promises of the Fathers must be sacredly fulfilled. This is the commanding rule, superseding all other rules. This is a great victory of the war,—perhaps the greatest. It is nothing less than the emancipation of the Constitution itself."[80]

Comparative Political Science

American revolutionary constitutionalism in 1787 was acutely self-conscious of its repudiation of the utility of classical republican models for the task of designing an enduring constitution for a commercial republic in a large territory committed to respect for human rights.[81] No American constitutionalist was a more profound student of the differences between ancient and modern republics or used it to more brilliant effect than James Madison in *The Federalist No. 10*. Madison did not draw explicit attention, however, to an implicit aspect of the contrast, namely, the central role of slavery in the ancient republics and its disfavored and hopefully declining status in a commercial republic committed to human rights.

The contrast, however, became absolutely central to the antebellum constitutional theories—in particular, those of Union and of moderate and radical antislavery—whose thought culminated in the Reconstruction Amendments. As we saw in Chapter 2, southern proslavery constitutional theory had, since Calhoun, embraced the ancient slave republics of Greece and Rome as models for its own conception of national identity, emphasizing heroism and imperialistic expansion led by a class accorded by slavery the

---

[79] See ibid., 13:210–11.

[80] See ibid., 13:234–35, 219.

[81] For fuller discussion, see Richards, *Foundations*, pp. 39–49, 55–64.

time and incentive to pursue public excellence and glory. Antislavery constitutional theory properly saw such southern theory as deeply anachronistic and fundamentally hostile, as it was, to both the political science and political and economic philosophy of Madisonian constitutionalism. Lincoln's clear articulation of discordant principles that doom the house divided made this point eloquently;[82] and leading social theorists of the age (John Stuart Mill[83] and Karl Marx)[84] used the same idea later to argue that the defeat of the South was necessary in the worldwide struggle for the advance of progressive values of modernity against a reactionary historicism. All the major proponents of radical antislavery—Goodell,[85] Spooner,[86] and Tiffany[87]—made the same point in the form of arguments based on the guarantee clause: that slavery was antirepublican. And Theodore Parker published a particularly well-argued form of the theory in 1858,[88] which much influenced Senator Charles Sumner, among others.[89]

Consistent with his views of Bible interpretation in light of values of ethical impartiality, Parker argued that the constitutional conception of American democracy—"government over all, by all, and for the sake of all"— must be best interpreted in terms of its background theory of the protection of inalienable human rights. Such rights were "founded not on Facts of Observation in Human History, but on Facts of Consciousness in human Nature itself." The constitutional conception of a republic in the guarantee clause must be interpreted in the same way that "the Somerset case" had construed British common law to invalidate slavery:

> There must be a Progressive Interpretation of many institutions and statutes. Thus the Common Law of England did not change, but ship-money became illegal; and slavery perished by interpretation. No number of decisions by learned Judges, no royal usage, no popular acquiescence for centuries, could withstand the demand for natural Justice made by the increased knowledge, virtue and humanity of the progressive People.[90]

For Parker, the interpretation of a written constitution such as that of

---

[82] See Abraham Lincoln, "'House Divided' Speech at Springfield, Illinois," delivered 16 June 1858, in Fehrenbacher, *Abraham Lincoln: Speeches and Writings, 1858–1865,* pp. 434.

[83] See John Stuart Mill, "The Contest in America" (1862) in Freidel, *Union Pamphlets,* 1:326–44.

[84] See Karl Marx, *On America and the Civil War,* ed. Saul K. Padover, (New York: McGraw-Hill, 1972).

[85] See Goodell, *Views,* pp. 44–47.

[86] See Spooner, *Unconstitutionality,* pp. 105–14.

[87] See Tiffany, *Treatise,* pp. 107–14.

[88] See Parker, *Relation of Slavery.*

[89] See Trefousse, *The Radical Republicans,* p. 267.

[90] See Parker, *Relation of Slavery,* pp. 5, 9, 11, 14.

the United States must make the best sense of the text in terms of a progressive understanding of human rights and the public interest in contemporary circumstances; such an interpretive attitude must ascribe to the text an abstract normative concept, sensitive to such a progressive understanding, and cannot for this reason anachronistically be reduced to how its Founders may have understood its concrete meaning in their circumstances. The classical republics were a radically inapposite precedent for the interpretation of the American republic because the American Constitution was, in contrast to the classical republics, clearly based on the protection of inalienable human rights:

> A constitutional representative Democracy did not exist in the old times. . . .
> I know there are men in Virginia and South Carolina, who quote Aristotle and
> Cicero in favor of American slavery; they seem to have read the translations
> of these authors only to get arguments against the Natural Rights of Mankind.
> Similar men have studied the Old Testament but to find out that Abraham
> was a slaveholder, that Moses authorized bondage; they have read the New
> only to find divine inspiration in the words of Paul, which they wrest into this:
> "Slaves, obey your masters!"[91]

The best interpretation of the guarantee clause, understood to be founded on the protection of basic human rights, now conferred power on Congress to abolish slavery in the states.

In the antebellum period, the conflicting constitutional interpretations of American republican government of a Calhoun and a Parker sketched out, to borrow Anne Norton's phrase, alternative Americas[92]—one nostalgic for the glories of the ancient world, the other committed to a self-consciously progressive conception of human rights. After the Civil War, Americans had to make the best sense they could of earlier events in light of the revolutionary constitutionalism to which the war had given rise. That perspective explains why the Reconstruction Congress chose Parker's alternative reading of America not only by adopting, as we have seen, the guarantee clause as the theory of reconstruction, but by taking the kind of interpretive and critical stance on American constitutionalism in general that his approach called for.

Parker had written of "a progressive demoralization of the Constitution,"[93] pointing, as Lincoln also did in his debates with Douglas, to both the politics of Douglas and the judiciary of Taney. Such interpretive distortion was a central concern of the revolutionary constitutionalists of 1865. Not all of them agreed with Charles Sumner's earlier discussed expansive

---

[91] See ibid., pp. 10–11, 14.

[92] See Anne Norton, *Alternative Americas: A Reading of Antebellum Political Culture* (Chicago: University of Chicago Press, 1986).

[93] See Parker, *Relation of Slavery*, p. 15.

reading of the guarantee clause (making unnecessary the fourteenth and fifteenth amendments). But Sumner provided a plausible metainterpretive analysis of how the demoralization of constitutional interpretation had taken place. The problem in both Bible and constitutional interpretation, Sumner argued, was that the sectarian conviction of the moral validity of slavery determined interpretation; textual authority for slavery and discrimination were only found "because they have first secured a license in his own soul."[94] Nothing in the text of the Constitution compelled Calhoun or Taney to read the Constitution in the positivistic way they did (Calhoun in terms of state sovereignty, Taney in terms of historical positivism). Rather, each brought to the Constitution a rights skepticism that distorted interpretation to protect fixed positions devoted to sectional interests. The only prophylaxis against the recurrence of such interpretive distortion was to demand that "from this time forward it [the Constitution] must be interpreted in harmony with the Declaration of Independence, so that Human Rights shall always prevail."[95]

American Political Experience

Americans had tested their constitutional minds in 1787 not only against comparative political science, but against their own democratic experience both before the revolution as colonies and after the revolution in a wide range of constitutional experiments at the state level and the Articles of Confederation at the national level. The 1787 Convention was motivated by the conviction that these experiments, state and federal, had not respected the principles of legitimacy they had invoked as revolutionaries against the British Constitution. The Constitution of 1787 accordingly transferred much political power from the states to the national government in order to render its exercise more legitimate.

I have already made reference to Madison's concern that, consistent with the theory of faction, sufficient constitutional power had not been accorded the national government to moderate the malign insularity and parochialism of state factions. American political experience during the antebellum period confirmed the wisdom of Madison's fears, and that experience played a central role in the deliberations on the Reconstruction Amendments. Such state factions had not only, as we have seen, distorted the interpretation of the Constitution itself, but had flagrantly violated without remedy their constitutional obligations both under the federal and their own state constitutions.

---

[94] See Charles Sumner, "The Antislavery Enterprise," in Sumner, *Complete Works*, 5:20. See also Charles Sumner, "The Barbarism of Slavery," in *Complete Works*, 6:223–27.

[95] See Sumner, *The Equal Rights of All*, in Sumner, *Complete Works*, 13:219.

The indictment of the slave power made both points. The slave power, operating in the states without federally enforceable constraints on it, had abridged basic inalienable human rights such as those to conscience, speech, and assembly, rights ostensibly guaranteed by the state constitutions. It had abridged as well rights guaranteed at the federal level. For example, constitutional rights of blacks and whites under the privileges and immunities clause had been violated;[96] and the rights of abolitionists to use the federal mails under the first amendment had been abridged, as well as their right to petition the Congress for redress of grievances.[97] From the perspective of Lockean political theory, all forms of political power—federal and state—must respect rights and pursue the public good; indeed, the Constitution had been justified in 1787 in such terms. Political experience over time had decisively shown that the Constitution had not only failed to meet these tests; its constitutional protection of slavery had led to the Constitution itself becoming an interpretive sword and shield for the aggressive violation of inalienable human rights.

The last chapter in this declension of the Constitution from its background republican morality was the appeal to the Constitution itself by the South as a justification for secession and civil war. Such southern proslavery constitutionalism had become a just object of the right to revolution on behalf of the Union (see Chapter 3). The task now—in the wake of the success of the revolution—was to preserve America's newly recovered revolutionary constitutionalism in a constitutionalism that would profit from America's bitter antebellum political experience of the devastating and malign consequences of a defective constitutionalism.

Constitutional Justification and Community

The deliberative procedures of both ratification and amendment of the U.S. Constitution marked its distinctive status as supreme law over all other law that was the product of ordinary politics. These procedures were an original contribution of the American Founders to constitutional thought and practice; their distinctive institutional procedures more closely approximated what Locke regarded as necessary to the legitimacy of any government,

---

[96] On South Carolina's exclusion of black sailors, see Freehling, *Prelude to Civil War*, pp. 111–16, 206–7; on the case of Prudence Crandall, who had been forbidden by Connecticut state law from teaching free blacks, see Hyman and Wiecek, *Equal Justice under Law*, pp. 94–95; for Chief Justice Taney on the issue of blacks having no status to claim protection under the privileges and immunities clause, see *Dred Scott*, pp. 404–5, 414–15, 416–17, 422–23.

[97] See Nye, *Fettered Freedom*.

namely, that the government must be reasonably acceptable to all as a protection of their inalienable human rights.[98]

Locke supposed that government could only feasibly be formed by the political decision procedure of majority rule.[99] But the American Founders—well familiar with the oppressions of majority rule in ordinary politics—innovated special procedures of constitutional ratification and amendment that would, as political decision procedures, more plausibly bear the interpretation of being reasonably acceptable to all in the required way. Constitutional law would be authoritatively supreme over all other law because it had been and would continue to be (if properly interpreted) subjected to more demanding and stringent tests (than other laws) of ultimate political legitimacy, namely, that it was reasonably justifiable to all as protecting rights and advancing the public interests of all alike.

The nature of constitutional ratification and interpretation had been one of the central items of interpretive controversy in the antebellum period between southern proslavery theories and the constitutional theory of Union (see Chapter 2). Southern advocates of the compact theory, as early as St. George Tucker in 1803 and as late as Alexander Stephens in 1868, had given ratification a positivistic interpretation, putting decisive weight on ratification by separate states, not by vote of the people as a whole. This was evidence of the ultimacy of state sovereignty with the interpretive consequences southern theorists variously drew from that fact: the narrow construction of national powers in favor of the broad reserved powers of the states. Proponents of the theory of Union (notably, Justice Story) emphasized, in contrast, the crucial significance of ratification by separately elected constitutional conventions wholly independent of the standing state governments. Story argued that such a historically unique procedure must be interpreted—consistent with the most natural reading of the words of the Preamble ("We, the People")—to rest the authority of the Constitution directly on the rights of the people that the Constitution preserved, protected, and defended against all governments, state and federal. Accordingly, the Constitution was to be interpreted to affirm a broad national power to protect such rights of the person.

The disagreement was not over facts, but an interpretive one that appealed, at bottom, to different understandings of how the Constitution should be interpreted in light of political theory, Lockean or otherwise. Calhoun's rights skepticism directly shaped his way of reading the relevant materials; other southern theorists, who accepted rights-based political theories (Tucker, Taylor of Caroline, Stephens), thought of such rights as best ultimately defended by state institutions and construed ratification and

---

[98] For further discussion, see Richards, *Foundations*, pp. 78–97, 140–42.
[99] See ibid., pp. 87–88.

constitutional interpretation accordingly. Proponents of the theory of Union identified the nation as the best ultimate vehicle for the articulation and enforcement of human rights, and thus thought of ratification and constitutional interpretation in the way they did.

From the perspective of the constitutional revolutionaries of 1865, the constitutional procedures of ratification and amendment were properly interpreted in terms of the theory of Union; and that carried with it a comparable view of constitutional interpretation. At the beginning of the Civil War, Lincoln,[100] Francis Lieber,[101] Edward Everett,[102] and Joel Parker[103] had all justified resistance to secession on grounds of the constitutional theory of Union. By the end of the war, the self-conscious constitutional revolutionaries of 1865 had to interpret the antebellum period and the Civil War itself in light of both the theory of Union and the moderate and radical antislavery views to which they increasingly turned to make sense of their responsibilities of constitutional reconstruction.

In terms of these views, secession and civil war by the southern states confirmed their antirepublican character. These states had obdurately refused to respect the inalienable right to freedom of their slaves and the rights of freemen to basic rights such as conscience and free speech. Finally, they made war on national institutions precisely because the ultimate moral and constitutional responsibility of the Union was to secure the equal rights of all. In such circumstances, procedures of constitutional amendment, themselves rooted in Lockean political theory, must be interpreted in light of both the guarantee clause and the background Lockean political theory of the Constitution (see Chapter 1). On the former ground, Congress could reasonably interpret its powers under the guarantee clause to secure a Union of republican states. Constitutional amendments might thus be proposed to ensure republican governments in the South; and Congress might reasonably exclude nonrepublican southern states from their constitutional position in the Union until they agreed to and conformed with the amendments. And on grounds of political theory, the Civil War had ultimately been politically justified on the basis of the revolutionary right of a people to recover its inalienable rights—both those of blacks and whites—from their political oppressors (who had dominated southern politics). The constitutionalism that gave ultimate vindication to that revolutionary right could not justifiably allow the oppressors to determine its terms. In light

[100] See Lincoln, "First Inaugural Address," in Fehrenbacher, *Abraham Lincoln: Speeches and Writings, 1858–1865*, pp. 217–18.

[101] See Lieber, "What Is Our Constitution—League, Pact, or Government?" in Lieber, *Miscellaneous Writings*, 2:87–136.

[102] See Edward Everett, "The Causes and Conduct of the Civil War" (1861), reprinted in Edward Everett, *Orations and Speeches* (Boston: Little, Brown, 1862), pp. 464–90.

[103] See Joel Parker, "The Right of Secession" (1861), in Freidel, *Union Pamphlets* 1:55–85.

of the events of the Civil War, it would not be reasonable to interpret the procedure of constitutional amendment, clearly meant to express the requirements of Lockean political legitimacy, to frustrate amendments that, for the first time in American history, permitted the Constitution to be justified to all as politically legitimate.

The Reconstruction Amendments were, in fact, the product of the most profound deliberation on American constitutionalism, from the perspective of its background political theory, since the Constitutional Convention of 1787. They reflect, in much more direct textual fashion than the Constitution of 1787, the impact of that political theory. The impact of political theory is evident both in the substantive terms of the amendments (in particular, those of the fourteenth) and in the national institutions accorded the central role in the interpretation and enforcement of those terms.

Both the citizenship clause[104] and the privileges and immunities clause[105] of the fourteenth amendment derived from the requirements of Lockean political theory that all persons in a political community sharing its benefits and burdens have a right to be treated as citizens and as equals with respect for their inalienable human rights. Weld had, of course, stated the argument as the basis for his criticism of American slavery, and Tiffany had put it in the form of a radical antislavery interpretation of the Constitution of 1787. The fourteenth amendment unambiguously constitutionalized these arguments on the Lockean terms of the respect for rights required, as Bingham put it, "to bear true allegiance to the Constitution and laws of the United States."[106] The textual adoption of the birthright theory of American citizenship must be understood against the background of the clear moral right of black Americans to be treated as citizens under a Lockean theory of justice[107] and the authoritative interpretation of the Constitution of 1787 to the contrary in *Dred Scott*. And the privileges and immunities clause extended to all citizens the protection of their basic human rights that is the very test, on Lockean grounds, of the legitimacy of any political power at all.

The revolutionary constitutionalists of 1865 clearly thought that the

---

[104] "All persons born or naturalized in the United States, and subject to the jurisdiction thereof, are citizens of the United States and of the State wherein they reside." U.S. Constitution, Amendment XIV, sec. 1.

[105] "No State shall make or enforce any law which shall abridge the privileges or immunities of citizens of the United States." U.S. Constitution, Amendment XIV, sec. 1.

[106] See Representative Bingham, *Congressional Globe*, 39th Cong., 1st sess., 10 May 1866, p. 2542.

[107] For an excellent study of various theories of American citizenship, see James H. Kettner, *The Development of American Citizenship, 1608–1870* (Chapel Hill: University of North Carolina Press, 1978). For a Lockean interpretation of the citizenship clause that controversially excludes illegal aliens, see Peter H. Schuck and Rogers M. Smith, *Citizenship without Consent: Illegal Aliens in the American Polity* (New Haven: Yale University Press, 1985).

terms of an amendment such as the fourteenth resulted from an assessment of the 1787 Constitution in light of such political theory. It is the theory Bingham assumed when he insisted that the fourteenth amendment "takes from no State any right that ever pertained to it. No State ever had the right, under the forms of law or otherwise to deny to any freeman the equal protection of the laws or to abridge the privileges or immunities of any citizen of the Republic, although many of them have assumed and exercised that power, and that without remedy."[108] The working assumption of the Constitution of 1787 had been that states could largely be depended on not to violate inalienable human rights. As Madison anticipated, the assumption proved false; and amendments were needed to ensure that this gaping lacuna of political legitimacy was filled.

The privileges and immunities clause extended to all American citizens federal protection of their inalienable human rights from abridgment by the states, the main source of the abuse of human rights in the antebellum period. The language of the clause, adapted from that of the privileges and immunities clause of Article IV,[109] reflected the interpretation of the latter as protecting what Bingham called "the inborn rights of every person."[110]

The clause of Article IV, sometimes called the comity clause, required each state to guarantee citizens of other states "all privileges and immunities of citizens in the several states." That phrase was ambiguous; it could extend only to such rights as a state in fact extended to its own citizens, or it could set a substantive standard of basic human rights owed to all citizens as such.

Bingham clearly interpreted the phrase in the latter way.[111] On this view, the privileges and immunities clause of the fourteenth amendment protected all human rights of citizens of the United States from abridgment by the states. Bingham's interpretation of Article IV reflected the construction of the clause given by Justice Bushrod Washington in *Corfield v. Coryell.*[112]

[108] See Representative Bingham, *Congressional Globe*, 39th Cong., 1st sess., 10 May 1866, p. 2542.

[109] "The citizens of each State shall be entitled to all privileges and immunities of citizens in the several States." U.S. Constitution, Art. IV, sec. 2, cl. 1.

[110] See Representative Bingham, *Congressional Globe*, 39th Cong., 1st sess., 10 May 1866, p. 2542.

[111] For Bingham's earlier expressed views to the same effect, see John A. Bingham, "The Constitution of the United States and the Proslavery Provisions of the 1857 Oregon Constitution" (delivered in the House of Representatives in 1859), in tenBroek, *Equal under Law*, pp. 321–41. Bingham said of the comity clause: "There is an ellipsis in the language employed in the Constitution, but its meaning is self-evident that it is 'the privileges and immunities of citizens of the United States in the several States' that it guaranties" (p. 333). He later specified these rights as "the equality of all to the right to live; to the right to know; to argue and to utter, according to conscience; to work and enjoy the project of their toil" (pp. 339–40).

[112] 6 Fed. Cases 546 (No. 3,230) C.C.N.J. (1823).

Indeed, relevant sections of Washington's opinion were cited to this effect by Senator Trumbull in the debates over the Civil Rights Act of 1866[113] and Senator Howard upon introducing the fourteenth amendment in the Senate.[114] Justice Washington had interpreted the clause in terms of the rights of American citizens as such: "We feel no hesitation in confining these expressions to those privileges and immunities which are, in their nature, fundamental; which belong, of right, to the citizens of all free governments."[115] As we have seen, Bingham referred to these as "the inborn rights of every person" and cited the prohibition on cruel and unusual punishments in the eighth amendment as an example.[116] Senator Howard in the Senate, after quoting *Corfield* on the nature of these rights, went on:

> To these privileges and immunities, whatever they may be—for they are and cannot be fully defined in their entire extent and precise nature—to these should be added the personal rights guarantied and secured by the first eight amendments of the Constitution; such as the freedom of speech and of the press; the right of the people peaceably to assemble and petition the Government for a redress of grievances, a right appertaining to each and all the people; the right to keep and to bear arms; the right to be exempted from the quartering of soldiers in a house without the consent of the owner; the right to be exempt from unreasonable searches and seizures, and from any search or seizure except by virtue of a warrant issued upon a formal oath or affidavit; the right of an accused person to be informed of the nature of the accusation against him, and his right to be tried by an impartial jury of the vicinage; and also the right to be secure against excessive bail and against cruel and unusual punishments.
>
> Now, sir, here is a mass of privileges, immunities, and rights, some of them secured by the second section of the fourth article of the Constitution, which I have recited, some by the first eight amendments of the Constitution; and it is a fact well worthy of attention that the course of decision of our courts and the present settled doctrine is, that all these immunities, privileges, rights, thus guarantied by the Constitution or recognized by it, are secured to the citizen solely as a citizen of the United States and as a party in their courts.[117]

It cannot do interpretive justice to the evident political theory that motivated the privileges and immunities clause to reduce it to the terms of

---

[113] See Trumbull, *Congressional Globe*, 39th Cong., 1st sess., 29 January 1866, p. 475.
[114] See Howard, *Congressional Globe*, 39th Cong., 1st sess., 28 May 1866, p. 2765.
[115] *Corfield*, p. 551.
[116] See Bingham, *Congressional Globe*, 39th Cong., 1st sess., 10 May 1866, p. 2542.
[117] See Howard, *Congressional Globe*, 39th Cong., 1st sess., 28 May 1866, p. 2765.

the incorporation debate between Justice Black[118] and Charles Fairman.[119] Fairman's cavalier attribution of confusion to a Bingham reflects less on Bingham than on Fairman's inability to take seriously the political theory Bingham propounded as the justification for extending a guarantee of basic rights against the states. Similarly, Justice Black's positivistic appeal to Senator Howard's illustrations does not engage Howard's essentially interpretive judgment of the basic rights that must, consistent with Lockean political theory, be secured to all as a condition of the legitimacy of political power. The privileges and immunities clause, so clearly based on political theory, must be interpreted in light of such theory (for further discussion, see Chapter 6).

The Constitution of 1787 had left interpretively open its relationship to the political theory stated in the Declaration of Independence; and that gap had been aggressively filled by forms of proslavery constitutional theory that denied the central role in constitutional interpretation of the political theory of human rights.

If both the citizenship clause and the privileges and immunities clause of the fourteenth amendment were grounded in such political theory, the equal protection clause was a direct and clear statement of it; it brought the implicit theory of the 1787 Constitution to center stage as the explicit governing theory of the Constitution. If the Constitution of 1787 was ultimately justified as a set of institutions that would overall tend to protect the equal rights of all, the fourteenth amendment imposed that justificatory requirement directly on the states, whose abuses of human rights had been the scandal and shame of the antebellum period. Because the fourteenth amendment in this way clarifies the general theory of the Constitution, the requirement of equal protection has been correctly construed to be applicable as well to the national government.[120] We have already seen that one deprivation of such equal rights, that grounded in racism, was a paradigm interpretive case for a violation of equal protection in 1866, and we must interpretively explore the jurisprudence of equal protection in light of that interpretive paradigm (see Chapter 5).

If the fourteenth amendment stated the affirmative principles of justice

---

[118] See *Adamson v. California*, 332 U.S. 46, 68 (Black, J., dissenting); *Duncan v. Louisiana*, 391 U.S. 145, 162 (Black, J., concurring).

[119] See Charles Fairman, "Does the Fourteenth Amendment Incoporate the Bill of Rights? The Original Understanding," *Stanford Law Review* 2 (December 1949): 5.

[120] See, e.g., *Bolling v. Sharpe*, 347 U.S. 497 (1954) (unconstitutionality of state-sponsored racial segregation applied to federal government). *Bolling* grounded its doctrine on the due process clause of the fifth amendment. Because of my own skepticism about the use of due process to protect substantive rights (see Chapter 7), I would argue that the result in this case would be better grounded on the implicit theory of justification of the 1787 Constitution, the nature and weight of which was clarified by the equal protection clause of the fourteenth amendment.

that undergirded the prohibition of the radical evil of slavery by the thirteenth amendment, the fifteenth amendment (forbidding abridgment of
the right to vote "on account of race, color, or previous condition of
servitude"[121]) expressed a companion judgment of the fair distribution of
political power required to support and sustain both the prohibitions of the
thirteenth amendment and the affirmations of justice of the fourteenth
amendment. The fifteenth amendment was much the most historically controversial of the Reconstruction Amendments. Its requirement of black suffrage had been repeatedly rejected in northern state votes during much of
the relevant period;[122] and only the more indirect procedures of constitutional amendment secured its ratification.[123]

All the substantive provisions of the Reconstruction Amendments were
subject to authoritative interpretation and enforcement by national institutions. It was Francis Lieber who, during the antebellum period, had most
deeply explored the connection between universal human rights and national identity; and his own influential proposals for constitutional amendments at the end of the Civil War centered on concepts of federally
enforceable guarantees of national citizenship and national rights as terms
of allegiance.[124] Many Republicans, as diverse as Bingham[125] and Sumner,[126]
defended constitutional reconstruction in Lieber's terms. The Civil War,
Lieber argued, enabled Americans as a people critically to assess the flaws
in their constitutionalism, "to see rugged ground or deep abysses where
from a distant view nothing but level plains had appeared." The main flaw
had been slavery and the associated doctrine of state's rights with their
attack on American nationality. Slavery must be abolished; and national
guarantees of equal rights must be imposed to protect black Americans
from a prejudice that Lieber, the German expatriate, analogized to European treatment of Jews.[127]

Almost all antebellum constitutional theorists (except notably Calhoun)

[121] U.S. Constitution, Amendment XV.

[122] See William Gillette, *The Right to Vote: Politics and the Passage of the Fifteenth
Amendment* (Baltimore: Johns Hopkins University Press, 1969), pp. 25–27, 167–68.

[123] See ibid.

[124] See Francis Lieber, "Amendments to the Constitution" (1865), in Lieber, *Miscellaneous
Writings*, 2:137–79.

[125] "Mr. Speaker, it appears to me that this very provision of the bill of rights brought in
question this day, upon this trial before the House, more than any other provision of the
Constitution, makes that unity of government which constitutes us one people, by which and
through which American nationality came to be, and only by the enforcement of which can
American nationality continue to be." Bingham, *Congressional Globe*, 39th Cong., 1st sess.,
22 February 1866, p. 1090.

[126] See Charles Sumner, "Are We a Nation?" (1867), in Sumner *Complete Works*, 16:7–65.

[127] See Lieber, "Amendments to the Constitution," in Lieber, *Miscellaneous Writings*,
2:147–48, 150, 169–72, 173–74.

paid at least lip service to political theories of human rights. But Lieber had not only seen the validity of Madison's 1787 worries about the Constitution; he had put the point on a more profound basis. The only legitimate basis for national political identity was the protection of the universal human rights of all persons subject to the political power of the relevant community. But universal human rights, by virtue of their abstract character and their demands on ethical impartiality, must be articulated, interpreted, and enforced as standards by the national institutions most capable of bringing to the task the kind of abstract and impartial justice that was required.

The southern doctrines of nullification, secession, and state's rights were a transparent mockery of these demands, a fact shown by the utility of such doctrines in shielding from scrutiny the radical evil of American slavery. Calhoun had justified his constitutionalism as a protection of minorities; in fact, his view gave regional majorities complete sovereignty over minorities, including, in South Carolina, the abridgment of the inalienable rights of the black slaves who were, numerically, a majority. Such intellectual obfuscation, ideological distortion of the language and thought of constitutionalism, and self-serving amoralism were made possible by the authority the Constitution had accorded the states over issues of human rights. The moral and constitutional meaning of the Civil War, for the generation who had fought it ultimately to defend the integrity of American revolutionary constitutionalism, must be that the protection of human rights be placed authoritatively in the hands of the nation.

Lieber's analysis fit securely in the framework of the great structures of American constitutionalism, which it left undisturbed. The task was not to change the federal system into a parliamentary democracy, but to make better use of the existing structures so that they might achieve their ends, yielding more impartial judgments on how to secure political power that respected rights and pursued the public interest. Congress had a general enforcement power under each of the three Reconstruction Amendments that, consistent with the constitutional theory of Union, was to be at least as broadly interpreted to advance human rights as the fugitive slave clause in *Prigg* had been interpreted by Justice Story (in the name of the theory of Union) to advance slavery. [128]

Importantly, the original draft of section 1 of the fourteenth amendment, which had focused on giving Congress power, had been changed to directly prohibit state power probably in response to a criticism of Representative Hotchkiss:

> It should be a constitutional right that cannot be wrested from any class of citizens, or from the citizens of any State by mere legislation. But this amend-

[128] See Wilson, *Congressional Globe*, 39th Cong., 1st sess., 9 March 1866, p. 1294.

ment proposes to leave it to the caprice of Congress; and your legislation upon the subject would depend upon the political majority of Congress, and not upon two thirds of Congress and three fourths of the States.

Now, I desire that the very privileges for which the gentleman is contending shall be secured to the citizens; but I want them secured by a constitutional amendment that legislation cannot override. [129]

The judiciary was the federal institution (much admired by Lieber) that, consistent with the theory of the 1787 Constitution, would afford an authoritative public forum for deliberative debate, articulation, and enforcement of these principles in the face of a nescient Congress. Of course, the judiciary, like any other branch of government, may make interpretive mistakes, and must be subject to constant critical scrutiny and public debate to maintain its ultimate accountability to the public community of reason, the ethical end of constitutional government. We know Lieber's views on the proper liberal construction of rights-protective constitutional provisions (see Chapter 2). It remains for us to explore how, in light of the argument here developed, interpretation of the Reconstruction Amendments should be understood, a discussion that will preface the substantive interpretive investigations of Chapters 5–7.

Of course, it does not follow from the fact that the authors of a constitution or some amendment thereof took a certain view of how it should be interpreted in the circumstances of the founding or even a view of how it should later be interpreted that those views are authoritative on how constitutional interpretation should be understood by a later generation. It is, of course, of interest that the Founders of the 1787 Constitution did not take the view of constitutional interpretation that I have called (in Chapter 1) originalist. [130] But a Lockean constitution, like that of the United States, rests on the reasonable consent of the present generation, not on the authority of a previous generation who are, from the perspective of Lockean political theory, no more authoritative than Filmer's fictive patriarchs. [131]

But Americans, in light of the arguments of *The Federalist No. 49* (see Chapter 2), have found reflection on the arguments of the Founders—made in a period of remarkable impartiality and public intelligence focused on the permanent problems of constitutional government—useful in understanding how the task of constitutional interpretation might best be understood by a contemporary generation. If we find this to be true of the

[129] See Representative Hotchkiss, *Congressional Globe*, 39th Cong., 1st sess., 28 February 1866, p. 1095.

[130] The now classic contemporary study is H. Jefferson Powell, "The Original Understanding of Original Intent," in Jack N. Rakove, *Interpreting the Constitution: The Debate over Original Intent* (Boston: Northeastern University Press, 1990), pp. 53–115.

[131] See Richards, *Foundations*, pp. 131–57.

Founders of 1787 (with the admitted tragic flaws in their work), it must be true, a fortiori, of the work of the founders of the Reconstruction Amendments, the most fundamental deliberation since 1787 on the flaws of American constitutionalism in the spirit of the founding and a self-conscious enterprise to bring that spirit to bear on the self-correcting reconstruction of the Constitution.

If the legitimacy of the American Revolution required a form of constitutionalism (in contrast to the corrupt British Constitution) adequate to its normative demands, the legitimacy of the Civil War required a comparable reflection on constitutional decadence (the Constitution of 1787) adequate to its demands for a rebirth of rights-based constitutional government. The critical analysis of antebellum constitutional decadence of radical antislavery met this need especially well because it was the most profound such reflection culturally available in the genre of American revolutionary constitutionalism forged by the Founders of 1787. Its great appeal for the American constitutional mind was both its radical insistence on the primacy of the revolutionary political theory of human rights central to American constitutionalism and its brilliant reinterpretation of the six ingredients of such constitutionalism in light of that political theory and the events of antebellum constitutional decadence and civil war.

In light of its analysis, radical antislavery supplied the most reasonable interpretation of the Civil War as the second American Revolution. And it offered, consistent with the genre of American revolutionary constitutionalism, remedies that plausibly could be and were regarded as the most justifiable way to correct central defects in the Constitution of 1787, some of which had been acknowledged by leading Founders such as Madison in 1787.[122] The Reconstruction Amendments, the most radical change in constitutionalism in our history, could thus be understood as a wholly reasonable conservative way to preserve the legitimacy of the longstanding project of American revolutionary constitutionalism.

The Reconstruction Amendments, thus understood, responded to the gravest crisis of constitutional legitimacy in our history; they are best understood and interpreted as negative and affirmative constitutional principles responsive to that crisis and any comparable such recurrent crisis in the legitimacy of the Constitution as supreme law. Our interpretive attitude today to these amendments must, consistent with the genre of American revolutionary constitutionalism, make the best sense of them in service of the narrative integrity of the story of the American people and their struggle for a politically legitimate government that respects, on terms of principle, the claim of each and every person to respect for their basic human rights—a community of principle.[133]

[132] See ibid., pp. 37–38.

[133] For further development of this idea, see ibid., pp. 145–57.

It cannot do justice to this enriched understanding of our interpretive responsibilities to trivialize our interpretation of the Reconstruction Amendments to some fictive search for the concrete exemplars to which some suitably described majority of the Reconstruction Congress or the ratifying states or, for that matter, advocates of radical antislavery would or would not have applied the relevant clause under interpretation. The political and constitutional theory of the Reconstruction Amendments was rooted in the antipositivist jurisprudence of radical antislavery, responding to the antebellum crisis of constitutional legitimacy by requiring an interpretive attitude toward the Constitution that would preserve its legitimacy on the grounds of the rights-based theory of human rights central to its claims to be the supreme law of the land.

Both Taney's originalism[134] and Stephen Douglas's majoritarian interpretation of popular sovereignty[135] were, from this perspective, equally illegitimate attempts to evade the interpretive responsibilities of making sense of the supremacy of the Constitution in terms of its protection of the human rights of all persons subject to political power. Taney's use of history and Douglas's majoritarianism substituted positivistic amoral facts or procedures for the deliberative rights-based normative judgments that could alone preserve the legitimacy of the Constitution as supreme law, namely, its principled protection of human rights to the fullest extent feasible. In light of the text and background of the Reconstruction Amendments, it would be, a fortiori, illegitimate today to make sense of these amendments in a comparably evasive positivistic way—by appeal to either the concrete intentions of the Founders (Bork[136]) or majoritarian democracy (Ely[137]) unconcerned with the reasonable demands of human rights in our circumstances.

The interpretive attitude that radical antislavery had taken toward the Constitution was insistent on the primacy of rights-based political theory in constitutional interpretation, disowning history and straining text in or-

---

[134] Taney argues in *Dred Scott*: "No one, we presume, supposes that any change in public opinion or feeling, in relation to this unfortunate race, in the civilized nations of Europe or in this country, should induce the court to give to the words of the Constitution a more liberal construction in their favor than they were intended to bear when the instrument was framed and adopted." *Dred Scott*, p. 426. In fact, as Justice Curtis points out in his dissent, Taney gets even his alleged originalist history of Founders' concrete intentions wrong; see pp. 572–74.

[135] Popular sovereignty, irrespective of constitutional or natural rights, allowed states to decide whether they would or would not have slavery. As one commentator observes, "Douglas looked upon popular sovereignty as essentially pragmatic and expedient." Johannsen, *Stephen A. Douglas*, p. 240.

[136] See Bork, *The Tempting of America*; for criticism, see Richards, "Originalism without Foundations."

[137] See Ely, *Democracy and Distrust*.

der to give maximum expression to the fullest possible protection of human rights. We, however, need neither disown history nor strain text to interpret the Reconstruction Amendments consistent with the requirements of rights-based political theory, for both the history and text of the Reconstruction Amendments make the best sense only understood in that way. Indeed, the enduring moral legacy of radical antislavery to American constitutionalism is that its once implausible interpretive attitude toward the Constitution of 1787 has been rendered, by virtue of the Reconstruction Amendments, the only plausible attitude toward the Constitution, as thus amended.

Rights-based contemporary egalitarian political theory must therefore play a central role in the interpretation of the requirements of the Reconstruction Amendments in contemporary circumstances; such interpretive responsibilities require us to take seriously what our rights are and how they are to be understood and elaborated today on terms of principle. The arguments of the most probing antebellum and Reconstruction analysts of constitutional interpretation (Theodore Parker, Francis Lieber, and Charles Sumner) support such an interpretive attitude, one based on interpreting constitutional traditions of respect for human rights in terms of what they took to be the best available contemporary theory of human rights, an anti-utilitarian neo-Kantian transcendentalism rooted in equal respect for basic moral powers. Our interpretive responsibilities must be understood in a similar way, making the best sense of what the Reconstruction Amendments clearly require (protection of human rights against certain political threats) in light of the best contemporary understanding of rights-based political legitimacy. If, for example, the kind of neo-Kantian rights-based argument emphasized by Lieber and Parker is today best articulated by a form of contemporary contractualism, as I have already suggested in Chapter 3 and hope to further show in Chapters 5–7, such argument should take its proper place in the interpretation of the enduring meaning of constitutional guarantees of basic human rights.

If the point of the idea of a written constitution was, as Madison argued in *The Federalist No. 49*, to memorialize normative demands in terms of which each generation of Americans must aspire to define its identity as a people, constitutional interpretation, consistent with this project, must ascribe to constitutional guarantees in general and the Reconstruction Amendments in particular that level of abstract moral understanding that allows such guarantees to be interpreted in this way, as a historically continuous strand of principles to which each generation must bring its best understanding of how such guarantees are most reasonably applied. This tendency to abstractness in the ascription of constitutional meaning preserves the continuity of the community over time; its normative demands can be seen to be continuous strands of principle at the core of our moral struggles and ethical growth as a people. Yet this interpretive attitude enables each generation to set and meet demanding standards of interpretive responsibility of bringing its own constructive internal powers of public reason and experience responsibly to bear on the articulation of the progressive meaning of human rights in its own circumstances.[138] The conservation of American constitutionalism, one of the greatest political legacies historically bequeathed to any people, is thus an interpretive challenge to each generation's creative powers of universal moral reason and imagination.

Such an aspiration does not dilute normative ideas, but like abolitionist political and constitutional theory, critically deepens them, constructing the larger patterns of justification that constitute the political community on the basis of a responsible understanding of what human rights are and require. The interpretation of equal protection in this way reveals, for example, a larger abstract structure of threats to basic human rights and the need for the same analysis, as a matter of principle, in contexts that might otherwise seem unrelated (for example, anti-Semitism, racism, sexism, and homophobia, discussed in Chapters 3 and 5). The nature and weight of basic human rights must, as a matter of principle, be analyzed in the same way; an abstract human right such as that to intimate personal life can reasonably be understood to raise issues of constitutional privacy in matters that might otherwise seem as disparate as contraception, abortion, and homosexual relations (see Chapter 6). Constitutional interpretation of this sort enriches the moral vocabulary and sensitivity of us all, enabling us to interpret our constitutional tradition in terms of basic ethical principles of legitimate government to which *all* persons, as a matter of principle, have a right.

The failure of constitutional interpretation to meet this demand is illustrated not only in the antebellum interpretive mistakes I have already noted, but in later interpretive mistakes that fail in comparable ways to make good sense of the Reconstruction Amendments themselves, a matter now to be explored (see Chapters 5–7). The positivism and rights-skeptical utilitarianism of Calhoun are echoed by those of Learned Hand; the popular sovereignty of Stephen Douglas by the majoritarianism of Ely; the originalism of Taney by that of Bork. To understand such recurrent temptations to interpretive mistake we must explore both their failure to interpret our history properly and their related failure to take seriously the rights-based political theory of American constitutionalism. As we shall see in Chapters 5–7, judicial interpretive mistakes regarding the meaning of

---

[138] On this tendency to abstractness, see Richards, *Foundations*, pp. 167–68, 170, 241, 271.

the Reconstruction Amendments rest on both failures. We need, as much as was needed in the antebellum period, to generate in our own terms and circumstances arguments of human rights adequate to identify and to challenge our corruptions, our decadent constitutionalism.

FIVE

A THEORY OF EQUAL PROTECTION

EQUAL PROTECTION expresses the general requirement, rooted in abolitionist political theory, that political power must be reasonably justifiable in terms of equal respect for human rights and the pursuit of public purposes (see Chapter 4).[1] It has various dimensions, including one demanding form of analysis associated with the protection of fundamental rights and another with the protection of suspect classes from oppression; outside these categories, its demand for reasonable justification is much more deferential to democratic politics.[2] Fundamental rights analysis under the equal protection clause was anticipated by the equality principles of the Constitution, as in the first amendment;[3] it will be best examined in the context of our later discussion of fundamental rights (see Chapter 6). Suspect classification analysis, however, is a distinctive doctrinal innovation under the equal protection clause, developed against the background of the revolutionary constitutionalism of the Reconstruction Amendments, and will be examined here in that light.

The American doctrine of equal protection in this dimension brings to bear an abstract normative judgment of political theory on a contextualized pattern of injustice with a certain history. I have already discussed some of the pertinent antebellum and Reconstruction Congress history (see Chapters 3–4). That discussion must now be widened to include pertinent later history (in particular, post-Reconstruction racial segregation in America) and the explanation of how and why this abstract mode of analysis ex-

---

[1] For the classic statement of equal protection as a form of public reasonableness, see Joseph Tussman and Jacobus tenBroek, "The Equal Protection of the Laws," *California Law Review* 37, no. 3 (September 1949): 341. For tenBroek's pathbreaking work on the abolitionist antecedents of equal protection, see tenBroek, *Equal under Law*.

[2] On the various modes of strict and rational basis analysis, see "Developments in the Law— Equal Protection," *Harvard Law Review* 82, no. 5 (March 1969): 82. For arguments for more aggressive rational basis review, see Gerald Gunther, "Newer Equal Protection," *Harvard Law Review* 86, no. 1 (November 1972): 86; Cass Sunstein, "Naked Preferences and the Constitution," *Columbia Law Review* 84, no. 7 (November 1984): 1689. I limit my discussion of equal protection to the demanding forms of equal protection review that do not defer to ordinary democratic politics.

[3] See Richards, *Foundations*, pp. 258–59. Rational basis analysis was also anticipated, namely, by the very similar requirement that, under the necessary and proper clause (U.S. Constitution, Art. I, sec. 8, cl. 18), congressional means must have a rational connection to legislative ends. See *McCulloch v. Maryland*, 17 U.S. (4 Wheat.) 316 (1819).

tends to other areas (gender) and should extend to still others (sexual preference).

A good interpretive theory of equal protection in this dimension must explain our interpretive mistakes (legitimating state-sponsored racial segregation) and how they have been corrected (invalidating such segregation). It advances such discussion to show how the abstract political theory of equal protection can be historically contextualized in different ways in America and Europe (for example, nineteenth- and twentieth-century American racism and European anti-Semitism). Not only were antebellum American and European racist thought mutually influential,[4] but the development of an American understanding of the political evil of racism prominently used anti-Semitism as an analogy (see Chapter 3). Later American interpretive developments also, as we shall see, profited from a similar comparison.

Racism as a Constitutional Evil

The normative theory of equal protection arose in the abolitionists' historically contextualized criticism of slavery and its underlying political pathology, racism (see Chapter 3). This criticism focused on the denial that blacks had the basic capacity to be even eligible to be bearers of the rights that were central to the moral identity of the culture: conscience, free speech, intimate personal and family life, free labor, and the like. These rights are, in their nature, culture-creating rights, forms of moral creativity through which people authenticate themselves, the larger meaning of their lives, and the culture of public reason required for exercise of their moral powers as persons. The systematic denial of these rights to any group by the dominant culture condemns that group to cultural death and deformed marginality, a form of denationalization.[5] The condition of the national identity of dominant white America was the construction of a negative identity (what an American is not) by means of a culturally defined image of a race-defined people accorded lower moral status on grounds that various rights were not in order because of underlying incapacity. Both Roger Taney and Alexander Stephens thus had argued that white supremacy was constitutive of American constitutional identity.

Under American slavery, the image of blacks as subhuman was constructed on the basis of alleged incapacities disqualifying them from basic rights. These included putative incapacities of moral reflection and delib-

[4] For example, on Nott's publication in the United States of a translation of Gobineau, see Stanton, *The Leopard's Spots*, pp. 174–75.

[5] For a related mode of analysis, see Orlando Patterson, *Slavery and Social Death* (Cambridge: Harvard University Press, 1982).

eration (no right to conscience), lack of reasoning skills such as literacy (no right of free speech), incapacity for responsible sexual intimacy and moral education of young (lack of privacy rights of sexual autonomy and family integrity), and lack of rational powers for many forms of work calling for independent exercise of rational powers (no right to free labor).[6] The underlying image of incapacity, constructed on the basis of the abridgment of such rights, was then alleged to be the reasonable basis (natural race differences) for American slavery. Only in this way could some Americans square their belief in human rights with the forms of total control that American slavery—in contrast to that in Latin America—peculiarly involved (including abridgments of legal rights to religious liberty, free speech, and family life, and restrictions on manumission).[7] A group, thus supposedly by nature not entitled to the basic rights constitutive of American nationality, could not, by definition, be part of American nationality.

The abolitionist criticism of American racism observed that the same definition of national identity that had rationalized slavery in the South also supported racial discrimination against free blacks both in the South and the North.[8] In the North the alleged inferiority of blacks could not perhaps justify slavery, but it could justify deprivations of rights aimed to exclude blacks from the political community. For example, states forbade blacks from entering their territory[9] and passed various discriminatory measures on voting rights, education, and the like that encouraged free blacks to

[6] On these features of American slavery, see Elkins, *Slavery*; Stampp, *The Peculiar Institution*; Eugene D. Genovese, *Roll, Jordan, Roll: The World the Slaves Made* (New York: Vintage Books, 1974); Genovese, *The World the Slaveholders Made*; Blassingame, *The Slave Community*; Herbert G. Gutman, *The Black Family in Slavery and Freedom, 1750–1925* (New York: Vintage Books, 1976). For a leading proslavery justification of many of these features of the institution, see Thomas R. R. Cobb, *An Inquiry into the Law of Negro Slavery in the United States of America* (1858; reprint, New York: Negro Universities Press, 1968).

[7] See works cited in note 6, especially Elkins, *Slavery*; see also Herbert S. Klein, *Slavery in the Americas: A Comparative Study of Virginia and Cuba* (Chicago: Elephant Paperbacks, 1989). It remains controversial, however, whether on balance slaves were treated worse in British than Latin America. See, e.g., David Brion Davis, "The Continuing Contradiction of Slavery: A Comparison of British America and Latin America," in Ann J. Lane, ed., *The Debate over Slavery: Stanley Elkins and His Critics* (Urbana: University of Illinois Press, 1971), pp. 111–36; Herbert S. Klein, "Anglicanism, Catholicism, and the Negro Slave," in Lane, *Debate*, pp. 137–90. For an important general study, see Degler, *Neither Black nor White*.

[8] On the South, see Berlin, *Slaves without Masters*. On the North, see Litwack, *North of Slavery*; Voegeli, *Free but Not Equal*. But for a balanced account of the improving treatment of blacks in the North prior to the Civil War, see Finkelman, "Prelude to the Fourteenth Amendment."

[9] Three states—Illinois, Indiana, and Oregon—incorporated such anti-immigration provisions into their state constitutions, which were overwhelmingly approved by white state electorates. See Litwack, *North of Slavery*, pp. 70–74.

leave.[10] Abolitionists such as Garrison and Maria Child saw that the natural expression of this view was the advocacy from Jefferson to Lincoln of abolition on terms of colonization abroad, confirming the basic racist image of the terms of American national identity. The theorists of radical antislavery drew the remedial inference that blacks must be fully included in the terms of a national citizenship that extended equal protection of basic rights to all.

Abolitionist analysis of the evil of racism focused on the corruption of public reason that its defense required. Its defense had, by the nature of the evil to be defended, required the deprivation of the basic rights of whites as well as blacks, for example, to free debate about the evils of slavery and racism. The abolitionists—the only consistent advocates of the argument for toleration in antebellum America—were for this reason pathbreaking moral and constitutional dissenters of conscience from and critics of the stifling tyranny of the majority of Jacksonian America. The ethical impulse that motivated abolitionists was the corruption of conscience that slavery and racism, like religious persecution, had worked on the spiritual lives of Americans. To sustain these practices and institutions, proslavery theorists had, consistent with the paradox of intolerance, repressed criticism precisely when it was most needed. Instead, they fostered decadent standards of argument in the use of history, constitutional analysis, Bible interpretation, and even in science, whose effect had been to corrupt the public sense of what ethics was. For abolitionists such as Garrison and Child, such attitudes could, consistent with respect for human rights, no more legitimately be allowed political expression than religious intolerance with its analogous corruption of public reason.

The original abolitionist aim was an ethical transformation of these public attitudes from their decadent to a more critically informed sense of the requirements of ethical impartiality by making public arguments that would deliberately persuade and enlighten the public conscience. In response to the brick wall of repression that met them, ethical persuasion remained their overriding aim. The abolitionists' commitment to nonviolence reflects this approach; only very late in the antebellum period did rational despair lead some of them (Theodore Parker and Henry David Thoreau, for example)[11] to support the armed revolution of John Brown.

---

[10] By 1840, some 93 percent of northern free blacks lived in states that either completely or as a practical matter excluded them from the right to vote. See Litwack, *North of Slavery*, pp. 74–75. Although some white schools admitted blacks especially before 1820, most northern states either excluded them from schools altogether or established racially separate and unequal schools for them. See Litwack, *North of Slavery*, p. 114.

[11] On Parker, see Commager, *Theodore Parker*; on Thoreau, for a good general treatment on this point, see Daniel Walker Howe, "Henry David Thoreau on the Duty of Civil Disobedience."

Most abolitionists turned to politics but politics as the best way effectively to make their ethical case, to forge through democratic politics a new moral consensus around sound ethical principles.

The task of the Reconstruction Amendments was not only, however, to set the terms of a desirable ethical transformation of American public opinion. It was also to undertake a more difficult task in which its abolitionist forebears had not taken much interest and some expressly disavowed, namely, to enforce constitutional standards of respect for rights against those who would flout them.[12] The aims of ethical transformation of public attitudes and constitutional enforcement to protect rights at risk were not necessarily coincident, at least in the short term. Indeed, one abolitionist, Maria Child, had prophetically worried, twenty-three years before the thirteenth amendment was ratified, about their possible antagonism: "Great political changes may be forced by the pressure of external circumstances, without a corresponding change in the moral sentiment of a nation; but in all such cases, the change is worse than useless; the evil reappears, and usually in a more aggravated form."[13] Those committed to the abolitionist ethical vision would have universally preferred that Americans both in the North and South had been persuaded to assent to the vision that condemned both slavery and racism. But the circumstances of the Reconstruction Amendments were those of a moral chasm in public opinion between the moral revolution the Civil War had worked in the North and a counterrevolution in the South of which the freedmen were the unjust victims.[14]

The moral revolution in American public opinion in the North worked by the Civil War rendered abolitionist arguments, regarded as so marginally radical in the antebellum period, the basic conservative principles of American revolutionary constitutionalism embodied in the Reconstruction Amendments.[15] The stark contrast of the black contribution to the Civil War and the South's intransigent attempts to return freedmen to the functional equivalent of slavery enabled the congressional leadership of the Republican party to forge a public opinion in the nation—despite a resisting president—that supported the central principles of the Reconstruction

[12] The leading criticism of the abolitionists, for not properly preparing the ground for what the Reconstruction Amendments required, is that of Stanley Elkins; see Elkins, *Slavery*, pp. 140–206; for a response to his criticism, see Aileen S. Kraditor, "A Note on Elkins and the Abolitionists," in Lane, *Debate*, pp. 87–101. For a good collection of essays that explore the issue, see Duberman, *The Antislavery Vanguard*.

[13] Cited Kraditor, "A Note on Elkins and the Abolitionists," in Lane, *Debate*, pp. 100-101.

[14] See Leon F. Litwack, *Been in the Storm So Long: The Aftermath of Slavery* (New York: Vintage Books, 1979). See also C. Vann Woodward, *The Strange Career of Jim Crow*, 3d rev. ed. (New York: Oxford University Press, 1974); *Origins of the New South, 1877–1913* (Baton Rouge: Louisiana State University Press, 1971); and *The Future of the Past*.

[15] See McPherson, *The Struggle for Equality*.

Amendments (see Chapter 4).[16] Black Americans were included in the American political community on terms of principles guaranteeing them equal protection of their basic human rights. The abolitionist vision of equal rights was realized.

Of course, it was not realized. A president of the exquisite political skill and moral principle and capacity for moral growth of a Lincoln might have stood some chance of bringing the nation (North and South) into some enduring consensus of principles about respect for the constitutional rights of black Americans.[17] But Andrew Johnson lacked both skill and principle, so polarizing the nation by his tragically misguided encouragement of southern racist resistance to the fourteenth amendment that "the South was united [on racism] as it had not been on slavery."[18] The constitutional abolition of slavery and guarantee of equal rights of citizenship to black Americans would, however, have been dead letters without some effective constitutional protection of the rights of black Americans against the populist racism that now flourished in the defeated South as the terms of southern sectional identity. The Reconstruction Amendments stood for an ethical vision of *national* identity based on respect for the human rights of all persons. Southern attempts to perpetuate racist subjugation through law (the Black Codes) were inconsistent with such respect and could not legitimately be allowed expression through public law.

The equal protection clause of the fourteenth amendment afforded a nationally applicable constitutional guarantee and enforcement power aimed to protect American citizens against such subjugation (see Chapter 4). The task now was the novel one, not really anticipated by the abolitionists, of how such guarantees were to be understood, interpreted, and implemented against those who would unconstitutionally abridge the rights of Americans to equal standing before the law. If the abolitionists (with their historical mission of persuasion by appeal to conscience) were unprepared for the task before them, the nation at large had even less understanding of what was required to achieve its publicly avowed constitutional aim of rectifying the American heritage of both slavery in the South and the cultural construction of racism nationwide.

The interpretive task required a theory of what counts or should count as racist subjugation from the terms of moral community, namely, what kinds of abridgments of equal standing have been pivotally responsible for

---

[16] For good general studies, see McKitrick, *Andrew Johnson and Reconstruction*; Benedict, *A Compromise of Principle*.

[17] See LaWanda Cox, *Lincoln and Black Freedom* (Urbana: University of Illinois Press, 1985); LaWanda Cox and John H. Cox, *Politics, Principles, and Prejudice, 1865–1866: Dilemma of Reconstruction America* (New York: Atheneum, 1976).

[18] C. Vann Woodward, "Emancipations and Reconstructions: A Comparative Study," in Woodward, *The Future of the Past*, p. 166.

the unjustifiable cultural construction of the subhuman status of a class of persons not eligible to be regarded as bearers of human rights. The transformation of religious persecution into racial degradation should be the key to this analysis (see Chapter 3).

The racist subjugation of blacks took root in America under the circumstances of the American institution of slavery combined with the denial that blacks, as "heathens," were within the ambit of the argument for toleration.[19] Religious persecution here took the form of enforcement at large of a politically entrenched view of religious truth that condemned "heathen" forms of cultural life as not reasonably entitled to respect. In effect, a political orthodoxy (concerned to maintain slavery as an institution) both imposed on the "heathen" sectarian standards of what counted as reasonable thought and inquiry and degraded them from the status of persons capable of exercising moral powers reasonably.

Religious persecution became racist subjugation when the sectarian enforcement of the political orthodoxy unreasonably interpreted the "heathens" as not merely willfully blind to religious truth (as Augustine supposed the Donatists to be),[20] but as incapable of the moral powers that entitle one to be regarded as a bearer of rights at all. The central mechanism of the cultural construction of racism was the radical isolation (through the institution of slavery and practices of racial discrimination) of a race-defined people from the culture-creating rights extended to all others. Such unjust exclusion from these rights (to conscience, free speech, education, family life, labor) was the unreasonable basis for condemning their culture and, ultimately, them as irrationally subhuman.

The normative theory of equal protection, when contextualized to this history, interpretively explains racist degradation as a constitutional evil, an insult to the status owed persons in a political community founded on equal human rights. The argument for toleration has played a central role in the analysis of this evil because the evil arose as a form of intolerance and was identified and attacked as an evil in such terms by its most acute critics. For the same reason that sectarian conviction could not be the measure of religious liberty, racist subjugation could not be the measure of the community of human rights. In both cases, attitudes inconsistent with respect for human rights must be denied expression through public law; and constitutional guarantees, rooted in respect for rights, must debar the legitimacy of laws and policies rooted in such attitudes.

[19] See, e.g., Jordan, *White over Black*, pp. 91–98; Morgan, *American Slavery, American Freedom*, p. 77; Davis, *The Problem of Slavery*, at pp. 170, 195, 207–8, 214, 246–47, 281, 473.

[20] See Richards, *Toleration*, pp. 86–88.

Abolitionists often made their point by analogy to anti-Semitism (see Chapter 3). It confirms the power of the analysis to show how it clarifies the related development of European anti-Semitism into racism.

Anti-Semitism as Racism

If American politics in the nineteenth century was preoccupied by the issue of the terms and scope of political community (including the status of blacks), the comparable political issue in Europe was posed by the emancipation of the Jews against the background of the principles of Enlightenment thought embodied in the French Revolution[21] and the ancient anti-Judaism and anti-semitism we earlier discussed (see Chapter 3). In the medieval period, both the expulsions of the Jews and their segregation were justified on the ground that they were legitimately the serfs or slaves of Christian princes because of their culpable failure to adopt Christian belief.[22] The segregation of Jewish communities from the life and occupations and responsibilities of Christian communities—intended, as it was, to stigmatize their culpability—created a Christian image of Jewish culture as inferior, the kind of cultural degradation that was, as we have seen in the case of American blacks, the context of American racism. It was, as we shall now see, also part of the historical background of the modern European form of racism we call anti-Semitism.

Modern European anti-Semitism, sometimes marked by its students as anti-Christian anti-Semitism,[23] arose in the context of the tense relationship between emerging European principles of universal human rights, sponsored by the French Revolution, and nineteenth century struggles for a sense of national identity and self-determination. When the French Revolution took the form of Napoleonic world revolution, these forces became fatally contradictory. The emancipation of the Jews occurred in this tense environment and became over time its most terrible victim. The Jews, whose emancipation was sponsored by the appeal to universal human rights, were identified with a culture hostile to the emergence of national self-determination. Their very attempts at assimilation into that culture were, according to this view, marks of their degraded inability for true national culture.

The struggles for national identity in nineteenth century Europe— against the background of balkanized Germany principalities, Italian king-

---

[21] See Arthur Hertzberg, *The French Enlightenment and the Jews* (New York: Columbia University Press, 1990).

[22] See Langmuir, *Toward a Definition of Antisemitism*, pp. 156–57.

[23] See Uriel Tal, *Christians and Jews in Germany*, trans. Noah Jonathan Jacobs (Ithaca: Cornell University Press, 1975).

doms, and imperialistic domination by non-Germans and non-Italians—were not obviously religious struggles. Indeed, many of them were self-consciously secular in nature and some of them deeply antireligious (thus, German anti-Christian anti-Semitism). Religion was not usually the rallying call of national identity, but culture was—culture often understood in terms of linguistic unity as the basis of a larger cultural and ultimate national unity (thus, Pan-Germanism). National unity, particularly in Germany, was increasingly identified with the forging of a cultural orthodoxy centering on the purity of the German language, its ancient "Aryan" myths,[24] its high culture. This search for cultural unity arose in part in reaction to the French imperialistic and assimilationist interpretation of universal human rights. That history invited the search for an alternative, linguistically and culturally centered concept of national unity.

But cultural unity—when hostile to universal human rights—is, as under southern slavery, an unstable, highly unprincipled, and sometimes ethically regressive basis for national unity. It may unreasonably enforce highly sectarian values by deadly polemical reaction to its imagined spiritual enemies; and it is all too comfortable to identify those enemies with a group already historically degraded as culturally inferior. Blacks were this group in America; in Europe, this role was performed by Jews, a highly vulnerable, historically stigmatized cultural minority—the paradigm case of cultural heresy. In the German case, where there was little solid, humane historical background of moral pluralism on which to build, romantic aesthetic values increasingly dominated over ethical ones. Italy's Mussolini, in contrast, had the history of Roman pluralistic toleration of Jews to appeal to in rebuking Hitler's very German anti-Semitism.[25] Richard Wagner, a major influence on the development of German anti-Semitism, thus preposterously regarded his artistic genius as sufficient to entitle him to articulate, as a prophetic moral leader such as Lincoln, an ethical vision for the German people in the Aryan myth embodied in *Parsifal*. Such a confusion of the categories of aesthetic and ethical leadership reflects the underlying crisis in ethical and political culture.[26]

These deadly confusions are brilliantly displayed in Houston Chamber-

---

[24] For a superb treatment, see Leon Poliakov, *The Aryan Myth: A History of Racist and Nationalist Ideas in Europe*, trans. Edmund Howard (London: Sussex University Press, 1971).

[25] See ibid., p. 70.

[26] See ibid. See also Poliakov, *The History of Anti-Semitism*, vol. 3, chap. 11. On Wagner's actual confused state of belief, see Jacob Katz, *The Darker Side of Genius* (Hanover, N.H.: University Press of New England, 1986). For good general studies of Wagner and Wagnerism (including their political uses by Hitler), see L. J. Rather, *Reading Wagner: A Study in the History of Ideas* (Baton Rouge: Louisiana State University Press, 1990); David C. Large and William Weber, eds., *Wagnerism in European Culture and Politics* (Ithaca: Cornell University Press, 1984).

lain's influential *The Foundations of the Nineteenth Century*,[27] a work much admired and indeed used by Hitler.[28] Chamberlain, Wagner's son-in-law, offered a cultural history of the world in which Aryan culture was the repository and vehicle of all value and Jews, as rationalists lacking creative imagination, the embodiment of negative value. In effect, Chamberlain called for a politically enforceable cultural orthodoxy centering on Aryan culture against corrupting non-Aryan (Jewish) culture.

Chamberlain's argument clearly exemplified the paradox of intolerance. He admitted that there were reasonable scientific doubts about the equation of language and race (which underlay his thesis), but resolved these doubts by appeal to a certitude expressive of the political irrationalism of the will: "Though it were proved that there never was an Aryan race in the past, yet we desire that in the future there may be one. That is the decisive standpoint for men for action."[29] Jesus of Nazareth, whom Chamberlain claimed to much admire, must, of course, be a non-Jew, an Aryan in fact. We are in the never-never land where wishes become, magically, facts.

As in the evolution of American racism, religious intolerance became racist subjugation under the impact of decadent standards of public reason. Chamberlain thus gave an essentially cultural argument a racial interpretation (transmogrifying religious or cultural intolerance into racism) at a time precisely when such scientific racism, as he (like Hitler)[30] clearly recognized, was under examination and attack among students of language and of culture more generally.

Franz Boas, a German Jew and anthropologist who emigrated to the United States, where he became a central architect of the modern human sciences of culture, had begun seriously to debunk the racial assumptions of European and American anthropology as early as the 1890s.[31] In a way

[27] Houston Stewart Chamberlain, *The Foundations of the Nineteenth Century*, trans. John Lees, 2 vols. (London: John Lane, 1911).

[28] See Adolf Hitler, *Mein Kampf* (New York: Reynal & Hitchcock, 1940), pp. 116, 307, 325, 359, 369, 395, 413, 605. On Chamberlain's admiration and support for Hitler, see Large and Weber, *Wagnerism*, pp. 124–25.

[29] Chamberlain, *The Foundations of the Nineteenth Century*, 1:266, n.

[30] For Hitler's clear recognition "that in the scientific sense there is no such thing as race," see Rather, *Reading Wagner*, p. 286 (quoting conversation with Hitler reported by Rauschning).

[31] See Franz Boas, "Human Faculty as Determined by Race," in George W. Stocking, Jr., ed., *A Franz Boas Reader: The Shaping of American Anthropology, 1883–1911* (Chicago: University of Chicago Press, 1974), pp. 221–42; originally published in American Association for the Advancement of Science, *Proceedings* 43 (1894): 301–27. For Boas's fullest statement of his views, see Franz Boas, *The Mind of Primitive Man* (1911; reprint, Westport, Conn.: Greenwood Press, 1963). On Boas's critical influence on modern social theory, see George W. Stocking, *Race, Culture, and Evolution: Essays in the History of Anthropology* (New York: Free Press, 1968); Degler, *In Search of Human Nature*. For a useful comparison of American and British antiracist thought and argument, see Elazar Barkan, *The Retreat of Scientific*

that had not been the case when the American ethnologists wrote, racial theory was now under sharp attack as scientifically unsound. Yet it was in this context that the increasingly well-understood irrationalism of racial thinking was accorded its fullest and most dangerous political expression in the legitimation of a new conception of the basis of political unity and identity.

The malignant consequences of the dynamic of such irrationalism, when it is actually harnessed to political power aggressively hostile to human rights, was played out in the history of modern political anti-Semitism and the racial genocide of some five million European Jews to which it ruthlessly led. [32] Political leaders obtained or retained populist political support for governments that violated human rights (and whose legitimacy was therefore in doubt) by appealing to racist fears as the basis of national unity. This strategy included the blatant falsification and distortion of facts that, consistent with Chamberlain and Hitler, inspired the national will with an unreasonable certitude (for example, the Dreyfus affair in France, and the Protocols of the Elders of Zion in Imperial Russia). [33]

In the German world, political anti-Semitism became, under Hitler's leadership, the very core of the success of Nazi politics in a nation humiliated by the triumphant democracies in World War I. [34] Reasonable standards of discussion and debate on issues of race and human rights were brutally suppressed by a government-sponsored pseudoscience of race enforced by totalitarian terror. [35] Nazism was self-consciously at war with the idea and practice of human rights, including the institutions of constitutional government motivated by the construction of a politics of public reason that respects human rights. [36] Its politics of an artificially constructed group solidarity of myth, ritual, and pseudoscience, having no basis whatsoever in public reason, starkly exemplifies the force of the paradox of intolerance; it was precisely when the alleged basis for national unity lacked any reasonable basis (and thus was most subject to reasonable doubt) that Nazi totalitarian power crushed the very possibility of raising or entertaining such doubts through the political manufacture of an ideological basis

---

Racism: Changing Concepts of Race in Britain and the United States between the World Wars (Cambridge: Cambridge University Press, 1992).

[32] See Raul Hilberg, *The Destruction of the European Jews,* 3 vols. (New York: Holmes & Meier, 1985), 3:1201–20. On anti-Semitism, see Leon Poliakov's magisterial *History of Anti-Semitism.*

[33] See Poliakov, *The History of Anti-Semitism,* vol. 4.

[34] See Peter Pulzer, *The Rise of Political Anti-Semitism in Germany and Austria,* rev. ed. (Cambridge: Harvard University Press, 1988); Jacob Katz, *From Prejudice to Destruction* (Cambridge: Harvard University Press, 1980).

[35] See Hannah Arendt, *The Origins of Totalitarianism* (New York: Harcourt Brace Jovanovich, 1973).

[36] See ibid.

for national unity, namely, the irrationalist will to believe in the fantasized, degraded evils of the Jews. The social construction of racism was carried in Nazi politics to its most irrationalist and immoral extremes because the basis of unity of Nazi politics was essentially a social solidarity of political unreason.

Racial Segregation as a Violation of Equal Protection

Events in America after the Civil War reveal a not dissimilar dynamic of increasingly powerful political racism. The principles of the Reconstruction Amendments could probably only have been effectively realized by a continuing national commitment to the ongoing federal enforcement of constitutional rights in the South. Such federal programs would have included land distribution and integrated education for the freedmen (of the sort suggested by Thaddeus Stevens in the House[37] and Charles Sumner in the Senate)[38] and active and ongoing federal protection of black voting rights.

Mainstream antebellum abolitionist thought, aside from radicals such as Stevens and Sumner, was unprepared for the task that reconstruction of the South would pose,[39] and the rest of the nation was even less prepared. The failure to accord such protection exposed the freedmen to the hostile environment of the South now committed with redoubled fury to the cultural construction of racism as the irrationalist symbol of southern sectional unity in defeat. Southern racism now evolved into a politically aggressive racism that the victory of the Union had, if anything, worsened. But even the inadequate federal congressional and executive commitment to black rights that there was (protecting voting rights and prosecuting the Ku Klux Klan) effectively ceased in 1877.[40]

The judiciary, for its part, did little better. We shall see in later discussions that it effectively aborted some of the central principles of the Reconstruction Amendments (notably, in its narrow and mistaken construction of the privileges and immunities clause of the fourteenth amendment[41] and

[37] On Stevens's abortive proposals for confiscation and distribution of southern plantations to the freedman, see Foner, *Reconstruction*, pp. 222, 235–36, 237, 245–46, 308–9, 310.

[38] On Sumner's proposals for federally sponsored land distribution and integrated education for the freedmen, see Foner, *Reconstruction*, pp. 236, 308.

[39] The key to much abolitionist thought during this period was the guarantee of voting rights to the freedmen (eventually realized through the fifteenth amendment), which would, it was hoped, accord them sufficient political power to defend themselves without the need for more extensive federal intervention in the South to protect them. See McPherson, *The Struggle for Equality*; Benedict, *A Compromise of Principle*.

[40] See C. Vann Woodward, *Reunion and Reaction: The Compromise of 1877 and the End of Reconstruction* (New York: Oxford University Press, 1966).

[41] See *Slaughter-House Cases*, 83 (16 Wall.) 36 (1873).

of state action under the equal protection clause of the amendment),[42] and we must examine now its misinterpretation of the guarantee of equal protection as applied to state-sponsored racial segregation.

The theory of illegitimate racist degradation—central to the understanding of equal protection—must be interpreted and applied in light of the circumstances relevant to its terms of reasonable justification of state power. The pivotal interpretive issue should be whether some law or policy by act or omission gives expression to an unreasonable exclusion of black Americans from one of the culture-creating rights central to the American public constitutional culture of equal rights.

One such issue should surely be state-sponsored racial segregation; such segregation perpetuates and reinforces the image of black Americans as outcasts from the common culture of the larger society—a point Charles Sumner (noting the analogy of European anti-Semitism) had forcefully made.[43] Illegitimate racist degradation should be understood against the background of the cultural intolerance fundamental to the social construction of American racism, in particular, the historical exclusion of the disfavored group from any of the rights of conscience, free speech, family life, and work that have been accorded other persons and the cultural groups with whom they identified. The task of equal protection, construed against that background, must be to refuse public recognition and enforcement of the attitudes of unjust exclusion on the basis of which racist degradation was rationalized. But state-sponsored racial segregation was precisely so motivated, expressing and legitimating a social construction of isolation and exclusion of the disfavored race-defined people that perpetuated the underlying evil of moral subjugation.[44]

The mission of the Reconstruction Amendments was and should have been the inclusion, on terms of equal rights, of black Americans into the American political community now understood to be a moral community of free and equal citizens, not two nations divided by a culturally constructed chasm of intolerance and subjugation supported by law.[45] In *Plessy*

---

[42] See *Civil Rights Cases*, 109 U.S. 3 (1883).

[43] See Charles Sumner, "Equality Before the Law," in Sumner, *Complete Works*, 3:51–100; for the analogy of anti-Semitism, see his discussion of the construction of anti-Semitism on the basis of compulsory segregation in ghettoes (p. 88). See also Charles Sumner, "The Question of Caste," in Sumner, *Complete Works*, 17:133–83; on anti-Semitism, see p. 158. For commentary on Sumner's attacks on racial segregation throughout his career, see David Donald, *Charles Sumner and the Coming of the Civil War* (New York: Knopf, 1960), pp. 180–81; Donald, *Charles Sumner and the Rights of Man*, pp. 152, 246–47, 298, 422.

[44] See, Woodward, *The Strange Career of Jim Crow*. For an interesting comparison of the comparable development of state-sponsored segregation in the United States and South Africa, see George M. Fredrickson, *White Supremacy: A Comparative Study in American and South African History* (Oxford: Oxford University Press, 1981).

[45] On the continuing power of this cultural construction today, see Andrew Hacker, *Two*

v. Ferguson,[46] the U.S. Supreme Court held state-sponsored racial discrimination to be consistent with the equal protection clause of the fourteenth amendment, one of the more egregious examples of grave interpretive mistake in the Court's checkered history. In this opinion the Supreme Court powerfully advanced the cultural construction of American racism.

The interpretive issue in *Plessy* was whether there was a reasonable basis for the racial distinction that the state law used. The Court's decision can be plausibly explained, as Charles Lofgren has recently shown,[47] against the background of the dominant racist social science of the late nineteenth century. I have already noted the importance of American ethnologists to antebellum proslavery thought.[48] The later development of this alleged science of natural race differences in moral capacity measured them in alleged physical differences (physically measured by brain capacity or cephalic indices);[49] these measures afforded a putatively scientific basis for making the allegedly reasonable judgment that the separation of races was justified. Segregation in transportation (the issue in *Plessy*) might thus discourage forms of social intercourse that would result in degenerate forms of miscegenation; and segregation in education would reflect race-linked differences in capacity best dealt with in separate schools, as well as discourage social intercourse.

The abolitionists had offered plausible objections to the scientific status of American ethnology, and similar objections were available at the time *Plessy* was decided in 1896. For example, Boas had already published his 1894 paper debunking the weight to be accorded race in the social sciences.[50] It is striking that the putative reasonable basis for *Plessy* was not, in fact, critically stated or discussed in the opinion, but rather conclusorily assumed. Even given the state of the human sciences at the time of *Plessy*, the interpretive argument in the decision did not meet the standards of impartial public reason surely due all Americans. Americans have a right to expect more of their highest court than the conclusory acceptance without argument of controversial scientific judgments hostage to an entrenched

---

Nations: Black and White, Separate, Hostile, Unequal (New York: Charles Scribner's Sons, 1992).

[46] See *Plessy v. Ferguson*, 163 U.S. 537 (1896).

[47] See Lofgren, *The Plessy Case.*

[48] See, Stanton, *The Leopard's Spots.*

[49] For good general treatments, see Stephen Jay Gould, *The Mismeasure of Man* (New York: W. W. Norton, 1981); Gossett, *Race*; Fredrickson, *The Black Image in the White Mind*; John S. Haller, Jr., *Outcasts from Evolution: Scientific Attitudes of Racial Inferiority, 1859–1900* (New York: McGraw-Hill 1971); Horsman, *Race and Manifest Destiny.*

[50] See Franz Boas, "Human Faculty as Determined by Race" (1894), in Stocking, *A Franz Boas Reader*, pp. 221–42.

political epistemology that protected the increasingly racist character of the American South. One justice (Justice Harlan, a southerner) powerfully made precisely this point in his dissent in *Plessy*.

It is surely not without importance that during this period southern blacks had been left by the federal government almost wholly at the mercy of southern state governments. These governments had (in violation of the spirit of the fifteenth amendment) effectively disenfranchised them, certainly not afforded them adequate educational opportunity, and cast a blind eye on, when they did not actively support, the informal forms of terrorism used to intimidate blacks from challenging their subjugated economic, social, and political position.[51] The Supreme Court, abandoning abolitionist ethical impartiality, supinely surrendered any semblance of morally independent critical testing in order to take instruction from bad and politically corrupt science to legitimate the further degradation of this already unconstitutionally victimized group. The consequence was what betrayal of the argument for toleration has taught us to expect. The political identity of the South, like its antebellum predecessor, immunized itself from serious discussion of its greatest evil,[52] and constituted its sense of political identity in racist subjugation. Consistent with the paradox of intolerance, such a failure of reason projectively fed on forms of political irrationalism (myth, factual distortion, deprivation of basic rights of conscience and free speech) based on the racist subjugation of its victims.

The consequences for the nation at large were felt not only in racist aspects of America's increasingly imperialist foreign policy, but in the racist immigration restrictions on Asians and, after World War I, on southern and eastern Europeans.[53] If race and culture were in this period so unreasonably confused, it is not surprising that American intolerance, to the extent legitimated by betrayal of constitutional principles, should turn from blacks to non-Christian Asians or Catholic Latins or Jewish Slavs whose cultures appeared, to nativist American Protestant public opinion, so inferior and (equating culture and race) therefore peopled by the racially inferior.

The long road to the overruling of *Plessy* by *Brown v. Board of Education*[54] in 1954 was the story of the critical testing and recasting of the assumptions that made *Plessy* possible. The great change in these background assumptions was in part achieved through the mobilization of a

---

[51] See, Woodward, *Reunion and Reaction; The Strange Career of Jim Crow*; and *Origins of the New South*.

[52] See, Cash, *The Mind of the South*.

[53] For a good general treatment, see John Higham, *Strangers in the Land: Patterns of American Nativism, 1860–1925* (New Brunswick: Rutgers University Press, 1988). See also Ronald Takaki, *Iron Cages: Race and Culture in 19th-Century America* (New York: Oxford University Press, 1990).

[54] See *Brown v. Board of Education*, 347 U.S. 483 (1954).

constitutional movement led by the NAACP.[55] Black Americans in the South and elsewhere asserted and were finally accorded some measure of national protection by the Supreme Court (reversing early decisions to the contrary)[56] in the exercise of their first amendment rights of protest, criticism, and advocacy.[57] The consequences were those to be expected by the liberation, on fair terms, of culture-creating moral powers.[58]

The interpretive substance of the argument against *Plessy* made extensive use of forms of social science research, some of it arguably of dubious analytic value for the purpose at hand.[59] But one strand of the argument based on social science reflected a structure of moral argument strikingly similar to abolitionist ethical analysis of these issues.

The eighteenth-century comparative science of human nature, developed by Montesquieu and Hume, had seen human nature as more or less constant subject to modification from the environment, history, institutional development, and the like. Both had discussed race differences from this perspective. Montesquieu's position was one of ironic skepticism (as noted in Chapter 3). Hume, however, departed from the model of a uniform human nature to suggest significant, constitutionally based race differences inferred from comparative cultural achievements.[60] The Humean suggestion of separate races had an antitheological significance; it was thus condemned, notably by James Beattie,[61] as one aspect of a larger repudiation of a Christian ethics of equality based on the biblical idea of one divine

---

[55] See Richard Kluger, *Simple Justice: The History of Brown v. Board of Education and Black America's Struggle for Equality*; (New York: Vintage, 1977) Genna Rae McNeil, *Groundwork: Charles Hamilton Houston and the Struggle for Civil Rights* (Philadelphia: University of Pennsylvania Press, 1983).

[56] See *Gitlow v. New York*, 268 U.S. 652 (1925) (first amendment held applicable to states under fourteenth amendment).

[57] See Harry Kalven, Jr., *The Negro and the First Amendment* (Chicago: University of Chicago Press, 1965).

[58] Even under the harsh terms of American slavery, black Americans—though brutally cut off from their native cultures as well as from the rights of American public culture—demonstrated remarkable creativity in giving ethical meaning to their plight, laying the foundations of their later interpretations of the religious and constitutional values of emancipatory freedom that they correctly understood to be at the basis of the public culture around them. On the black interpretation of Christian freedom under slavery, see Genovese, *Roll, Jordan, Roll*, pp. 159–284; on religious and political freedom under emancipation, see Litwack, *Been in the Storm So Long*, pp. 450–556; on the ideals of religious and constitutional freedom of Martin Luther King, see Taylor Branch, *Parting the Waters: America in the King Years, 1954–1963* (New York: Simon & Schuster, 1988).

[59] See Edmond Cahn's trenchant criticism along these lines, in "Jurisprudence," *New York University Law Review* 30 (January 1955): 150.

[60] See David Hume, "Of National Characters," in Hume, *Essays*, p. 208, n. 10.

[61] See Beattie, *An Essay on the Nature and Immutability of Truth*, pp. 479–84. See also James Beattie, *Elements of Moral Science* (1790; reprint, Delmar, N.Y.: Scholars' Facsimiles & Reprints, 1976), pp. 183–223.

creation of humans. Hume's suggestion was later developed in the nine-teenth century into polygenetic theories of human origins by the American ethnologists and others,[62] who thought of their theories as part of the battle of progressive science against reactionary religion.

In the nineteenth century, this artificially drawn contrast was hardened into one between certain approaches to the human sciences and nearly any-thing else. These approaches, very much under the influence of models of explanation drawn from the physical sciences, assumed that good expla-nations in the human sciences must be crudely reductive to some physical measure, such as brain capacity or cephalic indices. There was little atten-tion to, let alone understanding of, culture as an independent explanatory variable, and thus no concern with the interpretive dimension of human personality in general and of our moral powers in particular. To the extent culture was attended to at all, cultural transmission was thought of in La-marckian terms.[63] The efforts and resulting achievements of one generation were wired into the physical natures of the offspring of that generation. As a result, any cultural advantage that one people might have had was not only peculiarly its own (not necessarily transmissible to other peoples), but a matter of rational pride for all those born into such a people. Cultural advances were never accidents of time and circumstances, but products of the achieving will, with each generation playing its part in further acts of progressive will building on the achievements of the past generation.

These views not only failed to appreciate what culture is, let alone its explanatory weight in the human sciences. They confused culture with acts of will, failing to understand the nature of cultural formation and trans-mission, the role of contingency and good luck in cultural progress, and the complete impropriety of taking credit for such advances just by virtue of being born into such a culture. This whole way of thinking naturally created ethical space for explanations in terms of superior and inferior races as a proxy for the comparison between the remarkable scientific advances in Western culture in the nineteenth century in contrast to the putative lack of comparable advances nearly everywhere else.[64] If the least such progress appeared to be in African cultures, such peoples must be inferior; and if Egyptian culture clearly had been for some long period advanced and had an important impact on progressive cultures such as that of ancient Greece, then Egyptians could not be black.[65]

It was assumptions of these sorts that explain why the Supreme Court in *Plessy* could be so ethically blind, in the same way proslavery thinkers

[62] See Stanton, *The Leopard's Spots*; Fredrickson, *The Black Image in the White Mind*; Haller, *Outcasts from Evolution*; Gossett, *Race*.

[63] See Stocking, *Race, Culture, and Evolution*, pp. 47–48, 124, 234–69.

[64] See ibid., pp. 234–69.

[65] See, e.g., Stanton, *The Leopard's Spots*, p. 50.

had been blind, to the ignoble and unjust contempt that its legitimation of the further cultural degradation of blacks inflicted on black Americans. For the *Plessy* Court, race was not morally arbitrary, but a physical fact crucially connected with other physical facts of rational incapacity for which blacks, being from a nonprogressive culture, must be ethically responsible. In contrast, white Americans, taking rational ethical pride in their willed success in sustaining a progressive culture, should take the same pride in their race, and might reasonably protect their achievements from those of another race who were culpably non-progressive by nature. Race, a physical fact supposed to be causally connected to other physical facts, had been transformed into a trait of character. The highly moralistic mind of nineteenth-century America had no problem, once having bought the idea of such transformation, protecting people of good moral character from those who were culpably of unworthy character.

Abolitionist thought had taken the moral insularity of proslavery defenses as an example of the corruption of conscience so common in the history of religious persecution; and modern racism both in America and Europe comparably exemplified one of human nature's more artfully self-deceiving evasions of the moral responsibilities of liberal political culture—illustrated, in *Plessy*, by the way in which the culture's respect for science had been manipulated to serve racist ends. Fundamental public criticism of this view of the human sciences must, by its nature as a form of public reason bearing on constitutional values, reshape constitutional argument.

The pivotal figure in such criticism was a German Jew and immigrant to the United States, Franz Boas, who fundamentally criticized the racial explanations characteristic of both European and American physical anthropology in the late nineteenth century.[66] Boas argued that comparative anthropological study did not sustain the explanatory weight placed on race in the human sciences. In fact, there was more significant variability within races than there was between races.[67] Indeed, many of the human features, supposed to be unchangeably physical (such as the cephalic index), were responsive to cultural change. Boas had thus shown that the physical traits of recent immigrants to the United States had changed in response to acculturation.[68]

[66] See Boas, *The Mind of Primitive Man*; Stocking, *A Franz Boas Reader*. For superb commentary, see Stocking, *Race, Culture, and Evolution*; Degler, *In Search of Human Nature*, pp. 61–83. For a useful recent comparative study of comparable such developments in the United States and Britain, see Barkan, *The Retreat of Scientific Racism*.

[67] See Franz Boas, "Race," in *Encyclopaedia of the Social Sciences*, ed. Edwin R. A. Seligman (New York: Macmillan, 1937), 7:25–36; Boas, *The Mind of Primitive Man*, pp. 45–59, 179. For commentary, see Stocking, *Race, Culture, and Evolution*, pp. 192–94.

[68] See Franz Boas, "Changes in Immigrant Body Form," in Stocking, *A Franz Boas Reader*, pp. 202–14; Boas, *The Mind of Primitive Man*, pp. 94–96. For commentary, see Stocking, *Race, Culture, and Evolution*, pp. 175–80.

The crucial factor, heretofore missing from the human sciences, was culture. Its formation and transmission could not be understood in terms of the reductive physical models that had dominated scientific and popular thinking. In particular, Lamarckian explanation—having been discredited by Mendelian genetics in favor of random genetic mutation—was not the modality of cultural transmission, which was not physical at all but irreducibly cultural. One generation born into a progressive culture could take no more credit for an accident of birth than a generation could be reasonably blamed for birth into a less progressive culture. In fact, cultures advance often through accident and good luck and through cultural diffusion of technologies from other cultures. Such diffusion has been an important fact in the history of all human cultures at some point in their histories. No people has been through all points in its history the vehicle of the cultural progress of humankind, nor can any people reasonably suppose itself the unique vehicle of all such progress in the future.[69]

Boas's general contributions to the human sciences were powerfully elaborated in the area of race by his students Otto Klineberg[70] and Ruth Benedict.[71] They argued that the explanatory role of race in the human sciences was, if anything, even less important than the judicious Boas might have been willing to grant[72] (Boas's student, Margaret Mead, suggested that much the same might be true to some significant extent of gender)[73].

The most important study of the American race problem was not by an American but by the Swedish social scientist Gunnar Myrdal. His monumental *An American Dilemma* brought the new approach to culture powerfully to bear on the plight of American blacks who, from the perspective of the human sciences, now were increasingly well understood as victims of a historically entrenched cultural construction of racism.[74] In effect, the advances in morally independent critical standards of thought and analysis in the human sciences had enabled social scientists to make the same sort of argument that abolitionist theorists of race, such as Maria Child, had made earlier largely on ethical grounds (see Chapter 3).

Previously, the human sciences had been claimed on the side of race differences against regressive religion and ethics. Now, however, devel-

[69] See Boas, *The Mind of Primitive Man*. For commentary, see Stocking, *Race, Culture, and Evolution*.

[70] See Otto Klineberg, *Race Differences* (New York: Harper & Bros., 1935).

[71] See Ruth Benedict, *Race: Science and Politics* (New York: Viking Press, 1945).

[72] See e.g., Franz Boas, "Human Faculty as Determined by Race," in Stocking, *A Franz Boas Reader*, pp. 231, 234, 242; Boas, *The Mind of Primitive Man*, pp. 230–31.

[73] See Degler, *In Search of Human Nature*, pp. 73, 133–37.

[74] See Gunnar Myrdal, *An American Dilemma: The Negro Problem and Modern Democracy*, 2 vols. (1944; reprint, New York: Pantheon Books, 1972). For commentary, see David W. Southern, *Gunnar Myrdal and Black-White Relations: The Use and Abuse of an American Dilemma, 1944–1969* (Baton Rouge: Louisiana State University Press, 1987).

opments in the human sciences had cleared away as so much rationalizing self-deception the false dichotomy between science and ethics and revealed the ethically regressive uses to which even science may be put by politically entrenched epistemologies concerned to preserve the politics of race. Such political epistemologies, a modernist expression of essentially sectarian conceptions of religious and moral truth, cannot legitimately be the basis of political enforcement on society at large. Rather, legitimate political power must be based on impartial standards of reasonable discussion and debate not hostage to entrenched political orthodoxies. An old ethical point—that of the argument for toleration already used by the abolitionists against slavery and racism—was articulated yet again, now used in the service of an articulate argument of public reason against the force that American racism had been permitted to enjoy in the mistaken interpretation of equal protection in such cases as *Plessy*. Thus, a contractualist political theory of suspect classification analysis, rooted in the argument for toleration, affords an illuminating account of interpretive mistake and of the nature of the argument of public reason required to rectify that mistake.

This point of public reason was much highlighted in the American public mind by the comparable kind of racism that had flourished in Europe in the same period in the form of modern anti-Semitism. As we have seen, during this period both American racism and European anti-Semitism evolved into particularly virulent political pathologies under the impact of the respective emancipations of American blacks from slavery and European Jews from various civil disabilities keyed to their religious background. In both cases, the respective emancipations were not carried through by consistent enforcement of guarantees of basic rights (in the United States, despite clear constitutional guarantees to that effect).

The characteristic nineteenth-century struggles for national identity led, in consequence, to stark examples of the paradox of intolerance in which the exclusion of race-defined cultural minorities from the political community of equal rights became itself the irrationalist basis of national unity. Strikingly similar racist theorists evolved in Europe to sustain anti-Semitism (Houston Chamberlain)[75] and in America to sustain a comparable racism against the supposedly non-Aryan (Madison Grant).[76] American constitutional institutions were, as a consequence, misinterpreted, but nonetheless increasingly were the vehicle of black protest and dissent.[77]

[75] See Chamberlain, *The Foundations of the Nineteenth Century*.

[76] See Madison Grant, *The Passing of the Great Race or the Racial Basis of European History* (New York: Charles Scribner's Sons, 1919).

[77] See, e.g., McNeil, *Groundwork*. For good general studies, see John Hope Franklin and Alfred A. Moss, Jr., *From Slavery to Freedom: A History of Negro Americans*, 6th ed. (New York: Knopf, 1988); Donald G. Nieman, *Promises to Keep: African-Americans and the Constitutional Order, 1776 to the Present* (New York: Oxford University Press, 1991).

Certainly, American institutions did not collapse on the scale of the German declension into atavistic totalitarianism and the genocide of five million European Jews.[78] In both cases, however, the underlying irrationalist racist dynamic was strikingly similar in the ways already discussed at some length.[79]

Boas's important criticism of the role of race in the human sciences had, of course, been motivated as much by his own experience of European anti-Semitism as by American racism. The subsequent elaboration of his arguments by Klineberg, Benedict, and Myrdal had further raised the standards of public reason to expose the intellectual and ethical fallacies of racism both in America and Europe. In light of such criticism, the constitutional attack in the United States on the analytic foundations of *Plessy* began well before World War II.

But World War II, not unlike the Civil War, played an important role in stimulating the development of much more enlightened public attitudes on racial questions than had previously prevailed. Indeed, the allied victory raised corresponding questions about the state of American constitutionalism prior to the war not unlike those raised by the Reconstruction Amendments about antebellum American constitutionalism. The United States successfully fought the war in Europe against a nation that, like the American South in the Civil War, defined its world historic mission in self-consciously racist terms. The political ravages of such racism—both in the unspeakable moral horrors of the Holocaust of five million innocent European Jews and in the brutalities World War II inflicted on so many others—naturally called for a moral interpretation of that war, again like the Civil War, in terms of the defense of the political culture of universal human rights against its racist antagonists. In the wake of World War II and its central role in the allied victory and in the European reconstruction, the United States took up a central position on the world stage as an advocate of universal human rights. America was thus naturally pressed to examine not only at home but abroad as well such practices as state-sponsored racial segregation in light of the best interpretation of American ideals of human rights in contemporary circumstances.[80]

World War II played a role in American moral and political thought of a kind of Third American Revolution. American ideals of revolutionary constitutionalism were tested against the aggression on human rights of a nation, Nazi Germany, that attacked everything the American constitutional tradition valued in the idea and constitutional institutions of respect for

[78] See Hilberg, *The Destruction of the European Jews*, 3:1201–20.

[79] For related similarities between the United States and South Africa, see Fredrickson, *White Supremacy*.

[80] See Mary L. Dudziak, "Desegregation as a Cold War Imperative," *Stanford Law Review* 41, no. 1 (November 1988):61; Fredrickson, *The Black Image in the White Mind*, p. 330.

universal human rights.[81] The self-conscious American defense of human rights against the totalitarian ambitions of Nazi Germany required Americans, after the war, to ask if their own constitutionalism was indeed adequate to their ambitions.

In fact, the painful truth was what Boas and others had long argued, namely, that America had betrayed the revolutionary constitutionalism of its Reconstruction Amendments in ways and with consequences strikingly similar to the ways in which Germany had betrayed the promise of universal emancipation. Americans did not, however, have to reconstruct their constitutionalism in order to do justice to this sense of grievous mistake. Unlike the question that faced the nation in the wake of the Civil War, the problem was not one of a basic flaw in the very design of American constitutionalism. Rather, the issue was corrigible interpretive mistake. The judiciary had failed to understand and give effect to the moral ambitions fundamental to the Reconstruction Amendments themselves, namely, that the American political community should be a moral community committed to abstract values of human rights available on fair terms of public reason to all persons, not a community based on race.

The focus for such testing of American interpretive practice was, naturally, *Plessy v. Ferguson,* in which the Supreme Court had accepted the exclusion of black Americans from the American community of equal rights. But the intellectual and ethical foundations of *Plessy,* to the extent it ever had such foundations, had collapsed under the weight of the criticism we have already discussed at some length. The idea of natural race differences had been thoroughly discredited as the product of a long American history of the unjust cultural construction of racism in precisely the same way that European anti-Semitism had been discredited. State-sponsored racial segregation, once uncritically accepted as a reasonable expression of natural race differences, now was a clearly unreasonable way of excluding citizens from their equal rights as members of the political community. In *Brown v. Board of Education,* the U.S. Supreme Court articulated this deliberative interpretive judgment for the nation by unanimously striking down state-sponsored segregation as a violation of the equal protection clause of the fourteenth amendment.

A Theory of Suspect Classification Analysis

Brown v. Board of Education held that the racial classification expressly used in the relevant state statutes (namely, that persons of one race could not attend public school with those of another race) was constitutionally

---

[81] See, Arendt, *The Origins of Totalitarianism.*

suspect and, in the circumstances of that case, unjustified and therefore invalid.[82] The doctrinal issue of principle posed by *Brown* was twofold: what makes a classification constitutionally suspect under the equal protection clause, and what burden of justification, if any, could constitutionally justify the use of such a classification?[83] We need, consistent with the ethical aims of constitutional interpretation, an argument of abstract principle that can normatively justify the legitimate place of suspect classification analysis in our constitutional law (see Chapter 4).

Alexander Bickel formulated the principle of *Brown* as the abstract ethical ideal that state benefits and burdens shall never turn on an immutable characteristic such as race.[84] Bickel meant his principle to have the force of an intrinsically reasonable ethical standard. Many cases show it is not reasonable.[85] Handicapped persons are born with handicaps that often cannot be changed; nonetheless, people with such handicaps are certainly owed, on grounds of justice, a distinctive measure of concern aimed to accord them some fair approximation of the opportunities of nonhandicapped persons. It is no moral objection to such measures that they turn on immutable characteristics because the larger theory of distributive justice has identified such factors as here reasonably relevant to its concerns.

The example is not an isolated one; its principle pervades the justice of rewards and of fair distribution more generally. For example, we reward certain athletic achievements very highly, and do not finely calibrate the component of our rewards attributable to acts of self-disciplined will from those based on natural endowments. Achievement itself suffices to elicit reward, even though some significant part of it turns on immutable physical endowments that some have and others lack. Or we allocate scarce places in institutions of higher learning on the basis of an immutable factor such as geographic distribution, an educational policy we properly regard as sensible and not unfair. The point can be reasonably generalized to include that part of the theory of distributive justice concerned with both maintaining an economic and social minimum and with some structure of differential rewards to elicit better performance for the public good. The idea of a just minimum turns on certain facts about levels of subsistence, not on acts of will; we would not regard such a minimum as any the less justly due if some component of it turned on immutable factors. Differential rewards perform the role of incentives for the kind of performance required by mod-

---

[82] *Brown vs. Board of Education*, 347 U.S. 483 (1954).

[83] For a leading criticism of *Brown* for not properly articulating what its principle was, see Herbert Wechsler, "Toward Neutral Principles of Constitutional Law," *Harvard Law Review* 73, no. 1 (November 1959):1.

[84] See Alexander Bickel, *The Least Dangerous Branch* (Indianapolis: Bobbs-Merrill, 1962), pp. 56–65, 71–72, 187, 208.

[85] For a similar query and answer, see Dworkin, *Law's Empire*, pp. 393–97.

ern industrial market economies such as the United States and Western Europe; immutable factors such as genetic endowment may play some significant role in such performance. Nonetheless, we do not regard it as unjust to reward such performance so long as the incentives work out with the consequences specified by our theory of distributive justice. Our conclusion, from a wide range of diverse examples, must be that Bickel's principle is not an ethical principle we have reason to accept or believe. It is therefore an unworthy candidate for a fundamental ethical principle of constitutional morality of the sort required to interpret the equal protection clause of the fourteenth amendment.

Bickel's formulation of the principle of *Brown* at least has the virtue of a certain serious, even elevated ethical aspiration. It is no advance over Bickel to go to the other extreme and embrace what Bickel clearly deplored, a clearly political test, such as Ackerman's, for equal protection scrutiny.[86] As we have seen, Ackerman suggested a measure of relative group political powerlessness as the test for judicial protection under the equal protection clause (see Chapter 1). *Pace* Ackerman, it should not be relevant to such protection that a group, such as blacks, has now gained significant political power, or that another, homosexuals, is increasingly politically active and sometimes effective. Nor should the fact that any randomly identified group (say, dentists) may have less political power than some statistical norm for groups of that size elevate dentists to special equal protection concern. A political test for equal protection wrongly supposes that a just claim of this sort is for enhanced political power, when the point is the prohibition on expression through law of certain sorts of irrational prejudice. The political test, as Bickel would clearly have seen, fails to take seriously the ethical dimension of the concern of equal protection for respect for moral personality, confusing it with the different though related concern for the fair distribution of political power. One aspect of a deprivation of equal protection may be an unfair distribution of political power (for example, malapportionment),[87] but not all deprivations can be so understood; and we need to understand this more fundamental ethical dimension of equal protection.

To do so, we must formulate an ethical interpretation of equal protection that will afford a plausible alternative to the inadequacies in Bickel's interpretation. Race has been the paradigm interpretive exemplar of a suspect classification, and our analysis now has established that it is not the immutability of race that reasonably justifies this interpretive attitude. Bickel has confused the demands of ethical impartiality with the acontextuality of ethical principles; he wrongly supposes that a principle, contextually sensitive to the right factors, could not be impartially applied and

---

[86] See Bruce Ackerman, "Beyond *Carolene Products*."

[87] See, e.g., *Baker v. Carr*, 369 U.S. 186 (1962); *Reynolds v. Sims*, 377 U.S. 533 (1964).

objectively assessed in the required way. We need a formulation of the ethical content of the principle of *Brown* free of this confusion, one that is both ethically impartial and contextually sensitive to the right relevant factors in history and culture that make sense of the condemnation of racism as an interpretive exemplar of the evil that the equal protection clause condemns. On that interpretive basis, a more abstract principle of suspect classification analysis can later be constructively articulated applicable to other domains (gender, sexual preference), as we shall see.

The constitutional principle of equal protection identifies the presence of a political evil such as racial prejudice by means of the analysis and criticism, in light of the argument for toleration, of a historical and cultural construction of the unjust moral degradation of a class of persons from the community of equal rights. Racial prejudice, thus identified, must then be deconstructed as an effective political force in order (1) to protect inalienable rights placed at risk by such unconstitutional political prejudice, and (2) in order to construct over time a nonracist political consensus on the constitutional community as a moral community committed to the inalienable human rights of all persons subject to political power. As I have already suggested, mainstream abolitionist thought may never have clearly distinguished or realistically assessed these two purposes of equal protection or thought very carefully about the relationship between these purposes. After the Civil War, protection of the rights at risk of freedmen became an immediately pressing political issue; the more long-term moral transformation in racist attitudes would be a consequence of the credible and consistent enforcement of the rights of black Americans by national institutions under the powers conferred on the national government by the Reconstruction Amendments. One ingredient of such enforcement was the suspect classification principle of equal protection review, which would delegitimate the use of public institutions, by act or omission, to enforce racial prejudice.

Brown v. Board of Education correctly interpreted and applied this principle because state-sponsored racial segregation represented blatant state complicity with the cultural construction and perpetuation of a history and culture of racist subjugation. The haunting legacy of American racism was correctly analyzed and criticized by the abolitionists as colonization; the aim was either to colonize blacks away from the American community or, if compelled to keep them here, reduce them to a culturally degraded status as nonpersons unworthy of the inalienable rights central to the public culture defined by the argument for toleration. State-sponsored racial segregation was recognized by the Supreme Court in *Brown* as a constitutional evil because the state laws in question legitimated by public law precisely the kind of isolation from public institutions that was central to the cultural construction of racism as a political evil. Public education was the natural threshold context for the announcement and application of this principle (not in its nature limited to education). Its initial application to public education gave the most dramatic public announcement that could be given that the basic rights of conscience, speech, and association—so centrally developed through basic education—must be afforded in a public culture transparently open, available, and accessible to all persons as equal bearers of inalienable human rights.

It follows from this analysis of the principle of *Brown*, in contrast to Bickel's,[88] that affirmative action plans should not be mechanically invalidated by its principle. If the ethical principle of *Brown* were that no immutable characteristic may ever be the basis of state action, Bickel's conclusion would follow. But Bickel's principle is not ethically reasonable, and it follows that his principle can have no decisive ethical or constitutional force against such plans.

Affirmative action plans may be designed in many different ways. Their general design is to accord some independent weight to race among the factors to be taken into account in determining access to benefits such as education and job opportunities. Their purpose is both to take into account the social deprivations inflicted on blacks in determining qualifications and to deconstruct the historical culture of racism by promoting inclusion of blacks into the public culture in order to remedy the exclusion and marginalization that have been the historical nerve of American racism.

Some of these plans are more reasonable and more effective in achieving their aims than others; some may be unreasonable and ineffective and not worthy of adoption.[89] But as a matter of basic constitutional principle, affirmative action plans are not in their post-*Brown* nature grounded in racial prejudice, the moral degradation of a group through a continuing pattern of exclusion, exile, and colonized marginalization. To the contrary, these plans take reasonable steps that both acknowledge the nation's complicity with the construction of racism and its obligation to take steps to attack the nerve of the evil by promoting inclusion of blacks into the public culture.

[88] See Bickel, *The Least Dangerous Branch*, pp. 56–65, 71–72, 187, 208.

[89] Shelby Steele, a black academic, has recently made a claim along these lines about some affirmative action programs; see Shelby Steele, *The Content of Our Character* (New York: St. Martin's Press, 1990). Steele focuses on what he claims to be the damaging effects of such programs on blacks, namely, the failure of blacks to hold themselves to appropriately high standards of accomplishment and aspiration; in effect, the programs reinforce the sense of cultural inferiority they were meant to remedy. It would require much better argument than Steele affords to show that all such programs must, by their very nature, aggravate rather than ameliorate racism. At best, he articulates one negative feature in some such programs, which may be balanced over time by other positive factors of a more inclusive experience of respect as a participant in public culture, raising standards over time. Nothing in his argument shows that such programs are themselves the product of racism, and thus he has not shown that such programs should be suspect on grounds of constitutional principle.

As such, these plans should not be subject to the level of scrutiny required by the principle of *Brown*,[90] but to a lesser standard of reasonable review to assure they are untainted by racial prejudice.[91]

It is sometimes argued that, even if such plans are not actuated by racist hatred of blacks, they are objectionable because they inflict racist indignity on innocent members of nonminority white groups, depriving them on racial grounds of positions they would otherwise secure. The basic ethical force of this argument rests on Bickel's principle, and should enjoy no more and no less constitutional weight than the ethical principle to which it appeals. But the principle, on examination, has no fundamental ethical weight; and the corresponding constitutional argument is baseless.

The force that the argument appears to have depends on a confusion of the mechanical, acontextual impersonality of Bickel's principle with the demands of an ethical impartiality; it wrongly supposes that an ethical principle as such, like that condemning the political force of irrational prejudice, cannot be suitably contextualized to culture and history. In fact, the best interpretation of the abstract ethical force of the equal protection clause must be contextualized to the history and culture of American slavery and racism. From this perspective, the decontextualization of equal protection claims, on which the argument of nonminority white groups to injury from affirmative action plans depends, fails to take seriously the background of history and culture fundamental to the unjust American construction of racism, the complicity of American constitutional culture with that wrong, and the corresponding public responsibility of all to undo that wrong.

The construction of American racism is a fundamental flaw in our constitutionalism, one that enjoyed constitutional legitimation and support both in the antebellum period and into the modern period through the interpretive betrayals of the promise of the Reconstruction Amendments that I have now discussed at some length. Some white Americans, as immigrants, suffered, of course, from nativist prejudice; some such prejudice (as we saw in the case of southern and eastern European immigrants) was bizarrely racist in the style of Madison Grant's preference for "Aryan" over non-"Aryan" whites.[92] But their long-term acculturation into American public culture was not permanently barred by a constitutionally entrenched American history and culture of moral degradation. It is baseless for some of them now to claim that affirmative action plans are today grounded in

---

[90] For a striking judicial example of this interpretive mistake, see *Regents of University of California v. Bakke*, 438 U.S. 265 (1978), in which Justice Powell, writing for the Court, wrongly subjects affirmative action plans to strict scrutiny analysis.

[91] See ibid., opinion of Brennan, J. (concurring in the judgment in part and dissenting).

[92] See Grant, *The Passing of the Great Race*.

racism against them. This is bad history and self-serving distortion of facts, and should be bad constitutional law.

The constitutional test for suspect classifications under the equal protection clause should, *pace* Bickel, be contextually sensitive to relevant factors of history, culture, and dominant political motivation. The test of dominant political motivation is not a merely psychological inquiry, but must be interpreted against the background of a history and culture of moral degradation, the continuing political power of the social construction of racism today, and the high probability that some form of state action or omission has been dominantly motivated by such racial prejudice.[93] When these features are in place, the state policy is constitutionally suspect (that is, probably motivated by the unconstitutional motivation of racial prejudice), and should only be valid if it can be shown to be justified in fact by a compelling state purpose sufficient to purge the legislation of the taint of racist motivation.

My articulation of the principle of suspect classification review has been framed in terms of state action or omission.[94] This proposal addresses the interpretive question of how the state action requirement of the fourteenth amendment should be understood and the further issue of how constitutional proof of dominant racist motivation should be understood. The doctrine of equal protection imposes an ongoing ethical and constitutional responsibility on the nation to deconstruct the culture of American racism. That responsibility arises both from active support for such racism and from culpable inaction in not circumscribing its political power. In both cases, the Congress, the executive, and the judiciary failed to perform their obligations under the Reconstruction Amendments. The judiciary, deciding cases such as *Plessy*, legitimated racist segregation; and in related cases, it narrowly construed the state action requirement and hobbled the power of Congress reasonably to circumscribe public practices of exclusion and degradation that legitimated a public culture of racism.[95] Such complicity, based on both culpable action and omission, gives rise to a corresponding constitutional obligation to deconstruct the political force of the American culture of racism. That obligation must, in its nature, afford grounds for condemning both public actions supporting racism and omissions to take reasonable actions to circumscribe the force of racism in public life.

This argument of enforceable constitutional obligation condemns as interpretively mistaken the Supreme Court's early quite narrow construction of state action[96] and supports those more recent judicial attempts to expand

---

[93] Cf. Charles R. Lawrence, "The Id, the Ego, and Equal Protection: Reckoning with Unconscious Racism," *Stanford Law Review* 39 (January 1987): 317.

[94] For a similar view, see tenBroek, *Equal under Law*, pp. 119, 188, 221–23.

[95] See *Civil Rights Cases*, 109 U.S. 3 (1883).

[96] See ibid.

what can count as state action under the equal protection clause.[97] The narrow judicial construction of state action was of a piece with the judicial evisceration of the privileges and immunities clause[98] (further discussed in Chapter 6) and its legitimation of state-sponsored segregation in *Plessy*. American racism did not grow spontaneously outside the constitutional culture; it enjoyed, at crucial points, support, encouragement, and legitimation. A constitutional culture, now perhaps ethically capable of sustaining the vision of the Reconstruction Amendments, should fundamentally reexamine the conception of state action behind which it tried to conceal its culpable abdication of ethical and constitutional responsibility for the fetid growth of a characteristically American culture of racist exclusion and degradation.

The same conception of constitutional responsibility should extend to the interpretive issue of both the nature of unconstitutional motivation and the associated burden of argument appropriate to its proof. The focus of constitutional analysis should be not only on dominant racist political motivation, but on the forms of culpable political action and omission that have sustained a complex structure of social institutions constructive of racist culture, a structural racism with unjust disparate impact on the life chances of minorities.[99] To the extent the judiciary has not made room for standards of proof appropriate to such structural racism, its decisions are interpretively unsound and should be reexamined.[100] And to the extent affirmative action plans are a constitutionally reasonable way to remedy such structural racial disadvantage, they should be judicially encouraged, not hobbled.[101]

---

[97] See, e.g., *Marsh v. Alabama*, 326 U.S. 501 (1946) (company towns); *Evans v. Newton*, 382 U.S. 296 (1966) (private park); *Shelley v. Kraemer*, 334 U.S. 1 (1948) (enforcement of racially restrictive covenant); *Burton v. Wilmington Parking Authority*, 365 U.S. 715 (1961) (lessee of space for private restaurant from state); *Reitman v. Mulkey*, 387 U.S. 369 (1967) (state constitutional amendment forbidding fair housing laws).

[98] See *Slaughter-House Cases*, 83 (16 Wall.) 36 (1873).

[99] Cf. Owen M. Fiss, "The Fate of an Idea Whose Time Has Come: Antidiscrimination Law in the Second Decade after *Brown v. Board of Education*," *University of Chicago Law Review* 41, no. 4 (Summer 1974): 74; Fiss, "Groups and the Equal Protection Clause," *Philosophy and Public Affairs* 5, no. 2 (Winter 1976): 107.

[100] See, e.g., *Washington v. Davis*, 426 U.S. 229 (1976); *Arlington Heights v. Metropolitan Housing Corp.*, 429 U.S. 252 (1977). The Supreme Court has, however, employed such a test in the interpretation of the Title VII, the employment discrimination provision of the Civil Rights Act of 1964. See *Griggs v. Duke Power Co.*, 401 U.S. 424 (1971) (racially disparate impact of qualifications for employment must be shown to be job related). But see *Wards Cove Packing Co., Inc. v. Atonio*, 490 U.S. 642 (1989) (plaintiff's burden of proof must go beyond mere racial disparity in work force).

[101] See e.g., *City of Richmond v. J. A. Croson Co.*, 488 U.S. 469 (1989) (city of Richmond's 30 percent minority set-aside for construction contracts held unconstitutional). For an illuminating criticism of such decisions, see Michel Rosenfeld, *Affirmative Action and Justice: A Philosophical and Constitutional Inquiry* (New Haven: Yale University Press, 1991).

Gender as a Suspect Classification

The equal protection clause of the fourteenth amendment speaks in terms of an abstract normative concept, equal protection. Consistent with its abstract normative character, the Supreme Court has extended forms of suspect classification analysis to ethnic origin,[102] alienage,[103] illegitimacy,[104] and gender;[105] it has refused to extend it to poverty[106] and apparently would not extend it to sexual preference.[107] We must now bring our theory to bear on the interpretive question of the appropriate level of abstract principle that must, consistent with our rights-based analysis of arguments of principle (see Chapter 4), be ascribed to suspect classification analysis applicable to domains in addition to race. The interpretive and critical fertility of a general approach to equal protection should be evident in the areas of the greatest public interest and concern. Three such areas are gender, sexual preference, and poverty. I examine the question of gender and sexual preference as suspect classifications here; in Chapter 7 I discuss poverty.

Suspect classification analysis brings contractualist moral analysis to bear on politically entrenched structures of hierarchy and domination. The central issues are whether a history and culture has unjustifiably degraded a class of persons from the status of bearers of the inalienable culture-creating rights of public culture, and unjustly sustained and legitimated a cultural construction of inferior moral powers that rests on the history and culture of unjust deprivation of basic rights. The equal protection clause forbids public power, either by culpable act or omission, from giving expression to such unreasonable prejudice; laws or policies dominantly so motivated are suspect, and are unconstitutional unless sustained by a compelling burden of justification that expunges the taint of prejudice.

[102] See, e.g., *Hernandez v. Texas,* 347 U.S. 475 (1954) (discrimination against Mexican-Americans in jury selection).

[103] See, e.g., *Graham v. Richardson,* 403 U.S. 365 (1971) (state cannot deny welfare benefits to aliens).

[104] See, e.g., *Trimble v. Gordon,* 430 U.S. 762 (1977) (state law struck down governing intestate succession that barred inheritance by illegitimate children from their fathers).

[105] See, e.g., *Frontiero v. Richardson,* 411 U.S. 677 (1973) (federal law struck down on equal protection grounds permitting male, but not female, members of the armed services an automatic dependency allowances for their spouses); *Craig v. Boren,* 429 U.S. 190 (1976) (state statute struck down prohibiting sale of beer to males at age twenty-one and to females at age eighteen).

[106] See, e.g., *James v. Valtierra,* 402 U.S. 137 (1971) (state constitutional amendment involving wealth classification—special local referenda for low-rent housing projects—not suspect, and therefore constitutional).

[107] For two considered rejections of the claim on this ground by the Court of Appeals for the District of Columbia, see *Dronenberg v. Zech,* 741 F.2d 1388 (D.C. Cir. 1984) (Navy policy of mandatory discharge for homosexuality constitutional); *Padula v. Webster,* 822 F.2d 97 (D.C. Cir. 1987) (FBI rejection of lesbian as special agent held constitutional).

The constitutional analysis of gender as a suspect classification must begin with the required ethical analysis of the history and culture of gender hierarchy. By gender hierarchy, I understand the distribution of the basic goods of life (including rights and responsibilities) associated with social and political life in terms of dominant and often exclusive control of the most culturally valued goods by and at the discretion of men. The hierarchy of power and privilege is the consequence of masculine control over these goods, to which women have access only at the discretion of men.

The nature and defects of the justifications offered for the history and culture of gender hierarchy may be usefully examined in the arguments of presumptive public reason offered by philosophers of the Western tradition. If there is a notable and analyzable gap between their professions and their performance, its analysis affords constitutionally relevant insight into the nature and extent of the political corruption of public reason required to support gender hierarchy, which may have been pervasively influential on thought and practice.[108]

No one would ever suppose that an ancient political philosopher as communitarian as Aristotle or a modern philosopher as rights-based as Rousseau would have much in common on any question. Their structurally similar defenses of gender hierarchy, however, within political philosophies otherwise so radically different, suggest a pervasive rationalization for gender hierarchy throughout the Western political tradition.

Aristotle offered a functionalist account of women's nature inferred from the conventional roles as wife and mother defined for them in his society. He concluded, on that basis, that women have a moral nature inferior to men but superior to that of natural slaves[109] (persons, for Aristotle, so lack-

---

[108] A comparable analysis to similar effect might be extended to other arguments influential on the cultural construction of gender hierarchy, for example, those based on the interpretation of the Bible. See, e.g., Elaine Pagels, *Adam, Eve, and the Serpent* (New York: Random House, 1988); Rosemary Radford Ruether, *Womanguides: Readings toward a Feminist Theology* (Boston: Beacon Press, 1985); Rosemary Radford Ruether, *New Woman New Earth: Sexist Ideologies and Human Liberation* (San Francisco: Harper & Row, 1975); Mary Daly, *Beyond God the Father: Towards a Philosophy of Women's Liberation* (London: Women's Press, 1973); Daphne Hampson, *Theology and Feminism* (Oxford: Basil Blackwell, 1990); Uta Ranke-Heinemann, *Eunuchs for Heaven: The Catholic Church and Sexuality*, trans. John Brownjohn (London: Andre Deutsch, 1988); Susanne Heine, *Women and Early Christianity: Are the Feminist Scholars Right?* trans. John Bowden (London: SCM Press, 1987). On social background, see Gerda Lerner, *The Creation of Patriarchy* (New York: Oxford University Press, 1986).

[109] See Aristotle, *Politics*, trans. Ernest Barker (New York: Oxford University Press, 1962), pp. 35–36; for probing commentary, see Susan Moller Okin, *Women in Western Political Thought* (Princeton: Princeton University Press, 1979), pp. 73–96. See also Jean Ethke Elshtain, *Public Man, Private Woman: Women in Social and Political Thought* (Princeton: Princeton University Press, 1981), pp. 19–54.

ing moral capacity that they may be justly enslaved).[110] Rousseau demanded of men full commitment to both the equal rights of citizens and of mankind; however, he exempted women from both these rights and responsibilities on grounds of a romantic nature, as wife and mother, incapable of these demands.[111] In both Aristotle and Rousseau, public reason was interpreted in terms of a functionalist account of women's conventional social role as the measure of their natural and just place in the gender hierarchy.

Aristotle and Rousseau use the same basic functionalist analysis of women's nature to the same political effect, although they offer divergent general views of how justification in politics should be understood. Aristotle's basic ethical theory is perfectionist with a corresponding greater ethical weight accorded certain excellences of thought and action that are to be fostered by those incapable of such excellences, including (for Aristotle) those classes of persons justly deprived of rights by institutions such as slavery and the subjection of women.[112] But Rousseau's basic ethical theory is contractualist and egalitarian, with slavery ruled out as, in principle, inconsistent with respect for inalienable human rights.[113] How has contractualist political theory, understood by a rights-based interpreter such as Rousseau as antislavery, been rendered consistent with the legitimation of gender hierarchy?

This critical question is not uniquely aimed at the contractualism of Rousseau, though he gave the view the most extravagantly romantic expression it was to receive. Other leading expositors of contractualist political theory—whose use of it diversely included Hobbes's defense of political absolutism[114] and Locke's[115] and Kant's[116] defenses of rights-based consti-

[110] See Aristotle, *Politics*, p. 13.

[111] See, e.g., Jean Jacques Rousseau, *Emile*, trans. Barbara Foxley (London: J. M. Dent, 1961), pp. 321–56. For incisive commentary, see Okin, *Women in Western Political Thought*, pp. 140–94; see also Elshtain, *Public Man, Private Woman*, pp. 148–70; Carole Pateman, *The Sexual Contract* (Cambridge: Polity Press, 1988), pp. 96–99. For a general treatment, see Joel Schwartz, *The Sexual Politics of Jean-Jacques Rousseau* (Chicago: University of Chicago Press, 1984).

[112] See Aristotle, *Nicomachean Ethics*, trans. Martin Ostwald (Indianapolis: Bobbs-Merrill, 1961); for discussion of perfectionism and its normative implications, see Richards, *A Theory of Reasons for Action*, pp. 116–17.

[113] See Jean Jacques Rousseau, *The Social Contract*, in Rousseau, *The Social Contract and Discourses*, trans. G.D.H. Cole (New York: E. P. Dutton, 1950), p. 11.

[114] See Thomas Hobbes, *Leviathan*, ed. Michael Oakeshott (Oxford: Basil Blackwell, 1960). For illuminating commentary on Hobbes's acknowledgment of the equality of women and yet his justification for gender hierarchy, see Elshtain, *Public Man, Private Woman*, pp. 106–27; Pateman, *The Sexual Contract*, pp. 43–50; Okin, *Women in Western Political Thought*, pp. 197–99.

[115] See Locke, *Two Treatises*. For illuminating commentary on Locke's defense of gender

tutionalism—also ultimately legitimated gender hierarchy. How has contractualist political theory (particularly, the rights-based interpretation of it in Locke, Rousseau, and Kant) been, at once, so critical of slavery yet so legitimating of gender hierarchy?

Rousseau's political theory gave an arresting expression to this ethical paradox by means of his distinction between the pre-moral relationships of the state of nature and the ethical reconstruction and transformation of human nature in a political society organized on proper contractualist lines (in accord with his conception of the General Will).[117] Rousseau exempted women as a class from the ethical demands of contractualist political transformation because he took it to be a fact of their natures, qua women, that they were incapable of the transformation; indeed, their inclusion in it would imperil the only ethical transformation that was practicable—men's.

Rousseau's highly personal way of interpreting rights-based contractualism was rooted in the violent personal objection he took, very much in the spirit of Moliere's *Les Femmes Savantes*,[118] to women's participation in the explosive intellectual life of prerevolutionary France. No one during this period had a more trenchant and searing moral contempt for the illegitimacy of French monarchical absolutism and the way in which intellectuals of the French Enlightenment such as Voltaire often pandered to it or its companion absolutisms elsewhere.[119] Rousseau's contempt apparently embraced, as one of the causes of the intellectual degeneracy about him, what he regarded as the effeminization of French culture from the participation of women (especially Parisian women) in it.[120]

It is from the perspective of this analysis that Rousseau wholly excluded women from the ethical transformation of the General Will. The focal mistake of prerevolutionary France had been to include them in public culture.

---

hierarchy, see Okin, *Women in Western Political Thought*, pp. 199–201; Elshtain, *Public Man, Private Woman*, pp. 108–27; Pateman, *The Sexual Contract*, pp. 52–53.

[116] See Immanuel Kant, "On the Common Saying: 'This May Be True in Theory, but It Does Not Apply in Practice,'" in Kant, *Kant's Political Writings* ed. Hans Reiss (Cambridge: Cambridge University Press, 1977), pp. 61–92. For commentary on Kant's defense of gender hierarchy, see Pateman, *The Sexual Contract*, pp. 168–71; Okin, *Women in Western Political Thought*, p. 6.

[117] For illuminating general discussion, see Judith N. Shklar, *Men and Citizens: A Study of Rousseau's Social Theory* (Cambridge: Cambridge University Press, 1985); for comparable discussion focusing on Rousseau's treatment of gender, see Okin, *Women in Western Political Thought*, pp. 99–194.

[118] See Moliere, "The Learned Women," in Moliere, *The Misanthrope and Other Plays*, trans. Donald M. Frame (New York: New American Library, 1981), pp. 357–428.

[119] See Shklar, *Men and Citizens*, pp. 101–4, 108–10, 114, 116, 117, 123–24, 221–22, 229.

[120] See ibid., pp. 144–45. For a related argument, albeit certainly not in the defense of gender hierarchy, about nineteenth-century American culture, see Ann Douglas, *The Feminization of American Culture* (New York: Knopf, 1977).

The lesson to be learned was that their moral incapacities for public life required them to be forever kept in a private sphere of husband and family that would keep public life free of their corrupting taint. On this view, women's moral nature was exclusively suited to the private romantic attachments of family life and incapable of the impartial ethical demands of public life from which, for this reason of incapacity, they may and indeed must be totally excluded.

Rousseau's argument is remarkable not for its substance (other rights-based contractualists shared the view), but for the highly original and naive transparency of the revelatory way he expressed it.[121] If the legitimation of gender hierarchy on rights-based contractualist grounds was as tenuous as I believe it was, we need to understand the force of the assumptions (summarized in the idea of women's nature) that validated it for so many. Rousseau's way of expressing the point revealed its essentially reactionary motivations. The abstract ethical demands of public life must be protected and indeed immunized from the preethical realm of personal romantic spontaneity and attachment. In effect, the demands of abstract ethical argument—motivated by an emancipatory conception of public reason—required men, the bearers of public reason, sharply to divide their public lives as men with men from their private lives with wives and mothers.

Rousseau's arguments about the morally inferior nature of women, like the comparable arguments of antebellum proslavery thought and of European racist anti-Semitism, arose in the context of a long history and culture of patterns of hierarchy and subjugation, some of which (slavery and the subjection of women) had been philosophically justified by Aristotle, among others.[122] These patterns of political hierarchy and their philosophical supports were now, in light of the argument for toleration, subject to criticism in terms of ideas of human rights and to corrective political action on the ground of the revolutionary constitutionalism to which such ideas gave rise. Rousseau was one prominent advocate of such ethical criticism and revolutionary constitutionalism, but not in the area of gender hierarchy. Rousseau put his argument in the non-Aristotelian terms of protecting human rights. But he assumed, without reasonable contractualist justification, the good sense of Aristotle's functionalist account of women's moral nature.

That is the reason why, in my judgment, the comparison of Aristotle and Rousseau is so revealing. Aristotle, the great classical defender of natural hierarchies, has been repudiated in other areas (for example, slavery) on rights-based grounds; but he is uncritically accepted in the area of gender.

---

[121] For the importance of transparency in Rousseau's thought, see Jean Starobinski, *Jean-Jacques Rousseau: Transparency and Obstruction*, trans. Arthur Goldhammer (Chicago: University of Chicago Press, 1988).

[122] See Davis, *The Problem of Slavery*. On historical background, see Lerner, *The Creation of Patriarchy*.

In effect, women's traditional roles in the history and culture of gender hierarchy are taken to be the measure of their inferior moral capacities as persons, and that view of women's nature is then used as a pivotal assumption in the general contractualist analysis.

The interest of Rousseau's way of expressing the argument is its obvious reactionary motivations centered in special worries about the emancipatory consequences that the argument for toleration, so central to contractualist political theory, might be interpreted to have for women. Mary Wollstonecraft (an acute critic of Rousseau) made precisely this point when she criticized Rousseau's insistence that men must control women's religious conscience.[123] Rousseau did not, of course, object to the argument for toleration itself; it was as central to his rights-based contractualism as it was for Locke or Kant.[124] Indeed, he paid tribute to the argument by the very way in which he defended his exclusion of women from public culture. The exclusion was necessary in order to protect a political community of human rights from its subversion by the improper generalization of the argument for toleration to women, subversive consequences Rousseau thought he saw in prerevolutionary France.

But Rousseau's interpretation of the argument illustrates both the effects and motivations yet again of the paradox of intolerance that we earlier studied as a reactionary response to the American abolition of slavery and the European emancipation of the Jews. The context of Rousseau's argument was what he saw as the French Enlightenment's wrongheaded tendencies to emancipate women. Rousseau's reactionary response was, like that of American racism and European anti-Semitism, to offer a conception of the political community of human rights as necessarily masculine and to defend it on the basis of a thoroughgoing deprivation of the culture-creating rights of women, which would confirm the image of their degraded moral incapacity.

The key to the paradox of intolerance is the decadent uses to which it must, in order to rationalize intolerance, put the idea of public reason. The argument for toleration is in its proper nature emancipatory of public reason. It subjects political power that abridges basic rights to the test of impartial justification to all in terms not hostage to the entrenched political epistemology. In contrast, the paradox of intolerance, based on truncating the force that the argument of toleration should have, must unreasonably deny that whole classes of person have the moral powers to originate and deliberate about claims of public reason. The motivation of the intolerance effectively subverts the epistemic purposes of the argument it is inter-

---

[123] See Mary Wollstonecraft, *A Vindication of the Rights of Woman* (1792; reprint, New York: W. W. Norton, 1967), pp. 141, 147, 161, 281–82.

[124] See, e.g., Rousseau, *Emile*, pp. 228–78; cf. *The Social Contract*, pp. 129–41.

preting; it deprives public reason of precisely the discourse it most clearly demands and requires.

As we have seen in the case of American and European racism, this form of political argument must, in order to sustain its self-image of commitment to the argument for toleration, resort to forms of political irrationalism (cultivating bad arguments based on circularities or forms of allegiance antagonistic to free public reason). In this way it can construct an apparently reasonable image of the subhuman capacities of those excluded from the ambit of toleration; thus, its gargantuan appetite for bad science. Such irrationalism must in its nature both distort the very standards of reasonable argument and debate appropriate to the issues under discussion (the nature and role of blacks, or women) and correlatively deny that the persons excluded have the reasonable moral powers to originate claims and arguments relevant to that discussion. Both features mark the contractualist rationalization of gender hierarchy.

As we saw in Chapter 3, the argument for toleration rests not on ultimate epistemological and moral skepticism, but on a skepticism about the reliability of politically entrenched sectarian epistemologies as the exclusive measure of reasonable discussion and debate. Essentially sectarian views of fact and value thus immunize themselves from wider criticism in terms of independent reasonable standards of thought and inquiry; rather, they unreasonably and polemically make themselves the measure of what counts as reasonable inquiry and debate.

The political epistemology supportive of gender hierarchy was in this way epistemically and morally flawed; like the comparable circularity in the case of race, it took the consequences of unjust moral degradation as the measure of natural moral capacity. A political epistemology, thus wedded to the insular defense of a historically entrenched political orthodoxy, decisively shaped as well an alleged science of gender that was at least as epistemically unreliable as the comparable science of race. Indeed, the science of gender and race differences flourished together, used similar crude physical measures of moral capacity, and served similar ideological functions in the cultural construction of images of racist and sexist moral inferiority.[125] Such distortions of the alleged human sciences by the self-rationalizing requirements of a dominant, politically entrenched epistemology of gender were, of course, ancient. They took new forms under the

[125] See Gould, *The Mismeasure of Man*; Cynthia Eagle Russett, *Sexual Science: The Victorian Construction of Womanhood* (Cambridge: Harvard University Press, 1989); Londa Schiebinger, *The Mind Has No Sex? Women in the Origins of Modern Science* (Cambridge: Harvard University Press, 1989). For the continuing force of these political epistemologies today, see Anne Fausto-Sterling, *Myths of Gender: Biological Theories about Women and Men* (New York: Basic Books, 1985); Cynthia Fuchs Epstein, *Deceptive Distinctions: Sex, Gender, and the Social Order* (New Haven: Yale University Press, 1988).

impact of a growing public respect for the physical sciences in the nineteenth century, reinforcing a politically dominant cultural image of the basic moral incapacity of women.[126] These views were not held on the basis of impartial standards of critical reason that could be publicly justified to all, but were polemically entrenched modes of legitimating the established practices of gender hierarchy.

Distortions of fact and value were here motivated by the normative models of family roles at the heart of the dominant political epistemology. They took the form, in nineteenth-century America and Europe, of images of women as asexual, passive, essentially limited by their natures to their roles as wives and mothers, as caretakers of children and men.[127] The resulting distortion of value was the incomplete and truncated interpretation of contractualist political theory required to rationalize this political epistemology. Contractualist political theory that had, in the hands of Locke,[128] been used to criticize Filmer's appeal to patriarchalism to justify political absolutism among men,[129] was inhibited in its reasonable application to the family. As Carol Pateman has put the point, the social contract ideologically obfuscated the illegitimacy of the underlying sexual contract.[130] This truncation of contractualist analysis left the family essentially immune from scrutiny in light of arguments of political legitimacy.

The idea of women's nature was functionally interpreted in terms of uncritically accepted private family roles, and thus reflected and rationalized this failure of ethical and political analysis. Plato's argument in *The Republic* had shown that such a view of women's nature was not philosophically inevitable.[131] But the very context of his analysis (abolition of the private nuclear family) confirmed, if anything, the close links of the two questions, the family and women; in effect, the retention of the one required the inferior moral status of the other.[132] Even John Stuart Mill, who argued eloquently in *The Subjection of Women* for the rights of women in public life,[133] largely immunized the family itself from his analysis.[134]

[126] For a brilliant recent development of this theme of a continuity and even worsening of sexism through changing models of female sexuality, see Thomas Laqueur, *Making Sex: Body and Gender from the Greeks to Freud* (Cambridge: Harvard University Press, 1990).

[127] See Russett, *Sexual Science*.

[128] See Locke, *Two Treatises*.

[129] See Filmer, *Patriarcha*.

[130] See Pateman, *The Sexual Contract*.

[131] For Plato's argument that women were qualified to be guardians of his ideal state and for the abolition of the private family, see Plato, *Republic*, book 5, in *Plato: The Collected Dialogues*, ed. Edith Hamilton and Huntington Cairns (New York: Pantheon, 1961), pp. 688–720. For probing commentary, see Okin, *Women in Western Political Thought*, pp. 15–50.

[132] For incisive commentary on this point, see Jean Bethke Elshtain, *Public Man, Private Woman*, pp. 19–41.

[133] See John Stuart Mill, *The Subjection of Women*, in John Stuart Mill and Harriet Taylor

The consequence of this truncated interpretation of democratic political theory in general and contractualist theory in particular was an impoverishment of its analysis of the scope and meaning of human rights, a result clearly seen in Rousseau's unusually revealing statement of the view. Rousseau sharply separated the abstract human rights required for the public political life of men from the romantic absorption and partiality of private life, the world of women. This not only gave a falsely hypermasculinized image of the rights of public political life, but equally falsely failed to articulate the many issues of justice and human rights that arose in the context of the family, including justice between spouses, between parents and children, and between children and the political community at large.[135] The ethics of care, nurturance, and education in childrearing, for example, itself calls upon the exercise of the moral powers of both parents and children, at least some of which require sensitive concern for rights-based issues of fair respect for developmental independence and autonomy.[136]

It distorts both the ethics of human rights and the ethics of care to isolate them in hermetically sealed political compartments called, respectively, public and private life. Women's moral experience, as many abolitionists certainly believed,[137] may have much to teach political contractualism about the nature and weight of human rights and how both private and public life may be critically disencumbered of the vicious sexist significance Rousseau's contractualism accorded them.[138] Rousseau's truncated interpretation of contractualism did not make sense of many of these claims of

---

Mill, *Essays on Sex Equality*, ed. Alice S. Rossi (Chicago: University of Chicago Press, 1970), pp. 125–242.

[134] For incisive commentary along these lines, see Okin, *Women in Western Political Thought*, pp. 197–230.

[135] For a recent attempt to raise these issues within the context of a contractualist theory of justice, see Susan Moller Okin, *Justice, Gender, and the Family* (New York: Basic Books, 1989); cf. David A. J. Richards, "The Individual, the Family, and the Constitution," *New York University Law Review* 55, no. 1 (April 1980): 1.

[136] Cf. Sara Ruddick, *Maternal Thinking: Toward a Politics of Peace* (Boston: Beacon Press, 1989).

[137] For a powerful example of the systematic appeal to women's experience as a way of giving expression to an articulate sense of the moral evil of slavery, see Stowe, *Uncle Tom's Cabin*. On the importance of women and the woman question in antebellum abolitionist thought and practice, see Kraditor, *Means and Ends in American Abolitionism*, pp. 39–77. For commentary and primary sources reflecting the impact of women on abolitionist thought and the emergence of an independent feminist movement, see Rossi, *The Feminist Papers*, pp. 241–322, 378–470. For commentary, see DuBois, *Feminism and Suffrage*.

[138] For illustrations of this point, see Okin, *Justice, Gender, and the Family*; Elshtain, *Public Man, Private Woman*. For studies of the distinctive nature of women's moral experience, see Carol Gilligan, *In a Different Voice: Psychological Theory and Women's Development* (Cambridge: Harvard University Press, 1982); Eva Feder Kittay and Diana T. Meyers, eds., *Women and Moral Theory* (Totowa, N.J.: Rowman & Littlefield, 1987).

rights for the same reason that he made no sense of women as bearers of rights: he failed reasonably to apply contractualist analysis to the family and to women. In consequence, his contractualism gave a false picture of what rights were and, derivatively, of women's nature as bearers of human rights.

Such an unreasonable interpretation of human rights, based on an insular and parochial political epistemology enforced on society at large, further rationalized and was rationalized by the unreasonable exclusion of women from the political community of culture-creating rights, including the rights of conscience, free speech, and associational liberty, including the right to make decisions bearing on intimate personal life. The political epistemology that rationalized gender hierarchy was in its nature ascriptive; certain roles were mandatorily ascribed to women. But reasonable contractualist analysis suggests that such hierarchy reflected a history and culture of sexist degradation of the moral powers of women; it was a cultural construction of men during a period that unjustly excluded women from the culture-creating rights that respect their constructive moral powers as free persons. Mary Wollstonecraft's eloquent query was thus much to the point: "Absolute, uncontroverted authority, it seems, must subsist somewhere: but is not this a direct and exclusive appropriation of reason?"[139] The public culture of human rights and reason had been defined, in Rousseau's understanding of political community, as in its nature masculine. As a consequence, the paradox of intolerance had given rise to a sexist political epistemology that legitimated a cultural construction of gender hierarchy.

Simone de Beauvoir was thus correct when she called for a common analysis of the characteristics "ascribed to woman, the Jew, or the Negro."[140] In the terms of my analysis, a common pattern of cultural intolerance and marginalization, fostered by the paradox of intolerance, formed a sense of community based on the moral degradation of Jews, or blacks, or women, as the case may be. An understanding of political community in terms of Aryan or white or male supremacy rested on an irrationalist corruption of the political ethics of human rights, feeding on unreasonable stereotypes themselves based on the abridgment of human rights. De Beauvoir's characterization of men as transcendent and women as immanent[141] does not endorse, but describes this corruption of ethics in which men originate creative moral projects and women are its opposite, the Other[142]—inert

---

[139] See Wollstonecraft, A Vindication of the Rights of Woman, p. 141.

[140] See Simone de Beauvoir, The Second Sex, trans. H. M. Parshley (New York: Vintage Books, 1952), p. xvi. De Beavoir expressly invokes, as useful analogies, Myrdal on American blacks and Sartre on European anti-Semitism, (p. 144). See Myrdal, An American Dilemma; Jean Paul Sartre, Anti-Semite and Jew, trans. George J. Becker (New York: Grove Press, 1948).

[141] See de Beauvoir, The Second Sex.

[142] See ibid., p. xix.

and passive. The importance of her analysis is not her own view of appropriate remedies,[143] but her critical articulation of the depth and extent of
the ethical corruption that rests, like the comparable evils of anti-Semitism
and racism, on systematic historical exclusion from the public culture of
human rights.

A constitutional community committed to the protection of the inalienable human rights of all persons, like that of the United States, has a pre-
eminent obligation to extend to all persons the fair basis of social respect
that makes available to all a secure public culture of respect for their claims
of human rights. The forms of intolerance central to suspect classification
analysis are, in their nature, breaches of this obligation. The constitutional
order has itself been complicitous with the unjust and constitutionally illegitimate construction of forms of moral subjugation and contempt that
deny whole classes of person the fair basis of social respect that is their
right. Anti-Semitism, racism, and sexism all rest on such cultural intolerance, marginalization, and colonization: the denial of the very moral powers
by which persons could give authentic voice to the just claims of their creative moral powers of personality on their political community.

Such deadening of ethical sensibility is, in its nature, an incommensurable ethical wrong. In a constitutional community committed to human
rights, it is a constitutional wrong as well, one at the heart of suspect classification analysis. In the United States, a defective understanding of the
political community of equal rights had, as in the case of race, legitimated
the political construction of gender hierarchy that unjustly subjugated
women as bearers of human rights; and the political and constitutional community, as in the case of race, was unjustly complicitous with this cultural
construction of gender hierarchy.[144]

When the Supreme Court excluded women from the scope of equal protection in 1872, it did so in terms of a Rousseauean appeal to their "natural
and proper timidity and delicacy."[145] In a period when the Court clearly
acknowledged race as a suspect classification,[146] distinctions on the basis of
gender were ostensibly natural and therefore constitutionally reasonable.
The judiciary's complicity with the unjust construction of gender hierarchy
was thus both more blatant and more insidious than in the case of race.
Race was unquestionably a suspect classification, however wrongly inter-

[143] The view has been questioned as itself hypermasculinized. See Elshtain, *Public Man,
Private Woman*, pp. 306–10; Wendy Brown, *Manhood and Politics: A Feminist Reading of
Political Theory* (Totowa, N.J.: Rowman & Littlefield, 1988), p. 185.

[144] See, e.g., *Bradwell v. the State*, 83 U.S. (16 Wall.) 130 (1872) (woman denied admission
to state bar held consistent with equal protection).

[145] Ibid., p. 141.

[146] See e.g., *Strauder v. West Virginia*, 100 U.S. 303 (1880) (state law excluding blacks
from juries held unconstitutional).

preted (*Plessy*). The absence of any scrutiny of gender whatsoever rendered the extent and depth of the injustices wrecked by the dominant political epistemology of gender hierarchy invisible and all the more powerfully supportive of the cultural construction of sexist degradation.[147] Such degradation is, as we have seen, a basic insult to ethical integrity, a constitutional wrong more fundamental than that of unfair political power, and requiring, as such, independent treatment and remedy as a constitutional wrong.

Suspect classification analysis thus applies to gender for the same reasons it applies to race. In both cases, a background history and culture had morally degraded a class of persons from the community of equal rights, justifying in the one case gender hierarchy, in the other slavery.[148] The argument of toleration, central to the constitutional community of human rights, had not been fairly extended to either group, but the constitutional culture of equal rights had unjustly legitimated the cultural construction of the moral degradation of women and blacks as inferior. Suspect classification analysis requires that the state should, neither by action nor inaction, give expression to such an unjust cultural construction based on moral subjugation from the community of equal rights. Gender, like race, is and should be a suspect classification.[149]

The interpretation of gender as a suspect classification must be contextually sensitive, as in the case of race, to the features of history and culture that bear on the construction of sexist incapacity and the resulting unconstitutional political motivation of sexist subjugation. The political evil of sexism is keyed to the unjust cultural construction of gender hierarchy that limited women to mandatory roles in family life and, on that basis, excluded them from the political community of inalienable human rights. Accordingly, the constitutional test for sexist motivation must focus on any law or

[147] For recent studies of the still persisting political epistemology of gender hierarchy and its effects, see, e.g., Fausto-Sterling, *Myths of Gender*; Epstein, *Deceptive Distinctions*; Victor R. Fuchs, *Women's Quest for Economic Equality* (Cambridge: Harvard University Press, 1988); Claudia Goldin, *Understanding the Gender Gap: An Economic History of American Women* (New York: Oxford University Press, 1990). On its possible significance for contemporary science and the philosophy of science and for political theory, see Sandra Harding, *The Science Question in Feminism* (Ithaca: Cornell University Press, 1986); Sandra Harding and Jean F. O'Barr, *Sex and Scientific Inquiry* (Chicago: University of Chicago Press, 1987); Evelyn Fox Keller, *Reflections on Gender and Science* (New Haven: Yale University Press, 1985); Sandra Harding and Merill B. Hintikka, *Discovering Reality: Feminist Perspectives on Epistemology, Metaphysics, Methodology, and Philosophy of Science* (Dordrecht, Holland: D. Reidel, 1983); Alison M. Jaggar, *Feminist Politics and Human Nature* (Totowa, N.J.: Rowman & Allanheld, 1983).

[148] Cf. the opinion of Justice Brennan writing for a plurality of the Supreme Court in *Frontiero v. Richardson*, 411 U.S. 677 (1973).

[149] The Supreme Court, though often striking down gender classifications, has not accorded gender treatment full suspect classification on a par with race. See e.g., *Craig v. Boren*, 429 U.S. 190 (1976).

policy that, by act or omission, reinforces the culturally constructed incapacity of women keyed to the sexist interpretation of public and private life (including liability to sexual harassment). Under this interpretation, woman's access to culturally valued public goods turns on their dependent relations (including sexual relations) with the opposite gender, not their own independent and responsible origination of claims as free and rational persons. For example, the state should not legitimate the idea that access to state benefits turns on women's dependence on men,[150] nor should it accept as a legitimate basis for law an alleged factual distinction that reflects and legitimates the cultural construction of gender hierarchy.[151]

Under this view of gender as a suspect classification, there must be ongoing concern for any state-supported exclusion of women, grounded in gender hierarchy, from fair access to the public culture of human rights. This obligation must include the same concern for remedies for institutional structures (including those of education and employment) that, without any compelling justification, reinforce the sexist exclusion of women from fair access to the public culture of human rights.[152] Constitutional remedies for structural racism and sexism stand on the same reasonable ground. Forms of state-sponsored gender segregation may, for the same reason, be constitutionally disfavored;[153] and affirmative action plans may be constitutionally reasonable ways to balance the cultural deprivations from which women have suffered as well as to ensure the kind of access to public culture that will deconstruct the unreasonable cultural image of sexist incapacity.[154]

The constitutionally important issue is not ignoring gender differences as such (pregnancy, lactation), but the unreasonable interpretation of them,

---

[150] For correct applications of this principle, see *Frontiero v. Richardson*, 411 U.S. 677 (1973) (gender-based distinction in conditions for dependence allowance for spouses of servicemen and women unconstitutional); *Wengler v. Druggists Mutual Ins. Co.*, 446 U.S. 142 (1980) (gender-based distinction in criteria for receipt of death benefits unconstitutional); *Orr v. Orr*, 440 U.S. 268 (1979) (gender-based distinction in alimony imposition disallowed). For an incorrect application, see *Kahn v. Shevin*, 416 U.S. 351 (1974) (gender-based distinction in state property tax exemption held constitutional).

[151] For a correct application of this principle, see *Craig v. Boren*, 429 U.S. 190 (1976) (gender-based distinction in age for drinking, keyed to statistics of gender differences in alcohol use, held unconstitutional). For an incorrect application, see *Michael M. v. Superior Court*, 450 U.S. 464 (1981) (gender-based distinction in punishment for statutory rape, keyed to pregnancy as natural punishment for women, held constitutional).

[152] For the Supreme Court's contrary view consistent with its similar treatment of race, see *Personnel Administrator of Massachusetts v. Feeney*, 442 U.S. 256 (1979) (alleged disparate impact on women of absolute lifetime state preference in state employment for veterans held inadequate basis for constitutional attack).

[153] For a correct application of this principle, see *Mississippi University for Women v. Hogan*, 458 U.S. 718 (1982) (single-sex admission to state nursing school held unconstitutional).

[154] For a correct application of this principle, see *Johnson v. Transportation Agency, Santa Clara County*, 480 U.S. 107 (1987) (use of gender in promotions upheld).

which reinforces the unjust legitimation of the cultural image of sexist incapacity, of women as incapable of the responsible exercise of their moral powers.[155] Laws against contraception, for example, imposed a constitutionally unreasonable interpretation of sexuality on women; such laws deprived women on inadequate grounds of their right to control their reproductive life and to explore their intimate sexual life and love as an end in itself independent of the gender hierarchy's unjust requirement of mandatory procreational role.[156]

Traditional gender hierarchy has unethically failed to take seriously on fair terms the moral complexity of public and private ambitions that women, like men, may responsibly integrate into an ethically lived life; such responsibilities include a fair sharing of the burdens of childrearing consistent with the other ambitions of a life fully expressive of the range of one's moral powers. Rights and responsibilities within the family must be restructured consistent with this ethical analysis, including those forms of state regulation and support that equitably reallocate these roles consistent with a reasonable concern for the role of the history and culture of gender hierarchy in the unjust subjugation of women.[157]

Sexual Preference as a Suspect Classification

If there has been some measure of reasonable judicial concern for race and gender as suspect classifications under the equal protection clause, there has been little or none for sexual preference as a suspect classification.[158] My concern here, consistent with comparable treatments of this issue by others,[159] is with the best interpretive understanding of our traditions, which includes, when necessary, a critical theory of interpretive judicial mistake.

[155] Cf. Sylvia Law, "Rethinking Sex and the Constitution," *University of Pennsylvania Law Review* 132, no. 5 (June 1984): 955; Kenneth I. Karst, "Woman's Constitution," *Duke Law Journal* 1984, no. 3 (June 1984): 447.

[156] For further discussion, see Richards, *Toleration*, pp. 256–61; and *Foundations*, pp. 212–33.

[157] See Okin, *Justice, Gender, and the Family*; Deborah L. Rhode, *Justice and Gender* (Cambridge: Harvard University Press, 1989).

[158] See, e.g., *Dronenberg v. Zech*, 741 F.2d 1388 (D.C. Cir. 1984). For a good overview, see "Developments in the Law—Sexual Orientation and the Law," *Harvard Law Review* 102, no. 7 (May 1989): 1509.

[159] See "The Constitutional Status of Sexual Orientation: Homosexuality as a Suspect Classification," *Harvard Law Review* 98, no. 6 (April 1985): 1285; "An Argument for the Application of Equal Protection Heightened Scrutiny to Classifications Based on Homosexuality," *Southern California Law Review* (1984): 797; Seth Harris, "Permitting Prejudice to Govern: Equal Protection, Military Deference, and the Exclusion of Lesbians and Gay Men from the Military," *New York University Review of Law and Social Change* 17, no. 1 (1989–90): 171.

My general conclusion has been to discount the role that political powerlessness has been accorded by political process models of equal protection review. Lack of political power—measured either by some statistical
norm (Ackerman)[160] or by the utilitarian principle (Ely)[161]—does not cap-
ture the plane of ethical discourse fundamental to suspect classification
analysis. Correlatively, such analysis does not focus on all forms of public
political attitudes that reflect distaste for some persons or groups (some
such attitudes may be well justified). Rather, its focus is on the political
expression of irrational prejudices of a certain sort, namely, those rooted
in a history and culture of unjust exclusion of a certain group from the scope
of political community required by the argument for toleration. The fundamental wrong of racism and sexism has been the intolerant exclusion of
blacks and women from the rights of public culture, exiling them to cultural
marginality in supposedly morally inferior realms. Such unjust cultural
marginalization has, in my judgment, also victimized homosexuals, and
its rectification entitles sexual preference to be recognized as a suspect
classification.

The fact that sexual preference is not, like race or gender, an immutable
and salient personal characteristic has sometimes been taken to disqualify
sexual preference from treatment as a suspect classification.[162] The argument is controversial even on its own ethical terms. Sexual preference for
most people may be a largely settled and irreversible erotic preference long
before the age of responsibility.[163] The possible concealment or even
repression of the preference—as a reason for disqualifying it from treatment as a suspect classification—is not a reasonable condition of political
respect if sexual preference is integral to the authenticity of moral personality and the prejudice against it is as politically unreasonable as racism and
sexism. The sacrifice of moral authenticity is not a demand any person could
reasonably be asked to accept as the price for freedom from irrational prej-

[160] See Ackerman, "Beyond *Carolene Products.*"

[161] See Ely, *Democracy and Distrust.*

[162] See, e.g., Michael J. Perry, "Modern Equal Protection: A Conceptualization and Appraisal," *Columbia Law Review* 79, no. 6 (October 1979): 1066–67.

[163] On irreversibility, see Wainwright Churchill, *Homosexual Behavior among Males* (New
York: Hawthorn, 1967), pp. 283–91; C. A. Tripp, *The Homosexual Matrix* (New York:
McGraw-Hill, 1975), p. 251; D. J. West, *Homosexuality* (Chicago: Aldine, 1968), p. 266;
Michael Ruse, *Homosexuality* (Oxford: Basil Blackwell, 1988), pp. 59–62. On the early age
of its formation, see John Money and A. Ehrhardt, *Man & Woman, Boy & Girl* (Baltimore:
Johns Hopkins University Press, 1972), pp. 153–201. One study hypothesizes that gender
identity and sexual object choice coincide with the development of language, that is, from
eighteen to twenty-four months of age. See J. Money, J. G. Hampson, and J. L. Hampson,
"An Examination of Some Basic Sexual Concepts: The Evidence of Human Hermaphroditism," *Johns Hopkins Hospital Bulletin* 97 (1955): 301. Cf. Alan P. Bell, Martin S. Weinberg,
and Sue K. Hammersmith, *Sexual Preference* (New York: Simon & Schuster, 1978).

udice; and homosexual persons should no more be asked to make such a crippling sacrifice of self than any other person. In any event, the earlier discussion of the principle of *Brown v. Board of Education* rejected immutability as the principle of suspect classification analysis in favor of an analysis in terms of irrational political prejudice. From this perspective, the issue of the immutability of sexual preference should be irrelevant to its constitutional examination as a suspect classification, and the issue of irrational political prejudice (which does not turn on salience) should be central.

The essential points of the suspect classification analysis of sexual preference are (1) a history and culture of unjust moral subjugation of homosexuals, and (2) the political legitimation of such subjugation by the exclusion of homosexuals from the constitutional community of equal rights in a way that gives rise to the paradox of intolerance and the irrational political prejudice of homophobia.

The history and culture of the moral subjugation of homosexuals are ancient. Plato in *The Laws* gave influential expression to the moral condemnation in terms of two arguments: its nonprocreative character and (in its male homosexual forms) its degradation of the passive male partner to the status of a woman.[164] Homosexuality was, on this view, an immoral and unnatural abuse of the proper human function of sexuality, marking the homosexual as subhuman and therefore wholly outside the moral community of persons. The exile of homosexuals from any just claim on moral community was given expression by the striking moral idea of homosexuality as unspeakable. It was, in Blackstone's terms, "a crime not fit to be named: *peccatum illud horribile, inter christianos non nominandum*"[165] —not mentionable, let alone discussed or assessed. Such total silencing of any reasonable discussion rendered homosexuality a kind of cultural death, naturally thus understood and indeed condemned as a kind of ultimate heresy against essential moral values.[166]

The traditional moral condemnation of homosexuality was thus, in its historical nature, a form of intolerance that should have been subject to appropriate political and constitutional assessment in light of the argument for toleration. However, political contractualism, as in the related area of

---

[164] See Plato, *Laws*, book 8, 835d-842a, in *The Collected Dialogues*, pp. 1401–2. On the moral condemnation of the passive role in homosexuality in both Greek and early Christian moral thought, see Peter Brown, *The Body and Society: Men, Women, and Sexual Renunciation in Early Christianity* (New York: Columbia University Press, 1988), pp. 30, 382–83.

[165] See William Blackstone, *Commentaries on the Laws of England*, 4 vols. (Chicago: University of Chicago Press, 1979), 216.

[166] For further discussion of this point, see Richards, *Toleration*, pp. 278–79. For a useful historical overview on the social construction of homosexuality, see David F. Greenberg, *The Construction of Homosexuality* (Chicago: University of Chicago Press, 1988).

gender, not only failed to extend its analysis to sexual preference; it indulged the paradox of intolerance by accepting an unreasonable conception of constitutional community excluding homosexuals as subhuman and thus unworthy of the rights of conscience, free speech, and association central to the exercise of their moral powers.[167] The same defective political epistemology of gender and sexuality that unleashed the paradox of intolerance against women applied, a fortiori, to homosexuals, a group whose sexuality was, because morally unspeakable, even less well understood or fairly discussed or empirically assessed. The vacuum of fair discussion and assessment was filled by the fears and irrationalist stereotypes reflective of the long moral tradition that exiled homosexuals from moral community.

It is consistent with this argument about homophobia as a culturally constructed irrational prejudice (an insult to culture-creating rights) to observe the extraordinarily important role homosexuals have played in the construction of Western culture, including its arts.[168] An argument of essential human rights is not directed at saints, heroes, or persons of genius, who can find creative redemption in circumstances that crush the moral powers of other people. The cultural tradition of the West may honor its women and men of genius who are homosexuals, but not as homosexuals and not homosexuals as such. The bitter, plain truth is that ordinary people of good will, whose sexual preference was homosexual, could find in their culture only their denial as unspeakable, voiceless, dead.

The persisting political force of irrationalist homophobia, as an independent political evil, is apparent today when persons feel free to indulge their prejudices against homosexuals although neither of the two traditional moral reasons for condemning homosexuality can any longer be legitimately and indeed constitutionally imposed on society at large.

One such moral reason (the condemnation of nonprocreational sex) can, for example, no longer constitutionally justify laws against the sale to and use of contraceptives by married and unmarried heterosexual couples.[169] The mandatory enforcement of the procreational model of sexuality is, in circumstances of overpopulation and declining infant and adult mortality, a sectarian ideal lacking adequate secular basis in the general goods that can alone reasonably justify state power; accordingly, contraceptive-using heterosexuals have the constitutional right to decide when and whether their sexual lives shall be pursued to procreate or as an independent expression of mutual love, affection, and companionship.[170]

[167] For relevant historical background, see David A. J. Richards, *The Moral Criticism of Law* (Encino, Calif.: Dickenson-Wadsworth, 1977), pp. 78–82.

[168] See Wayne R. Dynes, ed., *Encyclopedia of Homosexuality*, 2 vols. (New York: Garland, 1990).

[169] See *Griswold v. Connecticut*, 381 U.S. 479 (1965); *Eisenstadt v. Baird*, 405 U.S. 438 (1972).

[170] For further discussion, see Richards, *Toleration*, pp. 256–61.

The other moral reason for condemning homosexual sex (the degradation of a man to the passive status of a woman) rests on the sexist premise of the degraded nature of women, which has, as we have seen, been properly rejected as a reasonable basis for laws or policies on grounds of suspect classification analysis.

Nonetheless, although each moral ground for the condemnation of homosexuality has been independently rejected as a reasonable justification for coercive laws enforceable on society, they unreasonably retain their force when brought into specific relationship to the claims of homosexuals.

These claims are today arguments of principle made by homosexuals for the same respect for their intimate love life, free of unreasonable procreational and sexist requirements, generously accorded heterosexual couples. Empirical issues relating to sexuality and gender are now subjected to more impartial critical assessment than they were previously; and the resulting light of public reason about issues of sexuality and gender should be available to all persons on fair terms. Such a claim of fair treatment (an argument of basic constitutional principle), however, was contemptuously dismissed by a majority of the U.S. Supreme Court in *Bowers v. Hardwick*.[171]

Traditional moral arguments, reasonably rejected in their application to heterosexuals, were uncritically applied to a group much more in need of constitutional protection on grounds of principle.[172] Reasonable advances in the public understanding of sexuality and gender, constitutionally available to all heterosexuals, were suspended in favor of an appeal to the sexual mythology of the Middle Ages.[173] The transparently unprincipled character of *Bowers* confirms the unjust continuing complicity of American constitutionalism with the legitimation of the cultural construction of the morally subjugated status of homosexuals. If the *Plessy* court illegitimately fostered the construction of American racism, the *Bowers* court has illegitimately advanced the construction of homophobia.

The issue in *Bowers* (the illegitimate criminalization of homosexual sex acts) is not the same issue as suspect classification analysis. Not all acts that should enjoy protection by the constitutional right to privacy would also call for suspect classification analysis; contraceptive-using heterosexual adults, who enjoy and should enjoy protection by the constitutional right to privacy, are not reasonably understood as a suspect class. And the scope

---

[171] *Bowers v. Hardwick*, 478 U.S. 186 (1986).

[172] For further criticism, see Richards, *Foundations*, pp. 209–47.

[173] Justice Blackmun put the point acidly: "Like Justice Holmes, I believe that 'it is revolting to have no better reason for a rule of law than that so it was laid down in the time of Henry IV. It is still more revolting if the grounds upon which it was laid down have vanished long since, and the rule simply persists from blind imitation of the past.'" *Bowers*, p. 199 (quoting Oliver Wendell Holmes, "The Path of the Law," *Harvard Law Review* 10 [1897]: 469).

of protection of groups properly regarded as suspect classes cannot be limited to the right to privacy or indeed to any fundamental right; it extends to all laws or policies actuated by irrational prejudice. Correspondingly, the issue of sexual preference, as a suspect classification, is much larger than the issue of *Bowers*. *Bowers* is an interpretive mistake as an analysis of the constitutional right to privacy (see Chapter 6). But even if *Bowers* had been rightly decided, the issue of sexual preference as a suspect classification would remain.[174]

The moral insult of homophobia, like that of racism and sexism, cannot be limited to any particular right, but to the denigration of one's status as a bearer of rights within the moral community of equal rights. Suspect classification analysis arose from the study of the radical political evil of a political culture, ostensibly committed to toleration on the basis of universal human rights, that unjustly denied a class of persons the cultural space in the political community that is their inalienable human right as persons with moral powers. To deny such a group, already the subject of a long history and culture of moral degradation, their culture-creating rights is to silence in them the very voice of their moral freedom, rendering unspoken and unspeakable the sentiments, experience, and reason that authenticate the moral personality a political culture of human rights owes each and every person. Sexual preference is a suspect classification because homosexuals are today victimized by irrational political prejudices rooted in this radical political evil, denying them the cultural resources of free moral personality.

Such political prejudice is an evil, subject to suspect classification analysis, whatever the form of erotic life in which a homosexual finds fulfillment.[175] Such erotic life may be embedded in complex, symbolically elaborated and idealized forms of intense, deeply loving relationships in which the sex acts that concern *Bowers v. Hardwick* are not in play. The political prejudice of homophobia remains the same evil of radical cultural intolerance, whatever the sex life in question, because it denies the cultural space through which persons of homosexual preference may reasonably define a life of personal and ethical self-respect on whatever terms best give expression to their free moral powers.

Another way of making the same point is to observe that homophobic prejudice, like sexism, unjustly distorts the idea of human rights applicable to both public and private life. If the political evil of sexism expressed itself in a morally degraded interpretation of private life (to which women, as morally inferior, were confined), the evil of homophobic prejudice is its

---

[174] For development of this analysis, see Janet E. Halley, "The Politics of the Closet: Towards Equal Protection for Gay, Lesbian, and Bisexual Identity," *UCLA Law Review* 37, no. 5 (June 1989): 915.

[175] See ibid.

degradation of homosexual love to the unspeakably private and secretive not only politically but intrapsychically in the person whose sexuality is homosexual. The political evil of this prejudice, based on the compulsory secrecy of the preference, is not always ameliorated and may indeed sometimes be aggravated by the growing practice of either not enforcing or repealing or otherwise invalidating criminal laws against homosexual sex. Such developments—without comparable antidiscrimination guarantees against homophobic prejudice—legitimate the ancient idea of something unspeakably and properly private, something all the more outrageous if given any public expression whatsoever (thus, legitimating sexist violence against forms of public expression of homosexual preference). But such compulsory privatization insults homosexuals in the same way it traditionally insulted women; it deprives them as moral persons of their right to speak and feel and live as whole persons on the terms of public and private life best expressive of their free moral powers. That is the moral right of every person in a free society, and homosexual persons have a right to it on equal terms.

It is for this reason that, in my judgment, appropriate constitutional remedies for homophobic prejudice include the range of remedies already discussed in the case of race and gender. I include among these remedies, in contrast to some commentators,[176] affirmative action because the underlying constitutional concern should be the deconstruction of the compulsory privatization of homosexual preference. Homosexuals cannot justly be required to be secretive as the condition of fair access to public goods; to the extent they are so required, they suffer unjust discrimination on grounds of prejudice. Such prejudice can, as in the case of race and gender, be remedied by appropriate affirmative action plans that ensure both that the qualifications of public homosexuals are fairly assessed and that the presence of such homosexuals in various positions undermines political prejudice in society at large.

Homophobia may be best understood today as a form of residual gender discrimination. The nonprocreative character of homosexual sexuality may be of relatively little concern, but its cultural symbolism of disordered gender roles excites anxieties in a political culture still sexist in its understanding of gender roles. Homosexuals—both lesbians and male homosexuals—are, under this view, in revolt against what many still suppose to be the "natural" order of gender hierarchy: women or men, as the case may be, undertaking sexual roles improper to their gender (for example, dominance in women, passivity in men). It is plainly unjust to displace such sexist

---

[176] See Ruse, *Homosexuality*, pp. 265–67. For a good general treatment of the need for antidiscrimination protections for homosexuals, see Richard D. Mohr, *Gays/Justice: A Study of Ethics, Society, and Law* (New York: Columbia University Press, 1988), pp. 137–211.

views, no longer publicly justifiable against heterosexual women, against a much more culturally marginalized and despised group—symbolic scapegoats of the feeble and cowardly sense of self that seeks self-respect in the unjust degradation of morally innocent people of goodwill. Homosexuals have the right, on grounds of suspect classification analysis, to be protected from such irrational prejudice.

It is prejudice of this sort that accounts, in my judgment, for the area of our national public life that is most conspicuously and unashamedly homophobic, the American military.[177] In the earlier discussion of gender, I noted the damage that political contractualism's complicity with sexism inflicted on the political culture's interpretation of basic human rights, that is, a hypermasculinized vision of the content and scope of human rights. Exclusion of women from the military surely reflects this misinterpretation,[178] and the exclusion of homosexuals is a variation on the same sexist theme.

People serving in the military must satisfy the reasonable requirements such service calls for, but these requirements have little to do with gender as such[179] and nothing to do with sexual preference.[180] The confusion of the military virtues of courage and competence with traditional ideas of manliness (including aggressive heterosexual virility) is, at bottom, transparently sexist (as if a woman or homosexual in the military must be either the perpetrator or victim of sexual harassment). It morally insults both women and homosexuals to ascribe to them incapacities of moral control or susceptibilities that reflect and reinforce irrational prejudice in this way. It also disfigures what military service is and should be in the defense of a constitutional culture of human rights.

Military service is a part of that culture and should reflect its best values and aspirations. Instead of distributing rights and responsibilities on terms that respect all persons as equal members of the political community, however, the military has been cordoned off from the larger fabric of constitutional principle, a judicially protected bastion of sexist prejudice exempt from reasonable constitutional analysis.[181] This is to make of military service not the defense of constitutional values, but their subversion in this last sectarian sanctuary of Rousseau's corruptly hypermasculinized contractualism.

[177] For excellent and probing analysis of this issue, see Harris, "Permitting Prejudice to Govern"; Kenneth I. Karst, "The Pursuit of Manhood and the Desegregation of the Armed Forces," *UCLA Law Review* 38, no. 3 (February 1991): 499.

[178] For the Supreme Court's insensitivity to this issue, see *Rostker v. Goldberg*, 453 U.S. 57 (1981) (gender-based statute, authorizing the registration for the draft of men but not women, held constitutional).

[179] Even the gender-based combat exclusion of women may in contemporary circumstances be largely unreasonable, as Kenneth Karst has recently argued with great force; see Karst, "The Pursuit of Manhood and the Desegregation of the Armed Forces," pp. 529–45.

[180] See ibid., pp. 545–63.

[181] See, e.g., *Rostker v. Goldberg*, 453 U.S. 57 (1981).

SIX

THE NATIONALIZATION OF HUMAN RIGHTS

THERE IS no area of current judicial interpretation of the Reconstruction Amendments more at war with their text and background history and political theory than the interpretation of the clauses of the fourteenth amendment bearing on the enforcement of fundamental rights against the states, in particular, the privileges and immunities clause. Text, history, and political theory all confirm that this clause should be broadly interpreted nationally to enforce against the states fundamental human rights including both enumerated and unenumerated such rights that had been enforceable against the federal government by the Constitution of 1787 and the amendments of 1791 that we call the Bill of Rights.[1]

Is this a worthwhile issue to discuss at all? Such analysis may appear idle and misplaced on the practical ground that the modern judiciary has reached most of the substantive results it would recommend, albeit not on the ground of the privileges and immunities clause but on the due process clause of the fourteenth amendment. The Supreme Court has on this ground almost completely incorporated the guarantees of the Bill of Rights against the states[2] and has also inferred and protected the unenumerated constitutional right to privacy in the area of contraception[3] and abortion.[4] If so, why should it matter that the judiciary has not grounded such decisions on their proper textual basis if such decisions can be reconstructed on some plausible textual basis?

There is, however, an interpretive integrity in the history, text, and political theory associated with all the great normative clauses of the U.S. Constitution, including those of the fourteenth amendment (the citizenship clause, equal protection clause, privileges and immunities clause, and due process clause). Clear interpretive mistake in one of these areas is not adequately remedied by transporting the correct interpretive analysis under one of these clauses (privileges and immunities) to another (due process). The due process analysis may be strained and for this reason muddy and even subvert public understanding of the basis for the result in question.

The due process clause of the fourteenth amendment is rooted in nor-

---

[1] See U.S. Constitution, Amendments I–X.

[2] For the Supreme Court's current methodology of selective incorporation, see *Duncan v. Louisiana*, 391 U.S. 145 (1968).

[3] See, e.g., *Griswold v. Connecticut*, 381 U.S. 479 (1965).

[4] See *Roe v. Wade*, 410 U.S. 113 (1973).

mative requirements taken from its background in the comparable clause of the fifth amendment of the Bill of Rights; that background largely emphasized procedural requirements.[5] Thus, when the Supreme Court interpreted the due process clause of the fifth amendment for the first time in 1856, it limited its scope to procedural connotations of proper notice and hearing derived from the settled usages and procedures of English law adapted to American conditions.[6] Against this background, a substantive interpretation of due process must appear without solid basis.

Historical evidence—both at the state and federal levels—on the other side does not convincingly rebut this reasonable sense of strain in the interpretation of due process as the repository for the national protection of basic substantive human rights. Antebellum state court opinions, calling for a substantive ingredient of due process under state constitutions,[7] cannot be the measure of a federal constitutional jurisprudence that at the time made little or no appeal to them. Antebellum arguments about substantive interpretations of the due process clause of the fifth amendment do not, on balance, convincingly ascribe such a meaning to the clause of the fourteenth amendment. Both proslavery and antislavery constitutional theorists had developed independent general arguments for their respective positions; they then offered an additional textual basis for their respective positions in a substantive interpretation of the due process clause;[8] Justice Taney in the controversial *Dred Scott Case* had used the proslavery substantive interpretation to justify his claim of the unconstitutionality of the Missouri Compromise.[9] But the interpretive vagaries of Justice Taney's thoroughly discredited opinion in *Dred Scott* hardly establish a reasonable basis for a substantive interpretation of due process at the national level. And the associated debate about substantive due process between antebellum pro- and antislavery constitutional theories turned on the background issue of whether the protection of slavery did or did not deprive persons of basic rights, an issue resolved constitutionally by the thirteenth amendment.

The antebellum debate over due process is thus peripheral to the essen-

---

[5] See Leonard Levy, "Due Process of Law," in Leonard Levy, Kenneth L. Karst, and Dennis J. Mahoney, eds., *Encyclopedia of the American Constitution*, 4 vols. (New York: Macmillan, 1986), 2:589–91.

[6] See *Murray's Lessee v. Hoboken Land & Improvement Co.*, 59 U.S. (18 How.) 272 (1856).

[7] See, notably, *Wynehamer v. People*, 13 N.Y. 378 (1856) (invalidating a state liquor prohibition law).

[8] For a general statement of a proslavery interpretation along these lines, see John C. Calhoun, "Speech on the Oregon Bill" (delivered in the Senate on June 27, 1848), in Calhoun, *Works*, 4:479–512; for Calhoun's explicit invocation of the fifth amendment as proslavery, see citations in Niven, *John C. Calhoun and the Price of Union*, pp. 204–6. For an antislavery interpretation of the due process clause, see Goodell, *Views*, pp. 57–63.

[9] See *Dred Scott*, p. 450.

tial issues in contention between the theories that are interpretively relevant to the fourteenth amendment. Those issues, as we have seen in Chapters 2–4, turn on the nature and weight of the background political theory of human rights in the interpretation of the Constitution. The fourteenth amendment constitutionalizes the general views of abolitionist constitutional theory in various clauses (see Chapter 4). One of these views was the nationalization of the protection of human rights. Of the relevant clauses, the privileges and immunities clause, as we shall see, forthrightly expressed the nationalization of human rights; the due process clause did not.

If the privileges and immunities clause did not exist and all other background factors were the same (including support for the nationalization of human rights), a case could at least be made that such nationalization should be reasonably ascribed to the due process clause in light of the overall historical purposes of the fourteenth amendment in the larger constitutional fabric.[10] But the privileges and immunities clause does exist; and the cavalier transportation from it to the due process clause of the nationalization of human rights has discredited the very idea of the nationalization of human rights. In effect, the idea appears as implausible as the interpretively unsound interpretation of due process to that effect.[11] In this spirit John Hart Ely sharply reminds us, lest we forget, "that 'substantive due process' is a contradiction in terms—sort of like 'green pastel redness.'" Ely understands perfectly well that, if necessary, a strained interpretive argument could be made for substantive due process.[12] But in view of the fourteenth amendment as it is, he regards such an argument as implausible and even bizarre.

Ely is correct on this interpretive point. But his own utilitarian rights skepticism about the enforcement of fundamental rights (see Chapter 1) motivates him not to explore its malign consequences for the proper interpretation of the fourteenth amendment's nationalization of the protection of human rights.[13] Such consequences are deep and real. The historical

[10] For an argument defending substantive due process as if this were the case, see Laurence H. Tribe, "Substantive Due Process of Law," Levy, *Encyclopedia of the American Constitution*, 4:1796–1803.

[11] Stanley Morrison, in the course of an attack on Justice Black's general views on the fourteenth amendment, thus concurs with the justice on one point: "When he thus seeks to abolish substantive due process, he is on solid ground historically. If the clause is to be interpreted in accordance with the meaning it had to the framers and others in 1868, the doctrine cannot be justified. It is . . . a later excrescence derived from natural-law sources." See Stanley Morrison, "Does the Fourteenth Amendment Incorporate the Bill of Rights?" *Stanford Law Review* 2 (December 1949): 166.

[12] See Ely, *Democracy and Distrust*, p. 18, 15–16.

[13] Ely cogently argues that the clear textual and historical ground for the nationalization of human rights is the privileges and immunities clause. See ibid, pp. 22–30.

flimsiness of substantive due process fails to anchor the interpretation of the nationalization of human rights in the historic antebellum constitutional debates that forthrightly bear on this question, including the debates over the privileges and immunities clause of Article IV, the model for the comparable clause of the fourteenth amendment (see Chapter 4). These debates included background arguments of constitutional and political theory about the nature and weight of basic human rights and how a constitution committed to such rights should be interpreted over time (see Chapters 2–4). The consequence has been a judicial interpretive attitude toward the nationalization of human rights that, while sometimes reaching the right results, lacks the cogency of argument that it can and should have, rendering judicial opinions much more vulnerable to criticism and public doubt than they should be.

The interpretation of a concept such as due process to protect substantive rights has required the Court to make judgments about both the content and weight of substantive rights in terms of either a stark appeal to abstract justice[14] or an equally vague appeal to essential American traditions.[15] One intrinsically vague and possibly incoherent idea (substantive due process) is thus interpretively explored in terms of even more vague ideas of justice or tradition that, apparently unmoored in the tradition that could make public sense of them, cast doubt on the impartiality of the judicial process; law has been, so the slogan goes, politically seduced.[16]

Even judges who defend some of the results reached in these opinions on the proper ground of the privileges and immunities clause do so in an interpretive spirit uninformed by background antebellum debates on political and constitutional theory. Justice Black, for example, correctly argued that these questions should be interpreted on the basis of privileges and immunities, not due process. He drew the conclusion, however, that the Bill of Rights should be fully incorporated against the states,[17] but that no unenumerated rights should be enforced against the states.[18] The nerve of Justice Black's position was a version of historical positivism (focusing, for example, on Senator Howard's speech cited in Chapter 4). He believed such positivism freed his position of the taint of natural law ideas that he condemned in others (both those who advocated selective incorporation of the Bill of Rights and those who defended the protection of unenumerated rights such as constitutional privacy).

But the way in which Black interpreted history was itself highly selective

[14] See, e.g., *Palko v. Connecticut*, 302 U.S. 319 (1937).

[15] See *Moore v. East Cleveland*, 431 U.S. 494 (1977).

[16] See Bork, *The Tempting of America*.

[17] See *Adamson v. California*, 332 U.S. 46, 68 (1947) (Black, J., dissenting); *Duncan v. Louisiana*, 391 U.S. 145, 162 (1968) (Black, J., concurring).

[18] See Justice Black's dissenting opinion in *Griswold v. Connecticut*, 381 U.S. 479 (1965).

and certainly was not value-free in the way that he claimed it was;[19] he ascribed to the historical record a command of total incorporation that is probably not there and a prohibition on the enforcement of unenumerated rights that is clearly not there. (Howard's speech, in fact, urged the full enforcement of such unenumerated rights.)[20] Black could not have misinterpreted history in this way if he had not been so uncritically wedded to a positivistic stance on constitutional interpretation at war with the political theory of human rights that he assumed. That theory would have required taking seriously the issue at the heart of abolitionist constitutional theory, the interpretation of the Constitution in light of a theory of inalienable human rights. Howard's speech expressed an interpretive judgment in his circumstances in that spirit, calling for comparable interpretive judgments by others in their circumstances, not a parroting of his conclusions. But Justice Black, the student of history, made no use of the history of antebellum constitutional theory most central to a sound understanding of the interpretive attitude appropriate to the Reconstruction Amendments. His great contribution to the proper interpretation of the amendments was, for this reason, flawed and incomplete.

Finally, the wrongheaded interpretation of the nationalization of human rights, in terms of due process, may have led to gravely mistaken acts of judicial interpretation and equally mistaken reactions: on the one hand, the interpretive mistake of *Lochner v. New York*[21] and, on the other, the equally mistaken overruling of the opinion by near total abdication of judicial review in the economic and social arena (see Chapter 7).[22] The very vagueness of substantive due process analysis may so invite the ideological distortion of constitutional interpretation exemplified by *Lochner* that the judiciary, like a cured drunk, seeks salvation in total interpretive abstinence. We need to ask whether a different approach to these matters (rejecting substantive due process) may afford a more sensibly temperate alternative.

Similarly, the apparently unmoored character of substantive due process analysis may lead to unjustified doubts about judicial interpretive developments such as the inference and elaboration of the unenumerated constitutional right to privacy,[23] including growing doubts within the Supreme

---

[19] See Fairman, "Does the Fourteenth Amendment Incorporate the Bill of Rights?" For Fairman's later elaboration of this position, see Charles Fairman, *Reconstruction and Reunion, 1864–88* (New York: Macmillan, 1971), pp. 1260–1300.

[20] See Ely, *Democracy and Distrust*, pp. 11–41. See also discussion following in the text.

[21] See *Lochner v. New York*, 198 U.S. 45 (1905).

[22] See, e.g., *Nebbia v. New York*, 291 U.S. 502 (1934); *West Coast Hotel v. Parrish*, 300 U.S. 379 (1937).

[23] See Bork, *The Tempting of America*. For objections to the specific application of the right to privacy to abortion, see Ely, "The Wages of Crying Wolf"; R. Kent Greenawalt, *Religious Convictions and Political Choice* (New York: Oxford University Press, 1988), p. 120.

Court about the application of such a right (for example, to abortion services.[24]) A different approach may here, as elsewhere, clarify the sound interpretive basis of such developments in the long American tradition of progressive protection of basic human rights.

Our interpretation of all these issues will be advanced by grounding our discussion of them on their proper basis in the privileges and immunities clause. I begin with a discussion of the decision that established the wrongheaded judicial framework within which these issues are currently analyzed, and then turn, on the basis of that analysis, to a discussion of the interpretation of enumerated and unenumerated rights on their proper basis. In Chapter 7, I examine constitutional claims grounded in economic injustice in light of this analysis.

Slaughter-House Cases

The pattern of judicial treatment of fundamental rights was set, apparently immovably, by one of the early decisions of the U.S. Supreme Court interpreting the meaning of the recently ratified Reconstruction Amendments: the *Slaughter-House Cases*. At constitutional issue in the case was an 1869 Louisiana law chartering a corporation and granting to it a twenty-five-year monopoly to maintain slaughterhouses in an area including the city of New Orleans. Under the law, the corporation was required to permit any person who wished to do so to slaughter in its houses at a reasonable fee. Four arguments, based on the Reconstruction Amendments, were made against the constitutionality of this law: involuntary servitude, equal protection, due process, and privileges and immunities. Justice Miller, writing for a five-four majority of a sharply divided Court, rejected all four arguments—three of them cursorily (involuntary servitude, equal protection, due process), one of them at more length (privileges and immunities).[25] The privileges and immunities clause argument was the only one that Miller took at all seriously; unlike other arguments in the opinion, it has enjoyed enduring precedential force.

Why did Miller take this argument, in contrast to the others, so seriously? The three concurring dissents of Justices Field, Bradley, and Swayne[26] explain why as a matter of text, history, and background political theory. Such grounds powerfully support the interpretation of the privileges and immunities clause as nationalizing the protection of human rights.

The relevant text of the fourteenth amendment states: "No State shall

[24] See e.g., *Webster v. Reproductive Health Services*, 492 U.S. 490 (1989).
[25] *Slaughter-House Cases*, 83 (16 Wall.) 36 (1873), pp. 66, 72, 80–81, 74–80.
[26] See ibid., 83, 111, 124.

make or enforce any law which shall abridge the privileges or immunities of citizens of the United States."[27] That text self-consciously uses concepts taken from Article IV, section 2, of the Constitution of 1787: "The citizens of each State shall be entitled to all privileges and immunities of citizens in the several States."[28] Since the privileges and immunities clause of the fourteenth amendment makes reference in this way to the comparable clause of Article IV, the interpretation of the substantive nature and weight of these privileges and immunities under the fourteenth amendment must in some important way draw upon the normative principles of Article IV.

These principles in their nature forbid the states to discriminate against the citizens of other states in terms of a benchmark of rights, namely, "all privileges and immunities of citizens in the several states." The jurisprudence of such rights had been authoritatively stated by Justice Bushrod Washington in his opinion in *Corfield v. Coryell,* an opinion not only much cited in the Reconstruction Congress debates (see Chapter 4), but cited as governing interpretive authority by both the majority and dissenters in the *Slaughter-House Cases.*[29] Justice Washington had defined the normative content of these privileges and immunities, in language expressly cited by Justices Miller, Field, and Bradley:

> The inquiry is, what are the privileges and immunities of citizens of the several States? We feel no hesitation in confining these expressions to those privileges and immunities which are *fundamental*; which belong of right to the citizens of all free governments, and which have at all times been enjoyed by citizens of the several States which compose this Union, from the time of their becoming free, independent, and sovereign. What these fundamental principles are, it would be more tedious than difficult to enumerate. They may all, however, be comprehended under the following general heads: protection by the government, with the right to acquire and possess property of every kind, and to pursue and obtain happiness and safety, subject, nevertheless, to such restraints as the government may prescribe for the general good of the whole.[30]

Justice Washington clearly thinks of these normative principles as embedded in a larger contractualist political theory of free government (defining rights "which belong of right to the citizens of all free governments"); this is the governing theory of American state and federal constitutionalism

---

[27] U.S. Constitution, Amendment XIV, sec. 1.

[28] U.S. Constitution, Art. IV., sec. 2, cl. 1.

[29] For the citation and discussion of the case by Justice Miller, see *Slaughter-House Cases,* pp. 75–77; by Justice Field, see pp. 97–98; by Justice Bradley, see *id.,* at pp. 116–18; by Justice Swayne, see p. 127.

[30] *Corfield v. Coryell,* 6 Fed. Case 546 (Case No. 3230) (C.C.E.D.Pa. 1823), pp. 551–52, cited by Justice Miller in *Slaughter-House Cases,* p. 76, by Justice Field at p. 97, by Justice Bradley at p. 117.

(thus, these rights "have at all times been enjoyed by citizens of the several States which compose this Union"). The natural inference from the textual transportation of this normative concept to the fourteenth amendment is that these principles, defined by the background political theory of free government, now are subject to national enforcement against the states.

The only puzzling *textual* gap between the language of the fourteenth amendment and that of Article IV is that the former speaks unambiguously of "the privileges or immunities of citizens of the United States," whereas the latter elliptically refers to "privileges and immunities of citizens in the several States." The puzzle is, however, not real if the privileges and immunities of Article IV are themselves to be understood, consistent with the dominant judicial understanding during the antebellum period,[31] as national rights of American citizens that must be respected, under Article IV, by states of which they were not citizens. The privileges and immunities of Article IV were, according to this view, rights of American citizens, and thus supplied the relevant normative standards in terms of which the command of the fourteenth amendment should be interpreted.

Relevant background history confirms this reading of the privileges and immunities clause of the fourteenth amendment. The background of the clause was the longstanding abolitionist criticism of systematic violations of the constitutional guarantees of Article IV both by southern and northern states. Such states had violated not only the rights of free blacks to travel[32] or to education,[33] but basic rights of whites to engage in the exercise of their rights to conscience and to free speech[34] and, indirectly through support of slavery, their right to free labor.[35]

Representative John A. Bingham—the main draftsman of the fourteenth amendment in general and the privileges and immunities clause in particular—had taken a public position in the House of Representatives in 1857 along these lines against the admission of Oregon to the Union. The Oregon state constitution prohibited nonresident blacks from entry into the state, holding property, making contracts, or bringing suit therein. The constitution thus violated, in Bingham's view, Article IV's guarantees of "natural rights . . . the right to know; to argue and to utter, according to conscience;

---

[31] See Kettner, *The Development of American Citizenship*, pp. 255–61.

[32] On South Carolina's exclusion of black sailors, see Freehling, *Prelude to Civil War*, pp. 111–16, 206–7; for Representative Bingham's objection on such grounds to Oregon's constitutional exclusion of blacks, see John A. Bingham, "The Constitution of the United States and the Proslavery Provisions of the 1857 Oregon Constitution," in tenBroek, *Equal under Law*, Appendix D, pp. 320–41.

[33] On the Prudence Crandall affair, see Hyman and Wiecek, *Equal Justice under Law*, pp. 94–95.

[34] See Nye, *Fettered Freedom*.

[35] For the general form of this argument, based on the tendency of the expansion of slavery to drive out free labor, see Foner, *Free Soil, Free Labor, Free Men*.

to work and enjoy the project of their toil." Article IV protected natural rights of this sort, not, Bingham insisted, "conventional" rights such as voting rights. Bingham took the view that the language of the privileges and immunities clause of Article IV refers

> not to the rights and immunities which result exclusively from State authority or State legislation; but to "all privileges and immunities" of citizens of the United States in the several States. There is an ellipsis in the language employed in the Constitution, but its meaning is self-evident that it is "the privileges and immunities of citizens of the United States in the several States" that it guaranties.[36]

Bingham brought that public understanding of the substantive nature and scope of privileges and immunities—reflecting the dominant judicial interpretation of Article IV—to bear on all stages of his proposals for what was eventually successfully approved by Congress as the language of the privileges and immunities clause of the fourteenth amendment. His February 3, 1866, proposal to the Joint Committee of Fifteen on Reconstruction offered language for the clause that directly tracked this understanding: "The Congress shall have power to make all laws which shall be necessary and proper to secure to the citizens of each state all privileges and immunities of citizens in the several states (Art. 4, Sec. 2); and to all persons in the several States equal protection in the rights of life, liberty and property (5th Amendment)."[37]

In introducing this proposal to the House of Representatives on February 26, 1866, Bingham argued that its principles were already guaranteed by the Constitution (in Article IV and the fifth amendment), but in a form that "rested for its execution and enforcement hitherto upon the fidelity of the States";[38] the new proposal would secure congressional enforcement power. That proposal was withdrawn largely in response to the objection that it rested enforcement of these principles too exclusively on the political vagaries of Congress; its principles should be "secured by a constitutional amendment that legislation cannot override."[39]

Bingham proposed the present form of the privileges and immunities clause to the Joint Committee on April 21, 1866. After initial rejection, it was finally accepted on April 28, 1866. Section 1 of the proposed fourteenth

---

[36] See Bingham, "The Proslavery Provisions of the 1857 Oregon Constitution," in tenBroek, *Equal under Law,* pp. 339–40, 333.

[37] See Benjamin B. Kendrick, *The Journal of the Joint Committee of Fifteen on Reconstruction* (1914; reprint, New York: Negro Universities Press, 1969), p. 61.

[38] See Representative Bingham, speech of February 26, 1866, *Congressional Globe,* 39th Cong., 1st sess., p. 1034.

[39] See Representative Hotchkiss, speech of 28 February 1866, *Congressional Globe,* 39th Cong., 1st sess. p. 1095.

amendment now took the following form: "No State shall make or enforce any law which shall abridge the privileges or immunities of citizens of the United States; nor shall any State deprive any person of life, liberty, or property without due process of law; nor deny to any person within its jurisdiction the equal protection of the laws."[40] In addition to the recasting of the language of the previous proposal as a constraint on state power, the new proposal clarified the nature of its main substantive provisions as an interpretation of the antecedent constitutional provisions to which they appealed. The privileges and immunities clause now textually adopted the unambiguous interpretation of its predecessor clause in Article IV as a guarantee of the basic human rights of American citizens; and the equal protection clause was now stated as a normative principle independent of the due process clause (previously, it was stated as an interpretation of due process).

In the discussion of the new proposal in the House of Representatives, Bingham characterized the guarantee of privileges and immunities, consistent with his 1857 public position, as securing "the inborn rights of every person"; that is, natural rights not conventional rights such as voting. Bingham offered both specific and general guidance on how such rights were to be understood. Specifically, he exemplified such protection of natural rights in terms of antebellum experience of state deprivation of such rights, for example: "Contrary to the express letter of your Constitution, 'cruel and unusual punishments' have been inflicted under State laws within this Union upon citizens, not only for crimes committed, but for sacred duty done, for which and against which the Government of the United States had provided no remedy and could provide none."[41]

More generally, Bingham characterized the nature and weight of the rights thus secured in terms of the familiar abolitionist contractualist theory of political legitimacy, namely, the more basic "right to bear true allegiance to the Constitution and laws of the United States, and to be protected in life, liberty, and property. Next, sir, to the allegiance we all owe to God our Creator, is the allegiance which we owe to our common country." The rights in question were thus to be identified in light of the general contractualist political theory of inalienable rights that must be guaranteed to each person subject to political power in order for that power to be regarded as politically legitimate. Bingham clearly regarded this political theory as the general justification for any legitimate political power at all; it is in light of that conviction that he insists that section 1 of the fourteenth amendment "takes from no State any right that ever pertained to it."[42] The

[40] See Kendrick, *Journal of the Joint Committee*, pp. 87, 98, 99–100, 106.

[41] See Representative Bingham, speech of 10 May 1866, *Congressional Globe*, 39th Cong. 1st sess., p. 2542.

[42] See ibid.

bitter lesson of antebellum constitutional controversy had been that a tragic gap existed between this political theory and the guarantees of the Constitution; and section 1 filled this gap by, among other things, nationalizing the protection of basic human rights. Accordingly, the understanding of such constitutionally protected privileges and immunities, must, as Bingham makes clear, now make reference to this political theory.

Senator Howard's speech introducing the proposed fourteenth amendment in the Senate was to similar effect. The privileges and immunities clause of the proposed fourteenth amendment must be understood in light of the requirements, properly understood, of the predecessor clause of Article IV.[43] Howard read Article IV as a radical constitutional theorist such as Joel Tiffany read it,[44] as a guarantee of basic human or natural rights (not voting rights[45]) to all persons legitimately subject to political power, including black Americans. This interpretation of Article IV is the basis for the later addition by the Senate of what is now the citizenship clause of the fourteenth amendment,[46] in effect, unambiguously adopting this interpretation of Article IV as an independent constitutional principle.

Howard introduced the privileges and immunities clause in light of this interpretation in order to make clear its basis in the contractualist political theory of legitimate government that, in fact, motivated that interpretation. His earlier cited discussion of the substantive scope of such privileges and immunities (see Chapter 4) rests, like Bingham's comparable discussion, on an interpretive appeal to background political theory. Howard illustrated the interpretive requirements of such political theory by reference to *Corfield v. Coryell*'s abstract characterization of such rights and by reference to "the personal rights guarantied and secured by the first eight amendments of the Constitution." Howard insisted that such human rights "are not and cannot be fully defined in their entire extent and precise nature";[47] he offered, in light of background political theory, an interpretive view of some concrete examples of how they should be understood. But his interpretations were self-consciously incomplete and illustrative; even his

[43] See Senator Howard, speech of 23 May 1866, *Congressional Globe*, 39th Cong., 1st sess., at pp. 2764–67.

[44] See Tiffany, *Treatise*, pp. 87–97.

[45] "The right of suffrage is not, in law, one of the privileges or immunities thus secured by the Constitution. It has always been regarded in this country as the result of positive local law, not regarded as one of those fundamental rights lying at the basis of all society and without which a people cannot exist except as slaves, subject to a despotism." Senate Howard, speech of 23 May 1866, *Congressional Globe*, 39th Cong., 1st sess., p. 2766.

[46] See speech of Senator Howard, 29 May 1866, *Congressional Globe*, 39th Cong., 1st sess., p. 2869, introducing the citizenship clause as an amendment to section 1 of proposed fourteenth amendment.

[47] See Senator Howard, speech of 23 May 1866, *Congressional Globe*, 39th Cong., 1st sess., p. 2765.

listing of the guarantees of the Bill of Rights does not mention each of them.[48]

The spirit of Howard's discussion is some interpretive clarification of how, in light of background political theory, privileges and immunities should be understood. It fundamentally distorts both the letter and spirit of Howard's speech to ascribe to it the meaning that Justice Black found there, namely, total incorporation of the enumerated rights of the Bill of Rights but no protection of unenumerated rights. Howard expressly repudiated the latter; and his discussion of the Bill of Rights does not require total incorporation, but invites interpretive reflection on them as candidates for basic human rights in light of background political theory. In short, Howard offered interpretive judgment, not, as Black supposed, positivistic lawmaking.

The spirit of Howard's argument is, consistent with its background in radical antislavery constitutional theory, antipositivistic; he appeals to the ultimate authority of human rights as the background for the interpretation of constitutional rights. No one who believes in such authority, as Howard, like Bingham, clearly did, could regard himself as having final positivistic authority to determine how such rights were to be reasonably understood by later generations for the same reason that Locke denied the authority of Filmer's fictive patriarchs to determine what counts as reasonable government for later generations.[49] The point, rather, was to invite each generation to reflect and enforce guarantees of basic human rights in light of the most reasonable public understanding available to them. Black's historical positivism thus ascribes to Howard an authority Howard's political theory would have denied; in so doing, as we have seen, Black falsifies (the repudiation of unenumerated rights) what he said.

Finally, the political theory of American constitutionalism supports the reading that the privileges and immunities clause nationalizes the protection of basic human rights. The absence of a national power comparable to this was, as we observed in Chapter 2, the basis for James Madison's privately expressed doubts about the legitimacy of the U.S. Constitution of 1787. The interpretation of the privileges and immunities clause as a national guarantee of human rights resolves these doubts.

For Madison, the Constitution was to be assessed in light of whether its substantive and procedural requirements (including its three great structural innovations—federalism, the separation of powers, and judicial review) could render the exercise of political power legitimate in terms of

---

[48] For example, his list does not include the religious liberty guarantees of the first amendment, or either the guarantee of a grand jury or the prohibition on double jeopardy of the fifth amendment, or the requirement of a trial by jury in civil cases of the seventh amendment.

[49] For further discussion of this point, see Richards, *Foundations*, pp. 135, 137, 143, 148, 171, 232.

contractualist political theory, that is, respect for inalienable human rights and the public good. This required some reasonable assessment of the likely effects of such institutions in light of the facts of group political psychology, for example, the political psychology of faction. Madison's argument to this effect in *The Federalist No. 10* was valid only to the extent that the most politically illegitimate propensities to faction were appropriately filtered through the structures of the constitutional system.

In fact, the worst propensities to faction were those that were most insular and parochially local, the least likely to take seriously the rights and interests of those outside the hegemonic local faction. But the Constitution did not impose effective controls on the political power of these factions exercised at the state level; the structures of the constitutional system, including the amendments known as the Bill of Rights, largely applied to the federal government, not to the states. In effect, the most politically illegitimate factions would in their nature run riot at the state level. A constitution not limiting the most illegitimate forms of faction could not, Madison privately mused to Jefferson in 1787, itself be legitimate.

Madison's private worries were about a Constitution not yet in action, about a gap, as he saw it in 1787, between its provisions and its political theory. That gap became the public basis for abolitionist moderate and increasingly radical antislavery constitutional theory and practice in the antebellum period; it also supported ultimate claims of the legitimacy of revolution against a Constitution that had proven so inadequate to the revolutionary constitutionalism called for by its background political theory.

The Constitution (including amendments one through twelve) and the Reconstruction Amendments must be interpreted in light of that political theory so that the Constitution, as thus amended, is politically legitimate. The key to the antebellum experience of radical constitutional illegitimacy had been state violations, both in the North and South, of the basic human rights of both blacks and whites. Madison's abortive proposal had been a national power that could be used to invalidate such state laws on the ground that the structures of the constitutional system would secure a more impartial deliberation over such issues (see Chapter 2). Francis Lieber had argued both in the antebellum period (see Chapter 2) and at the time of the Reconstruction Amendments (see Chapter 4) that basic human rights as such would only be impartially and adequately enforced by national institutions more capable of sustaining the kind and quality of argument of public reason that issues of universal human rights required; Lieber thought of the judiciary as playing a central role in this arena. The nationalization of the protection of human rights by the privileges and immunities clause, precisely because it better secures human rights from the most vicious factions, renders the Constitution legitimate by making the protection of such rights a central responsibility of national constitutional institutions; the clause should be interpreted to nationalize protection of these rights for this reason of political theory.

In the *Slaughter-House Cases*, Justice Miller took seriously the privileges and immunities argument of the dissenters because the reasons of text, history, and political theory in support of it were so strong. How well did Miller answer them?

Miller's argument rests on a sharp distinction between the privileges and immunities clause of Article IV and the comparable clause of the fourteenth amendment. The guarantee of Article IV is clarified by reference to *Corfield v. Coryell*; but *Corfield* is interpreted not, as Justice Washington's opinion clearly states, in terms of a federal constitutional standard of the fundamental rights of U.S. citizens, but in terms of whatever rights a state accords it own citizens.[50] Miller interprets the clause in this way, against the dominant judicial understanding to the contrary,[51] in order semantically to distinguish its meaning from any suggestion of the national rights of American citizens as such, an idea he argues must be limited entirely to the clause of the fourteenth amendment.

The argument for the separation of the meaning of the two clauses rests essentially on the citizenship clause's application of its birth or nationalization test for citizenship to "citizens of the United States and of the State wherein they reside."[52] The textual distinction between two kinds of citizenship suggests two distinct meanings of privileges and immunities: one, that of Article IV, arising from state citizenship; the other, that of the fourteenth amendment's guarantee of "privileges or immunities of citizens of the United States," arising from national citizenship. For Miller, "it is too clear for argument that the change in phraseology was adopted understandingly and with a purpose." Accordingly, the meaning of the clause of the fourteenth amendment has nothing to do with Article IV. Otherwise, Miller warns, the Supreme Court would be "a perpetual censor upon all legislation of the States."[53]

Finally, Miller ascribes to the clause of the fourteenth amendment a narrow list of national rights (rights to protection on high seas or when abroad, and rights of assembly, habeas corpus, use of navigable waters)[54] not at issue in the *Slaughter-House Cases*.

Miller's argument is studiously and exclusively textual because history and political theory are so powerfully opposed to his reading of the fourteenth amendment at every point. His interpretation of the privileges and immunities clause of Article IV, for example, ascribes to it only a require-

[50] See *Slaughter-House Cases*, p. 77.
[51] See Kettner, *The Development of American Citizenship*, pp. 255–61.
[52] See U.S. Constitution, Amendment XIV, sec. 1.
[53] See *Slaughter-House Cases*, p. 74, 78.
[54] See ibid., pp. 79–80.

ment of equality defined by state-defined rights, which is not the view Justice Washington takes in the excerpt Miller quotes. This is against the dominant judicial understanding of the clause, and is precisely the view not taken by both Bingham and Howard in publicly proposing the fourteenth amendment to Congress.

It would have been one thing for Miller to have argued, as Charles Fairman has,[55] that Justice Washington or Representative Bingham or Senator Howard were confused, and that the judiciary must ascribe a reasonable sense to their incoherence. That would, on its own terms, have been a bad argument; the views of all these exponents of privileges and immunities assumed and coherently interpreted a background theory of human rights. Fairman, a historian who fails to take seriously the powerful historical role of this political theory in their thought, can make no coherent sense of them because he apparently can make no sense of political theory. Incompetence thus breeds incoherence not in history but in the eye of the beholder. Miller's argument, had it followed Fairman's, would at least have taken seriously the public understanding underlying the fourteenth amendment. But Miller simply ignores whatever in the public record makes his position questionable, an unreasonable interpretive attitude by any standard.

Miller's sharp interpretive separation of the privileges and immunities clause of Article IV from that of the fourteenth amendment is even more remarkable. It makes a distinction between the clauses that no one in the Reconstruction Congress made, and many (Bingham and Howard) expressly denied.

For Miller, the distinction rests on the citizenship clause. But this clause was not part of Bingham's original proposal for the privileges and immunities clause in the House, and cannot thus be understood as primarily a narrowing qualification of its terms. Quite to the contrary, the citizenship clause was, as we have seen, added later in the Senate to constitutionalize an interpretive argument that Senator Howard, following radical antislavery constitutional theory, had earlier conspicuously ascribed to the privileges and immunities clause of Article IV as the basis for the comparable clause of the fourteenth amendment. The citizenship clause thus gave clearer constitutional force and support for the idea, taken to be implicit in the basic human rights accorded all Americans as privileges and immunities, that such rights were owed all persons reasonably subject to political power. It is interpretively willful, even perverse, in light of that history, to ascribe to the citizenship clause an intent, "understandingly and

---

[55] For Fairman on Judge Washington, see Fairman, *Reconstruction and Reunion*, pp. 1121–23; on Bingham, see pp. 1288–89, 1298; on Howard, see pp. 1291–97. For a comparable mode of analysis, see Fairman, "Does the Fourteenth Amendment Incorporate the Bill of Rights?"

with a purpose,"[56] on the one hand, to expand the class of persons owed national protection of their basic human rights and, on the other, shrink to a nullity the rights owed them. Both the citizenship clause and the privileges and immunities clause are thus rendered not mutually reinforcing expressions of a larger vision of inalienable human rights, but mutually trivializing.

Miller's argument makes little interpretive sense even on its own textualist terms. The citizenship clause speaks of "citizens of the United States and of the State wherein they reside," statuses conferred by being "persons born or naturalized in the United States, and subject to the jurisdiction thereof"; the privileges and immunities clause points to "privileges or immunities of citizens of the United States" that "no State . . . shall abridge." The former clause establishes common national constitutional standards of both federal and state citizenship, constitutionalizing the question of the scope of the American political community (both federal and state); the latter clause deprives the states of any power over the rights of American citizens as such. Such textual terms express a common constitutional concern for national standards of both citizenship and rights, and repudiate state power over citizenship and rights. Miller's interpretive argument, inventing a distinction not in the text, nullifies what the text is concerned with, national standards of rights.

The textual force of Miller's argument, to the extent it has any textual force, lies not in the citizenship clause, but in the earlier noted different textual terms of the privileges and immunities clause of Article IV and of the fourteenth amendment. There is a *textual* difference here, but not one that Miller himself can forthrightly exploit for he here acknowledges the relevance of interpretive tradition, for example, that of *Corfield v. Coryell*. Once Miller acknowledges the relevance of such tradition, he must open interpretive argument to reasonable discussion of the content of that tradition. He gets that tradition conspicuously wrong, and he fails to take seriously other publicly available traditions relevant to his interpretive responsibilities. His argument, in short, is at no point seriously textualist.

Miller's motivations are not interpretive; his interpretive performance is, by any reasonable measure of text, history, and political theory, incompetent. His motives, rather, are politically consequentialist worries that the dissenters' view of the privileges and immunities clause "radically changed the whole theory of the relations of the State and Federal governments."[57] Everything depends thus on what the interpreter takes the theory of American constitutionalism to be; Miller, however, offers not theory but antebellum historical practice as the measure of what counts as improper radical change.

[56] See *Slaughter-House Cases*, p. 74.
[57] See ibid., p. 78.

Federalism in the antebellum period was not, however, a freestanding value; its weight and scope were interpreted instrumentally, for example, in the context of a background theory of human rights and an institutional theory of which institutions (state or federal) best protected such rights. Both southern defenders of slavery and northern abolitionists would defend state's rights when they thought such arguments best protected their different understandings of such rights; similarly, the theory of Union and moderate antislavery defended expansive national power in service of their view of rights and how best to realize them (see Chapters 2–3). Antebellum historical practice, thus understood, cannot be the measure of how the Reconstruction Amendments should be interpreted, because that practice rests on background normative and institutional views that the amendments criticize and supplant.

At the heart of the amendments is the moral and constitutional meaning they ascribed to the Civil War and the antebellum constitutional controversies that culminated in that war, namely, that the failure to nationalize the protection of human rights in antebellum federalism had been responsible for the greatest political tragedy in the history of American constitutionalism. Under the Reconstruction Amendments, human rights are best protected by national institutions; and federalism must be interpreted against that background, not the now anachronistic background of antebellum controversy and constitutional tragedy. If some proponents of the Reconstruction Amendments interpretively believed their implementation would not require a thorough rethinking of antebellum American federalism, that concrete interpretive conviction may have been based on optimistic factual assumptions of full state compliance. Such convictions would not reasonably apply to the facts as they proved to be; for if they did apply to such facts, they would be inconsistent with the more abstract authoritative purposes of these amendments (preserving the rights-based legitimacy of political power). The reasonable interpretation of these amendments requires that such normatively fundamental purposes (national protection of basic human rights) must set the controlling interpretive framework for resolving ambiguities and contradictions in the relevant materials to be interpreted (see Chapter 4).[58]

[58] For an argument to the contrary based on the those supporters of the amendments who supposed that they basically preserved antebellum federalism, see Maltz, *Civil Rights, the Constitution, and Congress.* Maltz's interpretive argument rests on the implausible premise that the interpretation of the amendments should be established by the concrete interpretive convictions of the small group of members of Congress required to secure constitutional approval of the amendments by the required supermajorities. In fact, the concrete interpretive convictions of no proponents (whether the dominant supporters or some more conservative swing group) can reasonably be the measure of later constitutional interpretation (see Chapter 4). Even assuming originalism were a more defensible theory of constitutional interpretation than it is (see Chapter 1), an originalism resting on swing votes is surely less reasonable than one resting on dominant concrete interpretive convictions.

If Miller's fears may at least have made some sense in 1873 in view of the unchartered waters of unprecedented judicial activism that Miller apparently saw before him, they have no continuing weight today, after we have had a long and often brilliantly successful experience of judicial interpretation to similar effect under the due process clause. Miller's interpretive argument is entitled to no reasonable precedential weight; it is transparently incompetent, and its one shred of consequentialist support has been dissipated by our historical experience. It remains today only to blinker and confuse public understanding of legitimate constitutional principles and values that would be more responsibly articulated and elaborated without the blockage of its bad judgment. Miller's interpretation of the privileges and immunities clause should be overruled, placed on the dustbin of history among the interpretive mistakes judges have wrought when they confused serious interpretive responsibility with political fears.

Miller's mistaken interpretation of the privileges and immunities clause arguably was not even necessary to reach the judicial result he wanted in the *Slaughter-House Cases*. The state-imposed monopoly raised two related issues under the privileges and immunities clause: first, did the monopoly abridge a fundamental right? And if it did abridge such a right, was the abridgment justified by a sufficiently compelling state purpose?

Had Miller accepted the interpretive argument of the dissents regarding the meaning of the clause, he could not perhaps reasonably have denied that an issue of fundamental rights was involved, namely, the natural right to free labor. But he could have questioned whether the monopoly law, which required all butchers to be allowed access to slaughtering animals at reasonable fees, was a serious abridgment of that right of the sort that required compelling constitutional justification. In fact, Miller says as much early in the opinion: "It is difficult to see a justification for the assertion that the butchers are deprived of the right to labor in their occupation." In addition, Miller could have argued that, even if there was an abridgment of such a right, it was sufficiently justified by compelling state police purposes—namely, public health, convenience, and good urban planning—which justify zoning laws. In fact, Miller justifies the law as a reasonable way "to locate them where the convenience, health, and comfort of the people require they shall be located."[59]

The dissenting justices would have questioned both these arguments. Justice Field, for example, expressly denies that a monopoly, in contrast to a zoning law, is a constitutionally reasonable way to pursue legitimate police power interests without imposing a least restrictive burden on a basic right.[60] But within the framework of the privileges and immunities analysis

[59] See *Slaughter-House Cases*, pp. 61, 64. On this point, see the dissenting opinion of Justice Field, ibid., pp. 110–11.

[60] See ibid., pp. 87–88.

of the dissents, such argument would have been available. If so, Miller's interpretive argument was unnecessary to reach the result in the *Slaughter-House Cases*.[61]

A Theory of Privileges and Immunities

I have argued that, properly interpreted, the privileges and immunities clause of the fourteenth amendment nationalizes the protection of basic human rights. It is time now to explore the interpretive consequences of such a view for the protection of both enumerated and unenumerated constitutional rights.

The Constitution of 1787 and Bill of Rights of 1791 contain various guarantees of human rights, a few enforceable against the states,[62] most against the federal government alone.[63] That asymmetry in the constitutional protection of human rights gave rise to the antebellum crisis of constitutional legitimacy that I have discussed at length. Put simply, the Constitution, as amended, had failed to meet the demands for politically legitimate government set by its background contractualist political theory. Slavery had not been abolished, but rather entrenched and even expanded; the states—both in the South and North—had failed, often in connection with the defense of slavery and racism, to extend basic guarantees of human rights to both blacks and whites. Indeed, the Constitution itself had been misinterpreted by proslavery constitutional theory to protect slavery in the territories and to deprive blacks of American citizenship, a theory that became the law of the land in *Dred Scott*. The aim of the Reconstruction Amendments was, in light of an experience of constitutional decadence motored by state abridgment of basic human and constitutional rights, to restructure American constitutionalism to render it politically legitimate (see Chapter 4). Of the various interlocking provisions of the Reconstruction Amendments, the pivotal ones are the two great normative clauses of the fourteenth amendment that impose nationally enforceable constraints on state power: the privileges and immunities clause and the equal protection clause.

[61] For other comments on the opinion, see Nelson, *The Fourteenth Amendment*, pp. 155–81; Kaczorowski, *The Nationalization of Civil Rights*, pp. 253–74; Kaczorowski, *The Politics of Judicial Interpretation*, pp. 143–66; Hyman and Wiecek, *Equal Justice under Law*, pp. 472–82.

[62] See, e.g., U.S. Constitution, Art. I, sec. 10, cl. 1 (states prohibited from enacting bills of attainder, ex post facto laws, and laws impairing contracts).

[63] See, e.g., U.S. Constitution, Art. I, sec. 9, cl. 3; Amendments I–X. On the application of the Bill of Rights to the federal government alone, see *Barron v. the Mayor and City Council of Baltimore*, 32 U.S. (7 Pet.) 243 (1833).

Both these clauses express general requirements of the contractualist political theory of American constitutionalism, implicit as constraints largely on federal power in the Constitution of 1787, which are explicitly applied under the fourteenth amendment to the pathological source of the antebellum crisis of constitutional legitimacy, the power of the states. The normative requirement of equal protection states, as we saw in Chapters 4 and 5, the most abstract requirement of contractualist political legitimacy; political power can only legitimately make claims on allegiance if it extends to all persons reasonably subject to political power equal protection of their basic human rights and fair concern for their interests as part of the public good. The normative guarantee of privileges and immunities focuses on an aspect of this abstract requirement, protecting basic human rights as a necessary condition of contractualist political legitimacy. The Constitution had failed the tests of political legitimacy set by these normative requirements because it has not extended them to the power of the states; the normative clauses of the fourteenth amendment remedy this by applying these normative requirements, as nationally enforceable constitutional standards, to state power.

Equal protection, thus understood, elaborates a tradition of contractualist constitutional reflection long implicit in the American constitutional tradition, for example, in guarantees of basic rights such as those of religious liberty and free speech in the first amendment. Such guarantees secure to all persons respect for equal liberties of conscience and communication, the equal protection of basic rights that contractualist political theory requires. In my earlier discussion of equal protection (see Chapter 5), I observed that the fundamental rights test for equal protection review, in contrast to suspect classification analysis, rested on longstanding constitutional traditions protecting basic rights. The equal protection clause extends that analysis to state power, drawing on the longstanding principles and tests applicable to national power; thus, constitutional arguments of a content-biased regulation of speech may be made to precisely the same effect under this mode of equal protection scrutiny.[64] In contrast, suspect classification analysis, though certainly prefigured in the suspectness of classifications based on religious intolerance,[65] represents a more constitutionally novel concern for the moral subjugation of groups of persons on the basis of a history and culture of constitutional deprivations of their basic rights (see Chapter 5).

The privileges and immunities clause rests on the same foundation as equal protection analysis in terms of fundamental rights. Indeed, had the privileges and immunities clause been properly interpreted by the judi-

---

[64] See, e.g., *Erznoznik v. Jacksonville*, 422 U.S. 205 (1975).
[65] See Richards, *Toleration*, pp. 300–301; *Foundations*, pp. 259–60.

ciary, it would have afforded the interpretive basis for the identification of those basic human rights that are then subject to equal protection analysis as fundamental rights.[66] Properly understood, the clause elaborates the tradition of contractualist reflection on basic rights previously applicable largely to the federal government, calling for the national articulation and enforcement of principles of basic human rights against the states.

The interpretation of such principles must, in light of the aim of background political theory to render the Constitution legitimate, extend the national protection of such rights reasonably against those forms of state power that have pivotally undermined constitutional legitimacy. Such interpretation is in its nature not a simplistic application of the guarantees of rights of the Constitution and Bill of Rights to the states.

Many important interpretive debates did arise about the meaning of these guarantees during the antebellum period; the first amendment was at stake in the important constitutional controversy over the Alien and Sedition Act of 1798,[67] and the comparably important debates over the right of petition of, and use of federal mails by, abolitionists.[68] And as we have seen, controversies over the meaning of the privileges and immunities clause of Article IV of the Constitution were in their nature debates over the basic rights of American citizens. All these discussions do reasonably inform the interpretation of basic rights in general and rights of the first amendment in particular as basic human rights enforceable against the states under the privileges and immunities clause.

But the proper interpretation of the nature and weight of human rights can often only be clarified when they are appropriately contextualized in terms of political threats to them; and most of the important threats to human rights in the antebellum period came not from the federal government, but from the states. Indeed, most political power in the antebellum period was in the states;[69] the states had jurisdiction over many issues that were not regarded as federal (for example, rights of property and contract, the law of tort, crimes, and domestic relations law).

With the notable exception of Washington, D.C.,[70] American slavery was

[66] As it is, the judiciary has separated the analysis of substantive due process from that of fundamental rights in equal protection. The Supreme Court has thus treated voting rights as a matter of equal protection, not due process. See, e.g., *Harper v. Virginia Board of Elections*, 383 U.S. 663 (1966).

[67] See Richards, *Toleration*, pp. 174–75.

[68] See Nye, *Fettered Freedom*, pp. 32–69.

[69] For a sensitive study of the shift of political power to the national government initiated by the Civil War, see Paludan, *"A People's Contest."*

[70] Slavery in Washington, D.C., being subject to federal law, was a natural object of abolitionist constitutional criticism. For the classic such criticism, see Theodore Weld, "The Power of Congress over Slavery in the District of Columbia," in tenBroek, *Equal under Law*, pp. 243–80.

thus an institution based on state laws of property, contract, tort, crimes, and domestic relations.[71] Slavery in the states not only itself violated human rights, but its support and protection by states gave rise to many of the correlative violations of human rights by the states that were at the center of antebellum moral, political, and constitutional controversy. But most Americans (including advocates, such as Lincoln, of the constitutional theory of Union) regarded slavery and many other violations of rights by the states as immune from federal constitutional scrutiny. Certainly, such abridgments of human rights were not subject to constitutional assessment in terms of the Bill of Rights, which applied only to the federal government.

Federal constitutional jurisprudence, with the notable exception of Article IV (a constraint on state power), thus does not interpretively bear upon the most basic violations of human rights in the antebellum period; it does not reasonably clarify the nature and weight of the basic rights that were put at threat by state power—the rights that, in light of the privileges and immunities clause of the fourteenth amendment, require national protection. For this reason, the interpretation of these privileges and immunities, while drawing upon the Bill of Rights, must independently articulate the nature and weight of human rights worthy of national protection against the states. Many normative concepts and tests from the federal level may thus be reasonably used in this interpretive analysis, though their interpretation will often be best clarified by the state history of the gravest political threats to them. Some normative concepts (unenumerated rights) may take on a depth and urgency that they would not have had at the federal level, but do have at the state level where the political threats to such rights have been all too vividly real (for example, to the constitutional right to privacy). Some normative concepts of federal law may not correspond to basic human rights worthy of protection against the states.[72]

The interpretive fertility of this approach to the analysis of the national protection of human rights is best shown by illustration in terms of both enumerated and unenumerated rights. I do not propose here to repeat my extensive interpretive analysis of these matters elsewhere,[73] but rather to show how such analysis is the reasonable interpretive attitude to take in light of the approach to the privileges and immunities clause that I advocate. I turn in Chapter 7 to the implications of this approach for the understanding of claims of economic injustice as constitutional claims.

[71] See Cobb, *An Inquiry into the Law of Negro Slavery;* John Codman Hurd, *The Law of Freedom and Bondage in the United States,* 2 vols. (Boston: Little, Brown, 1858–62 (reprint, New York: Negro Universities Press, 1968).

[72] The seventh amendment to the Bill of Rights (guaranteeing a jury trial in civil cases) may be one of these.

[73] See Richards, *Toleration,* and *Foundations.*

Enumerated Rights

Interpretation of the privileges and immunities clause must give central place to those state abridgments of human rights that, from the perspective of the revolutionary constitutionalism of the Reconstruction Amendments, were pivotally responsible for antebellum constitutional decadence. As I have argued at length in Chapters 3 and 4, the argument for toleration, forged by abolitionists in their criticism of slavery and racism, pivotally framed the moral, political, and constitutional theory of the Reconstruction Amendments and its critical perspective on the antebellum period.

The principle of toleration was central to this criticism at two levels. Slavery and its underlying racism themselves rested on the radical political evil of depriving slaves of basic inalienable rights such as conscience and free speech; and the political support for slavery and racism required the systematic denial of both rights of conscience and free speech of anyone critical of the institution. The resulting tyranny of majoritarian racist opinion in Jacksonian America (observed by both de Tocqueville and Martineau) made possible, in turn, the declension in American constitutional morality that Lincoln so acutely analyzed in the politics of Stephen Douglas and the constitutionalism of Roger Taney.

State constitutions, of course, had in them guarantees of both religious liberty and free speech; but they were of no effect when state politics, especially in the South, was so dominated by hegemonic slave-owning interests that the interpretation of such guarantees gave no protection to any morally independent criticism of slavery as an institution. In effect, the measure of toleration was determined through the sectarian prism of a politically entrenched commitment to slavery as an institution; and any criticism of slavery as an institution was thus interpreted as the equivalent of violent incitement to slave rebellion and mass slaughter of the innocent.[74]

A reasonable interpretation of the nationalization of human rights requires that a constitutionally muscular conception of rights of conscience and free speech be articulated and enforced by national institutions against such illegitimate abuses of state power. If the historical nerve of the problem was the tendency of hegemonic local authorities parochially to entrench their own power, part of the solution must be the articulation of substantive national constitutional principles formulated to minimize the recurrence of such abuse. Two issues are crucial: the scope of protection and the burden of proof required to justify abridgment.

The scope of constitutionally protected conscience and speech must be broad enough to include all forms of morally independent exercises of conscience that bring facts and values to bear on public discourse and debate,

[74] See Nye, *Fettered Freedom*; Eaton, *The Freedom-of-Thought Struggle in the Old South*.

including conscientious criticism of the most fundamental institutions. From the contractualist perspective, the inalienable right to conscience must enjoy such broad protection in order to ensure the fullest possible exercise of free public reason, which may expose to fair pubic discussion and debate the ultimate issues of contractualist political legitimacy: respect for rights and the use of political power for the public good. Respect for rights, as a normative goal, is in its nature respect for the rights of each person; and such respect cannot be fairly tested by allowing majoritarian conceptions of value (including the putative value of basic political institutions) to be the measure of debate. From the perspective of contractualist revolutionary constitutionalism, subversive advocacy (the criticism of basic institutions as worthy of revolution and revolt) should be regarded as at the very core, not the periphery, of protected conscience and speech.[75] It is precisely such criticism, however despised by majoritarian opinion, that most fairly tests the underlying legitimacy of basic institutions.

The lesson to be learned from antebellum America is that there is no institution, however radically evil (like slavery), that majoritarian democratic opinion may not effectively legitimate by forbidding its criticism as a form of subversive advocacy. Slavery, a radical evil, came to be regarded as a positive good necessary to the integrity of republican institutions (see Chapter 2) within the framework of a prohibition on subversive advocacy of basic American institutions. The putative defense of "fundamental" or "basic" American constitutional institutions, by a prohibition on such advocacy, renders them often contemptibly unworthy of defense because based on doctrines and institutions that, untested by free debate, in fact rest on the violation of rights. Such prohibitions by their nature legitimate a delusive sense of what constitutional community is, a community not of principled respect for rights but of uncritical flag waving and sometimes fetishistic flag worship.[76]

The tragic contradiction of southern antebellum constitutionalism, the ideology behind southern intransigence, rests on this fact. An obsessive repression of any subversive advocacy turned a self-conscious appeal to a tradition of American rights-based revolutionary constitutionalism into a betrayal of that tradition by indulging shallow populist certitudes of racist group solidarity based on abridgment of rights. A congratulatory self-image, supposedly patriotically protecting rights-based constitutionalism, is not and cannot be self-authenticating; it may, rather, betray what it claims to love.

The same lesson is to be learned from our experience after the Civil War

---

[75] For a fuller defense of this position, see Richards, *Toleration,* pp. 178–87.

[76] For a correct application of this principle to a prosecution for desecrating the flag, holding the prosecution an unconstitutional abridgment of free speech, see *Texas v. Johnson,* 491 U.S. 397 (1989).

and the Reconstruction Amendments, when the failure to accord national protection for basic rights such as free speech (clearly required by the fourteenth amendment) fostered the same uncritical racist certitudes in the South and the nation at large, constructing a culture of racism that, in turn, interpretively betrayed the meaning and promise of the Reconstruction Amendments. A prohibition on subversive advocacy of basic institutions (such as state-supported racial segregation) had once again fostered political complacency about essential constitutional and political evils, debasing the public mind of a free people.[77] The long journey to correcting these mistakes was facilitated by the courageous assertion of these rights by the civil rights movement and the increasingly vigilant judicial protection of these rights, overruling the earlier view.[78]

For similar reasons, the abridgment of conscience and speech cannot reasonably be based on the fears of or hostility to what is thought or said, or on any rationale for abridgment that is interpreted to be substantially equivalent to such abridgment. Our reason for a broad conception of protected speech was to allow full scope for the exercise of the inalienable right to conscience not hostage to majoritarian judgments of the value of conscience or speech; it would undermine this rationale to allow the same majoritarian judgments to be the grounds for abridgment. Rather, the test for abridgment must be interpreted, as the Supreme Court currently interprets the clear and present danger test, to require a judicially impartial judgment of very grave harms that are both highly probable and not rebuttable by the normal pattern of dialogue and discourse in society at large.[79]

Finally, such strong national principles, protecting the rights of conscience and speech, must be articulated and enforced by national institutions, such as the federal judiciary, in a spirit that fosters a forum of free public reason that raises public appreciation of these issues to the highest level possible. If human rights rest, as the neo-Kantian Francis Lieber clearly saw and argued, on respect for the rational and reasonable powers of persons (see Chapters 3 and 4), the judiciary best performs its constitutional role under the privileges and immunities clause when it brings to its task the kind and quality of public reason that clarify for the American people an articulate sense of the rights and responsibilities of their status

---

[77] For a still brilliant analysis of the consequences, see Cash, *The Mind of the South*.

[78] See *Gitlow v. New York*, 268 U.S. 652 (1925) (due process clause of the fourteenth amendment extends protection of free speech to the states). For some of the important cases that protected black protest in the South, see *Herndon v. Lowry*, 301 U.S. 242 (1937); *Cox v. Louisiana*, 379 U.S. 536 (1965); *Shuttlesworth v. Birmingham*, 394 U.S. 147 (1969); but cf. *Walker v. Birmingham*, 388 U.S. 307 (1967). For a good general discussion of the significance of this judicial protection, see Kalven, *The Negro and the First Amendment*.

[79] See *Brandenburg v. Ohio*, 395 U.S. 444 (1969).

as free and equal persons in a historically continuous community of principle.

To the extent constitutional principles are often most politically threatened by local hegemonic factions active at the state level, the national judiciary should play a special interpretive role in protecting rights in this arena. Indeed, contrary to the views of some justices of the Supreme Court, the judiciary might justifiably bring more demanding standards for the protection of rights to bear on the state rather than the national level.[80]

Unenumerated Rights

The privileges and immunities clause is, in its nature, a national guarantee of basic human rights. Its text draws no distinction between enumerated and unenumerated human rights; its history (both antebellum discussion of the predecessor clause of Article IV and the statements of Bingham and Howard in Congress in 1866) draws no such distinction; indeed, *pace* Justice Black, it expressly eschews one. Its political theory makes no such distinction. As I have shown, its interpretation naturally draws upon normative ideas and tests of the Bill of Rights, but the Bill of Rights itself contains the ninth amendment, whose text, history, and political theory contemplate the articulation and enforcement of unenumerated rights.[81]

The interpretation of privileges and immunities must, in light of background contractualist political theory, articulate a nationally enforceable conception of basic rights in part informed by the human rights put at threat at the state level, as exemplified during the antebellum period. As I have suggested, the antebellum political power of the states was so much more extensive and pervasive than that of the federal government that the interpretation of basic rights at threat (in particular, unenumerated rights) takes on a more urgent and demanding character at the state than at the federal level.

Theodore Weld's classic indictment of slavery vividly characterizes such state abridgment of rights in terms of

plundering the slaves of all their inalienable rights, of the ownership of their own bodies, of the use of their own limbs and muscles, of all their time, liberty, and earnings, of the free exercise of choice, of the rights of marriage and parental authority, of legal protection, of the right to be, do do, to go, to stay, to think, to feel, to work, to rest, to eat, to sleep, to learn, to teach, to earn money, and to expend it, to visit, and to be visiting, to speak, to be silent, to

---

[80] For a defense of stronger free speech protections at the federal than state levels, see Justice Harlan's concurring opinion, *Roth v. United States*, 354 U.S. 476, 496 (1957).

[81] See Richards, *Toleration*, p. 256; and *Foundations*, pp. 214, 221–22, 228, 230.

worship according to conscience, in fine, their right to be protected by just and equal laws, and to be *amenable to such only.*[82]

Some of these rights were enumerated in the Bill of Rights (for example, rights of conscience and speech), but others were not (for example, the right to family life and to work freely). I concentrate here on the right to family life, examining the right to work in Chapter 7.

Both background history and political theory suggest that the right to marriage was thought of as one of the basic human rights not enumerated in specific provisions of the Bill of Rights but protected by the ninth amendment.[83] But the law of domestic relations, being state not federal, could not raise issues involving this right under guarantees of human rights only applicable to the federal government. The understanding of marriage as a human right, however, took on a new depth and urgency in the antebellum period at the state level in view of the peculiar nature of American slavery; such slavery failed to recognize the marriage or family rights of slaves,[84] and indeed inflicted on the black family the moral horror of breaking them up by selling family members separately.[85] One in six slave marriages thus were ended by force or sale.[86] No aspect of American slavery more dramatized its radical evil for abolitionists and Americans more generally than its brutal deprivation of intimate personal life, including undermining the moral authority of parents over children. Slaves, Weld argued, had "as little control over them [children], as have domestic animals over the disposal of their young."[87] Slavery, thus understood as an attack on intimate personal life,[88] stripped persons of essential attributes of their humanity.

The abolitionists' discussion of this issue was self-consciously drawn in terms of the argument for toleration so central to their general thought, as we saw in Chapter 3, on the radical political evil of slavery and racism. That argument had two interlinked components: first, the identification of certain inalienable rights of reasonable moral personality; and second, the requirement that politically legitimate government may regulate or limit such rights only on terms of public reason not hostage to entrenched political epistemologies based on the abridgment of such rights. Both components of the argument for toleration were in play in the searing aboli-

[82] Weld, *American Slavery as It Is*, p. 123; see also pp. 7–8, 143–44, 151.

[83] See Richards, *Toleration*, pp. 232–33, 256; and *Foundations*, at pp. 221–22, 224–26, 228, 230.

[84] See Stampp, *The Peculiar Institution*, pp. 198, 340–49; Genovese, *Roll, Jordan, Roll*, pp. 32, 52–53, 125, 451–58.

[85] See Stampp, *The Peculiar Institution*, pp. 199–207, 204–6, 333, 348–49; Gutman, *The Black Family in Slavery and Freedom*, pp. 146, 318, 349.

[86] See Gutman, *The Black Family in Slavery and Freedom*, p. 318

[87] See Weld, *American Slavery as It Is*, p. 56.

[88] See Walters, *The Antislavery Appeal*, pp. 95–96.

tionist indictment of state-supported slavery as an abridgment of the inalienable right to intimate family life.

First, contractualist thought, assumed by the Founders, had identified as one such natural right what Francis Hutcheson called "the natural right each one to enter into the matrimonial relation with any one who consents."[89] Indeed, relevant historical materials suggest that the right should be more abstractly stated; for example, John Witherspoon, whose lectures James Madison heard at Princeton, followed Hutcheson in listing as a basic human and natural right a "right to associate, if he so incline, with any person or persons, whom he can persuade (not force)—under this is contained the right to marriage."[90] The contractualist idea of a normatively protected sphere of associational choice, including intimate choices such as a marriage partner and having and caring for children, must be understood in the context of its general political skepticism about the enforcement on society at large of allegedly "natural" hierarchies that rest, in fact, on the unreasonable abridgment of basic rights of reasonable moral freedom.

The choice of marriage partner and child-rearing was an instance of one of these basic rights because essential moral powers of free people (powers of thought, deliberation, self-image, emotion, passion, imagination, moral growth and education, nurturance, caring, concern) are authenticated through the exercise of such choices. This contractualist understanding of marriage as a basic human right reflects and makes possible the historical conception of companionate marriage.[91] Such marriage is a voluntarily formed association of intimate friendship and love through which persons realize the complementary fulfillment of essential needs for the mutual support, companionship, and understanding that is often the very basis for sustaining enduring personal and ethical value in living a complete life. That new conception of marriage was rooted in a larger contractualist conception of self-governing people guaranteed the moral independence on reasonable terms to form the range of communities that are essential to the integral expression of their moral powers. Thus, Witherspoon correctly interprets the right to marriage as an instance of a larger right of association.

Second, this human right, like other such rights, may be regulated or limited only on terms of public reason not themselves hostage to an entrenched political hierarchy (for example, compulsorily arranged marriages)[92] resting on the abridgment of such rights. From the perspective of

---

[89] See Hutcheson, *A System of Moral Philosophy,* p. 299.

[90] James Witherspoon, *Lectures on Moral Philosophy* ed. Jack Scott (East Brunswick, N.J.: Associate University Presses, 1982), p. 123.

[91] See, e.g., Lawrence Stone, *The Family, Sex and Marriage* (New York: Harper & Row, 1977), pp. 325–404.

[92] See Werner Sollors, *Beyond Ethnicity: Consent and Descent in American Culture* (New York: Oxford University Press, 1986), p. 112.

the general abolitionist criticism of slavery and racism, the proslavery arguments in support of southern slavery's treatment of family life were transparently inadequate, not remotely affording public justification for the abridgment of such a fundamental right.

These arguments were in their nature essentially racist:

> His natural affection is not strong, and consequently he is cruel to his own offspring, and suffers little by separation from them.

> Another striking trait of negro character is lasciviousness. Lust is his strongest passion; and hence, rape is an offence of too frequent occurrence. Fidelity to the marriage relation they do not understand and do not expect, neither in their native country nor in a state of bondage.[93]

The blind moral callousness of southern proslavery thought was nowhere more evident than in its treatment of what were in fact agonizing, crushing, and demeaning family separations:[94]

> He is also liable to be separated from wife or child . . .—but from native character and temperament, the separation is much less severely felt.[95]

> With regard to the separation of husbands and wives, parents and children, . . . Negroes are themselves both perverse and comparatively indifferent about this matter.[96]

The irrationalist racist sexualization of black slaves was evident in the frequent justification of slavery as making possible the higher standards of sexual purity of southern white women.[97] Viewed through the polemically distorted prism of such thought, the relation of master and slave was itself justified as an intimate relationship, like husband and wife, that should similarly be immunized from outside interference.[98] In this Orwellian world of the distortion of truth by power, the defense of slavery became the defense of freedom.[99] Arguments of these sorts rested on interpretations of facts and values completely hostage to the polemical defense of entrenched political insti-

---

[93] Cobb, *An Inquiry into the Law of Negro Slavery*, pp. 39, 40.

[94] See Gutman, *The Black Family in Slavery and Freedom*.

[95] See William Harper, "Memoir on Slavery," in Faust, *Ideology of Slavery*, p. 110.

[96] See James Henry Hammond, "Letter to an English Abolitionist," in Faust, *Ideology of Slavery*, pp. 191–92.

[97] See, e.g., Harper, "Memoir on Slavery," in Faust, *Ideology of Slavery*, pp. 107, 118–19; Hammond, "Letter to an English Abolitionist," in Faust, *Ideology of Slavery*, pp. 182–84.

[98] See, e.g., Dew, "Abolition of Negro Slavery," in Faust, *Ideology of Slavery*, p. 65; Harper, "Memoir on Slavery," in Faust, *Ideology of Slavery*, p. 100 (citing Dew).

[99] For a good general discussion of such inversions, see Greenberg, *Masters and Statesman*.

tutions whose stability required the abridgment of basic rights of blacks
and of any whites who ventured reasonable criticism of such institutions.
Abolitionist moral thought about the family was itself in some respects limited by the dominant patriarchal assumptions of the age,[100] which, from our
perspective, may be questionable on the same grounds they questioned
proslavery thought (see Chapter 5). But the general abolitionist criticism
of slavery and racism, on grounds of the argument for toleration (see Chapter 2), justly applied to these proslavery arguments, which could no more
justify abridgment of the inalienable right to marriage than they could any
other of the slaves' comparable rights.

If the antebellum experience of state abridgments of basic rights must
inform a reasonable interpretation of the privileges and immunities clause,
the protection of intimate personal life must be one among the basic human
rights thus worthy of national protection. The constitutional right to privacy
correctly rests on this basis. Two interpretive issues must be separately
examined: the principle of constitutional privacy, and its application.

The principle of constitutional privacy interpretively rests on two cogent
grounds: first, the abstract fundamental human right to intimate personal
life; and second, threats to this right on the basis of arguments that cannot
be justified in contemporary circumstances in terms of public, secular reasons open and available to all. Both the right and its required burden of
justification are a reasonable interpretation of the American contractualist
tradition of protection of basic human rights in general and a justified interpretation of the privileges and immunities clause in particular. Such a
right must, in light of antebellum experience, be nationally protected from
likely unjust threats at the state level. The interpretive arguments in support of the principle of constitutional privacy are, I believe, the best reading
of the text, history, and political theory of the U.S. Constitution; the arguments against it cannot be sustained on any of these grounds.[101]

The proper scope of application of the principle of constitutional privacy
is much more controversial. The principle of the right was first applied by
the U.S. Supreme Court to contraception in *Griswold v. Connecticut*,[102]
extended to abortion services in *Roe v. Wade*,[103] and denied application to
consensual homosexual sex acts in *Bowers v. Hardwick*;[104] a related form
of analysis was used, albeit inconclusively, in a recent case involving the
right to die.[105] All these cases can be reasonably interpreted in terms of the

[100] See Gutman, *The Black Family in Slavery and Freedom*, pp. 293–95.

[101] On this point, see Richards, *Foundations*, pp. 202–47.

[102] See *Griswold v. Connecticut*, 381 U.S. 479 (1965).

[103] See *Roe v. Wade*, 410 U.S. 113 (1973).

[104] See *Bowers v. Hardwick*, 478 U.S. 186 (1986).

[105] See *Cruzan v. Director, Missouri Deptartment of Health*, 496 U.S. 261 (1990). Justice
Rehnquist, writing for a five-four majority, accepts that a right to die exists and applies to the
case but denies that the state has imposed an unreasonable restriction on the right on the
facts of the case.

kind of analysis of the privileges and immunities clause that I have argued is appropriate, three of them (contraception, abortion, homosexuality) on the grounds of a basic right to intimate personal life, one of them (death) involving another basic right (an aspect of the right to life or meaningful life).[106] I focus here on the first three cases.

The criminalization of the use of contraceptives in married life is clearly an abridgment of the basic human right to intimate life, to decide whether or when one's sexual life will lead to offspring, indeed, to explore one's sexual and emotional life in personal life as an end in itself. This can only be justified by a compelling public reason, not on the grounds of reasons that are today sectarian (internal to a moral tradition not based on reasons available and accessible to all). In fact, the only argument that could sustain such laws (namely, the Augustinian[107] and Thomistic[108] view that it is immoral to engage in nonprocreative sex) is not today a view of sexuality that can reasonably be enforced on people of large. Many people regard sexual love as an end in itself and the control of reproduction as a reasonable way to regulate when and whether they have children consistent with their own personal and larger ethical interests, that of their children, and of an overpopulated society at large. From the perspective of women in particular, the enforcement of an anticontraceptive morality on society rests on a sectarian conception of gender hierarchy in which women's sexuality is defined by a mandatory procreative role and responsibility. That conception, the basis of the unjust construction of gender hierarchy, cannot reasonably be the measure of human rights today (see Chapter 5).[109]

Similar considerations explain the grounds for doubt about the putative public, nonsectarian justifications for laws criminalizing abortion and homosexual sexuality. Antiabortion laws, grounded in the alleged protection of a neutral good such as life, unreasonably equate the moral weight of a fetus in the early stages of pregnancy with that of a person and abortion with murder, failing to take seriously the weight that should be accorded a woman's basic right to reproductive autonomy in making choices central

---

[106] For further discussion, see David A. J. Richards, *Sex, Drugs, Death, and the Law: An Essay on Human Rights and Overcriminalization* (Totowa, N.J.: Rowman and Littlefield, 1982), pp. 215–70.

[107] See Augustine, *The City of God*, trans. Henry Bettenson (Harmondsworth, Eng.: Penguin, 1972), pp. 577–94.

[108] Thomas Aquinas elaborates Augustine's conception of the exclusive legitimacy of procreative sex in a striking way. Of the emision of semen apart from procreation in marriage, he wrote: "After the sin of homicide whereby a human nature already in existence is destroyed, this type of sin appears to take next place, for by it the generation of human nature is precluded." Thomas Aquinas, *On the Truth of the Catholic Faith: Summa Contra Gentiles*, trans. Vernon Bourke (New York: Image, 1956), pt. 2, chap. 122(9), p. 146.

[109] For further discussion of the right to privacy and contraception, see Richards, *Toleration*, pp. 256–61.

to her most intimate bodily and personal life.[110] Antihomosexuality laws have, as I suggested in Chapter 5, no public justification that would be acceptably enforced on society at large; they brutally abridge the sexual expression of the companionate loving relationships to which homosexuals, like heterosexuals, have an inalienable human right. That right encompasses the free moral powers through which persons forge enduring personal and ethical value in living a complete life. The decision in *Bowers v. Hardwick* was, for this reason, an interpretively unprincipled failure properly to elaborate the right of constitutional privacy in an area of populist prejudice where the protection of that right was exigently required.[111]

In the background of the laws at issue in all these cases lies the view of gender roles and hierarchy that I earlier discussed in connection with the suspect classification analysis of gender (see Chapter 5). That is clear, as I earlier suggested, in the case of *Griswold v. Connecticut,* less so in *Roe v. Wade* and *Bowers v. Hardwick.* On analysis, however, the little weight accorded women's interests and the decisive weight accorded the fetus in antiabortion laws make sense only against the background of the still powerful traditional conception of mandatory procreational, self-sacrificing, caring, and nurturant gender roles for women; it is its symbolic violation of that normative idea that imaginatively transforms abortion into murder. Similarly, the failure of the majority of the Supreme Court in *Bowers* to accord *any* weight whatsoever to the right to privacy of homosexuals, and decisive weight to incoherently anachronistic traditional moralism, reflect a still powerful ideology of unnatural gender roles that renders homosexuals constitutionally invisible, voiceless, and marginal.

The privileges and immunities clause requires the national protection of basic human rights from local hegemonic factions in light of the highest standards of public reason that the nation can bring to bear on these matters. The political threats to constitutional privacy in modern mass society are deep and real, and require judicial interpretive performance with a lively and articulate sense of its institutional responsibilities. The performance of the U.S. Supreme Court in *Bowers* fails these responsibilities; and its growing internal skepticism about *Roe v. Wade* suggests a further interpretive declension in its standards of interpretive integrity and public reason.[112]

These interpretive responsibilities require an integrated understanding of the proper role of text, history, and political theory in the interpretation of the Constitution. Such an understanding requires, here as elsewhere, a reading of the Constitution as a historically continuous community of prin-

---

[110] For further discussion, see ibid., pp. 261–69.
[111] For further discussion, see ibid., pp. 269–80; Richards, *Foundations,* pp. 202–47.
[112] See *Webster v. Reproductive Health Services,* 492 U.S. 490 (1989).

ciple (see Chapter 4).[113] Each generation must bring to bear the full resources of public reason to extend to all persons the protection of their inalienable human rights. The task in America is, as we have seen, informed by the interpretation of normative principles implicit in our history of concern for threats to basic human rights, a history interpreted in light of each generation's contextualized best understanding of the ultimate values of human rights that render political power legitimate. To do justice to that task, the protection of human rights must be interpreted as what they are, abstract normative values that must be interpreted with sensitivity to each generation's most reasonable understanding of its circumstances and relevant matters of fact and value.

An earlier generation's concrete application of such values informs this understanding but cannot be interpretively dispositive for a later generation that finds them, by its lights and in its circumstances, unreasonable.[114] Indeed, to suppose that constitutional interpretation can or should be understood exclusively in terms of such concrete historical applications is to render the Constitution illegitimate, incapable of embodying the ethical demands that sustain the allegiance of the American people to the Constitution as supremely authoritative law.[115]

These considerations explain not only how and why normative concepts such as equal protection or the right to free speech or the right to intimate life must be given a different reasonable content in 1992 than in 1866, but how the very conception of abstract protected rights may change over time. The privileges and immunities clause, properly understood, invites such public reflection as an expression of the abolitionist interpretive attitude that Theodore Parker and Charles Sumner urged be taken both to the Bible and to the Constitution, namely, as embodying a progressive vision of human rights elaborated and articulated by the best sense of justice of each generation.

We have seen, for example, that it was a common view in 1866 (taken by both Representative Bingham and Senator Howard) that the privileges and immunities clause included natural rights, but not political rights such as voting. Natural rights, under this view, are the human rights owed all person as such; political rights are not, however, owed to all persons as such, but should be distributed in whatever way best leads to respect for natural rights.[116] The distinction can, of course, be sensibly drawn; but

---

[113] For further development of this idea, see Richards, *Foundations*, chap. 4.

[114] For further development of this view, see Richards, *Toleration*, pp. 20–45; and *Foundations*, pp. 131–71.

[115] For further criticism along these lines, see Richards, *Toleration*, pp. 20–45; and *Foundations*, pp. 78–171.

[116] For a defense of the distinction in the context of a general antebellum political theory, see Lieber, *Manual of Political Ethics*. For Lieber on natural or "primordial" rights, see 1:167–68, 191–214, 218–21.

historical experience and normative reflection may reasonably conclude that the guarantee of equal natural rights is most reasonably understood as requiring support by a comparable guarantee of equal political rights or at least a presumption of such a guarantee.[117] If so, the reasonable interpretation of privileges and immunities may include voting rights.[118]

A reading of the privileges and immunities clause along the lines I have suggested naturally must reopen the question answered negatively by the *Slaughter-House Cases*, namely, the application of this mode of analysis to economic rights such as the right to work. If the clause properly requires both enumerated and unenumerated rights to be enforced nationally against the states, does or should it protect economic rights? Have I defended constitutional privacy at the unacceptable price of resuscitating from unlamented death *Lochner v. New York*?

[117] For an important recent study, see Charles R. Beitz, *Political Equality* (Princeton: Princeton University Press, 1989).

[118] See, e.g., *Harper v. Virginia Board of Elections*, 383 U.S. 663 (1966); *Reynolds v. Sims*, 377 U.S. 533 (1964).

SEVEN

ECONOMIC JUSTICE AND THE CONSTITUTION

THE LEADING CASE taken today to define the interpretive limits of the Constitution as a vehicle for economic justice is a case that exceeded those limits, *Lochner v. New York*.[1] The issue in dispute in *Lochner* was a New York law prohibiting the employment of bakery workers for more than ten hours a day or sixty hours a week. In a five-four opinion, Justice Peckham, writing for the Supreme Court, held the statute unconstitutional on the ground that it abridged employers' and employees' right to contract, a substantive right protected by the due process clause of the fourteenth amendment. Peckham assessed the reasonableness of the law in light of what he took to be the only legitimate purposes such a law could have, namely, securing the health interests of consumers in good bread and the health interests of bakers in work conditions that were not physically harmful. He rejected the law as not reasonably related to these purposes.

Justices Harlan and Holmes wrote notable dissents to the opinion. Justice Harlan questioned both Peckham's characterization of legitimate state purposes and the appropriateness of a demanding standard of review for such legislation. One such legitimate state purpose, unacknowledged by Peckham, was the state's interest in the equalization of bargaining power "in the belief that employers and employes in such establishments were not upon an equal footing, and that the necessities of the latter often compelled them to submit to such exactions as unduly taxed their strength."[2] Judged in terms of this and its other legitimate state purposes, the judiciary should, Harlan argued, defer to the judgment of the legislature on reasonable regulations of work conditions in the bakery industry.

Justice Holmes, in his famous dissenting opinion, concentrated on what he took to be the economic theory motivating Peckham's opinion, a general "liberty of the citizen to do as he likes so long as he does not interfere with the liberty of others to do the same";[3] Holmes identified this theory with the Social Darwinian views of Herbert Spencer.[4] For Holmes, the appropriate interpretive question for a judge must be whether the alleged right

[1] *Lochner v. New York*, 198 U.S. 45 (1905).

[2] Ibid., 69 (Harlan, J., dissenting).

[3] See ibid., 75 (Holmes, J., dissenting).

[4] For the general impact of Spencer on American political thought, see Richard Hofstadter, *Social Darwinism in American Thought* (Boston: Beacon Press, 1955).

to contract is one that underlies American law; he adduced various examples to show that it was not a background right respected by American law (for example, laws dealing with Sunday closing, the post office, usury, compulsory school attendance and vaccination, taxation, monopolies). Holmes concluded that, since the right was not a principle of constitutional law, the majority could embody their contrary views in law. Spencer's economic theory—whatever its truth or the judge's agreement with it—was and should be interpretively irrelevant: "The 14th Amendment does not enact Mr. Herbert Spencer's Social Statics."[5]

Lochner v. New York was later repudiated by the Supreme Court not only on its facts, but as a more general kind or model of interpretive mistake;[6] in light of that mistake, the judiciary was to adopt an interpretive attitude in the area of economic regulation that was, to say the least, highly deferential.[7] The issue was not the rejection of substantive due process as such; the judiciary, notwithstanding its repudiation of the due process reasoning of *Lochner,* articulated and elaborated the substantive due process analysis of constitutional privacy. Even if the privacy cases were properly understood, as they should be, in terms of privileges and immunities, not due process (see chapter 6), *Lochner* would certainly be invoked by the judiciary to resist the use of the privileges and immunities clause to protect economic rights in the same way it was resisted by Justice Miller on the facts of the *Slaughter-House Cases.* The ground for this judicial resistance would be an interpretation of Justice Holmes's dissent in *Lochner.* The theory of the Constitution imposes no strong constraints on economic theories but is consistent with a number of them.

Under this now dominant view, claims of economic injustice, grounded on one or another theory of redistributive justice, are not judicially enforceable under the Constitution, but must be referred to democratic politics alone. This reading of *Lochner*'s mistake applies equally to proposed constitutional enforcement of antiredistributive theories from the Right (those, for example, of Richard Epstein[8] and Bernard Siegan)[9] and redistributive theories from the Left (Frank Michelman,[10] Joshua Cohen, and

[5] See *Lochner,* p. 75 (Holmes, J., dissenting).

[6] See *Nebbia v. New York,* 291 U.S. 502 (1934); *West Coast Hotel v. Parrish,* 300 U.S. 379 (1937).

[7] See, e.g., *Williamson v. Lee Optical Co.,* 348 U.S. 483 (1955) (state requirement that opticians fit lenses only on basis of prescription from licensed optometrist or ophthalmologist held constitutional).

[8] See Richard A. Epstein, *Takings: Private Property and the Power of Eminent Domain* (Cambridge: Harvard University Press, 1985).

[9] See Bernard H. Siegan, *Economic Liberties and the Constitution* (Chicago: University of Chicago Press, 1980).

[10] Frank Michelman, "Foreword: On Protecting the Poor through the Fourteenth Amendment," *Harvard Law Review* 83, no. 1 (November 1969):7; and "In Pursuit of Constitutional

Joel Rogers).[11] The Constitution is agnostic among all such theories and cannot therefore interpretively be used to enforce any of them.

The claim is not that constitutional interpretation should in all areas be uninformed by normative social theory. When it came to the first amendment, Justice Holmes made clear that the interpretation of free speech should use what he took to be the best political theory of free speech.[12] The claim, rather, is that the Constitution is agnostic on normative economic theory, in particular, on theories of economic justice; and for this reason, such claims of economic injustice should not be interpreted as grounds for judicially enforceable constitutional claims.

Theories of justice sometimes themselves make a distinction of this sort. John Rawls's contractualist theory of justice[13] can be elaborated to make the best contemporary sense of the contractualist political theory of the Constitution, including, as I have argued both in this book and elsewhere,[14] the interpretation of guarantees of free speech and religious liberty, constitutional privacy, federalism, equal protection, privileges and immunities, and the like. Rawls's theory however, makes, a sharp distinction between the first principle of justice (the greatest equal liberty of basic rights consistent with a like liberty for all) and the difference principle (distribution of economic goods is to be chosen that, in comparison with other distributions, makes worst off classes best off over time).[15]

Rawls thinks of the first principle as defining the proper distribution of the basic rights of the person embodied in the supreme law of the Constitution and thus legitimately the subject of judicial enforcement by institutions of judicial review such as those of the U.S. Constitution. The requirements of the difference principle, in contrast, "come into play at the stage of the legislature." As Rawls explains it, the reasonable enforcement of the first principle can be secured by constitutionalization, but not of the second principle:

> Now the question whether legislation is just or unjust, especially in connection with economic and social policies, is commonly subject to reasonable differences of opinion. In these cases judgment frequently depends upon speculative political and economic doctrines and upon social theory generally.

Welfare Rights: One View of Rawls' Theory of Justice," *University Pennsylvania Law Review* 121, no. 5 (May 1973):962.

[11] Joshua Cohen and Joel Rogers, *On Democracy* (New York: Penguin Books, 1983), pp. 158–61.

[12] For Holmes's liberal use of the ideas of John Stuart Mill's *On Liberty* in the interpretation of free speech, see *Abrams v. United States*, 250 U.S. 616, 624 (1919) (Holmes, J., dissenting).

[13] See Rawls, *A Theory of Justice*.

[14] See Richards, *Toleration*; and *Foundations*.

[15] For discussion, see Rawls, *A Theory of Justice*, pp. 195–257, 258–332.

Often the best that we can say of a law or policy is that it is at least not clearly unjust. The application of the difference principle in a precise way normally requires more information than we can expect to have and, in any case, more than the application of the first principle. It is often perfectly plain and evident when the equal liberties are violated. These violations are not only unjust but can be clearly seen to be unjust: the injustice is manifest in the public structure of institutions. But this state of affairs is comparatively rare with social and economic policies regulated by the difference principle.[16]

It is facile and untrue to claim that any role of contractualist political theory in constitutional interpretation is debarred on the ground, following Holmes, that the fourteenth amendment no more enacts Rawls than Spencer.[17] Holmes's point was not about the use of political theory as such (as his theory of the first amendment clearly shows), but about the use of normative social theory in a certain area of discourse (claims of economic injustice). The proposed theory played no background role in the discourse of American law, indeed, was flatly inconsistent with much of it. But contractualist theory not only makes sense of much of American constitutional law; at least in the hands of Rawls, it offers arguments on why one of its principles (the difference principle) was not and should not be constitutionalized.

Of course, no political theorist is the final authority on the best interpretation of her or his own views; and some theorists (notably, Michelman, Cohen, and Rogers), much under the influence of Rawls's general contractualist theory, have argued that at least some of its economically redistributive requirements would be properly constitutionalized. Are their arguments ruled out by a proper interpretation of *Lochner*'s mistake?

The now ritualistic incantation of *Lochner* to this effect is unsound. It does not follow, if the dissents in *Lochner* are correct, that no normative economic theory can properly inform constitutional interpretation; we might call this the nonsequitur of *Lochner*'s mistake. Neither of the dissents in *Lochner* warrants the nonsequitur.

Justice Holmes, author of the more famous of the dissents, put his point laconically with the type of gritty apothegm that has made him a favorite for commentators in search of quotable slogans: "The 14th amendment does not enact." But Holmes offered an interpretive argument for his conclusion, not just a conclusion. The conclusion was that a then certain current fad and fashion for Spencer's Social Darwinian ideas was not the measure of the interpretive responsibilities of the federal judiciary. The argument was that the interpretive relevance of any such theory must be tested against

---

[16] Ibid., pp. 198–99.

[17] For a form of this bad argument, see Ely, *Democracy and Distrust*, p. 58.

the benchmark of the historical traditions of American law; in short, did the theory fit the body of law it was meant to clarify?

Holmes's citation of a large and varied body of American laws and traditions—all unequivocally condemned by Spencer—showed that the theory failed this benchmark test; it was an interpretive nonstarter, as the majority would have seen if it had taken its interpretive responsibilities at all seriously. Holmes might have plausibly gone on to ask: If Spencer, why not Plato, or Gobineau, or Mohammed? Holmes's barely concealed impatience with the majority was at its interpretive nescience, introducing a normative theory—admittedly highly popular in the declining days of the gilded age[18]—to reach a result bizarrely unconnected with the larger fabric of American law. Thus understood, Holmes's dissent does not support the nonsequitur of Lochner's mistake. It delegitimates the use of one economic normative theory in the interpretation of the American Constitution; it offers no argument, in principle, against the interpretive relevance of all such theories.

Justice Harlan's dissent is, in comparison to that of Holmes, both fairer to the majority and more interpretively complex. The dissent is fairer because it does not ascribe to the majority a Spencerian radicalism that is, in fact, historically unrelated to the American traditions of laissez-faire constitutionalism that the majority elaborates. Spencer had "urged the elimination of public education, sanitation laws, and the public postal system, among other government institution" on the basis of immutable natural laws. Laissez-faire constitutionalism advocated none of these, but was based on an interpretation of the principle "that the power of government could not legitimately be exercised to benefit one person at the expense of others." That principle "received wide support in late nineteenth-century American not because it was based on widely adhered-to economic principles, and certainly not because it protected entrenched economic privilege, but rather because it was congruent with a well-established and accepted principle of American liberty."[19]

The principle had been invoked in the antebellum period in abolitionist criticism of the slave power conspiracy, an abuse of political power to advance the interests of slave owners and those economically dependent on them at the expense of both human rights and pursuit of the public good.[20]

---

[18] See Hofstadter, Social Darwinism; John A. Garraty, The New Commonwealth, 1877–1890 (New York: Harper & Row, 1968), pp. 309–35; Sean Dennis Cashman, America in the Gilded Age: From the Death of Lincoln to the Rise of Theodore Roosevelt, 2d ed. (New York: New York University Press, 1988).

[19] For an excellent general study, see Michael Les Benedict, "Laissez-Faire and Liberty: A Re-evaluation of the Meaning and Origins of Laissez-Faire Constitutionalism," Law and History Review 3, no. 2 (Fall 1985), pp. 294, 301, 298.

[20] For a good general study, see Davis, The Slave Power Conspiracy.

The slave power conspiracy was the paradigm interpretive example of private corruption of the public interest at the heart of antislavery political and constitutional thought, including its fruition in the great normative concepts of the fourteenth amendment, equal protection (see Chapter 5), and privileges and immunities (see Chapter 6).

One highly influential general expression of such antebellum political theory was that of Francis Lieber (see Chapters 3 and 4); and one strand of Lieber's interpretation of an unfair expression of private interests at the expense of public values was the activity of trade unions, a form of "aristocratic monopoly" that caused "enormous losses" to "the community at large."[21] Lieber, in turn, influenced the postbellum interpretation of basic constitutional principles of important constitutional thinkers such as Thomas Cooley.[22] Cooley gave great weight to protection of basic rights from state power (including conscience and free speech), to racial integration, and a general guarantee of due process that state power must be a reasonable regulation of basic rights, not the arbitrary expression of private interests.[23] It was this latter guarantee that laissez-faire constitutionalism identified as put at threat by unnecessary state economic regulation,[24] including the New York statute that the majority struck down on such grounds in *Lochner v. New York.*

Unlike the Holmes dissent, Harlan affirmed the general theory of the majority opinion that a right (such as the right to contract) cannot be violated arbitrarily, but must be subject to reasonable regulation. He offered, however, a different interpretation of what counted as a reasonable regulation on the facts of *Lochner,* one that rebutted the majority's suggestion of the perversion of public power by private interests.

The constitutional reasonableness of such a regulation must be assessed, Harlan argued, both from the perspective of its substantive ends and the means taken to pursue those ends. The majority opinion had narrowly construed the legitimate substantive ends of such legislation and then interpreted the legislation as not reasonably related to these narrow ends.

[21] See Lieber, *Manual of Political Ethics*, 2:344–50, esp. 349.

[22] See Alan R. Jones, *The Constitutional Conservatism of Thomas McIntyre Cooley: A Study in the History of Ideas* (New York: Garland, 1987), pp. 104–5, 197 n. 85.

[23] For Cooley on due process, see ibid., pp. 145–46; on conscience and free speech, see p. 161; on church-state separation, see p. 261; on desegregation see pp. 202–3, 311–12; on corporate regulation, see pp. 269–75, 336. See Thomas M. Cooley, *A Treatise on the Constitutional Limitations*, 6th ed. (Boston: Little, Brown, 1890); and *The General Principles of Constitutional Law in the United States of America* ed. Alexis C. Angell, 2d ed. (Boston: Little, Brown, 1891). Cooley did not question the authority of the *Slaughter-House Cases*; see T. M. Cooley, "The Fourteenth Amendment," in Story, *Commentaries*, 2:687–88. He therefore transported the reasoning of privileges and immunities to substantive due process.

[24] See Christopher G. Tiedeman, *A Treatise on State and Federal Control of Persons and Property in the United States*, 2 vols. (St. Louis: F. H. Thomas Law Book Co., 1900).

Harlan's analysis dissented from both grounds of the majority's analysis. The legislation had among its legitimate state purposes not only those mentioned by the majority, but a legislative concern for the unequal bargaining power of employers and employees that tainted the free market. The legislation's means to these ends were not unreasonable when assessed, as they should be, in terms of a standard of review that appropriately deferred to the superior fact-finding available to the legislature about the bakery industry and the best means to regulate that industry. If both ends and means were reasonable in this way, the New York statute's regulation of work hours in the bakery industry could be justified in terms of public values of both background fairness (equal bargaining power) and health; it was not, as Peckham's opinion suggested it was, an abuse of public power to pursue private ends of the labor movement.

In Chapter 6 I suggested that Justice Miller's opinion in the *Slaughter-House Cases* could be construed in a similar way. Both the New York statute and the Louisiana imposition of a monopoly for slaughtering animals required justification as regulations of the basic right of free labor, which was, like the right to intimate life, among the basic rights of the person appealed to by antebellum moral and political abolitionist thought in the criticism of slavery[25] and the slave power.[26] Such criticism is interpretively probative of the basic rights protected by the fourteenth amendment (see Chapter 6). But neither the New York nor the Louisiana statute totally abridged the right to work. Rather, they regulated its terms (the hours of work for bakers, the place of slaughtering animals for butchers) not on unacceptably sectarian grounds, but on grounds of legitimate public purposes such as fairness and health. Both were, therefore, arguably reasonable regulations and constitutional.

It is not necessary to this interpretive position that the argument for the constitutionality of these statutes is equally powerful in both cases; in fact, it is not. The New York statute rests on a concern for equality in the distribution of the right to work that complements the constitutional principle regulating that right; the Louisiana statute suggests constitutionally unjustified unequal treatment. It regulates the right to work by mandating a monopoly when legitimate state ends might have been just as well secured by a zoning law that was less restrictive of the right.

Nothing in Harlan's dissent legitimates the nonsequitur of *Lochner*'s mistake. If the New York statute is constitutional, Harlan's analysis does not suggest that all such statutes must be constitutional. For Harlan, the Constitution is consistent with a range of reasonable substantive legislative ends and certainly does not constitutionally condemn, as Peckham sup-

---

[25] See, e.g., Weld, *American Slavery as It Is*, pp. 7–8, 123, 143–44, 151.
[26] See Foner, *Free Soil, Free Labor, Free Men*.

posed, the ends underlying the New York statute. The thrust of Harlan's argument is that, in each case, the extent of the abridgment and the egalitarian merits of the legislative ends and means must be assessed; it would be consistent with this view that most statutes would pass constitutional muster, but some might not. For example, on the grounds of this analysis, the *Slaughter-House Cases* might be wrongly decided.

If neither of the dissents in *Lochner* warrants the nonsequitur of *Lochner's* mistake, both dissents emphasize the consistency of the Constitution with various economic theories and place, at best, only quite weak constitutional constraints on the scrutiny of legislation in this arena; both dissents are skeptical of constitutional delegitimation of legislative ends in the economic arena. Certainly, neither dissent warrants the claim that one theory of economic justice merits constitutional enforcement over others that the legislature might adopt. To make such an interpretive argument, we must move beyond *Lochner* and inquire more generally about the relationship between the theory of the Constitution and theories of economic justice.

Economic issues pervade the Constitution of 1787; both its text and historical background were preoccupied by limitations on abusive state regulations of the economy under the Articles of Confederation and with the need for sufficient national power to regulate commerce both nationally and internationally.[27] In *The Federalist No. 10*, Madison had defended the Constitution in terms of "its tendency to break and control the violence of faction," factions that he thought of as "adverse to the rights of other citizens, or to the permanent and aggregate interests of the community." Economic factions were prominently featured in the argument of *No. 10*, including those "for an equal division of property, or for any other improper or wicked project."[28] Madison had amplified these concerns about state economic factions at the Constitutional Convention in blunt terms: "No agrarian attempts have yet been made in this Country, but symptoms of a leveling spirit, as we have understood, have sufficiently appeared in a certain quarter to give notice of the future danger. How is this danger to be guarded agst. on republican principles?"

Such expressions of concern suggest that worries about unjust or imprudent threats to property rights were central motivations of the founding. The Constitution also extended constitutional protections to slavery, an institution understood by Madison (among others) to be itself an unjust violation of human rights. Madison's words on this point at the Convention were unambiguous and forceful: "We have seen the mere distinction of colour made in the most enlightened period of time, a ground of the most

---

[27] See U.S. Constitution, Art. I, sec. 8, cl. 3 (commerce clause); Art. I, sec. 10 (prohibitions on state power). For pertinent historical background, see Gordon S. Wood, *The Creation of the American Republic, 1776–1787* (New York: W. W. Norton, 1969).

[28] See *The Federalist No. 10*, pp. 56, 57, 65.

oppressive dominion ever exercised by man over man."[29] The constitutional protection of slavery (widely understood to violate human rights), combined with the other expressed worries about economic factions, leads to the not unreasonable inference that the dominant normative strand of the Constitution was the right to property as such, not human rights more broadly understood; indeed, the right to property was thought of as specifically antiredistributive.[30] This interpretive argument, if valid, would give us a reason to ascribe to the Constitution specifically antiredistributive economic principles of the sort endorsed by the majority in *Lochner*, only now not as a matter of Spencer's Social Darwinism but in terms of longstanding principles protecting the security of property.

The argument is, however, not valid. It ascribes to the historical records an interpretation they cannot bear and should not be made to bear. Madison's objections to an agrarian and an equal division of property were directed against what he took to be unjust and ill-considered aims of state factions, and specifically rejected only state-imposed absolute limits on amounts of property. The argument did not by its terms condemn reasonable aims of redistributive justice pursued through taxation at either the state or federal levels, aims that Madison elsewhere clearly endorsed.[31]

State-imposed property limits were unreasonable, even as redistributive policies, because they arbitrarily limited the kinds of incentives to work and productivity that would so enlarge the social product that everyone would be better off than under such misplaced egalitarian limits; or at least so Madison might, consistent with the background Lockean political theory he assumed,[32] reasonably have thought.[33] If Madison's thinking may thus plausibly be interpreted as motivated by reasonable redistributive concerns, it cannot be taken to forbid such redistributive concerns from exerting their proper role on public policy.

The argument from slavery is even weaker. Slavery was a topic leading Founders such as Madison could barely bring themselves to even mention,

[29] Farrand, *Records of the Federal Convention*, 1:422–23, 135.

[30] For a forceful recent argument to this effect, see Nedelsky, *Private Property*.

[31] Madison wrote in 1792 that "the great objection should be to combat the evil [of faction] by withholding *unnecessary* opportunities from a few, to increase the inequality of property, by an immoderate, and especially an unmerited, accumulation of riches. . . . By the silent operation of laws, which, without violating the rights of property, reduce extreme wealth towards a state of mediocrity, and raise extreme indigence towards a state of comfort." James Madison, "Parties," in Madison, *The Papers of James Madison, 1791–1793*, 14:197. See also Madison's 1821 note added to his record of his convention speech on rights of suffrage, in Farrand, *Records of Federal Convention*, 3:450–55.

[32] For a recent excellent discussion, see Stephen Buckle, *Natural Law and the Theory of Property: Grotius to Hume* (Oxford: Clarendon Press, 1991), pp. 125–90.

[33] For development of this argument, see Richards, *Foundations*, pp. 59–63.

acknowledging its constitutional protection by euphemism[34] and sorrowing indirection.[35] Its constitutional protection bespeaks not a general principle of the immunity of property as such from reasonable state regulation, but an immunity of one kind of property from federal interference. Such constitutional immunity is consistent with the view that this form of property, in fact, violated human rights, was undesirable, and should be abolished in due course in all states where it existed. Madison, following Jefferson's lead, clearly believed this;[36] and I earlier showed that the constitutional protection of slavery was consistent with such a view on the assumption that policies of emancipation would be most reasonably carried out with least injustice on balance at the state level (see Chapter 2). Even if Madison had not believed this, it would not be interpretively correct to infer from the constitutional protection of one kind of property (slavery) a well-understood general principle that property as such could and should not reasonably be regulated by the state in light of redistributive aims.

Consistent with Lockean political theory, Madison had argued in *The Federalist No. 10* that the underlying consideration in the protection of property was "the diversity in the faculties of men," and that "the protection of these faculties is the first object of Government."[37] Locke had thought of such faculties in terms of their exercise in creative workmanship, which would, justly protected and regulated by a politically legitimate government, encourage and stimulate greater productivity for the good of all. Such a theory, as Madison correctly interpreted it, would justify the regulation of property rights to secure justice and the public good, including redistributive measures to ensure that the gains from productivity were justly distributed. The protection of productive faculties is on a more fundamental level of political justification than the protection of property; as such, property arrangements are subject to reasonable regulations in service of more fundamental purposes.[38]

But if it would be wrong interpretively to ascribe to the Constitution of

---

[34] At the Constitutional Convention, Madison argued that the word *slaves* should not be used in the constitutional text: "Mr. Madison thought it wrong to admit in the Constitution the idea that there could be property in men." Farrand, *Records of the Federal Convention*, 2:417.

[35] Madison uses the word *slaves* in *The Federalist No. 42* (p. 281); but his descriptions are sometimes remarkably indirect: "an unhappy species of population abounding in some of the States" (p. 294).

[36] See Ralph Ketcham, *James Madison: A Biography* (Charlottesville: University Press of Virginia, 1971), pp. 148–49.

[37] *The Federalist No. 10*, p. 58.

[38] For a good discussion of Locke's argument along these lines, see Buckle, *Natural Law and the Theory of Property*, pp. 125–90. Locke somewhat confuses matters, as Buckle points out, by using the term *property* to cover all rights of the person. See, Locke, *Second Treatise*, pp. 341–42 (sec. 87).

1787 a constitutionally enforceable prohibition on redistributive policies, nothing in my argument shows that the Constitution of 1787 mandates such distribution either. The interpretive argument, at least to this point, shows only that the Constitution is consistent with such aims, not that it requires them. We have not, in short, advanced much beyond the dissents of *Lochner.*

If there is any plausible interpretive argument to be made that the Constitution enforces one theory of redistributive justice in part or in whole, it must rest on the Reconstruction Amendments and the revolutionary constitutionalism on which they rest. Two interpretive questions must, in this connection, be distinguished: substantive constitutional principles sponsored by the amendments and judicial enforcement of such principles. The political question doctrine is the usual example adduced in support of the distinction; substantive constitutional principles of republican government underlie the guarantee clause of Article IV,[39] but the clause is not judicially enforceable.[40] The interpretation of the substantive principles of the guarantee clause is the business not of the judiciary, but of the Congress and the president in those cases when they have taken action to enforce the clause.[41]

My colleague Lawrence Sager has persuasively argued that the idea of judicial unenforcement should be applied not only to an entire clause of the Constitution (such as the guarantee clause), but to parts of the interpretive jurisprudence arising under certain clauses (such as the equal protection clause of the fourteenth amendment). Some substantive principles underlying the equal protection clause are judicially enforceable, but others are not; he calls this latter phenomenon judicial underenforcement.[42] Of course, an interpretive theory is required to explain both substantive constitutional principles and their institutional enforceability by one institution or another. At this point, I want only to suggest that there is a distinction it may be worth drawing between principles and enforceability; if there is a distinction in fact worth drawing, an interpretive theory must eventually explain why. I begin with the discussion of substantive principles and then turn to enforceability.

I have argued that the Reconstruction Amendments express and should be interpreted in light of their background theory of revolutionary consti-

[39] See U.S. Constitution, Art. IV, sec. 4. For commentary on this clause, see Wiecek, *The Guarantee Clause.*

[40] See, e.g., *Luther v. Borden*, 48 U.S. (7 How.) 1 (1849).

[41] See Wiecek, *The Guarantee Clause.*

[42] See Lawrence G. Sager, "Fair Measure: The Legal Status of Underenforced Constitutional Norms," *Harvard Law Review* 91, no. 6 (April 1978):1212; and "Foreword: State Courts and the Strategic Space between Norms and Rules of Constitutional Law," *Texas Law Review* 63, no. 6 (March–April 1985):959.

tutionalism. The legitimacy of political power must be critically tested and testable in terms of the reasonable demands set by contractualist political theory for respect for inalienable human rights and pursuit of the public interest. It was in light of this vision that the abolitionists articulated their criticism of the political evils of slavery and racism and developed the radical antislavery constitutional theory that urged an antislavery interpretation of the Constitution as the only way to preserve its legitimacy, that is, so that it was not the just object of the right to revolution. The Reconstruction Amendments embody this vision in constitutional tests for political power that must be interpreted accordingly.

If the antebellum Constitution protected slavery (and, in the view of some, was property based and antiredistributive), the Reconstruction Amendments abolished slavery and required that political power must be justifiable to *all* subject to such power in light of their constitutionally inviolable status as bearers of equal human rights, not as property owners. If proslavery thought nostalgically took as its standard of comparison a historicist model of the slave republics of the ancient world, the antislavery vision of the post–Civil War amendments called for a progressive, emancipatory constitutional order of the sort Lincoln envisioned: "Let us hope . . . that by the best cultivation of the physical world, beneath and around us; and the intellectual and moral world within us, we shall secure an individual, social, and political prosperity and happiness, whose course shall be onward and upward, and which, while the earth endures, shall not pass away."[43]

Constitutional justification in this spirit must take as its normative benchmark an abstract ethical impartiality of respect for the rational and reasonable moral powers of each and every person and the justifiability to them, at least in principle, of forms of political power that each person, thus understood, would not reasonably reject.[44] That demand of principle cannot be explained reductively in terms of advancing each person's interests or their talents within a political framework not itself subject to such standards of impartial ethical assessment. Rather, the standard must be set in terms of a more abstract requirement of reasonable justification to all, defining the parameters for the distribution of basic resources within which the pursuit of people's interests or talents is politically legitimate.[45] It was assess-

[43] Abraham Lincoln, "Address to the Wisconsin State Agricultural Society, Milwaukee, Wisconsin," 30 September 1859, in Fehrenbacher, *Abraham Lincoln: Speeches and Writings, 1858–1865*, 101.

[44] See T. M. Scanlon, "Contractualism and Utilitarianism," in Amartya Sen and Bernard Williams, eds., *Utilitarianism and Beyond* (Cambridge: Cambridge University Press, 1982), pp. 103–28.

[45] For a form of contractualist argument that fails to do justice to this requirement, see David Gauthier, *Morals by Agreement* (New York: Oxford University Press, 1986); cf. Robert

ment in such terms that had made possible the condemnation of slavery and the slave power as unreasonable political structures of hierarchy and privilege that ostensibly advanced the interests of all (as proslavery theorists argued), but at the illegitimate cost of violating basic rights.[46]

Such condemnation would extend to other forms of economic injustice that also cannot be reasonably justified to all from the same abstract impartial perspective. The substantive principles of the Reconstruction Amendments should be interpreted accordingly to reflect such critical standards. Four interpretive possibilities along these lines are plausible.

First, the basic human rights, enforceable against the states under the privileges and immunities clause, must be interpreted to guarantee to each person not only equal respect for these rights, but also whatever ancillary protections are indispensable to maintaining for all the fair value of such rights as guarantees of their inviolable moral status as free persons in a community of equals.[47] Malnutrition, lack of shelter, inadequate medical care for disease, illiteracy, and the like debilitate and demean people subject to such deprivations and, for this reason, deprive them of the fair value of such rights as expressions of equal moral status. Accordingly, minimal guarantees of minimal subsistence, shelter, health care, education, and the like are reasonable contractualist requirements of constitutional principles of equal rights.[48]

Second, both enumerated and unenumerated basic rights are protected against the states as privileges and immunities. One such right is the equal right of free labor, the right to develop and exercise one's creative and productive faculties competently as the basis of self-respect (see Chapter 6). I have already suggested that this right may be unconstitutionally abridged by state-sponsored forms of economic monopoly lacking compelling public justification (arguably like that in the *Slaughter-House*

Nozick, *Anarchy, State and Utopia* (New York: Basic Books, 1974). For commentary on this inadequacy, see Samuel Freeman, "Contractualism, Moral Motivation, and Practical Reason," *Journal of Philosophy* 87, no. 6 (June 1991): 281.

[46] For standard rights-skeptical, utilitarian, proslavery justifications of southern slavery, see Albert Taylor Bledsoe, *Liberty and Slavery: or, Slavery in the Light of Moral and Political Philosophy*, in Elliott, *Cotton Is King*, pp. 286–87; Harper, "Memoir on Slavery," in Faust, *Ideology of Slavery*, pp. 88–90.

[47] See Norman Daniels, "Equal Liberty and Unequal Worth of Liberty," in Norman Daniels, ed., *Reading Rawls: Critical Studies of* A Theory of Justice (New York: Basic Books, 1974), pp. 253–81. A similar kind of analysis, in the context of an argument for education as a fundamental right, was suggested by Justice Marshall in his dissent in *San Antonio School District v. Rodriguez*, 411 U.S. 1, 118–20 (1973) (Marshall, J., dissenting). I have endorsed and elaborated this analysis in Richards, *The Moral Criticism of Law*, pp. 138–61.

[48] For a plausible argument that such a minimal floor principle is implicit in Rawls's theory of justice, see R. G. Peffer, *Marxism, Morality, and Social Justice* (Princeton: Princeton University Press, 1990), pp. 384–85, 404, 418, 420–21.

Cases); and the right is not unconstitutionally abridged by state regulations, like those in *Lochner,* themselves based on considerations of equality that better realize the underlying requirements of an equal right to free labor. The essence of *Lochner's* mistake, on Harlan's reading of it, is the cavalier way in which the majority delegitimates state purposes, in particular, equal bargaining power. Such a purpose is, in my judgment, not only legislatively permissible, but constitutionally compelled by the best interpretation of the guarantee of equal rights to labor, grounded in the interlocking requirements of the guarantees of privileges and immunities and equal protection. If so, constitutional principles regulate both state action and inaction bearing on this equal right (see Chapter 5). The failure to engage in economic policies that secure the broadest availability of diverse fair opportunities to work, including reasonable concern for full employment as an important state purpose, violates this constitutional right.

Third, suspect classification analysis under the equal protection clause of the fourteenth amendment delegitimates state purposes based on irrational prejudice reflecting a history and culture of abridgment of basic rights (see Chapter 5). Slavery and racism have been the interpretive exemplars of such prejudice in American constitutional experience, but historical analysis may show that contempt for the poor is a related feature of American historical and cultural experience. The historian Edmund Morgan thus has suggested such analysis as a legacy of slavery in his probing examination of Virginian republican ardor for equal rights, namely, such

> ardor was not unrelated to their power over the men and women held in bondage. In the republican way of thinking as Americans inherited it from England, slavery occupied a critical, if ambiguous, position: it was the primary evil that men sought to avoid for society as a whole by curbing monarchs and establishing republics. But it was also the solution to one of society's most serious problems, the problem of the poor. Virginians could outdo English republicans as well as New England ones, partly because they had solved the problem: they had achieved a society in which most of the poor were enslaved.[49]

Virginians could take this view of slaves because it complemented the larger classical republican idea that poverty was a mark of natural slavery.[50]

That idea may not only have outlived the abolition of slavery, but it may explain the constitutionally culpable failure of Radical Reconstruction responsibly to address the economic and social plight of the freedmen (ignoring the proposals to such effect of Sumner and Stevens; see Chapter 5). Lack of American concern for poverty as a suspect classification may, from

---

[49] See Morgan, *American Slavery, American Freedom,* p. 381.

[50] See ibid., pp. 322, 324–25, 381–87. Cf. Ian Shapiro, *The Evolution of Rights in Liberal Theory* (Cambridge: Cambridge University Press, 1986).

this perspective, reflect not a sound analysis of antislavery constitutional principles, but the influence of the inconsistent tradition of proslavery republicanism.[51] That tradition may unconstitutionally have been permitted political expression, legitimating the longstanding myopia in American republican theory and practice that sustains an irrational popular prejudice against the victims of poverty as natural slaves unworthy of full republican citizenship.[52]

If Morgan's suggestion can reasonably be interpreted in this way, a sound elaboration of antislavery constitutional principles should condemn both the history of such unjust subjugation and the cultural construction today of the poor as unworthy of public concern (reflected in public apathy toward homelessness). Indeed, to the extent the Constitution has itself been mistakenly interpreted to legitimate such unjust public attitudes, suspect classification analysis should aim to deconstruct the cultural legitimacy of such attitudes, condemning their expression through law. If so, poverty should be regarded as a suspect classification; laws that, by action or omission, reflect such prejudice should be struck down unless shown to rest on compelling public purposes.

Fourth, the equal protection clause rests on the abstract requirements of contractualist political theory (see Chapters 4 and 5) explicitly imposed by the fourteenth amendment on the states, the main loci of the decadence of constitutional values during the antebellum period. But the substantive principles of a political theory must occupy the full normative space required by its basic values. The best understanding of contractualist theory requires not only that basic equal rights be protected, but also that political power, to be legitimate, justifies the distribution of basic economic resources to all on terms of reasonable unanimity.[53]

The difference principle, as the basic principle of redistributive justice, affords a reasonable basis for such justification of inequality to all from the normative benchmark of their equal status as moral persons. From this position, inequalities in wealth will only be justifiable to all if both the advantaged and disadvantaged understand them to be a reasonable way to afford, in light of the lottery of natural talents, incentives to better performance. Such incentives are reasonably justifiable to all if they confer relative advantage as the necessary price to be paid for a distribution of goods overall that makes the disadvantaged better off than they would be under equality.[54] If so, the difference principle, required as it is by contractualist

---

[51] See *James v. Valtierra*, 402 U.S. 137 (1971).

[52] For a recent argument along these lines focusing on the black underclass, see Hacker, *Two Nations*.

[53] For a recent development of this basically Rawlsian analysis, to which I am indebted, see Thomas Nagel, *Equality and Partiality* (New York: Oxford University Press, 1991).

[54] For arguments to similar effect, see Rawls, *A Theory of Justice*, chaps. 2, 5; Richards, *A Theory of Reasons for Action*, chap. 8.

political theory, is the constitutional principle required by the fourteenth amendment.

I earlier made a distinction between substantive constitutional principles and their enforceability, and now must consider why and how this distinction should be drawn in the case of the four constitutional principles dealing with economic injustice that have now been articulated. Rawls offered such a theory when he argued that the reasonable enforcement of the difference principle, depending on controversial social and economic theories, was best performed through the deliberative procedures of the legislative process. Comparable arguments could be made in the case of the three other principles I have discussed, namely, their enforcement often turns on reasonable judgments best made through the legislative process or primarily through that process. If so, contractualist political theory will have explained the judicial underenforcement of economic rights.

Like others, I am, however, skeptical about the justifiability of this sharp distinction between the judicial nonenforcement of economic and enforcement of noneconomic rights.[55] Some of my skepticism is explained by my earlier remarks about the *Slaughter-House Cases,* in which the judiciary was well able to articulate and decide the issues, and the dissents may have had the better of the interpretive argument. There are, of course, many differences between the appropriate constitutional analysis of personal rights such as constitutional privacy and economic rights such as the right to work both in terms of the rights protected and the kinds of justification for their abridgment; but these differences are arrayed in a continuum, not in a normative difference in kind. Even if legitimate legislative regulatory judgments as to both ends and means are much broader in the economic area, that suggests not a wholesale immunity from judicial scrutiny, but only a correspondingly deferential standard of review well short of the current judicial abdication of any review at all.

If so, the judiciary could perform a constitutionally valid and valuable role by holding the legislative process to a less deferential standard of review than is currently the case; it could, for example, require the articulation and pursuit of acceptable public purposes in ways that do not unreasonably abridge basic economic rights, such as the right to work. It has recently done so in an ad hoc fashion in the economic area of the regulation of zoning,[56] and could legitimately do so in a more principled way.[57]

---

[55] See, e.g., Stephen Macedo, *Liberal Virtues: Citizenship, Virtue, and Community in Liberal Constitutionalism* (Oxford: Clarendon Press, 1990), pp. 185–89, 191–92, 197–99.

[56] See, e.g., *Cleburne v. Cleburne Living Center, Inc.,* 473 U.S. 432 (1975) (special-use permit for homes for mentally retarded held unconstitutional).

[57] Justice Brennan persuasively argued for such a more principled approach in his dissent in *U.S. Railroad Retirement Board v. Fritz,* 449 U.S. 166, 182 (1980) (Brennan, J., dissenting). Cf. Sunstein, "Naked Preferences and the Constitution."

There is, however, a more basic reason for concern about the justifiability of the sharpness with which the distinction is currently drawn. From the contractualist perspective, the normative point of making the distinction, in the way Rawls does, is to secure the best institutional division of power in enforcing the underlying vision of equality in all its dimensions, economic and noneconomic. But Thomas Nagel has recently argued that the usual tendency of democratic politics to enforce the difference principle has been undermined in the United States: "As things are, democracy is the enemy of comprehensive equality, once the poor cease to be a majority. The interests of the majority do not usually coincide with the interests of all, impartially weighed together, and they certainly do not coincide with the ideal of equality." On this basis, Nagel argues for the judicial protection of an economic and social minimum (in line with the first principle above discussed), but is skeptical about the constitutionalization of the difference principle because by its nature it is not likely to remain insulated from democratic politics.[58]

If Nagel's general position on the normative limits of contemporary politics is correct, it poses a crisis of democratic legitimacy along the same lines that absorbed the abolitionist movement in the antebellum period. The Constitution, as then interpreted and enforced, was increasingly seen to be illegitimate; constitutional ideals such as human rights and the public interest had been so degraded by pursuit of unjust private interests of lucre and domination (the slave power) that the Constitution itself, grounded on revolutionary constitutionalism, was the reasonable object of the right to revolution. A comparable sense of illegitimacy is very much Nagel's point about current American political apathy toward economic injustice.

In the antebellum period, this sense of illegitimacy led to political action, one form of which was radical antislavery constitutional theory (see Chapter 4). Such theory called for an interpretation of the constitutional *text* that, in light of background ideals of human rights, rendered slavery constitutionally illegitimate. As Joel Tiffany put the point, either interpret the Constitution in light of its political theory of legitimacy or justify the right to revolution against an illegitimate Constitution: "give us *change* or *revolution*."[59] The grounds for a new interpretation of the judicial underenforcement of economic rights are similar, but hardly as interpretively implausible.

Radical antislavery constitutional theory was resisted by the theorists of Union and of moderate antislavery because of its wholesale abandonment of *any* interpretive weight to be accorded either history or interpretive practice (see Chapters 2 and 3). The idea was not that history and interpre-

[58] See Nagel, *Equality and Partiality*, pp. 87–90.
[59] See Tiffany, *Treatise*, p. 99.

tive practice were dispositive; rather, they were interpretively relevant, and could not be simply ignored in the way radical antislavery ignored the great weight of evidence in history and interpretive practice that various clauses of the Constitution protected and were understood to protect the institution of state-endorsed slavery. There were, of course, significant interpretive disagreements between the theorists of Union and of moderate antislavery and proslavery theorists. They centered, however, not on the constitutionality of state-supported slavery, but on the proper interpretation of national power over slavery in the territories and over fugitive slaves in the free states. It was at one or another of these points that Lincoln and others regarded the Constitution as properly interpreted in light of its background political theory of human rights, and on this ground resisted the constitutional claims of the South.

The interpretive argument for abandoning the wholesale judicial underenforcement of economic rights, unlike the comparable interpretive arguments of radical antislavery, gives proper weight to both history and interpretive practice in constitutional interpretation. Indeed, as my argument about the privileges and immunities clause showed in Chapter 6, it does not ignore interpretive practice, but properly criticizes it internally in light of the interpretation of the relevant history and political theory that it often gets so egregiously wrong (for example, in Justice Miller's opinion for the Court in the *Slaughter-House Cases*). We need not even suppose that such interpretive practice has always been wrong in its understanding of judicial underenforcement of economic lights. In the circumstances of the overruling of *Lochner,* for example, much legislation both at the state and federal levels may have been in the proper redistributive direction. Consistent with Rawls's argument of contractualist political theory, such issues would therefore properly be in the jurisdiction of the legislatures. To the extent circumstances have changed today, a different interpretive judgment would be required in our circumstances.

We need not interpretively strain history and practice in the way radical antislavery did to reexamine judicial underenforcement of economic rights, but we do need to take seriously the revolutionary constitutionalism that is the enduring legacy of radical antislavery to the meaning of the Reconstruction Amendments. The Reconstruction Amendments constitutionalize such revolutionary constitutionalism, holding state political power accountable to its tests for politically legitimate power. Interpretive practice must, like other forms of political power, be tested against these demands when such practice leads to increasingly illegitimate forms of political power. Judicial underenforcement of such rights can no longer survive such analysis, and should be interpretively revised accordingly.

A good place to start would be at the point where the political illegitimacy is clearest, most susceptible to a judicially articulate standard of review, and most needed in light of a constitutionally decadent public opinion and sense of apathy, namely, the articulation and enforcement of standards of minimal welfare called for by the first constitutional principle (the fair value of equal rights) discussed above.[60] The important point in such a judicial development would be that principles in question should address uncontroversially minimal needs such as subsistence, shelter, health care, and education. Such principles could be reasonably articulated as standards of law and enforced at large as the minimal requirements of decent life in our society, a standard beneath which the public conscience would see or could reasonably come to see inhuman treatment inconsistent with a community committed to equal respect for moral persons.

The nonsequitur of *Lochner*'s mistake would, of course, debar such an interpretive development. But as I have argued, such an interpretation of *Lochner*'s mistake *is* a nonsequitur. To answer such sloganeering, I have sketched a constructive interpretation of the Reconstruction Amendments that, in light of their history and political theory, renders the judicial nonenforcement of economic rights into what it should be understood to be, the judicial underenforcement of substantive economic constitutional rights. The grounds for judicial underenforcement, while arguably once valid, no longer are; therefore such underenforcement should be reconsidered. Constitutional guarantees of minimal welfare rights would be a good place to start.

[60] See Michelman, "Foreword: On Protecting the Poor"; "In Pursuit of Constitutional Welfare Rights."

EIGHT

CONSCIENCE AND

CONSTITUTIONAL INTERPRETATION

THE INTERPRETIVE PROJECT of this book is now complete and should be assessed in terms of the tests for adequacy that I set out in Chapter 1. These tests were, first, whether the theory clarified the general normative purposes of the Reconstruction Amendments; and second, whether it advanced public understanding of the central interpretive questions that arise in connection with these amendments.

It is against the antebellum background of prolonged controversies over issues of political theory, constitutional interpretation, and their relationship that the basic normative purposes of the Reconstruction Amendments should be understood. Proslavery constitutional thought had featured both rights-based political theories (John Taylor of Caroline) and rights-skeptical theories (John C. Calhoun), and had interpreted the Constitution in light of them to require local state control over most issues (see Chapter 2). The basic normative purposes of the Reconstruction Amendments, drawing on the insights of abolitionist political and constitutional theory (see Chapter 3), responded to these claims. First, rights-based contractualist political theory was directly invoked by the amendment, requiring that all Americans reasonably subject to political power were citizens and subjecting state power (the loci of antebellum constitutional decadence) directly to the essential demands of contractualist political legitimacy: respect for basic human rights and equal protection. Second, national institutions were given the constitutional power and responsibility to articulate and enforce the principles required by this political theory. These normative purposes reflect a shrewd Madisonian diagnosis of the sources of antebellum constitutional decadence.

This account affords, in contrast to other views, a perspicuous and compelling understanding not only of the normative aims of the Reconstruction Amendments, but of the proper role political theory plays in their historical interpretation and their interpretation more generally (see Chapter 4). The interpretation of history plays a role in understanding these amendments because they bring political theory to bear on the interpretation and diagnosis of the antebellum constitutional decadence to which they were so clearly a response. In short, the amendments used political theory to understand a certain tragic history and to forge constitutional principles that would, in light of that history, yield a more adequate (because polit-ically legitimate) constitutionalism. Contemporary political theory plays such a central role in the interpretation of the Reconstruction Amendments because it gives the best account of their text, history, and interpretive practice over time, including interpretive mistakes. Such political theory enables us to interpret the historically continuous principles of these amendments in the way that most reasonably articulates how their endur-ing abstract values of inviolable human rights are best understood and implemented as conditions of politically legitimate government in our cir-cumstances. The mission of the Reconstruction Amendments, to render political power legitimate, is thus met.

I have tried to show how this approach illuminates the interpretation of equal protection (see Chapter 5) and the nationalization of human rights (see Chapter 6). For example, the interpretation of antebellum argument (in particular, abolitionist use of the argument for toleration to criticize slavery and racism) suggests surprising but clarifying analogies between religious and racial intolerance (American racism and European anti-Semitism) and casts a flood of light on suspect classification analysis in terms of which controversies about its interpretation both in the past and today are better understood. The nature of race as a suspect classification is given a more secure basis than Ely or Ackerman afford it (see Chapter 1); and some of the proposed extensions of the analysis by Ackerman (to women, homosexuals, and the poor), not well explained by his account, are better illuminated in terms of the account proposed here (see Chapters 5 and 7). And the interpretation of the terms of antebellum abolitionist moral, political, and constitutional criticism explains the nature, weight, and scope of the human rights protected against state power by the privileges and immunities clause of the fourteenth amendment (see Chapter 6).

The interpretive fertility of an account of this sort is shown not only by clarification of the interpretive strands of our current jurisprudence of equal protection or basic rights, but by the critical standards it offers in terms of which current interpretive practices may be assessed and sometimes found wanting. I have offered various criticisms along these lines—for example, judicial failure to acknowledge the suspectness of classifications in terms of sexual preference (see Chapter 5), its use of due process rather than privileges and immunities as the ground for the enforcement of human rights (see Chapter 6), the judiciary's wavering enforcement of the consti-tutional right to privacy (see Chapter 6), and its failure to enforce any eco-nomic rights (see Chapter 7).

These criticisms raise a final and important point about the kind of ac-count I have offered, a point rooted in its origins in a vision of independent conscience and ethical impartiality and in the strenuous interpretive de-mands this vision imposes on public conscience and the public reason of the nation today. The moral, political, and constitutional arguments—central to the theory and principles of the Reconstruction Amendments—did not originate in the judiciary or, for that matter, in the Congress or the president or the state governments, but in a despised group of political outcasts. The abolitionists defended and demanded the right to conscience in an age of stupefying majoritarian complacency. They insisted on holding the public mind of the nation accountable to the reasonable demands of a morally independent assessment of slavery and racism. They held a clear ethical mirror up to the conscience of the nation, and did not quail before the rage and anger and even violence their integrity unleashed on them.

The abolitionists achieved the level of ethical impartiality they did because they more consistently understood and more courageously upheld the intellectual and ethical standards of thought and action that the argument for toleration required of a community ostensibly committed to respect for human rights as its theory of political legitimacy. Both their intellectual standards and their ethical rigor and courage made them the conscience of American constitutionalism and the prophets and architects of our moral and constitutional growth as a people.

The Reconstruction Amendments rest on their demanding ethical vision of a political community of human rights, a vision that, when properly interpreted and enforced, has been and can be the same instrument of ethical struggle and growth for our generation that it had been in the hands of the abolitionists in antebellum America. It is not surprising that American political institutions, including the judiciary, should so often have failed to meet the demands of this vision (see Chapters 5–7), rooted, as it is, not in mainstream political majoritarianism, but in the demands of conscience and public reason for a community of human rights. That vision of American constitutional community consecrates it as a moral community, a community of persons founded not in race or nationality or gender or sexual preference, but in the abstract ethical demands of principles of mutual respect on the basis of public reason.

Such ethical demands, based in a political theory of revolutionary constitutionalism, can never be entirely domesticated to the measure of any political institution since the legitimacy of all political institutions must be independently tested by a free people in terms of those demands. It is true that the background political theory of the Reconstruction Amendments looks to national institutions in general and the federal judiciary in particular as the political institutions most likely to bring public reason to bear on the elaboration of these issues. But it is no part of this theory—indeed it contradicts its demands—that any political institution (including the judiciary) is the exhaustive measure of these ethical demands. National political institutions may afford a more impartial forum for these issues than state institutions, but the argument of this book surely shows that even national institutions may prove interpretively inadequate to the demands of ethical impartiality and must be held accountable to public reason for making such interpretive mistakes. Two other sorts of appeals have at this point proved crucial (one to external sources, the other to internal). Both of them are well explained by the interpretive theory I have here proposed.

If national standards have sometimes proved inadequate, criticism from the vantage of a larger international culture has sometimes stimulated a more impartial ethical standard of constitutional argument here. The American abolitionists undoubtedly profited enormously from the earlier success of the abolitionist movement in Great Britain.[1] And I have made reference at several points to how much American constitutional theory and practice profited from European insights into our culture brought sometimes by immigrants such as Francis Lieber and Franz Boas; sometimes by visiting social critics such as Martineau, de Tocqueville, and Myrdal; and sometimes by Americans such as Theodore Parker who brought to bear on their life and work the ethical and historical insights of European thought. Finally, the pressure of America's international stature as a constitutional democracy undoubtedly stimulated the nation, in the wake of World War II, to rethink its racist distortions of the moral meaning and promise of the Reconstruction Amendments.

Such prods to ethical impartiality are, I believe, consistent with the argument I have offered about the normative purposes of these amendments. Their interpretive demands are those of public reason, demands that know no race or nationality or ethnicity. We have profited, as a constitutional people, from our receptivity to the larger public culture of universal reason, accessible to and articulated by all peoples, to the extent its arguments have better enabled us to articulate and to meet the demands of public reason that are central to our interpretive responsibilities to understand our ethical ideals and aspirations as a people. Indeed, from this perspective, the development of larger international institutions protective of human rights might afford relevant tests of impartiality in terms of which we might better meet our interpretive responsibilities.[2]

Our study of the Reconstruction Amendments shows that the understanding of our own law is best understood in the context of the larger

---

[1] See James Walvin, ed., *Slavery and British Society, 1776–1846* (London: Macmillan, 1982); R.J.M. Blackett, *Building an Antislavery Wall: Black Americans in the Atlantic Abolitionist Movement, 1830–1860* (Ithaca: Cornell University Press, 1983); Douglas Charles Stange, *British Unitarians against American Slavery, 1833–65* (London: Associate University Presses, 1984); Christine Bolt and Seymour Drescher, eds., *Anti-Slavery, Religion and Reform* (London: Wm. Dawson & Sons., 1980).

[2] For the benign impact of European institutions of this sort on Great Britain and the need to render the protection of rights even more secure, see Ronald Dworkin, *A Bill of Rights for Britain* (London: Chatto & Windus, 1990).

ethical and constitutional movement of which it is an important part—the movement that, for the first time in recorded human history, abolished slavery and aspired to extend human rights to all persons. Both the aspirations and the bitter failures of that great movement have been played out in the law and life of many nations; and our study confirms the interpretive wisdom of placing American constitutionalism in that larger context in which American racism and European anti-Semitism appear as the common sadistic worm in the bud of our emancipatory hopes. The study of American constitutional law thus becomes continuous with the study of the humane political and constitutional imagination of humankind, as one great experiment, among others, in bringing public reason to bear on politics.

If one source of ethical impartiality has been thus external, the other has been, as we have seen, the articulate voice of the internal exile. Sometimes, like the abolitionists, the voice of ethical impartiality and constitutional interpretive responsibility has been the demanding voice of morally independent radical dissent, protest, and challenge. Such often despised internal exiles from the then dominant American political mainstream have often, precisely by virtue of their outcast status, looked more critically into the foundations of American constitutionalism, understood our decadence, and more fully and fairly brought public reason to bear on the proper understanding of constitutional principles in contemporary circumstances. Their work has sometimes not been obviously political (some abolitionists, the disunionists, refused even to vote; see Chapter 3). Nonetheless, their efforts were always crucially engaged with holding the American public mind to more rigorous intellectual and ethical standards; they recognized, like Lincoln, that the corruption of public opinion was the key to antebellum constitutional decadence. The mission of the internal exile of conscience has been, consistent with the political theory of our revolutionary constitutionalism, to maintain the highest standards of intellectual and ethical discourse about public values independent of dominant political epistemologies that often corrupted them.

American universities were usually as hostile to the abolitionists as were all other dominant political and social institutions of the age.[3] But surely a political community, now capable of mature ethical reflection on the meaning of the Reconstruction Amendments, should today sustain institutions of academic freedom that could foster and sustain the kind and quality of intellectual and ethical standards that the interpretation of these amendments requires. The interdisciplinary study of American constitutional law—uniting, as it should, political philosophy, history, and law—must be

---

[3] For example, Charles Follen, a German immigrant and professor at Harvard, lost his professorship because of his outspoken antislavery views. For the quality of Follen's thought, see Charles Follen, "Speech before the Anti-Slavery Society," in Pease and Pease, *The Antislavery Argument*, pp. 224–56.

at the center of such responsibilities. It may be a symptom of decadence that it is not; the study of constitutional law remains isolated in law school discourse hermetically sealed off from the larger discourse of their universities.[4]

A constitutional theory that makes the challenge of international public culture and of radical dissent central to its analysis of the interpretive demands of American constitutionalism better explains our self-correcting interpretive experience. It makes sense of the fact that, during the long periods when American political institutions (state and federal) miserably failed their interpretive responsibilities under the Reconstruction Amendments, radical ethical dissent by black Americans, supported by European immigrant intellectuals of the stature and standards of a Boas, played a preservative and ultimately transformative role as the measure of interpretive responsibility.

The role that American blacks—an unconstitutionally subjugated group —have played as constitutional leaders to a nation suggests the importance of this point to any reasonable understanding of the interpretive responsibilities imposed by the Reconstruction Amendments. The ethical and constitutional visions of Frederick Douglass[5] and Martin Luther King,[6] articulated in the face of rejection by and exile from the constitutional community, gave fuller voice to the moral vision of the Reconstruction Amendments, and thus were its best interpreters. Our revolutionary constitutionalism, when interpreted by those whose visions are adequate to it, gives the voice of prophecy to the outcast, and renders law the transformative agency of the moral growth of a people into a public conscience worthy of their constitutionalism.

For this reason, the critical dimension of a constitutional theory may be more important than its interpretive dimension (that is, the dimension aimed at making sense of current interpretive practice). It helps set and maintain the standards of interpretive responsibility of citizens of a moral community of human rights. It reminds a free people of the dangers of majoritarian complacency in light of the consequences of recurrent failures of interpretive responsibility—the constitutional decadence advanced through the rights skepticism of Calhoun, the majoritarianism of Stephen

---

[4] For further discussion of this point, see Richards, *Foundations*, pp. 287–99.

[5] See Foner, *Life and Writings*. For commentary, see David W. Blight, *Frederick Douglass' Civil War: Keeping Faith in Jubilee* (Baton Rouge: Louisiana State University Press, 1989); William S. McFeely, *Frederick Douglass* (New York: W. W. Norton, 1991); Eric J. Sundquist, *Frederick Douglass: New Literary and Historical Essays* (Cambridge: Cambridge University Press, 1990).

[6] See James Melvin Washington, ed., *A Testament of Hope: The Essential Writings of Martin Luther King, Jr.* (San Francisco: Harper & Row, 1986); for commentary, see Branch, *Parting the Waters*; Derek Q. Reeves, "Beyond the River Jordan: An Essay on the Continuity of the Black Prophetic Tradition," *Journal of Religious Thought* 47 (1990–91): 42.

Douglas, the mangled originalism of Justice Taney in *Dred Scott*. It renders the public mind properly critical today of politicians who find it to be in their transient political interest to advance as competent judicial interpreters of the Constitution contemporary advocates of such positions.[7]

The lesson of the study of the Reconstruction Amendments is that its ideals of revolutionary constitutionalism, like those of the Constitution of 1787, may also be perverted by an inadequate constitutionalism or interpretive attitude into self-deceiving political evil worked through and in the name of a decadent and betrayed constitutionalism. Our task surely is to be intellectually and morally worthy of the American tradition of independent conscience and dissent. We must aspire to embody in our thought and practice the standards of moral, political, and constitutional independence and courage that will generate in our own terms and circumstances arguments of human rights adequate to identify and to challenge our corruptions, our decadent constitutionalism—whether the originalism of Bork or the majoritarianism of Ely.

If necessary, a free people must stand ready to reclaim the people's Constitution, as Lincoln did, from its political and judicial corruptions. Constitutional law, properly understood, empowers people to be self-governing, responsible moral agents, not the victims of the manifold modes of their historic subjugation. To be thus worthy of their freedoms, they must critically understand and demand in their own terms and circumstances the enduring ethical meaning of a constitutionalism forged by its Founders to protect universal human rights in light of public reason.

That is a vision of the founders of 1787 that Lincoln in his youth memorialized, in the epigraph to this book, as "the political religion of the nation." It is the vision that, in his maturity, he died for, and for which he is now justly consecrated a founder of our constitutional rebirth. It is the flaming vision of our youth that, tempered by understanding of the history and experience of our maturity, must guide our interpretive responsibilities as free people under the rule of constitutional law.

[7] The most striking recent example of this phenomenon was the abortive nomination of Robert Bork to the Supreme Court. For Bork's views, see Bork, *The Tempting of America*; for criticism, see Richards, "Originalism without Foundations;" see also Richards, *Foundations*, pp. 202–47, 288–99.

APPENDIX I

CONSTITUTION, STATUTES, AND LEGISLATIVE HISTORY

CONSTITUTION AND STATUTES

U.S. Constitution (1787).
The Fugitive Slave Act of 1793, chap. 7, 1 Stat. 302 (1793) (repealed 1850).
The Fugitive Slave Act of 1850, chap. 60, 9 Stat. 462 (1850) (repealed 1864).
The Civil Rights Act of 1866, chap. 31, 14 Stat. 27 (1866).

LEGISLATIVE HISTORY

Thirteenth Amendment

Representative Ashley, *Congressional Globe*, 38th Cong., 2d sess., 6 January 1865, p. 138.

Representative Smith, *Congressional Globe*, 38th Cong., 2d sess., 12 January 1865, p. 237.

Representative Farnsworth, *Congressional Globe*, 38th Cong., 2d sess., 10 January 1865, p. 200.

Representative Davis, *Congressional Globe*, 38th Cong., 2d sess., 7 January 1865, p. 154.

Representative James Wilson, *Congressional Globe*, 38th Cong., 1st sess., 19 March 1864, pp. 1199–1206.

Fourteenth Amendment

First draft, *Congressional Globe*, 39th Cong., 1st sess., 26 February 1866, p. 1034.

Second draft, *Congressional Globe*, 39th Cong., 1st sess., 8 May 1866, p. 2461.

Representative Bingham, *Congressional Globe*, 39th Cong., 1st sess., 22 February 1866, p. 1090.

Representative Bingham, *Congressional Globe*, 39th Cong., 1st sess. 26 February 1866, p. 1034.

Representative Bingham, *Congressional Globe*, 39th Cong., 1st sess., 28 February 1866, p. 1088.

Representative Bingham, *Congressional Globe*, 39th Cong., 1st sess., 9 March 1866, pp. 1291–92.

Representative Bingham, *Congressional Globe*, 39th Cong., 1st sess., 10 May 1866, p. 2542.

Senator Henderson, *Congressional Globe*, 39th Cong., 1st sess., 8 June 1866, p. 2034.

Representative Hotchkiss, *Congressional Globe*, 39th Cong., 1st sess., 28 February 1866, p. 1095.

Senator Howard, *Congressional Globe*, 39th Cong., 1st sess., 23 May 1866, pp. 2765–69.

Senator Lyman Trumbull, *Congressional Globe*, 39th Cong., 1st sess., 29 January
  1866, pp. 474–75.
Representative Wilson, *Congressional Globe*, 39th Cong., 1st sess., 9 March 1866,
  pp. 1294–95.

APPENDIX II

CASE LAW

Abrams v. United States, 250 U.S. 616 (1919).

Adamson v. California, 332 U.S. 46 (1947).

Arlington Heights v. Metropolitan Housing Corp., 429 U.S. 252 (1977).

Baker v. Carr, 369 U.S. 186 (1962).

Barron v. Mayor and City Council of Baltimore, 32 U.S. (7 Pet.) 243 (1833).

Bolling v. Sharpe, 347 U.S. 497 (1954).

Bowers v. Hardwick, 478 U.S. 186 (1986).

Bradwell v. Illinois, 83 U.S. (16 Wall.) 130 (1872).

Brandenburg v. Ohio, 395 U.S. 444 (1969).

Brown v. Board of Education, 347 U.S. 483 (1954).

Burton v. Wilmington Parking Authority, 365 U.S. 715 (1961).

City of Richmond v. J. A. Croson Co., 488 U.S. 469 (1989).

Civil Rights Cases, 109 U.S. 3 (1883).

Cleburne v. Cleburne Living Center, Inc., 473 U.S. 432 (1975).

Corfield v. Coryell, 6 Fed. Cas. 546 (No. 3230) (C.C.E.D.Pa. 1823).

Cox v. Louisiana, 379 U.S. 536 (1965).

Craig v. Boren, 429 U.S. 190 (1976).

Cruzan v. Director, Missouri Department of Health, 496 U.S. 261 (1990).

Dred Scott v. Sanford, 60 U.S. (19 How.) 393 (1857).

Dronenberg v. Zech, 741 F.2d 1388 (D.C.Cir. 1984).

Duncan v. Louisiana, 391 U.S. 145 (1968).

Eisenstadt v. Baird, 405 U.S. 438 (1972).

Erznoznik v. Jacksonville, 422 U.S. 205 (1975).

Evans v. Newton, 382 U.S. 296 (1966).

Frontiero v. Richardson, 411 U.S. 677 (1973).

Gitlow v. New York, 268 U.S. 652 (1925).

Graham v. Richardson, 403 U.S. 365 (1971).

Griggs v. Duke Power Co., 401 U.S. 424 (1971).

Griswold v. Connecticut, 381 U.S. 479 (1965).

Harper v. Virginia Board of Elections, 383 U.S. 663 (1966).

Hernandez v. Texas, 346 U.S. 475 (1954).

Herndon v. Lowry, 301 U.S. 242 (1937).

James v. Valtierra, 402 U.S. 137 (1971).

Johnson v. Transportation Agency, Santa Clara County, 480 U.S. 107 (1987).

Kahn v. Shevin, 416 U.S. 351 (1974).

Lochner v. New York, 198 U.S. 45 (1905).

Luther v. Borden, 48 U.S. (7 How.) 1 (1849).

McCulloch v. Maryland, 17 U.S. (4 Wheat.) 316 (1819).

Marsh v. Alabama, 326 U.S. 501 (1946).

Michael M. v. Superior Court, 450 U.S. 464 (1981).

Mississippi University for Women v. Hogan, 458 U.S. 718 (1982).

Moore v. East Cleveland, 431 U.S. 494 (1977).

Murray's Lessee v. Hoboken Land & Improvement Co., 59 U.S. (18 How.) 272 (1856).

Nebbia v. New York, 291 U.S. 502 (1934).

Orr v. Orr, 440 U.S. 268 (1979).

Padula v. Webster, 822 F.2d 97 (D.C. Cir. 1987).

Palko v. Connecticut, 302 U.S. 319 (1937).

Personnel Administrator of Massachusetts v. Feeney, 442 U.S. 256 (1979).

Plessy v. Ferguson, 163 U.S. 537 (1896).

Prigg v. Pennsylvania, 41 U.S. (16 Pet.) 539 (1842).

Regents of University of California v. Bakke, 438 U.S. 265 (1978).

Reitman v. Mulkey, 387 U.S. 369 (1967).

Reynolds v. Sims, 377 U.S. 533 (1964).

Richmond. *See* City of Richmond

Roe v. Wade, 410 U.S. 113 (1973).

Rostker v. Goldberg, 453 U.S. 57 (1981).

Roth v. United States, 354 U.S. 476 (1957).

San Antonio School District v. Rodriguez, 411 U.S. 1 (1973).

Shelley v. Kraemer, 334 U.S. 1 (1948).

Shuttlesworth v. Birmingham, 394 U.S. 147 (1969).

Slaughter-House Cases, 83 (16 Wall.) 36 (1873).

Sommersett v. Stuart, 99 Eng. Rep. 499 (K.B. 1772).

Strauder v. West Virginia, 100 U.S. 303 (1880).

Texas v. Johnson, 491 U.S. 397 (1989).

Trimble v. Gordon, 430 U.S. 762 (1977).

U.S. Railroad Retirement Board v. Fritz, 449 U.S. 166 (1980).

Walker v. Birmingham, 388 U.S. 307 (1967).

Wards Cove Packing Co., Inc. v. Atonio, 490 U.S. 642 (1989).

Washington v. Davis, 426 U.S. 229 (1976).

Webster v. Reproductive Health Services, 492 U.S. 490 (1989).

Wengler v. Druggists Mutual Ins. Co., 446 U.S. 142 (1980).

West Coast Hotel v. Parrish, 300 U.S. 379 (1937).

Williamson v. Lee Optical Co., 348 U.S. 483 (1955).

Wynehamer v. People, 13 N.Y. 378 (1856).

BIBLIOGRAPHY

Ackerman, Bruce A., "Beyond *Carolene Products*," *Harvard Law Review* 98, no. 4 (February 1985): 713–46.

———, "Constitutional Politics/Constitutional Law," *Yale Law Journal* 99, no. 3 (December 1989): 453–548.

———, *Social Justice in the Liberal State* (New Haven: Yale University Press, 1980).

———, "The Storrs Lectures: Discovering the Constitution," *Yale Law Journal* 93, no. 6 (May 1984): 1023–72.

———, *We the People* (Cambridge: Harvard University Press, 1991).

Adams, Alice Dana, *The Neglected Period of Anti-Slavery in America, 1810–1831* (Boston: Ginn & Co., 1908).

Adams, Charles Francis, ed., *The Works of John Adams*, 10 vols. (Boston: Little Brown, 1851–1856).

Adams, John Quincy, *An Oration Addressed to the Citizens of the Town of Quincy* (Boston: Richardson, Lord, & Holbrook, 1831).

Amar, Akhil Reed, "Of Sovereignty and Federalism," *Yale Law Journal* 96, no. 7 (June 1987): 1425–1520.

———, "Philadelphia Revisited: Amending the Constitution Outside Article V," *University of Chicago Law Review* 55, no. 4 (Fall 1988): 1043–1104.

Anderson, Benedict, *Imagined Communities: Reflections on the Origin and Spread of Nationalism* (London: Verso, 1983).

Aptheker, Herbert, *American Negro Slave Revolts* (New York: International Publishers, 1952).

———, ed., *A Documentary History of the Negro People in the United States*, 4 vols. (New York: Citadel Press Books, 1990).

Aquinas, Thomas, *On the Truth of the Catholic Faith: Summa Contra Gentiles*, trans. Vernon Bourke (New York: Image, 1956).

Arendt, Hannah, *The Origins of Totalitarianism* (New York: Harcourt Brace Jovanovich, 1973).

"An Argument for the Application of Equal Protection Heightened Scrutiny to Classifications Based on Homosexuality," *Southern California Law Review* 57 (1984): 797.

Arieli, Yehoshua, *Individualism and Nationalism in American Ideology* (Cambridge: Harvard University Press, 1964).

Aristotle, *Nicomachean Ethics*, trans. Martin Ostwald (Indianapolis: Bobbs-Merrill, 1961).

———, *Politics*, trans. Ernest Barker (New York: Oxford University Press, 1962).

Ashcraft, Richard, *Locke's Two Treatises of Government* (London: Allen & Unwin, 1987).

Augustine, *The City of God*, trans. Henry Bettenson (Harmondsworth, Eng.: Penguin, 1972).

Baer, Judith A., *Equality under the Constitution: Reclaiming the Fourteenth Amendment* (Ithaca: Cornell University Press, 1983).

Bailyn, Bernard, *Faces of Revolution* (New York: Knopf, 1990).

———, ed., *Pamphlets of the American Revolution, 1750–1776*, vol. 1 (Cambridge: Belknap Press, Harvard University Press, 1965).

Barkan, Elazar, *The Retreat of Scientific Racism: Changing Concepts of Race in Britain and the United States between the World Wars* (Cambridge: Cambridge University Press, 1992).

Barnes, Gilbert Hobbs, *The Antislavery Impulse, 1830–1844* (New York: D. Appleton-Century Co., 1933).

Bauer, Elizabeth Kelley, *Commentaries on the Constitution, 1790–1860* (New York: Columbia University Press, 1952).

Bayle, Pierre, *Philosophical Commentary*, trans. Amie Godman Tannenbaum (New York: Peter Lang, 1987).

Beard, Charles A., and Mary R. Beard, *The Rise of American Civilization* (New York: Macmillan 1930).

Beattie, James, *Elements of Moral Science* (1790; reprint, Delmar, N.Y.: Scholars Facsimiles & Reprints, 1976).

———, *An Essay on the Nature and Immutability of Truth*, ed. Lewis White Beck (1770; reprint, New York: Garland, 1983).

Beeman, Richard, Stephen Botein, and Edward Carlos Carter, eds., *Beyond Confederation: Origins of the Constitution and American National Identity* (Chapel Hill: University of North Carolina Press, 1987).

Beitz, Charles R., *Political Equality* (Princeton: Princeton University Press, 1989).

Bell, Alan P., Martin S. Weinberg, and Sue K. Hammersmith, *Sexual Preference* (New York: Simon & Schuster, 1978).

Bemis, Samuel Flagg, *John Quincy Adams and the Union* (New York: Knopf, 1956).

Benedict, Michael Les, *A Compromise of Principle: Congressional Republicans and Reconstruction, 1793–1869* (New York: W. W. Norton, 1974).

———, "Laissez-Faire and Liberty: A Re-evaluation of the Meaning and Origins of Laissez-Faire and Constitutionalism," *Law and History Review* 3, no. 2 (Fall 1985): 294–332.

Benedict, Ruth, *Race: Science and Politics* (New York: Viking Press, 1945).

Bentham, Jeremy, *The Works of Jeremy Bentham*, book 2, ed. John Bowring (Edinburgh: W. Tait, 1843).

Berger, Raoul, *Government by Judiciary: The Transformation of the Fourteenth Amendment* (Cambridge: Harvard University Press, 1977).

Berlin, Ira, *Slaves without Masters: The Free Negro in the Antebellum South* (New York: Pantheon Books, 1974).

Bickel, Alexander, *The Least Dangerous Branch* (Indianapolis: Bobbs-Merrill, 1962).

Birney, James G., *Letter on Colonization Addressed to the Rev. Thornton J. Mills, Corresponding Secretary of the Kentucky Colonization Society* (New York, 1834)

Blackett, R.J.M., *Building an Antislavery Wall: Black Americans in the Atlantic Abolitionist Movement, 1830–1860* (Ithaca: Cornell University Press, 1983).

Blackstone, William, *Commentaries on the Laws of England*, 4 vols. (1768–69; reprint, Chicago: University of Chicago Press, 1979).

Blassingame, John W., *The Slave Community: Plantation Life in the Antebellum South*, rev. ed. (New York: Oxford University Press, 1979).

Blight, David W., *Frederick Douglass' Civil War: Keeping Faith in Jubilee* (Baton Rouge: Louisiana State University Press, 1989).

Boas, Frank, *The Mind of Primitive Man*, rev. ed. (1911; reprint, Westport, Conn.: Greenwood Press, 1963).

————, "Race," in *The Encyclopaedia of the Social Sciences*, ed. Edwin R. A. Seligman (New York: Macmillan, 1937), 7:25–36.

Bolt, Christine, and Seymour Drescher, eds., *Anti-Slavery, Religion and Reform* (London: Wm. Dawson & Sons, 1980).

Bork, Robert, *The Tempting of America: The Political Seduction of the Law* (New York: Free Press, 1990).

Bowditch, William, *The Constitutionality of Slavery* (Boston: Coolidge & Wiley, 1848).

Branch, Taylor, *Parting the Waters: America in the King Years, 1954–1963* (New York: Simon & Schuster, 1988).

Brown, Bernard Edward, *American Conservatives: The Political Thought of Francis Lieber and John W. Burgess* (New York: Columbia University Press, 1951).

Brown, Peter, *The Body and Society: Men, Women, and Sexual Renunciation in Early Christianity* (New York: Columbia University Press, 1988).

Brown, Wendy, *Manhood and Politics: A Feminist Reading of Political Theory* (Totowa, N.J.: Rowman & Littlefield, 1988).

Brownson, Orestes Augustus, *Brownson on the Rebellion* (1861), reprinted in Frank Freidel, ed., *Union Pamphlets of the Civil War, 1861–1865* (Cambridge: Belknap Press, Harvard University Press, 1967), 1:128–65.

Buchanan, Allen, *Secession: The Morality of Political Divorce from Fort Sumter to Lithuania and Quebec* (Boulder: Westview Press, 1991).

Buckle, Stephen, *Natural Law and the Theory of Property: Grotius to Hume* (Oxford: Clarendon Press, 1991).

Burke, Edmund, *The Works of Edmund Burke*, vol. 2, 6th ed. (Boston: Little, Brown, 1880).

Cahn, Edmund, "Jurisprudence," *New York University Law Review* 30 (January 1955): 150–69.

Calhoun, John C., *A Disquisition on Government*, ed. Richard K. Cralle (1853; reprint, New York: Peter Smith, 1943).

————, *The Works of John C. Calhoun*, 6 vols; ed. Richard K. Cralle (New York: D. Appleton, 1861–64).

Carlyle, Thomas, *Latter-day Pamphlets* (London: Chapman & Hall, 1850).

Carpenter, Jesse T., *The South as a Conscious Minority, 1789–1861* (New York: New York University Press, 1930).

Cash, W. J., *The Mind of the South* (New York: Vintage Books, 1969).

Cashman, Sean Dennis, *America in the Gilded Age: From the Death of Lincoln to the Rise of Theodore Roosevelt*, 2d ed. (New York: New York University Press, 1988).

Chamberlain, Houston Stewart, *The Foundations of the Nineteenth Century*, trans. John Lees, 2 vols. (London: John Lane, 1911).

Channing, William E., *The Works of William E. Channing* (1882; reprint, New York: Burt Franklin, 1970).

Chase, Salmon P., and Charles Dexter Cleveland, *Anti-Slavery Addresses of 1844 and 1845* (1867; reprint, New York: Negro Universities Press, 1969).

Child, L. Maria, *An Appeal in Favor of Americans Called Africans* (1833; reprint, New York: Arno Press and the New York Times, 1968).

Churchill, Wainwright, *Homosexual Behavior among Males* (New York: Hawthorn, 1967).

Cleveland, Henry, *Alexander H. Stephens, in Public and Private* (Philadelphia: National Publishing Co., 1866).

Cobb, Thomas R. R., *An Inquiry into the Law of Negro Slavery in the United States of America* (1858; reprint, New York, Negro Universities Press, 1968).

Cohen, I. Bernard, ed., *Puritanism and the Rise of Modern Science: The Merton Thesis* (New Brunswick, N.J.: Rutgers University Press, 1990).

Cohen, Joshua, and Joel Rogers, *On Democracy* (New York: Penguin Books, 1983).

Commager, Henry Steele, *Theodore Parker* (Boston: Little, Brown, 1936).

"The Constitutional Status of Sexual Orientation: Homosexuality as a Suspect Classification," *Harvard Law Review* 98, no.6 (April 1985): 1285–1309.

Cooke, Jacob E., ed., *The Federalist Papers* (Middletown, Conn.: Wesleyan University Press, 1961).

Cooley, Thomas M., *The General Principles of Constitutional Law in the United States of America*, ed. Alexis C. Angell, 2d ed. (Boston: Little, Brown, 1891).

———, *A Treatise on the Constitutional Limitations*, 6th ed. (Boston: Little, Brown, 1890).

Cover, Robert, *Justice Accused: Antislavery and the Judicial Process* (New Haven: Yale University Press, 1975).

Cox, LaWanda, *Lincoln and Black Freedom* (Urbana: University of Illinois Press, 1985).

Cox, LaWanda and John H. Cox, *Politics, Principle, and Prejudice, 1865–1866: Dilemma of Reconstruction America* (New York: Atheneum, 1976).

Curtis, Michael Kent, *No State Shall Abridge: The Fourteenth Amendment and the Bill of Rights* (Durham, N.C: Duke University Press, 1986).

Daly, Mary, *Beyond God the Father: Towards a Philosophy of Women's Liberation* (London: Women's Press, 1973).

Daniels, Norman, ed., *Reading Rawls: Critical Studies of* A Theory of Justice (New York: Basic Books, 1974).

Davis, David Brion, *The Problem of Slavery in the Age of Revolution, 1770–1823* (Ithaca: Cornell University Press, 1975).

———, *The Problem of Slavery in Western Culture* (Ithaca: Cornell University Press, 1967).

———, *The Slave Power Conspiracy and the Paranoid Style* (Baton Rouge: Louisiana State University Press, 1969).

———, *Slavery and Human Progress* (New York: Oxford University Press, 1984).

Davis, Jefferson, *The Rise of Fall of the Confederate Government*, 2 vols. (Richmond, Va.: Garret & Massie, 1938).

de Beauvoir, Simone, *The Second Sex*, trans. H. M. Parshley (New York: Vintage Books, 1952).

Degler, Carl N., *In Search of Human Nature: The Decline and Revival of Darwinism in American Social Thought* (New York: Oxford University Press, 1991).

———, *Neither Black nor White: Slavery and Race Relations in Brazil and the United States* (Madison: University of Wisconsin Press, 1986).

———, *Out of Our Past: The Forces That Shaped Modern America*, 3d ed. (New York: Harper & Row, 1984).

Delbanco, Andrew, *William Ellery Channing: An Essay on the Liberal Spirit in America* (Cambridge: Harvard University Press, 1981).

d'Entremont, John, *Southern Emancipator: Moncure Conway, the American Years, 1832–1865* (New York: Oxford University Press, 1987).

de Tocqueville, Alexis, *Democracy in America*, 2 vols., ed. Phillips Bradley (New York: Vintage Press, 1945).

"Developments in the Law—Equal Protection," *Harvard Law Review* 82, no. 5 (March 1969): 1065–1192.

"Developments in the Law—Sexual Orientation and the Law," *Harvard Law Review* 102, no. 7 (May 1989): 1509–1671.

Dillon, Merton L., *The Abolitionists: The Growth of a Dissenting Minority* (New York: W. W. Norton, 1974).

Dirks, John Edward, *The Critical Theology of Theodore Parker* (New York: Columbia University Press, 1948).

Donald, David, *Charles Sumner and the Coming of the Civil War* (New York: Knopf, 1960).

———, *Charles Sumner and the Rights of Man* (New York: Knopf, 1970).

Douglas, Ann, *The Feminization of American Culture* (New York: Knopf, 1977).

Douglas, Stephen A., "The Dividing Line between Federal and Local Authority: Popular Sovereignty in the Territories," *Harper's New Monthly Magazine* (September 1859): 519–37.

Duberman, Martin, ed., *The Antislavery Vanguard: New Essays of the Abolitionists* (Princeton: Princeton University Press, 1965).

DuBois, Ellen Carol, *Feminism and Suffrage: The Emergence of an Independent Women's Movement in America, 1848–1869* (Ithaca: Cornell University Press, 1978).

Dudziak, Mary L., "Desegregation as a Cold War Imperative" *Stanford Law Review* 41, no. 1 (November 1988): 61–120.

Dumond, Dwight Lowell, *Antislavery: The Crusade for Freedom in America* (Ann Arbor: University of Michigan Press, 1961).

———, *Antislavery Origins of the Civil War in the United States* (Ann Arbor: University of Michigan Press, 1939).

Dunne, Gerald T., *Justice Joseph Story and the Rise of the Supreme Court* (New York: Simon & Schuster, 1970).

Dworkin, Ronald, *A Bill of Rights for Britain* (London: Chatto & Windus, 1990).

———, *Law's Empire* (Cambridge: Harvard University Press, 1986).

———, "What Is Equality? Part I: Equality of Welfare," *Journal of Philosophy and Public Affairs* 10, no. 3 (Summer 1981): 185–246.

———, "What Is Equality? Part II: Equality of Resources," *Journal of Philosophy and Public Affairs* 10, no. 4 (Fall 1981): 283–345.

———, "What Is Equality? Part III: The Place of Liberty," *Iowa Law Review* 73, no. 1 (October 1987): 1–54.

———, "What Is Equality? Part IV: Political Equality," *University of San Francisco Law Review* 22, no. 1 (Fall 1987): 1–30.

Dynes, Wayne R., ed., *Encyclopedia of Homosexuality*, 2 vols. (New York: Garland, 1990).

Eaton, Clement, *The Freedom-of-Thought Struggle in the Old South* (New York: Harper & Row, 1940).

Elkins, Stanley M., *Slavery: A Problem in American Institutional and Intellectual Life*, 3d rev. ed. (Chicago: University of Chicago Press, 1976).

Elliot, Jonathan, *The Debates in the Several State Conventions on the Adoption of the Federal Constitution*, 5 vols. (Philadelphia: J. B. Lippincott, 1836).

Elliott, E. N., *Cotton Is King, and Pro-Slavery Arguments: Comprising the Writings of Hammand, Harper, Christy, Stringfellow, Hodge, Bledsoe, and Cartwright, on This Important Subject* (Augusta, Ga.: Pritchard, Abbott & Loomis, 1860).

Ellis, Richard E., *The Union at Risk: Jacksonian Democracy, States' Rights, and the Nullification Crisis* (New York: Oxford University Press, 1987).

Elshtain, Jean Ethke, *Public Man, Private Woman: Women in Social and Political Thought* (Princeton: Princeton University Press, 1981).

Ely, John Hart, *Democracy and Distrust: A Theory of Judicial Review* (Cambridge: Harvard University Press, 1980).

———, "The Wages of Crying Wolf: A Comment on *Roe v. Wade*," *Yale Law Journal* 82, no. 5 (April 1974): 920–49.

Epstein, Cynthia Fuchs, *Deceptive Distinctions: Sex, Gender, and the Social Order* (New Haven: Yale University Press, 1988).

Epstein, Richard A., *Takings: Private Property and the Power of Eminent Domain* (Cambridge: Harvard University Press, 1985).

Everett, Edward, *Orations and Speeches*, vol. 4 (Boston: Little, Brown, 1892).

Fairman, Charles, "Does the Fourteenth Amendment Incorporate the Bill of Rights? The Original Understanding" in *Stanford Law Review* (December 1949): 5–173.

———, *Reconstruction and Reunion, 1864–88* (New York: Macmillan, 1971).

Farrand, Max, ed., *The Records of the Federal Convention of 1787*, 4 vols. (New Haven: Yale University Press, 1966).

Faust, Drew Gilpin, *James Henry Hammond and the Old South: A Design for Mastery* (Baton Rouge: Louisiana State University Press, 1982).

———, *A Sacred Circle: The Dilemma of the Intellectual in the Old South, 1840–1860* (Philadelphia: University of Pennsylvania Press, 1977).

———, ed., *The Ideology of Slavery: Proslavery Thought in the Antebellum South, 1830–1860* (Baton Rouge: Louisiana State University Press, 1981).

Fausto-Sterling, Anne, *Myths of Gender: Biological Theories about Women and Men* (New York: Basic Books, 1985).

Fehrenbacher, Don E., *Constitutions and Constitutionalism in the Slaveholding South* (Athens, Ga.: University of Georgia Press, 1989).

———, *The Dred Scott Case: Its Significance in American Law and Politics* (New York: Oxford University Press, 1978).

———, *Prelude to Greatness: Lincoln in the 1850's* (Stanford: Stanford University Press, 1962).

———, ed., *Abraham Lincoln: Speeches and Writings, 1832–1858* (New York: Library of America, 1989).

———, ed., *Abraham Lincoln: Speeches and Writings, 1858–1865* (New York: Library of America, 1989).

Filler, Louis, *The Crusade against Slavery, 1830–1860* (New York: Harper & Row, 1960).

Filler, Louis, ed., *Abolition and Social Justice in the Era of Reform* (New York: Harper & Row, 1972).

———, ed., *Wendell Phillips on Civil Rights and Freedom* (New York: Hill & Wang, 1965).

Filmer, Robert, *Patriarcha and Other Writings*, ed. Johann P. Sommerville (Cambridge: Cambridge University Press, 1991).

Finkelman, Paul, "The Constitution and the Intentions of the Framers: The Limits of Historical Analysis," *University of Pittsburg Law Review* 50, no. 2 (Winter 1989): 349–98.

———, *An Imperfect Union: Slavery, Federalism, and Comity* (Chapel Hill: University of North Carolina Press, 1981).

———, "Prelude to the Fourteenth Amendment: Black Rights in the Antebellum North," *Rutgers Law Journal* 7 (1986): 415–82.

———, ed., *Antislavery* (New York: Garland, 1989).

Fisher, Sidney George, *The Trial of the Constitution* (Philadelphia: J. B. Lippincott, 1862).

Fiss, Owen, "The Fate of an Idea Whose Time Has Come: Antidiscrimination Law in the Second Decade after *Brown v. Board of Education*," *University of Chicago Law Review* 41, no. 4 (Summer 1974): 742–73.

———, "Groups and the Equal Protection Clause," *Philosophy and Public Affairs* 5, no. 2 (Winter 1976): 107–77.

Fitzhugh, George, *Cannibals All! or, Slaves without Masters*, ed. C. Vann Woodward (1857; reprint, Cambridge: Belknap Press, Harvard University Press, 1960).

Flack, Horace Edgar, *The Adoption of the Fourteenth Amendment* (Baltimore: Johns Hopkins University Press, 1908).

Fogel, Robert William, *Without Consent or Contract: The Rise and Fall of American Slavery* (New York: W. W. Norton, 1989).

Foner, Eric, *Free Soil, Free Labor, Free Men: The Ideology of the Republican Party before the Civil War* (New York: Oxford University Press, 1970).

———, *Nothing but Freedom: Emancipation and Its Legacy* (Baton Rouge: Louisiana State University Press, 1983).

———, *Reconstruction: America's Unfinished Revolution, 1863–1877* (New York: Harper & Row, 1988).

Foner, Philip S., ed., *The Life and Writings of Fredrick Douglass*, 5 vols. (New York: International Publishers, 1975).

Franklin, John Hope, *The Militant South, 1800–1861* (Cambridge: Belknap Press, Harvard University Press, 1956).

Franklin, John Hope, and Alfred A. Moss, Jr., *From Slavery to Freedom: A History of Negro Americans*, 6th ed. (New York: Knopf, 1988).

Fredrickson, George M., *The Black Image in the White Mind: The Debate on Afro-American Character and Destiny, 1817–1914* (Middletown, Conn., Wesleyan University Press, 1971).

———, *White Supremacy: A Comparative Study in American and South African History* (Oxford: Oxford University Press, 1981).

Freehling, William W., *Prelude to Civil War: The Nullification Controversy in South Carolina, 1816–1836* (New York: Harper & Row, 1968).

———, *The Road to Disunion: Secessionists at Bay, 1776–1854* (New York: Oxford University Press, 1990).

Freeman, Samuel, "Contractualism, Moral Motivation, and Practical Reason," *Journal of Philosophy* 87, no. 6 (June 1991): 281–303.

Freidel, Frank, *Francis Lieber: Nineteenth-Century Liberal* (Baton Rouge: Louisiana State University Press, 1947).

———, ed., *Union Pamphlets of the Civil War, 1861–1865*, 2 vols. (Cambridge: Belknap Press, Harvard University Press, 1967).

Fuchs, Victor R., *Women's Quest for Economic Equality* (Cambridge: Harvard University Press, 1988).

Gager, John A., *The Origins of Anti-Semitism: Attitudes toward Judaism in Pagan and Christian Antiquity* (New York: Oxford University Press, 1983).

Gallie, W. B., *Philosophy and the Historical Understanding*, 2d ed. (New York: Schocken Books, 1968).

Garraty, John A., *The New Commonwealth, 1877–1890* (New York: Harper & Row, 1968).

Garrison, Wendell Phillips, and Francis Jackson Garrison, *William Lloyd Garrison, 1805–1879*, 4 vols. (New York: Century Co., 1885–89).

Garrison, William Lloyd, *Selections from the Writings and Speeches of William Lloyd Garrison* (Boston: R. F. Wallcut, 1852).

———, *Thoughts on African Colonization* (1832; reprint, New York: Arno Press and the New York Times, 1968).

Gauthier, David, *Morals by Agreement* (New York: Oxford University Press, 1986).

Gellner, Ernest, *Nations and Nationalism* (Ithaca: Cornell University Press, 1983).

Genovese, Eugene D., *From Rebellion to Revolution: Afro-American Slave Revolts in the Making of the Modern World* (Baton Rouge: Louisiana State University Press, 1979).

———, *Roll, Jordon, Roll: The World the Slaves Made* (New York: Vintage Books, 1974).

———, *The World the Slaveholders Made: Two Essays in Interpretation* (Middletown, Conn.: Wesleyan University Press, 1988).

Gerteis, Louis S., *Morality and Utility in American Antislavery Reform* (Chapel Hill: Univerity of North Carolina Press, 1987).

Gienapp, William E., *The Origins of the Republican Party, 1852–1856* (New York: Oxford University Press, 1987).

Gillette, William, *The Right to Vote: Politics and the Passage of the Fifteenth Amendment* (Baltimore: Johns Hopkins University Press, 1969).

Gilligan, Carol, *In a Different Voice: Psychological Theory and Women's Development* (Cambridge: Harvard University Press, 1982).

Goldin, Claudia, *Understanding the Gender Gap: An Economic History of American Women* (New York: Oxford University Press, 1990).

Goodell, William, *Slavery and Anti-Slavery: A History of the Great Struggle in Both Hemispheres, with a View of the Slavery Question in the United States* (New York: William Goodell, 1855).

——, *Views of American Constitutional Law in its Bearing upon American Slavery* (1845; reprint, Freeport, N.Y.: Books for Libraries Press, 1971).

Gossett, Thomas F., *Race: The History of an Idea in America* (New York: Schocken Books, 1965).

Gougeon, Len, *Virtue's Hero: Emerson, Antislavery, and Reform* (Athens, Ga.: University of Georgia Press, 1990).

Gould, Stephen Jay, *The Mismeasure of Man* (New York: W. W. Norton, 1981).

Graham, Howard Jay, *Everyman's Constitution* (Madison: State Historical Society of Wisconsin, 1968).

Grant, Madison, *The Passing of the Great Race or the Racial Basis of European History* (New York: Charles Scribner's Sons, 1919).

Grant, Ruth W., *John Locke's Liberalism* (Chicago: University of Chicago Press, 1987).

Greenawalt, R. Kent, *Religious Convictions and Political Choice* (New York: Oxford University Press, 1988).

Greenberg, David F., *The Construction of Homosexuality* (Chicago: University of Chicago Press, 1988).

Greenberg, Kenneth S., *Masters and Statesmen: The Political Culture of American Slavery* (Baltimore: Johns Hopkins University Press, 1985).

Grimke, Frederick, *The Nature and Tendency of Free Institutions* (1848; reprint, Cambridge: Belknap Press, Harvard University Press, 1968).

Gunther, Gerald, "Newer Equal Protection," *Harvard Law Review*, 86, no. 1 (November 1972): 1–49.

Gutman, Herbert G., *The Black Family in Slavery and Freedom, 1750–1925* (New York: Vintage Books, 1976).

Hacker, Andrew, *Two Nations: Black and White, Separate, Hostile, Unequal* (New York: Charles Scribner's Sons, 1992).

Haller, John S., Jr., *Outcasts from Evolution: Scientific Attitudes of Racial Inferiority, 1859–1900* (New York: McGraw-Hill, 1971).

Halley, Janet E., "The Politics of the Closet: Towards Equal Protection for Gay, Lesbian, and Bisexual Identity," *UCLA Law Review* 37, no. 5 (June 1989): 915–76.

Hampson, Daphne, *Theology and Feminism* (Oxford: Basil Blackwell, 1990).

Hand, Learned, *The Bill of Rights* (New York: Atheneum, 1968).

Harding, Sandra, *The Science Question in Feminism* (Ithaca: Cornell University Press, 1986).

Harding, Sandra, and Merill B. Hintikka, *Discovering Reality: Feminist Perspec-*

tives on Epistemology, Metaphysics, Methodology, and Philosophy of Science (Dordrecht, Holland: D. Reidel, 1983).

Harding, Sandra, and Jean F. O'Barr, *Sex and Scientific Inquiry* (Chicago: University of Chicago Press, 1987).

Harris, Seth, "Permitting Prejudice to Govern: Equal Protection, Military Deference, and the Exclusion of Lesbians and Gay Men from the Military," *New York University Review of Law and Social Change* 17, no. 1 (1989–90): 171–223.

Harrison, Ross, *Bentham* (London: Routledge & Kegan Paul, 1983).

Hartz, Louis, *The Liberal Tradition in America* (New York: Harcourt, Brace & World, 1955).

Heine, Susanne, *Women and Early Christianity: Are the Feminist Scholars Right?* trans. John Bowden (London: SCM Press, 1987).

Herndon, William H., and Jesse W. Weik, *Herndon's Life of Lincoln* (1889; reprint, New York: Da Capo Press, 1983).

Hertzberg, Arthur, *The French Enlightenment and the Jews* (New York: Columbia University Press, 1990).

Higginbotham, A. Leon, Jr., *In the Matter of Color: Race and the American Legal Process: The Colonial Period* (New York: Oxford University Press, 1978).

Higham, John, *Strangers in the Land: Patterns of American Nativism, 1860–1925* (New Brunswick: Rutgers University Press, 1988).

Hilberg, Raul, *The Destruction of the European Jews*, 3 vols. (New York: Holmes & Meier, 1985).

Hitler, Adolf, *Mein Kampf* (New York: Reynal & Hitchcock, 1940).

Hobbes, Thomas, *Leviathan*, ed. Michael Oakeshott (Oxford: Basil Blackwell, 1960).

Hobsbawm, E. J., *Nations and Nationalism since 1780* (Cambridge: Cambridge University Press, 1990).

Hoemann, George H., *What God Hath Wrought: The Embodiment of Freedom in the Thirteenth Amendment* (New York: Garland, 1987).

Hofstadter, Richard, *Social Darwinism in American Thought* (Boston: Beacon Press, 1955).

Hopkins, Samuel, *Timely Articles on Slavery* (1776; reprint, Miami: Mnemosyne, 1969).

Horowitz, Robert H., *The Moral Foundations of the American Republic*, 3d ed. (Charlottesville: University Press of Virginia, 1986).

Horsman, Reginald, *Race and Manifest Destiny: The Origins of American Racial Anglo-Saxonism* (Cambridge: Harvard University Press, 1981).

Howe, Daniel Walker, "Henry David Thoreau on the Duty of Civil Disobedience," *An Inaugural Lecture Delivered before the University of Oxford on 21 May 1990* (Oxford: Clarendon Press, 1990).

———, *The Unitarian Conscience: Harvard Moral Philosophy, 1805–1861* (Middletown, Conn.: Wesleyan University Press, 1988).

Hume, David, *Essays Moral Political and Literary*, ed. Eugene F. Miller (Indianapolis: Liberty Classics, 1987).

Hurd, John Codman, *The Law of Freedom and Bondage in the United States*, 2 vols. (Boston: Little, Brown, 1858–62) (reprint, New York: Negro Universities Press, 1968).

Hutcheson, Francis, *A Short Introduction to Moral Philosophy* (1747; reprint, Hildesheim: Georg Olms Verlagsbuchhandlung, 1969).

———, *A System of Moral Philosophy* (1775; reprint, Hildesheim: Georg Olms Verlagsbuchhandlung, 1969).

Hyman, Harold M., *A More Perfect Union: The Impact of the Civil War and Reconstruction on the Constitution* (New York: Knopf, 1973).

———, ed., *The Radical Republicans and Reconstruction, 1861–1870* (Indianapolis: Bobbs-Merrill, 1967).

Hyman, Harold M., and William M. Wiecek, *Equal Justice under Law: Constitutional Development, 1835–1875* (New York: Harper & Row, 1982).

The Influence of the Slave Power with Other Anti-Slavery Pamphlets (1836–48; reprint, Westport, Conn.: Negro Universities Press, 1970).

Inikori, Joseph E., and Stanley L. Engerman, eds., *The Atlantic Slave Trade: Effects on Economies, Societies, and Peoples in Africa, the Americans, and Europe* (Durham: Duke University Press, 1992).

Jaffe, Harry V., *Crisis of the House Divided: An Interpretation of the Issues in the Lincoln-Douglas Debates* (Chicago: University of Chicago Press, 1982).

Jagger, Alison M., *Feminist Politics and Human Nature* (Totowa: N.J.: Rowman & Allanheld, 1983).

James, Joseph B., *The Framing of the Fourteenth Amendment* (Urbana: University of Illinois Press, 1956).

Jay, William, *Miscellaneous Writings on Slavery* (1853; reprint, New York: Negro Universities Press, 1968).

Jefferson, Thomas, *Notes on the State of Virginia*, ed. William Peden (New York: W. W. Norton, 1982).

Jenkins, William Sumner, *Pro-slavery Thought in the Old South* (Chapel Hill: Univerity of North Carolina Press, 1935).

Johannsen, Robert W., *The Lincoln-Douglas Debates of 1858* (New York: Oxford University Press, 1965).

———, *Stephen A. Douglas* (New York: Oxford University Press, 1973).

Jones, Alan R., *The Constitutional Conservatism of Thomas McIntyre Cooley: A Study of the History of Ideas* (New York: Garland, 1987).

Jordon, Winthrop D., *White over Black: American Attitudes toward the Negro, 1550–1812* (New York: W. W. Norton, 1977).

Julian, George W., *The Life of Joshua R. Giddings* (Chicago: A. C. McClurg, 1892).

Kaczorowski, Robert J., *The Nationalization of Civil Rights: Constitutional Theory and Practice in a Racist Society, 1866–1883* (New York: Garland, 1987).

———, *The Politics of Judicial Interpretation: The Federal Courts, Department of Justice and Civil Rights, 1866–1876* (New York: Oceana, 1985).

———, "Revolutionary Constitutionalism in the Era of the Civil War and Reconstruction," *New York University Law Review* 61, no. 5 (November 1986): 863–909.

———, "Searching for the Intent of the Framers of the Fourteenth Amendment," *University of Connecticut Law Review* 5, no. 5 (Winter 1972–73) 368–98.

Kalven, Harry, Jr., *The Negro and the First Amendment* (Chicago: University of Chicago Press, 1965).

Kant, Immanuel, *Kant's Political Writings,* ed. Hans Reiss (Cambridge: Cambridge University Press, 1977).

Karst, Kenneth L., *Belonging to America: Equal Citizenship and the Constitution* (New Haven: Yale University Press, 1989).

———, "The Pursuit of Manhood and the Desegregation of the Armed Forces," *UCLA Law Review* 38, no. 3 (Febuary 1991): 499–582.

———, "Woman's Constitution," *Duke Law Journal* 1984, no. 3 (June 1984): 447–508.

Katz, Jacob, *The Darker Side of Genius* (Hanover, N.H.: University Press of New England, 1986).

———, *From Prejudice to Destruction* (Cambridge: Harvard University Press, 1980).

Keller, Evelyn Fox, *Reflections on Gender and Science* (New Haven: Yale University Press, 1985).

Kendrick, Benjamin B., *The Journal of the Joint Committee of Fifteen on Reconstruction* (1914; reprint, New York: Negro Universities Press, 1969).

Kent, James, *Commentaries on American Law,* ed. Oliver W. Holmes, Jr., 12th ed. (1826–30; reprint, Boston: Little, Brown, 1873).

Ketcham, Ralph, *James Madison: A Biography* (Charlottesville: University Press of Virginia, 1971).

Kettner, James, *The Development of American Citizenship, 1608–1870* (Chapel Hill: University of North Carolina Press, 1978).

Kittay, Eva Feder, and Diana T. Meyers, eds., *Women and Moral Theory* (Totowa, N.J.: Rowman & Littlefield, 1987).

Klein, Herbert S., *Slavery in the Americas: A Comparative Study of Virginia and Cuba* (Chicago: Elephant Papberbacks, 1989).

Klineberg, Otto, *Race Differences* (New York: Harper & Bros., 1935).

Kluger, Richard, *Simple Justice: The History of Brown v. Board Of Education and Black America's Struggle for Equality* (New York: Vintage, 1977).

Kolchin, Peter, *Unfree Labor: American Slavery and Russian Serfdom* (Cambridge: Harvard University Press, 1987).

Kraditor, Aileen S., *Means and Ends in American Abolitionism: Garrison and His Critics on Strategy and Tactics, 1834–1850* (1967; reprint, Chicago: Elephant Paperbacks, 1989).

Lane, Ann J., ed., *The Debate over Slavery: Stanley Elkins and His Critics* (Urbana: University of Illinois Press, 1971).

Langmuir, Gavin I., *History, Religion, and Antisemitism* (Berkeley: University of California Press, 1990).

———, *Toward a Definition of Antisemitism* (Berkeley: University of California Press, 1990).

Laqueur, Thomas, *Making Sex: Body and Gender from the Greeks to Freud* (Cambridge: Harvard University Press, 1990).

Large, David C., and William Weber, eds., *Wagnerism in European Culture and Politics* (Ithaca: Cornell University Press, 1984).

Law, Sylvia, "Rethinking Sex and the Constitution," in *University of Pennsylvania Law Review* 132, no. 5 (June 1984): 955–1040.

Lawrence, Charles R., "The Id, the Ego, and Equal Protection: Reckoning with Unconscious Racism," *Stanford Law Review* 39 (January 1987): 317–88.

Lerner, Gerda, *The Creation of Patriarchy* (New York: Oxford University Press, 1986).

Levy, Leonard W., *Establishment Clause: Religion and the First Amendment* (New York: Macmillan, 1986).

———, *Judgments: Essays on American Constitutional History* (Chicago: Quadrangle Books, 1972).

Levy, Leonard, Kenneth L. Karst, and Dennis J. Mahoney, eds., *Encyclopedia of the American Constitution*, 4 vols. (New York: Macmillan, 1986).

Lieber, Francis, *Legal and Political Hermeneutics*, ed. William G. Hammond, 3d ed., (1837–38; reprint, St. Louis: F.H. Thomas, 1880).

Lieber, Francis, *Manual of Political Ethics*, 2 vols. (Boston: Little, Brown, 1838–39).

———, *The Miscellaneous Writings of Francis Lieber*, 2 vols. (Philadelphia: J. B. Lippincott, 1880).

———, *On Civil Liberty and Self-government* (Philadelphia: J. B. Lippincott, 1859).

Litwack, Leon F., *Been in the Storm So Long: The Aftermath of Slavery* (New York: Vintage Books, 1979).

———, *North of Slavery: The Negro in the Free States, 1790–1860* (Chicago: University of Chicago Press, 1961).

Locke, John, *Two Treatises of Government*, ed. Peter Laslett (Cambridge: Cambridge University Press, 1960).

———, *The Works of John Locke*, 10 vols. (London: Tomas Tegg, 1823).

Locke, Mary Stoughton, *Anti-Slavery in America from the Introduction of African Slaves to the Prohibition of the Slave Trade, 1619–1808* (Boston: Ginn & Co., 1901).

Lofgren, Charles A., *The Plessy Case: A Legal-Historical Interpretation* (New York: Oxford University Press, 1987).

Lovejoy, Arthur O., *The Great Chain of Being* (Cambridge: Harvard University Press, 1964).

Lowell, James Russell, *The Anti-Slavery Papers of James Russell Lowell*, 2 vols. (Boston: Houghton Mifflin, 1902).

McClellan, James, *Joseph Story and the American Constitution* (Norman: University of Oklahoma Press, 1971).

McCoy, Drew R., *The Last of the Fathers: James Madison and the Republican Legacy* (Cambridge: Cambridge University Press, 1989).

Macedo, Stephen, *Liberal Virtues: Citizenship, Virtue, and Community in Liberal Constitutionalism* (Oxford: Clarendon Press, 1990).

McFeely, William S., *Frederick Douglass* (New York: W. W. Norton, 1991).

McKitrick, Eric L., *Andrew Johnson and Reconstruction* (New York: Oxford University Press, 1960).

———, ed., *Slavery Defended: The Views of the Old South* (Englewood Cliffs, N.J.: Prentice-Hall, 1963).

MacLeod, Duncan J., *Slavery, Race and the American Revolution* (Cambridge: Cambridge University Press, 1974).

McNeil, Genna Rae, *Groundwork: Charles Hamilton Houston and the Struggle for Civil Rights* (Philadelphia: University of Pennsylvania Press, 1983).

McPherson, James M., *Abraham Lincoln and the Second American Revolution* (New York: Oxford University Press, 1990).

———, *Battle Cry of Freedom: The Civil War Era* (New York: Ballantine Books, 1988).

———, *The Struggle for Equality: Abolitionists and the Negro in the Civil War and Reconstruction* (Princton: Princeton University Press, 1964).

Madden, Edward H., *Civil Disobedience and Moral Law in Nineteenth-Century American Philosophy* (Seattle: University of Washington Press, 1968).

Madison, James, *Letters and Other Writings of James Madison*, 4 vols. (New York: R. Worthington, 1884).

———, *The Papers of James Madison*, ed. William T. Hutchinson, and William M. E. Rachal, Robert A. Rutland, Charles F. Hobson, and Fredrika J. Teute, 10 vols. (Chicago: University of Chicago Press, 1962–77).

———, *The Papers of James Madison*, Robert A. Rutland, Charles F. Hobson, Thomas A. Mason, and Jeanne K. Sisson, 5 vols. (Charlottesville: University of Virginia Press, 1977–85).

Maltz, Earl M., *Civil Rights, the Constitution, and Congress, 1863–1869* (Lawrence: University Press of Kansas, 1990).

Martineau, Harriet, *Society in America*, 3 vols. (London: Saunders & Otley, 1837).

Marx, Karl, *On America and the Civil War*, ed. Saul K. Padover, (New York: McGraw-Hill 1972).

Mellen, G.W.F., *An Argument on the Unconstitutionality of Slavery* (Boston: Saxton & Peirce, 1841).

Meyer, D. H., *The Instructed Conscience: The Shaping of the American National Ethic* (Philadelphia: University of Pennsylvania Press, 1972).

Meyers, Marvin, *The Mind of the Founder: Sources of the Political Thought of James Madison*, rev. ed. (Hanover, N.H.: University Press of New England, 1981).

Michelman, Frank, "Foreword: On Protecting the Poor through the Fourteenth Amendment," *Harvard Law Review* 83, no. 1 (November 1969): 7–59.

———, "In Pursuit of Constitutional Welfare Rights: One View of Rawls' Theory of Justice," *University of Pennsylvania Law Review* 121, no. 5 (May 1973): 962–1019.

Mill, John Stuart, and Harriet Taylor Mill, *Essays on Sex Equality*, ed. Alice S. Rossi (Chicago: University of Chicago Press, 1970).

Miller, Harris M., II, "An Argument for the Application of Equal Protection Heightened Scrutiny to Classifications Based on Homosexuality," *Southern California Law Review* 57, no. 5 (July 1984): 797–836.

Miller, John C., *The Federalist Era, 1789–1801* (New York: Harper & Row, 1960).

Miller, John Chester, *The Wolf by the Ears: Thomas Jefferson and Slavery* (New York: Free Press, 1977).

Mohr, Richard D., *Gays/Justice: A Study of Ethics, Society, and Law* (New York: Columbia University Press, 1988).

Moliere, *The Misanthrope and Other Plays,* trans. Donald M. Frame (New York: New American Library, 1981).

Money, John, and A. Ehrhardt, *Man & Woman, Boy & Girl* (Baltimore: Johns Hopkins University Press, 1972).

Money, John, J. G. Hampson, and J. L. Hampson, "An Examination of Some Basic Sexual Concepts: The Evidence of Human Hermaphroditism," *Johns Hopkins Hospital Bulletin* 97 (1955): 301.

Montesquieu, Baron de, *The Spirit of the Laws,* trans. Thomas Nugent (New York: Hafner, 1949).

Moore, R. I., *The Formation of a Persecuting Society: Power and Deviance in Western Europe, 950–1250* (Oxford: Basil Blackwell, 1987).

Morgan, Edmund S., *American Slavery, American Freedom: The Ordeal of Colonial Virginia* (New York: W. W. Norton, 1975).

Morrison, Stanley, "Does the Fourteenth Amendment Incorporate the Bill of Rights?" *Stanford Law Review* 2 (December 1949): 140–73.

Myrdal, Gunnar, *An American Dilemma: The Negro Problem and Modern Democracy,* 2 vols. (1944; reprint, New York: Pantheon Books, 1972).

Nagel, Thomas, *Equality and Partiality* (New York: Oxford University Press, 1991).

Nedelsky, Jennifer, *Private Property and the Limits of American Constitutionalism: The Madisonian Framework and Its Legacy* (Chicago: University of Chicago Press, 1990).

Nelson, William, E., *The Fourteenth Amendment: From Political Principle to Judicial Doctrine* (Cambridge: Harvard University Press, 1988).

Newmyer, R. Kent, *Supreme Court Justice Joseph Story: Statesman of the Old Republic* (Chapel Hill: University of North Carolina Press, 1985).

Nieman, Donald G., *Promises to Keep: African-Americans and the Constitutional Order, 1776 to the Present* (New York: Oxford University Press, 1991).

Niven, John, *John C. Calhoun and the Price of Union: A Biography* (Baton Rouge: Louisiana State University Press, 1988).

Norman, Andrew E., ed., *The Autobiography of Martin Van Buren* (New York: Confucian Press, 1981).

Norton, Anne, *Alternative Americas: A Reading of Antebellum Political Culture* (Chicago: University of Chicago Press, 1986).

Norton, Charles Eliot, ed., *Orations and Addresses of George William Curtis* (New York: Harper & Bros., 1894).

Nozick, Robert, *Anarchy, State and Utopia* (New York: Basic Books, 1974).

Nye, Russel B., *Fettered Freedom: Civil Liberties and the Slavery Controversy, 1830–1860,* (East Lansing: Michigan State College Press, 1949).

Okin, Susan Moller, *Justice, Gender, and the Family* (New York: Basic Books, 1989).

———, *Women in Western Political Thought* (Princeton: Princeton University Press, 1979).

O'Neill, Onora, *Constructions of Reason* (Cambridge: Cambridge University Press, 1989).

Orth, John V., *The Judicial Power of the United States: The Eleventh Amendment in American History* (New York: Oxford University Press, 1987).

Pagels, Elaine H., *Adam, Eve, and the Serpent* (New York: Random House, 1988).

Paludan, Phillip Shaw, *A Covenant with Death: The Constitution, Law, and Equality in the Civil War Era* (Urbana: University of Illinois Press, 1975).

———, *"A People's Contest": The Union and Civil War* (New York: Harper & Row, 1988).

Parker, Theodore, *A Discourse of Matters Pertaining to Religion,* ed. Thomas Wentworth Higginson (Boston: American Unitarian Association, 1907).

———, *The Relation of Slavery to a Republican Form of Government* (Boston: William L. Kent, 1858).

———, *The Rights of Man,* ed. F. B. Sanborn (Boston: American Unitariam Association, 1911).

———, *Saint Bernard and Other Papers,* ed. Charles W. Wendte (Boston: American Unitarian Association, 1911).

———, *The Slave Power,* ed. James K. Hosmer (Boston: American Unitarian Association, 1916).

———, *Social Classes in a Republic,* ed. Samuel A. Eliot (Boston: American Unitarian Association, n.d.).

———, *The Transient and Permanent in Christianity,* ed. George Willis Cooke (Boston: American Unitarian Association, 1908).

———, *The Trial of Theodore Parker* (1855; reprint, Freeport, N.Y.: Books for Libraries Press, 1971).

———, *The World of Matter and the Spirit of Man,* ed. George Willis Cooke (Boston: American Unitarian Association, 1907).

Pateman, Carole, *The Sexual Contract* (Cambridge: Polity Press, 1988).

Patterson, Orlando, *Slavery and Social Death* (Cambridge: Harvard University Press, 1982).

Pease, William H., and Jane H. Pease, *The Antislavery Argument* (Indianapolis: Bobbs-Merrill, 1965).

Peffer, R. G., *Marxism, Morality, and Social Justice* (Princeton: Princeton University Press, 1990).

Perry, Lewis, *Radical Abolitionism: Anarchy and the Government of God in Antislavery Thought* (Ithaca: Cornell University Press, 1973).

Perry, Michael J., "Modern Equal Protection: A Conceptualization and Appraisal," *Columbia Law Review* 79, no.6 (October 1979): 1023–84.

Phillips, Wendell, *Can Abolitionists Vote or Take Office under the United States Constitution?* (New York: American Anti-Slavery Society, 1845).

———, *The Constitution a Pro-Slavery Compact* (1844; reprint, New York: Negro Universities Press, 1969).

———, *Review of Lysander Spooner's Essay on the Unconstitutionality of Slavery* (1847; reprint New York: Arno Press and the New York Times, 1969).

———, *Speeches, Lectures, and Letters* (Boston: Lothrop, Lee & Shepard, 1863).

———, *Speeches, Lectures, and Letters,* 2d ser. (Boston: Lee & Shepard, 1905).

Plato, *Plato: The Collected Dialogues,* ed. Edith Hamilton and Huntington Cairns (New York: Pantheon, 1961).

Poage, George Rawlings, *Henry Clay and the Whig Party* (Chapel Hill: University of North Carolina Press, 1936).

Poliakov, Leon, *The Aryan Myth: A History of Racist and Nationalist Ideas in Europe,* trans. Edmund Howard (London: Sussex University Press, 1971).

―――, *The History of Anti-Semitism,* trans. Richard Howard, Natalie Gerardi, and Miriam Kochan, vols. 1-3 (New York: Vanguard Press, 1965–75); trans. George Klin, vol. 4 (Oxford: Oxford University Press, 1985).

Potter, David M., *The Impending Crisis, 1848–1861,* ed. Don E. Fehrenbacher (New York: Harper & Row, 1976).

―――, *Lincoln and His Party in the Secession Crisis* (New Haven: Yale University Press, 1942).

Pulzer, Leon, *The Rise of Political Anti-Semitism in Germany and Austria,* rev. ed. (Cambridge: Harvard University Press, 1988).

Quarles, Benjamin, *Black Abolitionists* (London: Oxford University Press, 1969).

Rakove, Jack N., *Interpreting the Constitution: The Debate over Original Intent* (Boston: Northeastern University Press, 1990).

―――, "The Madisonian Moment," *University of Chicago Law Review* 55, no. 2 (Winter 1988): 473–505.

―――, "The Madisonian Theory of Rights," *William & Mary Law Review* 31, no. 2 (Winter 1990): 245–66.

Randall, J. G., *Constitutional Problems under Lincoln,* rev. ed. (Gloucester, Mass.: Peter Smith, 1963).

Ranke-Heinemann, Uta, *Eunuchs for Heaven: The Catholic Church and Sexuality,* trans. John Brownjohn (London: Andre Deutsch, 1988).

Rather, L. J., *Reading Wagner: A Study in the History of Ideas* (Baton Rouge: Louisiana State University Press, 1990).

Rawle, William, *A View of the Constitution of the United States of America* (Philadelphia: H. C. Carey & I. Lea, 1825).

Rawls, John, *A Theory of Justice* (Cambridge: Harvard University Press, 1971).

Reeves, Derek Q., "Beyond the River Jordan: An Essay on the Continuing of the Black Prophetic Tradition," *Journal of Religious Thought* 47 (1990–91): 42.

Reiman, Jeffrey, *Justice and Modern Moral Philosophy* (New Haven: Yale University Press, 1990).

Reiss, Hans, ed., *Kant's Political Writings* (Cambridge: Cambridge University Press, 1970).

Rhode, Deborah L., *Justice and Gender* (Cambridge: Harvard University Press, 1989).

Rice, C. Duncan, *The Rise and Fall of Black Slavery* (New York: Harper & Row, 1975).

Richards, David A. J., *Foundations of American Constitutionalism* (New York: Oxford University Press, 1989).

―――, "The Individual, the Family, and the Constitution," *New York University Law Review* 55, no. 1 (April 1980): 1–62.

―――, *The Moral Criticism of Law* (Encino, Calif.: Dickenson-Wadsworth, 1977).

―――, "Originalism without Foundations," *New York University Law Review* 65, no. 5 (November 1990): 1373–1407.

―――, "Revolution and Constitutionalism in America and France," *University of Mississippi Law Journal* 60, no. 2 (Fall 1990): 331–56.

————, *Sex, Drugs, Death, and the Law: An Essay on Human Rights and Over-criminalization* (Totowa, N.J.: Rowman & Littlefield, 1982).

————, *A Theory of Reasons for Action* (Oxford: Clarendon Press, 1971).

————, *Toleration and the Constitution* (New York: Oxford University Press, 1986).

Richards, Leonard L., *"Gentlemen of Property and Standing": Anti-Abolition Mobs in Jacksonian America* (New York: Oxford University Press, 1970).

Robinson, Donald L., *Slavery in the Structure of American Politics, 1765–1820* (New York: Harcourt Brace Jovanovich, 1971).

Rosenfeld, Michel, *Affirmative Action and Justice: A Philosophical and Constitutional Inquiry* (New Haven: Yale University Press, 1991).

Rossi, Alice S., ed., *The Feminist Papers: From Adams to de Beauvoir* (Boston: Northeastern University Press, 1988).

Rousseau, Jean Jacques, *Emile*, trans. Barbara Foxley (London: J. M. Dent, 1961).

————, *The Social Contract and Discourses*, trans. G.D.H. Cole (New York: E. P. Dutton, 1950).

Ruchames, Louis, *The Abolitionists: A Collection of Their Writings* (New York: Capricorn Books, 1964).

Ruddick, Sara, *Maternal Thinking: Toward a Politics of Peace* (Boston: Beacon Press, 1989).

Ruether, Rosemary Radford, *New Woman New Earth: Sexist Ideologies and Human Liberation* (San Francisco: Harper & Row, 1975).

————, *Womanguides: Readings toward a Feminist Theology* (Boston: Beacon Press, 1985).

Ruse, Michael, *Homosexuality* (Oxford: Basil Blackwell, 1988).

Russett, Cynthia Eagle, *Sexual Science: The Victorian Construction of Womanhood* (Cambridge: Harvard University Press, 1989).

Sager, Lawrence G., "Fair Measure: The Legal Status of Underenforced Constitutional Norms," *Harvard Law Review* 91, no. 6 (April 1978): 1212–65.

————, "Foreword: State Courts and the Strategic Space between Norms and Rules of Constitutional Law," *Texas Law Review* 63, no. 6 (March–April 1985): 959–76.

Sandel, Michael J., *Liberalism and the Limits of Justice* (Cambridge: Cambridge University Press, 1982).

Sartre, Jean Paul, *Anti-Semite and Jew*, trans. George J. Becker (New York: Grove Press, 1948).

Scanlon, T. M., "Preference and Urgency," *Journal of Philosophy* 72, no. 19 (November 6, 1975): 655–69.

Schiebinger, Londa, *The Mind Has No Sex? Women in the Origins of Modern Science* (Cambridge: Harvard University Press, 1989).

Schlesinger, Arthur M., Jr., *The Age of Jackson* (Boston: Little, Brown, 1945).

Schuck, Peter H., and Rogers M. Smith, *Citizenship without Consent: Illegal Aliens in the American Polity* (New Haven: Yale University Press, 1985).

Schwartz, Bernard, *The Great Rights of Mankind* (New York: Oxford University Press, 1977).

Schwartz, Joel, *The Sexual Politics of Jean-Jacques Rousseau* (Chicago: University of Chicago Press, 1984).

Sen, Amartya, *The Standard of Living* (Cambridge: Cambridge University Press, 1987).

Sen, Amartya, and Bernard Williams, eds., *Utilitarianism and Beyond* (Cambridge: Cambridge University Press, 1982).

Sewell, Richard H., *Ballots for Freedom: Antislavery Politics in the United States, 1837–1860* (New York: Oxford University Press, 1976).

Shakespeare, William, *Shakespeare: Complete Works*, ed. W. J. Craig (London: Oxford University Press, 1966).

Shapiro, Ian, *The Evolution of Rights in Liberal Theory* (Cambridge: Cambridge University Press, 1986).

Shklar, Judith, *Men and Citizens: A Study of Rousseau's Social Theory* (Cambridge: Cambridge University Press, 1985).

Siegan, Barnard H., *Economic Liberties and the Constitution* (Chicago: University of Chicago Press, 1980)

Smelser, Marshall, *The Democratic Republic, 1801–1815* (New York: Harper & Row, 1968).

Sollors, Werner, *Beyond Ethnicity: Consent and Descent in American Culture* (New York: Oxford University Press, 1986).

Solow, Barbara L., ed., *Slavery and the Rise of the Atlantic System* (Cambridge: Cambridge University Press, 1991).

Southern, David W., *Gunnar Myrdal and Black-White Relations: The Use and Abuse of an American Dilemma, 1944–1969* (Baton Rouge: Louisiana State University Press, 1987).

Spain, August O., *The Political Theory of John C. Calhoun* (New York: Bookman Associates, 1951).

Spooner, Lysander, *The Unconstitutionality of Slavery* (New York: Burt Franklin, 1860).

Stampp, Kenneth M., *The Peculiar Institution* (New York: Vintage, 1956).

Stanton, William, *The Leopard's Spots: Scientific Attitudes toward Race in America, 1815–59* (Chicago: University of Chicago Press, 1960).

Starobinski, Jean, *Jean-Jacques Rousseau: Transparency and Obstruction*, trans. Arthur Goldhammer (Chicago, University of Chicago Press, 1988).

Steele, Shelby, *The Content of Our Character* (New York: St. Martin's Press, 1990).

Stephens, Alexander, *A Constitutional View of the Late War Between the States*, 2 vols. (Philadelphia: National Publishing Co., 1868–70).

Stewart, James Brewer, *Holy Warriors: The Abolitionists and American Slavery* (New York: Hill & Wang, 1976).

———, *Joshua R. Giddings and the Tactics of Radical Politics* (Cleveland: Case Western Reserve University Press, 1970).

Stocking, George W., Jr., *Race, Culture, and Evolution: Essays in the History of Anthropology* (New York: Free Press, 1968).

———, ed., *A Franz Boas Reader: The Shaping of American Anthropology, 1883–1911* (Chicago: University of Chicago Press, 1974).

Stone, Lawrence, *The Family, Sex and Marriage* (New York: Harper & Row, 1977).

Story, Joseph, *Commentaries on the Constitution of the United States*, ed. Melville M. Bigelow, 2 vols., 5th ed. (1833; reprint, Boston: Little, Brown, 1891).

Stowe, Harriet Beecher, *The Key to Uncle Tom's Cabin* (1854; reprint, Salem, N.H.: Ayer Company, 1987).

————, *Uncle Tom's Cabin or, Life Among the Lowly*, Ann Douglas ed. (1852; reprint, New York: Penguin, 1981).

Strange, Douglas Charles, *British Unitarians against American Slavery, 1833–1865* (London: Associate University Presses, 1984).

Stuart, Moses, *Conscience and the Constitution* (1850; reprint, New York: Negro Universities Press, 1969).

Sumner, Charles, *Charles Sumner: His Complete Works,* 20 vols. (1900; reprint, New York: Negro Universities Press, 1969).

Sundquist, Eric J., *Frederick Douglass: New Literary and Historical Essays* (Cambridge: Cambridge University Press, 1990).

Sunstein, Cass, "Naked Preferences and the Constitution," *Columbia Law Review* 84, no. 7 (November 1984): 1689–1732.

Takaki, Ronald, *Iron Cages: Race and Culture in 19th-Century America* (New York: Oxford University Press, 1990).

Tal, Uriel, *Christians and Jews in Germany*, trans. Noah Jonathan Jacobs (Ithaca: Cornell University Press, 1975).

Tappan, Lewis, *The War, Its Cause and Remedy: Immediate Emancipation: The Only Wise and Safe Mode* (New York, 1861), reprinted in Frank Freidel, ed., *Union Pamphlets of the Civil War* (Cambridge: Belknap Press, Harvard University Press, 1967), 1:102–17.

Taylor, John, *Arator*, ed. M. E. Bradford (1818; reprint, Indianapolis, Liberty Classics, 1977).

————, *Construction Construed and Constitutions Vindicated* (1823; reprint, New York: Da Capo Press, 1970).

————, *An Inquiry into the Principles and Policy of the Government of the United States* (1814; reprint, New Haven: Yale University Press, 1950).

————, *New Views of the Constitution of the United States* (1820; reprint, New York: Da Capo Press, 1971).

Taylor, William R., *Cavalier and Yankee: The Old South and American National Character* (New York: George Braziller, 1961).

tenBroek, Jacobus, *Equal under Law* (New York: Collier, 1969).

Thomas, Emory M., *The Confederate Nation, 1861–1865* (New York: Harper & Row, 1979).

Thomas, John L., *Slavery Attacked: The Abolitionist Crusade* (Englewood Cliffs, N.J.: Prentice-Hall, 1965).

Thoreau, Henry D., *Henry D. Thoreau: Reform Papers*, ed. Wendell Glick, (Princeton: Princeton University Press, 1973).

Tiedeman, Christopher G., *A Treatise on State and Federal Control of Persons and Property in the United States*, 2 vols. (St. Louis: F. H. Thomas Law Book Co., 1900).

Tiffany, Joel, *A Treatise on the Unconstitutionality of American Slavery* (1849; reprint, Miami: Mnemosyme, 1969).

Tise, Larry E., *Proslavery: A History of the Defense of Slavery in America, 1701–1840* (Athens Ga.: University of Georgia Press, 1987).

Trefousse, Hans L., *The Radical Republicans: Lincoln's Vanguard for Racial Justice* (New York: Knopf, 1969).

Tripp, C. A., *The Homosexual Matrix* (New York: McGraw-Hill, 1975).

Tucker, St. George, *Blackstone's Commentaries with Notes of Reference to the Constitution and Laws of the Federal Government of the United States and of the Commonwealth of Virginia*, 5 vols. (Philadelphia: Birch & Small, 1803).

———, *A Dissertation on Slavery with a Proposal for the Gradual Abolition of It, in the State of Virginia* (1796; reprint, Westport, Conn.: Negro Universities Press, 1970).

Tussman, Joseph, and Jacobus tenBroek, "The Equal Protection of the Laws," *California Law Review* 37, no. 3 (September 1949): 341–81.

Upshur, Abel P., *A Brief Enquiry into the True Nature and Character of Our Federal Government: Being a Review of Judge Story's Commentaries* (1840; reprint, Philadelphia: John Campbell, 1863).

van der Berghe, Pierre, *Race and Racism* (New York: John Wiley & Sons, 1967).

Van Buren, Martin, *Inquiry into the Origin and Course of Political Parties in the United States* (New York: Hurd & Houghton, 1867).

Voegeli, V. Jacque, *Free but Not Equal: The Midwest and the Negro during the Civil War* (Chicago: University of Chicago Press, 1967).

Walker, Peter F., *Moral Choices: Memory, Desire, and Imagination in Nineteenth-Century American Abolition* (Baton Rouge: Louisiana State Univerisity Press, 1978).

Walters, Ronald G., *The Antislavery Appeal: American Abolitionism after 1830* (New York: W. W. Norton, 1978).

Walvin, James, ed., *Slavery and British Society, 1776–1846* (London: Macmillan, 1982).

Washington, James Melvin, ed., *A Testament of Hope: The Essential Writings of Martin Luther King, Jr.* (San Francisco: Harper & Row, 1986).

Wayland, Francis, *The Elements of Moral Science*, ed. Joseph L. Blau (1835; reprint, Cambridge: Belknap Press, Harvard University Press, 1963).

———, *The Limitations of Human Responsibility* (New York: D. Appleton & Co., 1838).

Wechsler, Herbert, "Toward Neutral Principles of Constitutional Law," *Harvard Law Review* 73, no. 1 (November 1959): 1–35.

Weld, Theodore, *American Slavery as It Is* (1839; reprint, New York: Arno Press and the New York Times, 1968).

———, *The Bible against Slavery* (1838; reprint, Pittsburgh: United Presbyterian Board of Publication, 1864).

West, D. J., *Homosexuality* (Chicago: Aldine, 1968).

Whipple, Edwin P., *The Great Speeches and Orations of Daniel Webster* (Boston: Little, Brown, 1899).

Wiecek, William M., *The Guarantee Clause of the U.S. Constitution* (Ithaca: Cornell University Press, 1972).

———, *The Sources of Antislavery Constitutionalism in America, 1760–1848* (Ithaca: Cornell University Press, 1977).

Wiltse, Charles M., *John C. Calhoun: Sectionalist, 1840–1850* (Indianapolis: Bobbs-Merrill, 1951).

Wish, Harvey, ed., *Antebellum: Writings of George Fitzhugh and Hinton Rowan Helper on Slavery* (New York: Capricorn Books, 1960).

Witherspoon, James, *Lectures on Moral Philosophy,* ed. Jack Scott (East Brunswick, N.J.: Associate University Presses, 1982).

Wolf, Susan, *Freedom within Reason* (New York: Oxford University Press, 1990).

Wollstonecraft, Mary, *A Vindication of the Rights of Woman* (1792; reprint, New York: W. W. Norton, 1967).

Wood, Gordon S., *The Creation of the American Republic, 1776–1787* (New York: W. W. Norton, 1969).

Woodward, C. Vann, *The Future of the Past* (New York: Oxford University Press, 1989).

———, *Origins of the New South, 1877–1913* (Baton Rouge: Louisiana State University Press, 1971).

———, *Reunion and Reaction: The Compromise of 1877 and the End of Reconstruction* (New York: Oxford University Press, 1966).

———, *The Strange Career of Jim Crow,* 3d rev. ed. (New York: Oxford University Press, 1974).

Zarefsky, David, *Lincoln, Douglas and Slavery in the Crucible of Public Debate* (Chicago: University of Chicago Press, 1990).

Zilversmit, Arthur, *The First Emancipation: The Abolition of Slavery in the North* (Chicago: University of Chicago, 1967).

INDEX

"Abolition of Negro Slavery," 28, 111n
abolitionist constitutional theory. *See* moderate antislavery; radical antislavery; radical disunionism; Union, constitutional theory of
abolitionist dissent, 3, 8, 19, 254, 256–57
abolitionists, 58ff.; British vs. American, 119–20, 255; feminist, 89, 186; nonviolence of, 92, 93
abortion, 147, 199, 203–4, 229, 230
Abrams v. United States, 235n
Ackerman, Bruce, 9, 12–16, 172, 192, 253
Adams, John, 4, 5, 29, 30, 43, 123
Adams, John Quincy, 43–44, 47, 95
Adamson v. California, 140n, 202n
affirmative action, 174–75, 177, 190, 197
Agassiz, Louis, 88
Alien and Sedition Act, 29, 219; Taylor of Caroline on, 30
alienage, as suspect classification, 178
Amar, Akhil Reed, 13n
American Civil War, 6, 15, 21, 80, 81; impact on Reconstruction Amendments, 109; as second American Revolution, 15, 21, 109, 110, 116–18, 121, 134, 136–37, 144
American Dilemma, 167
American Revolution, 4, 17, 27, 37, 44, 103, 109, 110, 117, 144
American revolutionary constitutionalism, six ingredients of, 5, 17, 18, 27, 42, 43, 47, 56, 59, 104, 114–15, 121, 129, 130, 144, 221, 243, 250, 254–55, 258
—: inalienable rights (first ingredient), 5, 21, 27, 30–31 (Taylor of Caroline), 32 (Calhoun), 47–48 (Lieber), 52–56 (Lincoln), 60 (Weld), 61–62, 91 (Channing), 90–91, 95, 97–98 (Weld), 97–104 (radical antislavery), 119–23 (Reconstruction Amendments), 129–30, 132–33 (Sumner), 131–32 (Parker)
—: constitutional analysis (second ingredient), 5, 21, 27, 30–31 (Taylor of Caroline), 32 (Calhoun), 48 (Lieber), 52–53 (Lincoln), 62, 91 (Channing), 95, 97–98 (Weld), 97–104 (radical antislavery), 115–19 (Reconstruction Amendments), 129–30, 132–33 (Sumner), 131–32 (Parker)
—: political psychology (third ingredient), 5, 21, 27, 30–31 (Taylor of Caroline), 32–33 (Calhoun), 48 (Lieber), 53–56 (Lincoln), 60–61 (Weld), 62 (Channing), 97–104 (radical antislavery), 123–30 (Reconstruction Amendments), 129–30, 132–33 (Sumner), 132–33 (Parker)
—: comparative political science (fourth ingredient), 5, 21, 27, 30–31 (Taylor of Caroline), 33 (Calhoun), 91 (Channing), 48 (Lieber), 53 (Lincoln), 62 (Channing), 97–104 (radical antislavery), 130–33 (Reconstruction Amendments), 129–30, 132–33 (Sumner), 132 (Parker)
—: political experience (fifth ingredient), 5, 21, 27, 30–31 (Taylor of Caroline), 33 (Calhoun), 48 (Lieber), 53–57 (Lincoln), 62 (Channing), 97–104 (radical antislavery), 129–30, 132–33 (Sumner), 132 (Parker), 133–34 (Reconstruction Amendments)
—: constitutional argument (sixth ingredient), 5, 21, 27, 30–31 (Taylor of Caroline), 33 (Calhoun), 48–49 (Lieber), 53–57 (Lincoln), 62 (Channing), 95, 97–98 (Weld), 97–104 (radical antislavery), 129–30, 132–33 (Sumner), 132 (Parker), 134–48 (Reconstruction Amendments)
American Slavery as It Is, 59, 90, 224–25
anarchism, moral, 93, 106
antiabolitionist mobs, 59
antiestablishment principle, 50n
anti-Judaism, 67–68, 156
antimiscegenation laws, 83
anti-Semitism, 147, 156, 188; abolitionist critique of, 19, 59–63, 68; anti-Christian, 156, 157; Channing and analogy of, 62–63; Christian, 67–68, 85, 156; Curtiss and analogy of, 63; Douglass and analogy of, 63; European, 150, 156–60, 168–70, 183, 253, 256; Lieber and analogy of, 141; Lowell and analogy of, 63; political, 159–60; as racism, 156–60, 182; Sumner and analogy of, 63, 161